Additional Praise for *Keep Your Donors: The Guide to Better Communications and Stronger Relationships*

"*Keep Your Donors* serves as a reminder that what really counts in these donor relationships is the ability to communicate our organization's vision in such a clear, relevant, compelling and passionate way that they actually look forward to hearing from us. This book offers a practical prescription for many nonprofit ailments, from failure to actively listen to failure to inspire action. It should be on every thoughtful practitioner's bookshelf."

—Sandra A. Adams, Senior Vice President, External Affairs
National Breast Cancer Coalition Fund

"Every single person who considers themselves to be part of building donor relationships must read this book. Truly superb concrete, research based information. You will wish you had it with you all along!"

—Patricia M Dowling, MSW, Executive Director of The Shoreline Soup Kitchens & Pantries, and past Board President of Interval House.

"This book isn't about gimmicks, taste or (what we all secretly fear) manipulating relationships to take advantage of others. Simone and Tom synthesize the body of knowledge and research on fundraising to teach you to communicate so someone can tell if your organization is worthy of his or her interest-and gift. Your relationship with donors is based on their desire to make the world better in some way, and your organization's ability to accomplish it. They transformed how I write (and I was good before) and made it more comfortable for myself and board members to ask."

—Stephen Slaten, Ph.D., Executive Director
Jewish Family Service of Worcester, Inc.

"With inspired precision, energy and passion, Tom and Simone have set a new milestone and raised the bar for fundraisers around the world. *Keep your Donors* throws down the gauntlet–it is now up to us to share their vision and step outside our comfort zones to meet the challenges of the flat philanthropic world head on!"

—Jon Duschinsky, Fundraiser
France

"This book is a "must-have" for those who want to move beyond competence to excellence, beyond formula to strategy, beyond immediate "fix" to long-term stability."

—Sarah C. Coviello, CFRE, President
Coviello and Associates

Keep Your
Donors

Keep Your Donors

The Guide to Better Communications & Stronger Relationships

TOM AHERN

SIMONE JOYAUX

BICENTENNIAL
1807
WILEY
2007
BICENTENNIAL

John Wiley & Sons, Inc.

Library of Congress Cataloging-in-Publication Data:

ISBN: 978-0-470-08039-9

10 9 8 7 6 5 4 3 2 1

The AFP Fund Development Series

The AFP Fund Development Series is intended to provide fund development professionals and volunteers, including board members (and others interested in the nonprofit sector), with top-quality publications that help advance philanthropy as voluntary action for the public good. Our goal is to provide practical, timely guidance and information on fundraising, charitable giving, and related subjects. The Association of Fundraising Professionals (AFP) and Wiley each bring to this innovative collaboration unique and important resources that result in a whole greater than the sum of its parts. For information on other books in the series, please visit:

http://www.afpnet.org

THE ASSOCIATION OF FUNDRAISING PROFESSIONALS

The Association of Fundraising Professionals (AFP) represents 28,000 members in more than 185 chapters throughout the United States, Canada, Mexico, and China, working to advance philanthropy through advocacy, research, education, and certification programs.

The association fosters development and growth of fundraising professionals and promotes high ethical standards in the fundraising profession. For more information or to join the world's largest association of fundraising professionals, visit www.afpnet.org.

2006-2007 AFP Publishing Advisory Committee

To Tim Burchill

There is no man easier to praise than one you didn't know especially well but liked immensely each time you met; of whom no one has anything but loving, admiring things to say.

This book is dedicated to Tim Burchill, that man.

I am here to praise him, to throw him a brief Irish wake in words, something I am qualified by my family tree to attempt.

I am writing this dedication for my wife, Simone Joyaux. She *did* know Tim well and loved him deeply. As a learned, venturesome, impeccably ethical colleague. As a steady, comforting, generous, and wise friend. He had her utter respect and faith, neither given easily; her standards for conduct are inhumanly high, I'll attest. But Tim met them.

The news came near midnight, an evil time for unbidden phone calls. Simone pawed up the phone in the dark. She heard a close colleague, Guy Mallabone, sob out the rumor of Tim's sudden death a few hours earlier. By heart attack, not Tim's first. A good man down. Gone between one sentence and the next.

This book is in praise of Tim. This book is in many ways *because* of Tim, as fabric is *because* of thread. His ideas, his principles, his beliefs, his practice, his observations, his enthusiasm, his advice, his urging are here, woven into these pages.

Morgean Hirt knew Tim well from his work as a board member and item writer for the Certified Fund Raising Executive program. She was amazed by her memories of him. "It is quite the thing to be both overwhelmingly saddened and unspeakably delighted in the same instant when I think of Tim."

Dozens of Tim's colleagues and past students posted loving farewells on a memorial blog created by Saint Mary's University of Minnesota. Among his other ventures, Tim founded Saint Mary's highly regarded master's degree program in philanthropy and development.

Morgean summed up many sentiments in her posting to the blog. "He will be terribly, deeply missed for a long time to come but the world is a much better place for him having been here."

Thomas J. "Tim" Burchill, III. Born March 30, 1947. Died February 20, 2007.

Beyond our reach now. But remembered with love and gratitude. For the proverb reminds us, "Good men must die. But death cannot kill their names."

About the Authors

SIMONE P. JOYAUX, ACFRE

Simone P. Joyaux, ACFRE, is recognized internationally as an expert in fund development, board and organizational development, and strategic planning. She is the author of *Strategic Fund Development: Building Profitable Relationships That Last.*

After having worked for 13 years inside nonprofits, first as an executive director and then as chief development officer at a major regional theater, Simone left to establish her own consulting practice in 1988. She has worked with hundreds of nonprofit organizations of all types and sizes since.

Simone presents all over the world, including the prestigious International Fundraising Congress held annually in The Netherlands. She has also presented—in French—at the conference of the Association Française des Fundraisers.

Simone is a faculty member in the Master's Program in Philanthropy and Development at Saint Mary's University, Minnesota. She also teaches in the nonprofit program at Rhode Island College.

Simone serves regularly on boards; is the founder and a former chair of the Women's Fund of Rhode Island; and is the former chair of CFRE International, the baseline certification program for fundraisers worldwide. Simone is the recipient of the 2003 Rhode Island Outstanding Philanthropic Citizen Award for her commitment as a volunteer and donor. In 1987 she was recognized as Rhode Island's Fundraising Executive of the Year.

She and her life partner, Tom Ahern, give at least 10 percent of their income to charitable causes annually and have bequeathed 100 percent of their estate to charity, mostly through their local community foundation. On a related note, they have no children, but they do own a second home in France.

TOM AHERN, ABC

Tom Ahern is considered one of North America's top authorities on fundraising communications. He has published two previous books, one on donor newsletters in 2005, and in 2007, *How to Write Fundraising Materials That Raise More Money.*

Tom presents dozens of workshops a year. His easy-to-follow, practical advice has made him a popular speaker at fundraising conferences internationally.

He began his consulting practice in 1990. Before that, he had been marketing communications chief for a multinational technology firm, public relations director for a state arts agency, and an oral historian, and had written several books of short fiction. He's received an NEA Fellowship in fiction.

His work for nonprofits includes several specialties. Tom evaluates and helps improve the yield from donor communications programs. He writes case statements for capital campaigns; on average, one a month. And he adds punch to donor newsletters. His clients range in size from national advocacy groups and universities, to local grassroots organizations.

His nonprofit work has won several prestigious Gold Quill awards, given annually to the most effective communications programs submitted to IABC's formidable worldwide competition. He is also an award-winning magazine journalist.

Contents

Preface

This was supposed to be a book about fundraising communications.

But that begs the question: communications to what end? So we changed it a bit.

In this book, we're trying to fix a problem we see too often: organizations—and here we mean staff and board—launching into space without sufficient preparation. These organizations focus on *how-to* and are impatient with *why*. (By the way, our colleague Alexcia WhiteCrow has this view of the problem: "I'm not sure they focus on how-to either. I think they focus on mission, which is wonderful. They are impatient with how-to *and* why. They want to skip those steps and get right to fixing the problem the mission solves.")

Our promise: This book will help you—no matter your level of experience. This book will help your organization—no matter its size or mission. And we think this book will help you and your organization—no matter your country or your culture or your life experience.

How can we make this promise?

Because this book incorporates the experience and knowledge of countless of professionals and organizations working around the world, in both the nonprofit/NGO and for-profit sectors. Because every day, both of us use these strategies and tactics. But more important, we reflect on the larger context. Every day, we question and learn and imagine that you do, too.

This book is a paean to all the great professionals, researchers, and organizations we know. We learn from you. We borrow shamelessly from you and lavishly give you credit. Thank you.

By the way, we also used the job analyses conducted by CFRE International and the Association of Fundraising Professionals to make sure this book covers what fundraisers need to know. Whether you're preparing for fundraising certification (and we believe that you should; we're both certified in our fields) or not, this book is intended to advance you as a professional.

And finally, this book is full of questions. The best questions stimulate new thinking and produce change. So every chapter includes meaningful and cage-rattling questions to challenge your learning and encourage change.

Please let us know what you think. And thank you for your commitment to philanthropy.

Tom Ahern, ABC, Ahern Communications, www.aherncomm.com

Simone P. Joyaux, ACFRE, Joyaux Associates, www.simonejoyaux.com

P.S. We'd like to extend a special apology to our readers outside North America. The majority of the examples chosen to illustrate the points made in our book come from American and Canadian charities. Those choices imply nothing negative about the quality of fund development in other countries, merely the availability. On the contrary. We are deeply impressed and excited by what we see charities outside North America doing. It's evolutionary. It's revolutionary. And it's happening worldwide.

We continue to seek examples from clients and our workshop attendees around the world. Please send us examples of your best fund development communications, so we can incorporate them into our teaching.

Acknowledgments

We are profoundly indebted to the many generous, thoughtful individuals and organizations who helped us form and improve this book—by sharing their hard-won knowledge, by reviewing and editing the manuscript in progress, and by granting us permission to reprint materials. They include: Sandra Adams, ACFRE; Ron Arena; Tracey Biles; Jeff Brooks; Lisa Bousquet; Penelope Burk; Marcia Coné-Tighe; Marci Cornell Feist; Sarah Coviello, CFRE; Patty Dowling; Jon Duschinsky; Peter Duschinsky; Carol Golden; Kathe Grooms; Nisia Hanson; Ted Hart, ACFRE; Sally Kirby Hartman; Kris Hermanns; Morgean Hirt, ACA; Jim Hoyt; Dianna Huff; Louise Jakobson; Patricia Kern; Guy Mallabone, CFRE; Ari Matusiak; Rose McIlvane; Harvey McKinnon; Barbara Mulville, CFRE; Tony Myers, CFRE; Tina Palmer, CFRE; Jerry Panas; Bob Parks; Shawn Poland; Jim Rattray; Martha Rennie, CFRE; Susan Rice, ACFRE; Richard Radcliffe; Adrian Sargeant and Elaine Jay; Gene Scanlan, CFRE; Rick Schwartz; Steve Slaten; Lisa Smolski; Larry Taft; Clovis Thorn; Phil Valentine; Nondas Hurst Voll; Mal Warwick; Colin Wheildon; Alexcia WhiteCrow, CFRE; and Wendy Zufelt-Baxter.

CHAPTER 1

Beginning at the Beginning

THE CONTEXT FOR EVERYTHING ELSE

The capacity to learn is a gift; the ability to learn is a skill; the willingness to learn is a choice.

—Brian Herbert and Kevin J. Anderson,
Dune: House Harkonnen

DEAR READER As the title promises, this book focuses on increasing donor loyalty by nurturing relationships and using communications to help nurture those relationships.

But—and it's a big but—something else comes first: the context for this work. For Tom and me, this context is the heart and soul of the book. We believe this context is critical, and that's where we begin.
Simone ■

WHY THE LARGER CONTEXT MATTERS

I'm one of the forest-and-trees people. I embrace the big picture as well as the smaller items inside the picture. I believe in keeping both in my mind at one time, despite the occasional difficulty! As both business theory and self-help guides proclaim, it's important to have a vision to know where you are going. That's the forest picture. With that big picture in mind, it's easier to understand why and how the trees—the smaller items—fit inside.

For me, everything is linked. That's systems thinking. Ignoring one part of the system doesn't work. It's like a prospective client who wants me to help raise more money but doesn't want me to talk about mission and values, governance, and management. I explain it's like a house, one system. You've asked me to fix the plumbing, but you won't let me fix the heating system that causes the plumbing to freeze. I can fix the plumbing but it will freeze and break again. We have to fix the heating system, too.

Just about every problem I've ever encountered in fund development arises because the organization or the staff (including the fundraiser) doesn't understand the larger context. It's like wearing blinders. For many fundraisers, no one talks with them enough about the larger context. For others, they're focused on the trees and don't respect the forest. Still others suspect there's a forest and want to understand it, but are stymied by unsupportive leadership.

I'm not alone in this perception. Fund development colleagues around the world tell me that the larger context is critical but isn't talked about enough. Well, this book talks about that, just like I do always.

> *I suspect we all need a larger context; otherwise, complacency sets in. We stay in our comfort zone. Perhaps the larger context can serve as a touchstone—or a lens or frame—to help us venture where we are less comfortable; to challenge us.*

For me, the larger context includes two elements: (1) a philosophical framework for philanthropy and (2) effective organizations that create an environment conducive to effective fund development. I believe these two elements position organizations to develop better fund development programs.

Relationship building (which includes communications) is embedded within this larger context. In my experience, the ability to move back and forth through the layers of context—or preferably integrate them fully and seamlessly—affect all the work that nonprofits and nongovernmental organizations (NGOs) do.

PHILOSOPHICAL FRAMEWORK

I begin with the first element of the larger context: the philosophical framework.

I think that most professionals ask themselves this question: Why do I choose to do "this work"? I imagine that a doctor asks that question, so does a teacher, so does any professional. And each of them answers the question personally.

I imagine those working in the nonprofit/NGO sector answer that question by saying "I believe in the mission." For example, someone working in an environmental organization might say, "I do this work in order to make sure we have clean air to breathe." Or maybe "I'm fighting to reduce carbon emissions so we can reduce global warming and protect the planet and its species."

But I think there is another question that those of us who focus on the nonprofit/NGO sector must ask and answer: Why do I choose to work *in this sector?*

I think this sector demands leaders who are committed to more than their organization's particular mission. I believe this sector requires a broader commitment, to philanthropy and civil society. I call that a philosophical framework.

Who are these leaders with this broader commitment? I'm referring to fundraisers and executive directors at least, and hopefully many others in the organization. And in my experience, it's often the fundraisers who have to lead the executive directors to this understanding.

Here's my philosophical frame, part of the heart and soul of this book about relationships and communications.

This I Believe

This is my really big picture.

I believe in "the inherent dignity and the equal and inalienable rights of all members of the human family," because this is the "foundation of freedom, justice and peace in the world," as it says in the United Nations' Universal Declaration of Human Rights. And nonprofits the world over fight for these rights.

I believe in the European Constitution, described as

> the first [governmental] document of its kind to expand the human franchise to the level of global consciousness, with rights and responsibilities that encompass the totality of human existence on Earth. ... The language throughout the text is one of universalism, making it clear that its focus is not a people, or a territory, or a nation, but rather the human race and the planet we inhabit. If we were to sum up the gist of the document, it would be a commitment to respect human diversity, promote inclusivity, champion human rights and the rights of nature, foster quality of life, pursue sustainable development, free the human spirit for deep play, build a perpetual peace, and nurture a global consciousness.[1]

And NGOs around the globe struggle to make these changes.

> *We cannot seek achievement for ourselves and forget about progress and prosperity for our community. ... Our ambitions must be broad enough to include the aspirations and needs of others, for their sakes and for our own.*
>
> —César Chavez, 1927 – 1993, Co-Founder, United Farm Workers

I hope that, together, we can build these communities. I believe that, together, we must try. And the nonprofit/NGO sector is critical to this community-building process.

Building Community

John Gardner's 1991 monograph, "On Building Community," remains one of my favorite writings.[2] Gardner understands community as place and as belonging.

"Where community exists it confers upon its members identity, a sense of belonging, a measure of security." He recognizes communities of all types: workplace, school, religious organization, club, trade union, town, neighborhood, and so forth.

He talks about the importance of community: "Families and communities are the ground-level generators and preservers of values and ethical systems . . . the ideals of justice and compassion are nurtured in communities."

He reminds us that the word "community" itself "implies *some* degree of wholeness." The opposite, fragmentation, stops us from thinking or acting as a community. Gardner describes the breakdown of community and some of the causes.

A decade later, using the metaphor of "bowling alone" (where previously people bowled in teams), Robert Putnam echoes similar causes that erode social connectedness and community involvement: pressures of time and money, mobility and sprawl, technology and mass media, breakdown of the old-time traditional family unit, and generational, gender, and ethnic issues. All this contributes to "isolation, alienation, estrangement," which means there is "no longer a web of reciprocal dependencies."[3]

> *Philanthropy is uniquely able to build strong communities and improve people's lives.*

Yet there's hope. Despite the collapse of community, renewal happens, too. Ingredients critical for building any kind of community include shared values, diversity, effective communications, broad participation, and systems to reinforce connections, among other things.

While Gardner's writing is still applicable, other language is more common today. For example, a community's ability to regenerate itself is often called "civic capacity." Gardner's "web of reciprocal dependencies" is today's "social capital." And "civil society" refers to all the organizations that, together with government, help build strong communities.

Here's an overview of building community, using today's vocabulary. Think about this as a philosophical framework for philanthropy.

Civic Engagement   That's me and you, our neighbors and friends involved in our communities, whether it's our town or some other group we belong to. The word "civic" refers to the obligations each of us have by belonging to a community.

Civic engagement means people vote and volunteer. They participate in politics and advocate on behalf of others. They band together to build a stronger community.

Of course, the degree of civic engagement goes up and down in any community or society at large. For years the United States has had one of the lowest records of voter turnout in any voting nation. That's an example of bad civic engagement. Around the world, growing numbers of people volunteer; that's good civic engagement.

The nonprofit/NGO sector plays a critical role in civic engagement. People get together to form nonprofits to help others. NGOs bring people together for public discourse. And NGOs recruit people to volunteer their time and money to support important causes. All of this is civic engagement, a virtuous circle that happens when positive results continuously reinforce positive results.

Social Capital   Social capital is the theory that a person's networks have value. Made popular by Robert Putnam, the term "social capital" refers to the people we know (networks) and what we do for each other (reciprocity).

You use social capital everyday. You meet with some of your work colleagues to solve a problem. You borrow your friend's car because yours is in the garage. You attend an event to meet corporate executives, recognizing that this expanded network might help your nonprofit in the future. Social capital makes individuals and organizations more productive.

Each of us has personal and public networks based on reciprocity, which produce mutually beneficial results. Social capital identifies two kinds of reciprocity. One is the exchange of favors: "You do this for me and then I'll do this for you." This form of reciprocity always worries me because it smacks of some form of "payoff."

The second kind of reciprocity is more like philanthropy, a general commitment to help others. "I'll do this without expecting anything specific in return—because someday when I need it, maybe someone will help me." For example, you donate money to the hospital because someday you expect to use its services. I volunteer at the homeless shelter because I imagine how easy it would be to lose my job and default on my mortgage.

This kind of reciprocity recognizes mutual dependence and shared accountability for healthy communities. All this connecting reminds me of the "webs of interconnectedness," from Peter Senge, learning organization guru.

Here's how social capital works, inspired by Putnam's descriptions in *Bowling Alone*.[4]

- *Social capital helps people work together to solve problems they all share.* A lack of social capital would mean that most of us just sat back and waited till others (perhaps too few) tried to solve the problem. I think of climate change and its effect on the planet. Regulations like car emission standards can make things better; that's social capital. But we need a norm at the citizen level. Imagine a day when the peer pressure would be so great that no one would buy a gas-guzzling Hummer. And then our social capital would require that General Motors stop making them. I'll bet a nonprofit is working on this right now.

- *The goodwill generated through social capital helps the community work smoothly.* We buy things at stores assuming that the cashier isn't cheating us. I get into a taxi expecting the driver to take me to my destination, not a different one. Your donors assume you're using their gifts as directed. To behave otherwise would produce dysfunction in daily lives.

- *Social capital helps us lead happier and more productive lives.* Trusting connections and deep bonds actually help us "develop or maintain character traits that are good for the rest of society." Both experience and research show that social ties reduce isolation and stress, provide feedback to mitigate negative impulses, and help people develop empathy. Research even verifies the health effects of volunteering and giving money.

- *Social capital also helps us learn and change.* Through our networks, we meet diverse people and connect with different life experiences. We pass information around, often increasing its usefulness through our conversations. That same information exchange helps individuals, organizations, and communities achieve their goals. Effective nonprofits join this information exchange to support their own progress.

> There was this joke that when the women who worked in the lab were stressed, they came in, cleaned the lab, had coffee, and bonded. . . . When the men were stressed, they holed up somewhere on their own. . . . The "tend and befriend" notion developed by Drs. Klein and Taylor may explain why women consistently outlive men. Study after study has found that social ties reduce our risk of disease by lowering blood pressure, heart rate, and cholesterol. "There's no doubt," says Dr. Klein, "that friends are helping us live."[5]

Not only do you use social capital yourself, you watch its use daily. From religious congregations to school boards, sports leagues to civic groups, Internet networks to professional associations and your own favorite nonprofits—all this is social capital in action, carried out through all those civil society organizations. Social capital produces civil society.

Civil Society   "Civil society" refers to all the things people and organizations do together, without being forced to do so. The term itself is very old, and commonly used everywhere in the world except the United States.[6] Just visit the International Fundraising Congress, hosted annually in The Netherlands by the Resource Alliance (www.resource-alliance.org). You'll hear "civil society" all the time.

I think it's easiest to understand the term "civil society" as those organizations and individuals that come together voluntarily to build stronger communities. Or, as Alexis de Tocqueville said, "proposing a common object for the exertions of a great many men [and women] and inducing them voluntarily to pursue it."[7]

Most important, these people come together outside the boundaries of government. The "outside of government" piece is critical. Government doesn't make us get together to build the hospital or found a museum. Government doesn't form trade unions or professional associations. In fact, many civil society organizations fight government, for example, the struggle for civil rights and the right to vote.

For some, civil society includes the broadest array of collective action: every kind of nonprofit/NGO including charities, religious institutions, professional associations, trade unions, civic groups, academia, the arts, businesses, the media, and more. Others define a more limited view of civil society, focusing primarily on the nonprofit/NGO sector.

But no matter what you include or exclude, civil society helps build stronger communities. And many of us believe that it's the spread of civil society worldwide that produces the most significant change.

> *Peace and prosperity cannot be achieved without partnerships involving Governments, international organizations, the business community, and civil society.*
>
> —UNITED NATIONS, WWW.UNORG/ISSUES/CIVILSOCIETY

Civic Capacity   Without civic engagement, there is no civic capacity. And without the sector called "civil society," there is reduced civic capacity.

Civic capacity is the ability of a community to identify its challenges and opportunities, overcome the problems, and capitalize on the opportunities. Inherent in the concept is the coming together of diverse community voices, not just the select few who traditionally wield privilege and power.

The term "civic capacity" most typically relates a town or city and the duties and obligations belonging to that community. The nonprofit/NGO sector has modified the term to "organizational capacity," referencing the capacity of an organization to identify and solve its challenges and identify and capitalize on its opportunities—in other words, achieve its mission.

Civic capacity depends on social capital and civic engagement. It depends on a strong civil society to partner with or fight against government.

Building Community Redux

In sum, building community relies on the ability of individuals and groups to connect, to build bridges, to nurture relationships, and to work together for change. Healthy communities depend on civic capacity. Civic capacity is built through social capital (which helps increase civic engagement), civil society, and government (which are not discussed in this book). All this together produces a virtuous circle to build community.

Yet we've all encountered the exact opposite: insular people and organizations. For example, I know fundraisers who pay little attention to what's happening in the field. I've watched nonprofits with similar missions ignore cooperative opportunities.

Insular people and organizations focus only on their own interests and issues, disregarding anything beyond self-imposed boundaries. Those who are insular ignore new ideas or different experiences. Their inward, narrow-minded approach limits their own possibility for success and distances them from connections that could generate meaningful relationships and build healthy communities.

> *Individuals acquire a sense of self from their continuous relationships to others, and from the culture of their native place. . . . Humans need communities—and a sense of community. . . . An understanding of the mutual dependence of individual and group has existed below the level of consciousness in all healthy communities from the beginnings of time.*
>
> —JOHN GARDNER, "ON BUILDING COMMUNITY"

EFFECTIVE ORGANIZATIONS

Here's my mantra: Effective organizations are more likely to produce effective fund development. To reiterate my earlier metaphor about systems thinking: Your organization is the house. Fund development is the plumbing. The whole house has to work, not just the plumbing.

Key Components of Effective Organizations

Chapter 3 describes, in detail, five components that help make organizations effective and then directly impact fund development. They are:

1. Organizational development specialists
2. Culture of philanthropy
3. Value of research
4. Qualified opinions
5. Commitment to conversation and questions, learning and change

There are more, but I picked these five because they are of particular value to fund development. Also, they're central to fund development, the most effective organizations recognize the value of relationships. And I'm talking about relationships beyond donors.

In Chapter 4 I describe four types of relationships. I do *not* intend to discuss all these relationships, although I believe that the first three are essential to all organizations. The fourth is optional, but you'll see my bias soon enough! The general concepts of relationship building and communications in this book apply to any of these relationships:

1. **Philanthropic relationships.** How your organization relates to its donors of time and money. That is the focus of the book, discussed in detail in subsequent chapters.

2. **Relationships with other organizations.** How your organization relates to other organizations and to government. All organizations must build relationships with other organizations in order to fulfill the promise of building community and civic capacity and to be more effective. This relationship is referenced periodically in the book.

3. **Relationships within your organization.** How the various internal parts of your organization relate in order to create an effective organization. This relationship, which is required by all organizations to ensure effectiveness, is discussed briefly in this book.

4. **Advocacy and public policy relationships.** How your organization promotes public policy that fosters healthy communities. Some of us believe that ensuring democracy and freedom is the ultimate role of the nonprofit/NGO sector. This topic is discussed briefly in this book.

EFFECTIVE FUND DEVELOPMENT

The sad truth is, you *can* raise money without an effective organization. You *can* raise money without embracing my key components of effective organizations.

Many successful fundraisers ignore the larger context that Tom and I describe in this book. But our experience shows you can raise more money more easily by embracing this larger context. And we're convinced you won't be so frustrated if you expand your view beyond the trees to the forest—and accept the power and responsibility you have for the forest.

Everyone looks to the development staff to make fund development effective. But too often, people ignore how organizational effectiveness impacts fund development.

Fundraisers are the most powerful voice to point out why and how organizational effectiveness affects fund development effectiveness. As a fundraiser, your power comes from this one truth: You work in the fund development office; therefore, you control money.

Here's my theory: Everyone else in the organization fantasizes that you print money in the basement. Even though they realize that's merely a fantasy, they count on you to raise money. That gives you the right, the power, and the responsibility to explain what compromises—or helps—the raising of money.

In Conclusion

Philanthropy is in a unique position to build both civil society and civic capacity. But not, I think, without this larger context. A philosophical framework coupled with an effective organization produces the best fund development program.

For me, these remarks from Paul Pribbenow, CFRE capture the larger context: "Simply put, a focus on bold ideals often leaves us with vacuous principles untethered to the reality of our daily work, while a focus on the cold technique and 'dull' work of fundraising leads to a set of transactional rules and guidelines devoid of a sense of context. . . . We will not resolve this tension, but we must understand it and look for ways to develop a framework . . . that links the real and ideal in an integrated whole."[8]

ENDNOTES

1. Jeremy Rifkin, *The European Dream: How Europe's Vision of the Future is Quietly Eclipsing the American Dream* (New York: Tarcher Penguin, 2004) p. 113.
2. John Gardner, "On Building Community," occasional paper published by the Independent Sector, www.independentsector.org. Quotes from pp. 5, 15, 8.
3. Robert D. Putnam, *Bowling Alone: The Collapse and Revival of American Community* (New York: Simon & Schuster, 2000) p. 8.
4. Ibid., p. 288
5. Gale Berkowitz, "UCLA Study on Friendship Among Women," posted at www.anapsid.org/cnd/gender/tendfend.html. Original source, Taylor, S.E., Klein, L.C., Lewis, B.P. Gruenewald, T.L., Gurung, R.A.R., and Updegraff, J.A., "Female Responses to Stress: Tend and Befriend, Not Fight or Flight," *Psychological Review,* 107(3): 41–429
6. Used by Adam Ferguson in his "An Essay on the History of Civil Society," published in 1767.
7. Nineteenth-century Frenchman Alexis de Tocqueville talked about "the principle of association" while traveling in the United States. His writings have long inspired the nonprofit and philanthropic movements in this country and, by extension, to civil society around the world. This quote is from his *Democracy in America,* The Henry Reeve Text as Revised by Francis Bowen and Further Corrected by Phillips Bradley, Abridged with an Introduction by Thomas Bender (New York: The Modern Library, 1945), p. 404.
8. Paul Pribbenow, Ph.D., CFRE, speaking at the Ethics Think Tank, Washington D.C., September 2005, quoted in "The President's Report," *Advancing Philanthropy,* May/June 2006. Copyright© Association of Fundraising Professionals (AFP) 2006. *Advancing Philanthropy* is the bi-monthly publication of AFP, which promotes philanthropy through advocacy, research, education and certification programs (www.afpnet.org). All rights reserved. Reprinted with permission.

Why?

It's any day anywhere on planet earth. A child asks, "Why?" And the designated adult has an answer.

Which of course begs another question from the child: "Why?"

Another answer.

Another question.

Why? Why? Why? On and on.

Concluding sooner or later with, "Because."

We are great little probers as kids. It's one way we navigate our strange new world. Psychology calls this phase, or pathological examples of it, *folie du pourquoi*. a mania to ask why.

Too bad we outgrow it.

School tests soon teach us there is one "right" answer to every question. Questioning in the workplace or on boards may be seen as threatening or disloyal. Jobs in fund development soon teach us to adopt "high-probability solutions" that pretty much always produce some kind of result. "Lessons learned," case studies, professional development—they all aim to give us better answers than we currently have.

Sometimes, though, better answers aren't the answer.

What would really help are better *questions*.

Reactivate your childhood *folie du pourquoi*. Stop assuming there are answers. Instead, start relentlessly asking questions. Of your donors. Of your prospects. Of your fundraising methods. Of your organization. Questions like "Why did you give us that first gift?" Or "What could we do better in your opinion?" Or "What happens when the grantmakers change their priorities?" Or "Are we still relevant?"

We believe that a question-driven fund development program lodged inside a questioning organization will *always* outperform and certainly outlast a complacent program inside a complacent organization.

And you probably agree, if not from your own experience, at least instinctively. Science and art, after all, advance by asking questions, often rude, stupid, improper questions that no reasonable person would ask.

Here's our advice to you: Don't be a reasonable person. Being reasonable won't tell you anything explosively new. Reasonable people already know the answers. Or assume those answers exist *somewhere.*

Well, they don't. Each organization is different. Different time, different place, different needs, different mission, different vision, different leadership.

For sure, *this* book doesn't have all the answers. We are well aware of our limits. Oh, it has plenty of information, examples, tips, good advice from dozens of honest-to-goodness experts, sound theory and practice.

But you will also notice lists of questions without answers. We know what you might be thinking: Aren't books like this *supposed* to explain things? Isn't that why you purchase a book like this?

Not this time. This book is a bit different. This is a *folie du pourquoi* book. A "why-to" as well as a "how-to" book. "It's about going someplace fundamentally different. Remember, it's not the activities that lead to success. It's the understanding that produces success."[1]

We think the best, most profitable habit we can promote is an itch to ask lots of questions. Cage-rattling questions. Questions without known answers. Questions that turn your brain upside down and shake it until the coins fall out.

ENDNOTE

1. Remarks made by Eddie Thompson, Ed.D., Thompson & Associates, at the April 2007 Kaiser Institute.

CHAPTER 2

The Red Pants Factor

A STORY ABOUT THE POWER OF QUESTIONING

You sure get a lot of questions in the world, without exactly getting the same number of answers. In fact, there was a huge gap between the two numbers.

—GUY GAVRIEL KAY, YSABEL.

In theory, there is no difference between theory and practice. In practice, there is.

—ATTRIBUTED TO BOTH YOGI BERRA, AMERICAN BASEBALL PLAYER AND TEAM MANAGER, AND JAN L. A. VAN DE SNEPSCHEUT, COMPUTER SCIENTIST AND EDUCATOR

DEAR READER As Tom and I wrote this book, we kept asking ourselves "Why?" "Why are we writing this book and what do we want to achieve? Why do we keep talking about why?" Our answer? The "Red Pants" factor.

Simone ▪

In 2006, Red Pants was born. This is her story.

Since 2000, I have spent a glorious, transforming week each summer at Saint Mary's University in Winona, Minnesota. I serve as a faculty member in Saint Mary's Master's Program for Philanthropy and Development. It's an intense learning experience for everyone. Adult students, many of them seasoned fundraisers, come from all types and sizes of organizations around North America and beyond.

I arrived on campus Monday, July 17, 2006. I wore my traveling clothes: loose light pants in shameless red, T-shirt, summer tennis shoes. I lugged along my teaching materials for two courses, Volunteerism and Governance; and Relationships, Communications and Philanthropy.

I arrived. The luggage I'd checked did not.

For four days I wore the same red pants to class. Where we explored volunteerism and governance, plus topics above and beyond, things like:

- Candor and risk taking
- Diversity, pluralism and inclusion
- Conversation and learning
- Organizational development
- Subversive topics, such as challenging assumptions, questioning the status quo, privilege and power, and speaking out

We talked and disagreed. Students questioned me and I questioned them. The course was all about the why, with a few how-tos thrown in. It was great.

Then one day, I gave them an evaluation form for small-group work. I was pretty proud of this form. After all, I'd been using and modifying it for the previous six years. Students periodically made suggestions to improve the form, but no one ever questioned using it—at least not out loud to me!

That is, not until Black Dress (aka Wendy). She respectfully asked me the purpose of the form. I responded, but my response didn't seem to work well for Black Dress. She questioned me again.

And at that moment, I thought, "What a perfect metaphor for governance and management. Just imagine a board meeting where the board chair announces something and a fellow board member questions it." And even better: "What a perfect example of power dynamics and the courage of questioning."

Throughout the course, I'd been suggesting that our class was a group, much like a board. We had been talking about effective and ineffective groups and group dynamics.

I regularly raised the course themes and challenged the students to question and disagree and argue. I asked about hierarchy and privilege and power.

So here was Black Dress, taking a risk and speaking out. She didn't settle for my explanations. She didn't let my presumed power as the instructor stop her. Yeah, this was what I was trying to promote!

And you know how sometimes you have a flash of brilliance? Well, I had a flash at that moment—despite the stress of missing my clothes and sundries!

I was watching Wendy and the others. And they were watching Wendy and me.

So I said to the class: "Here we are at a board meeting. And Black Dress is questioning Red Pants, the board chair. Does Black Dress have the right to do so?"

Then I asked: "Can student Black Dress question Red Pants the instructor?"

And Red Pants was born. The avatar. The alternate ego allowed us to talk about difficult issues—such as power–without focusing on the real individual.

This wasn't about Simone the instructor or a board chair. This wasn't about Wendy the student. Instead, Red Pants was there. And later, Wendy told me she was separate, and protected, as Black Dress.

Finding Your Own "Red Pants" Factor

In October 2006, one of my Saint Mary's students, Shawn Poland, Cohort 15, (The term Cohort refers to a group of students that stay together for the 3 years of the program) sent me his final project. In the paper's opening, he introduced a concept he called "the red pants" factor. I shared the introduction with my coauthor Tom, and he immediately saw a link: "That's the spirit of this book. That's what this book is about."

Here's Shawn's introduction:

> There's something about spending four days with "red pants." In retrospect, there is little that can be done in preparation save ensuring that both an open mind and a mental parachute—for those unforeseen emergency rescues—accompany you through the classroom door.
>
> From cage-rattling questions that rattle more than cages, to asking "why" and "how" to just about everything in the volunteer governance world, to discovering that the answers never come easy nor are they clear-cut, to embracing mavericks and taking the bluster out of rogues, and finding post-meeting solace and forgiveness in the most unlikely places.
>
> Time with "red pants" is as much about self-discovery as it is about issues in governance, volunteerism, and leadership. In fact, I would suggest that time with "red pants" places the not-for-profit philanthropic professional within the swirling vortex between governance, volunteerism, and leadership ... starting one on a road of discovery that places the "self" within a seemingly endless cycle of "what-ifs, how-comes, and oh my gawd, what the hell am I gonna do nows?"

Now substitute "fund development and communications and relationships" for governance and leadership. Substitute "philanthropy and fund development." Think about all the meaningful whys. Consider each possible cage-rattling question. Why and how-to. A swirling vortex of connecting and integrated issues.

By the way, my class at Saint Mary's set up a task force to resolve the issue of the evaluation form. Black Dress served on the task force with other colleagues, but Red Pants refused to serve because it was a conflict of interest.

A Postscript from Black Dress

> There is theory and there is practice. Putting theory into practice is an evolutionary process. It takes effort and trust and leaps of faith. It takes a group effort and cooperation.

This process is about creating a non-threatening environment and highly-engaging conversation. It's coaching and mentoring, and breaking down walls and assumptions. It's about giving away positions of power.

This evolutionary process isn't easy. It isn't a destination but a journey. A journey that you may take with others or, at times, you may be on your own.

But it is a journey worthy of your effort. The moving destination is unpredictable but more rewarding in the long run. And there's a greater chance of bringing others along on the journey instead of using power to push people through.

That's what Red Pants did for Black Dress.[1]

ENDNOTE

1. Wendy Zufelt-Baxter, Cohort 15, Masters in Philanthropy and Development, Saint Mary's University, Winona, Minnesota.

What Do All the Words Mean?

I want to define two key words that tend to get "lost in translation": philanthropy and fund development.

Let's start with philanthropy. My favorite definition is "voluntary action for the common good." Robert L. Payton, first professor of philanthropics in the United States, coined this. People give time and money to make things better in their communities. Serving as a board member, for instance, is philanthropy. So is making a financial gift.

Philanthropy is all about dreaming. Through philanthropy, we change communities. As Lee Kaiser says, "I love philanthropy because it allows me to substitute realities. Philanthropy is the motor that drives social change."[1]

Philanthropy is a transformational act for donors, nonprofits, and the communities served by both. These transformational gifts have a "unique capacity to alter the programs, perceptions, and future of an organization."[2]

When it comes to the "f" word, Tom and I wish people would use "fund development" rather than "fundraising" to describe the industry we're all in. Of course, we're as guilty as the next person: We use both terms in this book. But "fund development" seems to us bigger and better. It includes the concepts of process, activity over time, planning, growth, and change. Fund development makes us think about more than asking for the gift. And asking for the gift is one of the smallest portions of this work.

So here's how Tom and I explain fund development:

Philanthropy means voluntary action for the common good. Fund development is the essential partner of philanthropy. Fund development makes philanthropy possible by bringing together a particular cause and donors and prospects who are willing to invest in the cause. The goal is to acquire donors of time and money who stay with the charity. This is done through the process of relationship building. With the donor at the center, fund development nurtures loyalty and lifetime value, thus facilitating philanthropy. You know if your relationship building works because your retention rates rise and the lifetime value of your donors and volunteers increases.

ENDNOTES

1. Leland R. Kaiser, Ph.D., is founder and president of Kaiser Consulting, a healthcare consulting firm located in Brighton, Colorado. Writer, lecturer, health policy analyst, and futurist, Dr. Kaiser sparks the imagination of audiences worldwide to change obsolete mind-sets. He made this statement at the April 2007 Kaiser Institute in Ponte Vedra, Florida.

2. Kay Sprinkel Grace and Alan L. Wendroff, *High Impact Philanthropy: How Donors, Boards, and Nonprofit Organizations Can Transform Communities* (Hoboken, NJ: John Wiley & Sons, 2001), p. 2.

CHAPTER 3

Key Components of Effective Organizations

PART OF THE LARGER CONTEXT FOR THIS WORK

To know anything well involves a profound sensation of ignorance.

———JOHN RUSKIN, 1819–1900, ENGLISH CRITIC AND ESSAYIST

DEAR READER   For more than three decades, I've studied what makes fund development productive and what makes organizations effective. As promised in Chapter 1, I'm describing five components that are of particular value to fund development: organizational development specialists; culture of philanthropy value of research; qualified opinions; and commitment to conservation and questions, learning and change. Together and individually, these five things make a powerful contribution to your organization's success in fund development.
Simone

ADOPT AN ORGANIZATIONAL DEVELOPMENT APPROACH

Most fundraising problems are not fundraising problems at all. They are organizational development problems that poison fundraising success.[1] To solve these problems, professionals must become organizational development specialists.

> *Guaranteed: To survive and flourish, every organization needs its own in-house organizational development specialists. And the fundraising executive should be one of these specialists.*

Consider these income-depleting possibilities:

- **Your organization is blindsided by some event that happens externally or internally.** (What happens, for instance, if your executive director suddenly quits?) How will that event affect your fund development activities and your donors and volunteers? Someone has to raise and own this question. And guess what? That's you.

- **There's major fundraising congestion in your community.** Your organization cannot distinguish itself with a better letter or a more special special event. Instead, you may need to overhaul fund development. You may need to change the way you do the business of your organization, and even what that business is.

- **Your organization's mission may be out-of-date and your programs may no longer be important to the community.** Eventually your stakeholders/constituents will notice and leave. Your donors will stop giving.

- **Your donors may not feel close enough to your organization.** Small gifts will not become larger ones, and donors may not renew their gifts.

Finally, fund development has never been solely about money. It's always been about relationships. And that means understanding someone's interests and finding a match with your organization. Or accepting people's disinterest and moving on. Simply focusing on dollar goals, response rates, and prospect research won't work without forging a deep relationship between the organization and the prospect.

None of these situations is new. They were true yesterday and will be true tomorrow. The only difference may be the speed and frequency with which these situations occur, the time and effort it takes to recover, and the increasing frustration experienced by donors, volunteers, clients, and staff.

Limitations of Technical Fundraising

Technical fundraisers abound. They focus almost exclusively on how-tos and on managing tactics to produce more money. These technicians are good at isolating a fundraising challenge or opportunity and devising an appropriate response. Every fund development team needs great technicians. And all fundraisers need to stay up-to-date on the latest how-tos and tactics.

But being a technician is not enough. It never has been. Since most fundraising challenges stem from the organization and its operations, not from fund development, you must be able to discern the true nature of the situation in order to solve it. Focusing on fund development, as technicians do, doesn't solve the nonfund development problems. Healthy charitable gifts income is a by-product of doing lots of things other than fund development well.

> *Whereas fundraising technicians can, and often do, succeed, remaining merely a technician leaves you and your organization vulnerable.*

You can always find a great technician. But organizational development demands broader learning and a commitment to leadership beyond fund development.

Turning You into an Organizational Development Specialist

Organizational development specialists garner respect and access throughout the organization, probing deeply into areas that ordinary fundraising technicians would consider out of bounds. These areas include board recruitment and performance expectations, organization-wide planning and community needs assessment, program quality and customer service, mission drift and communications, and more.

Organizational development specialists are change agents. They are critical thinkers; they analyze, they critique, and they work out solution with others. These professionals ask the tough questions about fund development and every other area of operation. They track down challenges and opportunities facing the organization. These leaders observe how things link across the organization and then figure out how to suggest and facilitate change.

> *Are you in charge of hiring a fund development executive, either staff or consultant? Make sure you pick an organizational development specialist.*

As strategists, organizational development specialists help the organization decide where it wants to go and how to get there. They identify relevant information and help others understand the implications of the information.

These accomplished fundraisers are often the first to question whether the organization is still relevant to the community, because irrelevance cramps the ability to build donor loyalty and raise money. But it's more than a financial question; it's an ethical question. Organizational development specialists know that without sufficient relevancy, an organization has no right to exist and drain community resources.

As pivotal players in the agency, these accomplished individuals are consummate enablers, empowering volunteers and staff to participate meaningfully on behalf of the organization. See Appendix A for a brief overview of enabling. For further detail, see my book *Strategic Fund Development: Building Profitable Relationships That Last.*[2]

What the Organizational Development Specialist Needs to Know

Take a look at my list. You don't have to be an expert in all the areas, but you have to be pretty darn knowledgeable. And some of this will be familiar to you if you check out the CFRE test content outline, the baseline certification for fundraisers worldwide.

- General business management and governance
- Group dynamics and organizational behavior
- Learning organization and systems thinking theories
- Strategic and operational planning
- Fiscal planning and management
- Volunteer and staff role delineation and performance appraisal
- Marketing and communications
- Values clarification and mission and vision
- Enabling

Skills of organizational development specialists include:

- Conflict resolution and facilitation
- Critical and strategic thinking
- Proficient teacher and learner
- Effective communicator and motivator

For more details about organizational development specialists, visit the Free Library (located in the Resources section) on my Web site at www.simonejoyaux .com. For help making all this theory work, see Exhibit 3.1. Also see Exhibit 3.2, tips about your fund development committee meeting, which can help make theory practical.

EXHIBIT 3.1   HELPING YOUR ORGANIZATION IMPLEMENT THEORIES AND IDEAS

Much of the information and many of the ideas in this book are not new. You may know all or lots of this. In that case, the repetition affirms that you are on a good track. Or the repetition stimulates a new insight for your own application.

Often the challenge is implementation. Not conceiving the idea but actually translating it into action and making it work.

Professionals—especially organizational development specialists—enable others to do the work. These leaders explain the why behind the how-to. These professionals translate ideas into action. They give practical, tangible examples so others understand.

I call this "operationalizing" the idea or the concept. (You can only imagine how disgusted Tom was with that word! But hey, what other word would you pick? How about "making an idea tangible"? Then the verb would be even more awkward, "to tangibilize"! Anyway, "operationalize" is actually a term in science.)

Think about all those directions that accompany various products. You know, assembly required! Now imagine those directions without any illustrations (I got that from *The Big Moo.* Pretty neat, eh?) That's your job. You operationalize for others through your explanations and examples. You enable staff, board members, and other volunteers to operationalize.

And finally, you help your organization institutionalize these new ways of thinking and acting. The term "institutionalizing" means to make something a custom, an accepted part of the organization's structure, systems, and practice.

BUILD A CULTURE OF PHILANTHROPY

Concept of Corporate Culture

Research finds that the so-called culture inside an organization dramatically impacts its effectiveness. This includes for-profit and nonprofit corporations and government entities.

What does "culture" mean? Generally speaking, the term "culture" refers to the particular attitudes, beliefs, customs, practices, and social behaviors that characterize a group of people.

What does the term mean when referring to an organization or group? The same thing. A strong culture exists when people within the organization share values. This alignment allows them to work together, share experiences, and move forward. A weak culture results when there is little alignment of values. In such organizations, control typically is enforced through bureaucracy, systems, and rules.

All groups, large and small, develop a culture. Culture is pervasive. It impacts all areas of the organization including fund development effectiveness and results.

Of course, organizational culture can be either positive or negative, or somewhere in between. You've seen toxic organizations and so have I. And I've also

EXHIBIT 3.2   **ASK THESE QUESTIONS AT THE END OF EVERY FUND DEVELOPMENT COMMITTEE MEETING**

Ask these three questions at the end of every fund development committee meeting (or for that matter, any committee):

1. What information—translated into trends and implications—needs to be shared with the board, and why?

2. What trends and implications require strategic dialogue with the board—or with different individuals and groups within the organization—and why? What background information—and strategic questions—should be provided in advance to prepare for the strategic dialogue? How will you facilitate the dialogue?

3. What decisions need to be made by which individuals or groups within the organization? What kind of information and questions must be provided in advance, to set the context for the decision-making dialogue?

seen strong cultures that perpetuate negativity. The people in those organizations aren't happy or supportive. These aren't good places to work or volunteer.

In this book, we focus on strong organizations that perpetuate a positive culture. These organizations carefully define and nurture the kind of culture that builds effective and more productive organizations.

For me, a culture of philanthropy is an essential component of a positive corporate culture in the nonprofit/NGO sector. In my experience, professionals and organizations that nurture a culture of philanthropy are more likely to succeed.

> *Everything else can fall away; the industry and products and circumstances may change; but an abiding culture can serve as the custodian of dreams for your company team, and for the customers on whose faith you build your house of business. It is an unchanging constant in the midst of a tornado of change, and it is something people want badly. It allows us to offer choice to those who work here and for those we want to work here...to live and work by their values, and who will toil together toward something larger than themselves.... The company, at its best, can be a vehicle for everyone to make a difference.*
>
> —DAVID S. POTTRUCK AND TERRY PEARCE, *CLICKS AND MORTAR*

Culture of Philanthropy

More and more fundraisers talk about a culture of philanthropy. Just Google the term! I first started writing about a culture of philanthropy in the late 1990s, and focused on it in the second edition of *Strategic Fund Development*.

But what, exactly, is this culture of philanthropy? Like any culture, it's that generally unconscious personality of your organization. It's a feeling that infiltrates everyone and everything in your organization.

I think a culture of philanthropy looks like this: Everyone in the organization accepts and celebrates these points:

- Philanthropy means giving time and/or money.
- A philanthropist is anyone who gives time and/or money, regardless of the amount.
- Philanthropy is not merely a means to carry out the organization's mission. Instead, everyone embraces philanthropy as an essential component of civic engagement and healthy community.

The culture of philanthropy is the perfect blending of philanthropy and fund development—and only the positive words and feelings echo forth. The philanthropic culture embraces the two sides of the coin, donor-centrism and donor loyalty. This culture embodies the virtuous circle of relationships.

In my ideal culture of philanthropy, people in the organization break the obsession with transactions and mechanics and learn to cherish interests and emotions. Organization representatives reach out to stakeholders, describing the value of giving. Each person in the organization serves as an ambassador promoting both the organization's mission and the concept of philanthropy. Each person honors all donors—whether of time or money, no matter the amount—as central figures in the organization's mission.

Remember "Beginning at the Beginning," that larger context and philosophical framework for philanthropy ad fund development? Our work is about building community, creating civil society, and nurturing civic capacity. How can we do that without believing in and living a culture of philanthropy?

And by the way, to achieve maximum donor revenue and sustain that maximum indefinitely, nonprofits/NGOs depend upon a strong culture of philanthropy. Effective leaders of these organizations help define and then consciously nurture this culture.

Meaningful Questions   This book is about one thing above all: asking lots of questions. As you think about organizational culture and a culture of philanthropy, take a look at the questions proposed here.

But before you review the questions, think about this: How will you even get your colleagues to talk about the most meaningful questions? Try these tips:

- If you're the executive director, introduce the topic of corporate culture at your next staff meeting. Talk a bit about it. Let people share examples. And at the next staff meeting, begin discussing these questions.

- If you're not the executive director, take him or her to lunch and introduce the topic of corporate culture. Talk about how the staff—and even the board—could have this kind of discussion.

Now begin working on these eight questions in your organization. How would you answer these questions where you work or volunteer? How do you think your colleagues would respond?

1. How would you describe your organization's culture, its personality? How does it feel to work there?

2. How does this culture affect your enthusiasm and commitment, and your behaviors and interactions?

3. How do you think your colleagues define the organization's culture? How do you think their perception affect the work environment? (You actually have to ask colleagues these questions, not just trust your judgment about what they think.)

4. What kind of process would help your organization examine and evaluate its organizational culture, define any desired changes, and then make the change?

5. How would a culture of philanthropy look and feel to your staff colleagues, your donors, and your volunteers?

6. How would you nurture this culture of philanthropy in your organization?

7. How would you distinguish a culture of philanthropy from a culture of giving?

8. How is a culture of philanthropy different from a culture of greed?

After a session with me in January 2005, the AFP Southern Minnesota Chapter developed seven culture-defining questions to ask internally:

1. Is building a culture of philanthropy any different from building a culture of excellence?

2. How do we engage linear thinkers in culture building, because they don't always value process? (Linear thinking proceeds in an obvious sequential manner, without in-depth understanding.)

3. How well do we understand ourselves and our own motivations for giving?

4. How does a culture of philanthropy apply to soliciting low-income clients, and who makes these decisions?

5. Do we have the courage to treat everyone the same? Do we treat our donors better than our clients? Do we treat all donors the same?

6. How can we ease people's fears, anxieties, and discomforts about money (e.g., board member discomfort about solicitation; donor discomfort about the size of their gifts)?

7. How do employment practices impact a culture of philanthropy?

PERSONAL AND ORGANIZATIONAL COMMITMENT TO CONVERSATION AND QUESTIONING, LEARNING AND CHANGE

"Conversation," "questioning," "learning," and "change" are familiar words.

But in business theory, these terms take on special urgency because they are all recognized now as secrets behind organizational success. Of course, merely giving lip service to these high-powered concepts achieves nothing. It's past time for fundraisers and their organizations to make these concepts a core part of their professional behavior. And it might be left to you as the organizational development specialist to help your agency incorporate these concepts as an established part of operations.

Learning Organization Theory

According to the experts like learning organization guru Peter Senge, learning means building the capacity of an organization and its individuals to achieve results. Learning is more than acquiring information; it's about re-creating yourself. This requires new ways of thinking, and often, as Yoda, the Jedi character in George Lucas's *Star Wars* films, says: "You have to unlearn what you've learned."

Senge uses the word "metanoia," which means shift of mind, to describe the learning organization. "To grasp the meaning of 'metanoia' is to grasp the deeper meaning of 'learning,' for learning also involves a fundamental shift or movement of mind."[3]

> *The attributes of entrepreneurship—risk taking, innovation, vision —are both cultural and learned.*
>
> —GROUP OF 33, *THE BIG MOO*

Learning is a prerequisite to change. Change is a fact of existence. So ultimately, your organization's effectiveness and results depend on how fast, how well you learn and change.

Film director, producer, and screenwriter Francis Ford Coppola was *not* working in a learning organization environment when he said, "I've found in dealing with people, with society, that you barely get an idea out into the room before there are four or five reasons why it should be killed. Sometimes good

---

EXHIBIT 3.3   AIM FOR A MIND SHIFT, YOUR OWN METANOIA

How to start? Try Einstein's approach: "I have no special talents. I am only passionately curious." But how can you develop your curiosity? How can you stimulate new thinking in your organization?

Here's some inspiration from *The Big Moo*:

> "[G]et as serious, rigorous, and creative about renewing yourself as any other aspect of your business. So get out. Get out of your comfort zone...we preserve and revere experience when we should be challenging and renewing it...invite naïveté, passion, and new talent into the organization...Pick up a new tool...Try something you've never done before...without judgment. Get out of your frame of reference. The best way to open your mind is to apply a jolt of unfamiliarity...seek out new sources, mix up your milieus, and rearrange your references. Go on a field trip. Go somewhere you've never been before...Think contrast...Let your questions lead...Get out of your own skin...stir up your passions, dreams, and projects lying dormant inside yourself... "

Group of 33, *The Big Moo: Stop Trying to Be Perfect and Start Being Remarkable*, ed. Seth Godin, New York: Portfolio (Penguin Group) 2005

---

reasons, sometimes not. Nonetheless, if you kill off an idea too early, then you never get to places you would have gotten to."[4]

Clearly Coppola expects to experiment and welcomes the risk and potential reward. He knows that creating something new involves risk and requires courage. I imagine Coppola applauding Irish novelist and playwright Samuel Beckett, who said, "No matter. Try again. Fail again. Fail better." I suspect that those who accept learning organization theory see mistakes as Joyce's "portals of discovery."

Now it's up to you. Create your own mind shift or new viewing lens (see Exhibit 3.3).

Systems Thinking, the Cornerstone of Learning Organizations

Here's a mini-primer. An organization, like your own body, operates as a single system. What happens in one part of the system affects other parts of the system, either sooner or later.

Systems thinking means you see the whole: your entire organization and all its departments and activities. You understand how the individual parts relate and operate for a common purpose. You know that what happens in one part of the system (e.g., your organization) affects what happens elsewhere in the system, maybe not immediately, but certainly eventually. For example, program quality and board recruitment affect fund development, values affect board and staff recruitment, and so forth. The systems thinking approach helps you figure out the best place you can push or manipulate in complex situations. Think of these places as leverage points to produce learning and make change.

Conversation at Work

According to dictionaries, "conversation" is the informal way that we exchange opinions, ideas, and feelings. Obviously individuals do this. As social beings, humans connect through conversation.

But in learning organization theory, conversation is a core business practice as well. Widely-respected business journalist Alan Webber says conversations are the way that workers "discover what they know, share it with their colleagues, and in the process create new knowledge for the organization. The panoply of modern information and communication technologies . . . can help knowledge workers in this process. But all depends on the quality of the conversations that such technologies support."[5] Learning organizations use conversation (also called dialogue) and questioning to stimulate learning and change.

In both personal and business realms, conversation circulates information and nurtures relationships. Conversation helps generate commitment, thus producing a sense of community. And this feeling of community is characteristic of highly functioning organizations. Think about those Three Musketeers, "all for one and one for all." Now that's commitment!

> It is in how we speak with one another that we experience respect from others and [know] whether we are being heard.
>
> —LINDA ELLINOR AND GLENNA GERARD, *DIALOGUE: REDISCOVER THE TRANSFORMING POWER OF CONVERSATION*

As a core business practice, the informal conversation around the photocopier can help individuals understand why donor recognition is important. Maybe in a lunchroom a colleague talks about how she was recognized as a donor to her mosque and suddenly a wonderful new idea for donor recognition pops into your head. Conversations with clients offer important insights to improve your service quality.

The most effective organizations actively promote conversation in order to optimize learning and change. See the tips in Exhibit 3.4.

Conversation produces individual and organizational learning by:

- Gathering information and identifying trends
- Interpreting the implications of the information
- Identifying possible choices and the consequences of those choices
- Sharing knowledge
- Questioning assumptions
- Identifying conflict and commonalities
- Generating ideas

EXHIBIT 3.4	HOW TO PROMOTE MORE CONVERSATIONS IN YOUR ORGANIZATION

Examine the conversations in your organization. How does your organization use conversation as a core business practice? Do you see lots of conversations, both formal and information, structured and casual? Explore the questions below. How would you modify them for your organization? What would you add?

- Where do the best conversations happen in your organization—and why?
- What do your board and committees talk about, and why?
- How do your conversations extend between departments and across areas of operation?
- How do you ensure that your conversations are inclusive, welcoming diverse people and perspectives?
- How do your conversations encourage questioning and stimulate innovation?
- How do you use information to stimulate questioning and expand conversation?
- What changes must happen—and why—to nurture conversation in your organization?

- Creating shared meaning
- Building understanding and ownership and alignment
- Supporting change
- Creating a sense of community and shared purpose

Asking the Essential Questions

Now think about conversation and asking questions. Usually you start a conversation, and continue it, with a question. You learn by asking a question. You stimulate thinking—your own and that of others—with questions. You help people reflect on their own assumptions by questioning them yourself. And you expect others to help you think by questioning your assumptions.

> *Pursuit of knowledge is based on asking questions, questioning answers, and asking the right questions in the first place.*
>
> —KARLA A. WILLIAMS ACFRE AND SIMONE P. JOYAUX ACFRE

How does this work?

An important question makes you pause. You question your own assumptions. This can be difficult. After all, personal assumptions are based on life experience and knowledge. These assumptions often define us. Yet questioning one's own assumptions and the assumptions of others is essential to stimulate learning and change, thus helping to build an effective organization.

Asking meaningful questions is not a rhetorical exercise, where the questioner is attempting to make a point. Nor is it an attempt at sabotage or a test. Instead, the best questioning is stubbornly open-ended. It promotes conversation, learning, innovation, and change. And the truly essential questions take you to a new place entirely.

> *A good question is never answered. It is not a bolt to be tightened into place but a seed to be planted and to bear more seed toward the hope of greening the landscape of the idea.*
>
> —JOHN CIARDI, QUOTED IN *75 CAGE-RATTLING QUESTIONS TO CHANGE THE WAY YOU WORK*

However, questions can be risky. Some of the best questions cause conflict and discomfort. But that's good! In a board meeting, Alfred Sloan, a former CEO of General Motors Corporation, supposedly said about an important decision: "I take it that everyone is in basic agreement about this decision?" When everyone nodded yes, Sloan replied, "Then I suggest we postpone the decision. Until we have some disagreement, we don't understand the problem."

Handled well, the conflict and discomfort of great questions stimulates conversation and encourages deeper thinking. Sadly, too many organizations suffer from dysfunctional politeness. Avoiding disagreement and discomfort, though, is a real quick way to disempower your board, pacify your staff, stifle innovation, and—bottom line—ruin your organization. Yes, *ruin* your organization. Dysfunctional politeness stops you from talking about the difficult issues. Avoiding unpleasant questions and conversations is a bad and unhealthy habit. Eventually it will ruin your organization, rest assured.

> *The best way to strengthen your organization is getting people to ask the "why" questions and working hard to answer them.*

The Best Questions Rattle the Most Cages   What do you think are the most important questions your organization should discuss? What are the most difficult questions your organization must confront? These are your "cage-rattling questions," a phrase borrowed from authors Dick Whitney and Melissa Giovagnoli in their book *75 Cage-Rattling Questions to Change the Way You Work*.[6] This book can help craft questions for you and your organization. Here are some of my favorites. How would you modify them for your organization?

- "Pretend your organization (or department) is an organized religion. What are the core beliefs? What constitutes a sin?" (From Simone: Think organizational values.)

- "What drives your best customers crazy and what makes them exceedingly happy?" (From Simone: Think donors and volunteers and those you serve.)

- "If your crystal ball told you that most of the products or services you work with will be obsolete in five years, how would you react?" (From Simone: Think strategic planning and the process to define your organization's relevance.)

- "If you came up with a brilliant idea, who or what might prevent you from implementing it?" (From Simone: Think organizational development.)

- "If you could snap your fingers and turn your boss into a member of the opposite sex (or another race, or change his or her age by 30 years), what workplace issues might he or she become more sensitive to? (From Simone: Think about diversity and cultural competence.)

- "Top management is wiped out by a tidal wave at their annual retreat in Bora Bora; when your team is put in charge of the company, how would you change things and who would be in charge?" (From Simone: Wow.)

Composing Good Questions, Whether Business or Personal Composing good questions is hard work. Good questions focus on the important issues, not the inconsequential ones. Good questions are open enough to kindle thinking and useful conversation.

Use these tips to help develop good questions:

- **Avoid questions with yes/no answers.** They shut down thinking and stop conversation.

- **Create open-ended questions.** They stimulate thinking and produce more conversation.

- **Focus on strategic issues with significant implications.** Don't waste people's time with frivolous questions that don't really matter.

- **Remove bias in your questions.** Make sure your own assumptions are not embedded.

- **Aim for simplicity.** Overly complex questions distract people.

> *What assumptions are you making that stop you from changing?*

This book includes lots of strategic questions—questions intended to surprise, cause discomfort, stimulate novel thinking, and reinforce risk taking. You'll find more questions (including questions about boards, philanthropy and fund development, and volunteerism) in my book *Strategic Fund Development* and at www.simonejoyaux.com.

For example:

- How will you help your board members overcome their discomfort with fund development?
- How can you create meaningful relationships with your donors?
- How can you value all donors regardless of gift size?
- And here's a cage-rattler: If your mission is no longer relevant, how should your organization change?

Chapter 17 focuses on conversations with your prospects and donors and includes lots of questions for these conversations.

This Is Hard Work

The theories of conversation and questioning, learning and change are often threatening. In my experience, this approach requires a certain comfort with complexity, disagreement, and conflict. There are lots of whys and then *more* whys. Things don't always proceed sequentially, in an obvious linear manner. And all this is accompanied by hassles and anxiety. And rest assured, Tom and I feel the hassles and anxiety too!

Sometimes it's hard to identify the questions that matter the most. And it's even harder to risk the asking. It's also difficult to design questions that take you or your organization to a really new place.

VALUE OF RESEARCH—YOUR OWN AND THAT OF OTHERS

Research is as close as the real world comes to owning a crystal ball. You ignore research at your organization's peril.

Where were you, for instance, the day direct mailed died? That's an exaggeration, of course. It's not dead yet. But it is in flux, as you know if you keep up with the research. Given that flux, what are your plans for direct mail?

Where were you when women inherited the money and controlled gift giving? That one's old news, eh? But have you adjusted your relationship building and solicitation according to the research?

Just imagine if you missed either of those announcements. And imagine what other useful insights you miss unless you follow the research.

The bottom line: Quality information helps make quality decisions. The right information is essential to getting the job done well. Equally important, the right information produces questioning, learning, and change. Indeed, information, question, and conversation are interdependent.

Research replaces assumptions, which often lead you astray. Research can countermand the personal opinions of others. Research helps you anticipate and avoid problems. When analyzed and interpreted, research data explain the why and justifies the how-to.

Accomplished professionals seek opportunities for information. These professionals follow news reports about research, go to the original source, and read the details. These professionals seek research sessions at conferences.

> *The farmer who has never ventured beyond his field says his own methods are the best.*
>
> —POPULAR SAYING FROM THE ANLO-EWE TRIBAL GROUP OF GHANA

By the way: Don't be country-centric in your examination of research. If you're from the United States, you should know that some of the best research is being done elsewhere. Visit major Web sites in other countries to find out what's going on elsewhere. See examples at www.simonejoyaux.com. Ask colleagues. Search the Internet. How would you answer the questions in Exhibit 3.5?

EXHIBIT 3.5   HOW WOULD YOU AND YOUR ORGANIZATION ANSWER THESE QUESTIONS?

1. Are you passionate about philanthropy and fund development, not just your organization's mission?

2. Are you passionate about the whys, not just the how-tos?

3. Why is best practice best practice?

4. Which best practice is appropriate for your organization now?

5. What preparation must you do with your organization before it is ready to confront some parts of best practice?

6. How will you customize best practice for your organization?

7. What knowledge and skills are necessary for you and your organization to carry out best practice? What should reside within you and your organization? What already resides within you and your organization? How will you acquire what you do not yet have?

8. What's the difference between a right and a wrong decision, and a preferred decision for this time in your organization?

9. What can be outsourced without compromising that which you and your organization should know?

10. How will you explain all this to your organization?

11. What modifications of best practice would you propose for the sector, and why?

12. What do you anticipate as next practice for the sector, and why?

Collecting Data from Your Organization

The best fundraisers also collect meaningful data within their own organizations. What data does your organization currently collect, and what is the data good for? Consider these eight questions:

1. What information do you gather internally about your own strategies, tactics, and results? What information do you gather from comparable organizations that might prove helpful?

2. How do you analyze and present trends as objectively as possible, but with the added value of your expertise?

3. How do you present information in a way that opens rather than ends conversation?

4. What data are available in the philanthropic sector that can help assess and inform your organization?

5. What societal information would be useful in your deliberations—for example, economic, regulatory, lifestyle, workplace, demographics, and so on?

6. What questions arise as you analyze and interpret the trends through various lens: for example, gender and sexual orientation, age and ethnicity/race, socioeconomics, and so on?

7. How will you facilitate strategic dialogue about the implications of these trends?

8. How will you enable your organization to make the best decisions regarding strategies and tactics?

Translating Data into Useful Information

The best fundraisers know that information is useless without an analysis of the trends and implications, followed by strategic conversation about the meanings and consequences. Unfortunately, too much information is presented without analysis and void of strategic conversation.

> *Data itself is nothing unless one uses it as a resource from which to draw conclusions.*
>
> —BRIAN HERBERT AND KEVIN J. ANDERSON, *DUNE: THE MACHINE CRUSADE*

A caveat: Beware about jumping to conclusions. Evaluate and interpret data through diverse lens and multiple areas of expertise. See Chapter 24 for more about translating data into useful information.

QUALIFIED OPINIONS ONLY, PLEASE!

Depend on the documented body of knowledge and research, not a single person's opinion. Read publications. Attend workshops. Apply the lessons learned. Ask questions and question assumptions. With all this, you will understand the "why" behind each how-to. Then you have the knowledge and experience to question current practice. And with your own experience and learning, you can propose and anticipate next practice.

Seems sensible, eh? Yet how often do you hear someone's opinion—stated with great assurance—that contradicts the body of knowledge? How often do you try to explain why someone's personal opinion actually conflicts with best practice and is problematic rather than helpful?

For example:

- Your wonderful volunteer offers the opinion that direct mail is better than a face-to-face request. But you know that face-to-face solicitation is estimated to be many times more effective than direct mail. You suspect the volunteer's opinion is based on personal discomfort. But the board credits the opinion and wastes time discussing the comparative value of solicitation strategies rather than talking about how to develop its capacity to do face-to-face solicitation.

- Perhaps a great graphic designer has just re-created your newsletter. You're thrilled with how good it looks. Then you find out that the design reduced readability by 500%.

- Or the marketing/public relations department in your university keeps writing bad headlines and poor photo captions. You explain the body of knowledge and you're told that's "just your opinion."

Opinion just got you into trouble. The volunteer doesn't know the body of knowledge for fund development. The graphic designer isn't familiar with readability standards. And your marketing/public relations staff don't understand written communications.

A Curious Conundrum

We face a curious conundrum in the philanthropic sector. We engage volunteers. We enable them to help raise charitable gifts. And suddenly some of those volunteers assume that their opinion is equal to the documented body of knowledge.

We hire well-trained graphic designers who create really pretty materials. But these professionals never learned the science of readability—and some don't want to learn it. So their design frustrates easy reading and people don't read your publications—but they all think your stuff is pretty.

Curiously, no one would dare tell a builder that the short nails are cuter so "let's use them instead of the long ones." No one but another experienced surgeon would discuss which scalpel to use in brain surgery. And the electrician generally gets more respect than the fundraiser!

Opinions can be big trouble. How valuable is someone's view when it is based solely on personal judgment rather than an understanding of the body of knowledge and experience? How valuable is someone's technical opinion without a solid understanding of the myriad intersecting whys?

Personal opinions about personal issues are fine. But opinions about business issues—which are not qualified through sufficient technical expertise coupled with an understanding of why—are baseless and useless, and often cause problems.

However, keep in mind this special warning: Asking strategic questions and questioning assumptions is different from offering an opinion. Everyone has the right to ask questions and question assumptions, whether his or hers or those of others. So here's the bottom line: Encourage questioning and discourage unqualified opinions.

> *Learning is a paradox. It is life affirming and often painful, because you care, and without it you're literally dead.*
>
> —GROUP OF 33, *THE BIG MOO*

Corollary of the Curious Conundrum

Or, as Tom asked in his February 2007 e-news, "Who's blessing YOUR stuff?

Who approves your solicitation letters or your written case statement or your newsletters? Absolutely NOT NOT NOT your board of directors or your fund development committee or your board chair or your committee chair, or any other volunteer that I can think of.

This is staff work—whether you write it yourself or hire an expert to write it; whether you design it in house or hire designers. This work is not board work.

The problem isn't whether the board or board member liked the four-page letter or not. The problem is scope of authority and who does what. Fix that problem first. Distinguish between staff work and board work, typically described as management and governance. Define the limits of authority between management and governance. That's the real problem to solve.

Now, if your board chair complains after receiving the solicitation letter, saying "I throw away such long letters," then quote best practice. Show the body of knowledge. Explain the research. But most important, graciously say, "I'm the expert, that's why I was hired. I know the body of knowledge and best practice. I read the books and the research. You can count on me to do my job correctly."

Staff members are supposed to be the in-house authorities on all things within the management purview. They should know what they're doing, or they hire that expertise, or they have on hand expert books that demonstrate how to do things the right way. As Tom notes, "I can't think of any topic in fund development or advocacy communications that can't claim a book written by a credible expert." (And by the way, that goes for everything else in management too.)

Instincts just aren't enough, and nonprofessionals use the wrong criteria. (Car manufacturer Henry Ford once said, "If we'd asked the public what they wanted, they would have said 'a faster horse.'")

Combine the curious conundrum of unfounded opinions and its corollary, inappropriate authority, and here's the summary: It's irresponsible to cede authority to those who do not actually have the authority. It's irresponsible to cede expertise and experience to uninformed opinions and second-guessing. Without malice or intent, this inappropriate input can easily ruin competent work and undermine your ability to nurture relationships and raise charitable gifts. When untrained and ill-informed people have the final say on what goes out the door, you run a serious risk.

> *When love and skill work together, expect a masterpiece.*
>
> —JOHN RUSKIN

IN CONCLUSION

Accomplished professionals position themselves as reliable experts and resources, competent teachers, and trusted advisors. These professionals hold organizations and colleagues accountable to a higher standard than short-term, quick-fix approaches. The whys help guide choices, focus effort, justify time spent, challenge strategies and tactics, and reinforce learning and change.

> *Good information and process—coupled with a strong understanding of why and how-to—makes for better decisions. The absence of these elements dramatically increases the likelihood of "what the hell am I gonna do now" moments.*
>
> —PARAPHRASING SHAWN POLAND, COHORT 15, MASTER'S PROGRAM, PHILANTHROPY AND DEVELOPMENT, SAINT MARY'S UNIVERSITY

The evolution of the profession provides unique opportunities to apply the body of knowledge, expand research, and adapt technical expertise to diverse cultures around the world. But we must not ignore forgotten whys. Long-term significant fund development results depend on professionals and organizations that embrace both the whys and the how-tos.

ENDNOTES

1. The term "organizational development" refers to all the elements of your organization, including governance, management, communications, and how it all fits together.
2. *Strategic Fund Development: Building Profitable Relationships That Last 2nd Ed.* (Sudbury, MA: Jones & Bartlett, 2001).
3. Peter M. Senge, *The Fifth Discipline* (New York: Doubleday, 1990), p. 13.
4. Cited in *The Rolling Stone Book of Life: Wisdom for Survival* (Philadelphia: Running Press, 1997), from original interview with Coppola in *Rolling Stone,* February 7, 1991.
5. Quoted in Linda Ellinor and Glenna Gerard, *Dialogue: Rediscover the Transforming Power of Conversation* (New York: John Wiley & Sons, 1998), p. 282.
6. Dick Whitney and Melissa Giovagnoli, *75 Cage-Rattling Questions to Change the Way You Work* (New York: McGraw-Hill, 1997), p. 75.

CHAPTER 4

What Relationships Are and Why We Have Them

THE ART OF HUMAN INTERACTION

I do not believe in things, I believe in relationships.

—GEORGES BRAQUE, 1882–1963, FRENCH PAINTER AND SCULPTOR

Learning to communicate and build relationships more effectively will influence just about every hot-button aspect of your personal and professional life.[1]

—TOM KRAMLINGER ET AL., *THE SOCIAL STYLES HANDBOOK*

DEAR READER Relationships are bigger than "getting something from someone" or collaborating with some organization because a funder expects it. I agree with my colleague Tony Myers, CFRE, from Alberta, Canada, when he says, "Relationships are the core to everything. My life. Your life. Our work." Tony goes on to ask: "Why are we building relationships? What is our purpose?" His answer: "It's about community building, a key pillar of philanthropy. It's about building bridges before we need them."

Simone

RELATIONSHIPS ARE EVERYTHING

Your organization isn't an isolated fiefdom. Instead, it operates as part of a community. No matter your specific mission, your organization exists to make the community a better place. Nonprofits/NGOs exist to build communities.

It's also a two-way street. While your organization helps build community, your organization needs community to survive and flourish. You need clients, volunteers, and donors. You need partner organizations. All of this is social capital, civil society, and civic capacity, described in Chapter 1.

> *In a synergistic relationship, those involved are transformed so that they get more out of the relationship than they originally put into it.*
>
> —G. CLOTAIRE RAPAILLE,
> *7 SECRETS OF MARKETING IN A MULTI-CULTURAL WORLD*

Highly successful people demonstrate an openness and curiosity. Their external focus helps them develop a growing number of relationships with other individuals and with organizations. The diversity of these relationships nourishes the individual.

Highly effective organizations do the same. Their external focus enables them to be flexible and able to adapt. The diversity of their relationships moves organizations forward to ever-stronger performance (see Exhibit 4.1). These relationships build a positive power base and expand influence.

EXHIBIT 4.1   REASONS FOR DEVELOPING RELATIONSHIPS

Examine these reasons for developing relationships. What would you add?

1. Expand your network of connections so that your organization becomes an indispensable element in the fabric of the community. For example: An international development agency partners with local government, religious leaders, and doctors and nurses to build a hospital.

2. Engage more people and businesses, thus increasing word of mouth. Also, their involvement with your organizations suggests they think you're credible.

3. Increase your organization's diversity in order to broaden your perspective. Management theory reinforces that diversity—of life experience, demographics, opinions, and the like—makes organizations stronger by challenging the status quo and introducing new ideas.

4. Increase your community connections so you regularly get more feedback, new information, and innovative ideas.

5. Bring together people and groups to test your ideas and programs and ensure your organization's relevance.

6. Extend your reach into new communities, acquiring additional clients, volunteers, and donors.

7. Increase your financial and human resources.

A Radical Notion

Here's my radical notion: Pursue relationships with no motive but to have them. Justify relationships as a desirable result rather than a strategy to produce money or volunteers or anything else.

If you're reading this book to learn more about donor relationships and communications, don't panic. The book does that. I'm just saying that if we broaden our horizons, more could result. I touch on this "radical notion" again in Chapter 11. Bet you can't wait!

Relationships Require Choice

Don't expect a response if you don't give people a choice. Just because you want a relationship with them doesn't mean they want one with you. Too often, organizations ignore this fact.

Take a look at these typical examples:

- I keep getting a newsletter from some organization that I don't care about. I'm not sure where the organization got my name. I'm choosing *not* to be in a relationship with that organization. Leave me alone. Don't add people to your mailing list unless you're darn sure they want a relationship with you! And clean your list regularly by asking people if they care to remain on board.
- You insist your board members set up meetings with their wealthy friends, even though those friends have never expressed an interest in your cause.

While developing relationships is central to effective organizations, the effort is time consuming. Furthermore, maintaining meaningful connections requires significant time from volunteers and staff.

How will you convince your organization that the return warrants the investment? What added value will you keep in mind as you prioritize your workload and cajole sufficient organizational investment?

Return to Chapter 1, on the larger context; that's the main reason for relationships. Explain that to your organization. Review the seven reasons for relationships from Exhibit 4.1. Personalize these with examples specific to your organization.

Don't treat people as objects to get something from.

—LEE KAISER

TYPES OF RELATIONSHIPS IN THE NONPROFIT/NGO SECTOR

As previewed in Chapter 1, I propose four relationships important to organizations in the nonprofit/NGO sector. Specifically:

1. Philanthropic relationships
2. Relationships with other organizations
3. Relationships within your organization
4. Advocacy and public policy relationships

Smart nonprofits maintain a strong network of these different relationships. For sure, an organization cannot flourish without the first three. And I think that without the last relationship, organizations don't achieve maximum value.

Your Philanthropic Relationships: How Your Organization Relates to Its Donors of Time and Money

Your organization is the means by which donors and volunteers live out their philanthropic interests and aspirations. But many organizations ignore this relationship. They place their mission first, making little room for the donor except as a source of cash or labor.

Relationships with Other Organizations: How Your Organization Relates to Other Community Organizations

Consider these relationships that benefit the organizations and their communities:

- Religious organizations partner with each other to feed the hungry.
- A city's arts organizations team up to promote cultural activities.
- A coalition of social justice organizations advocate for welfare legislation.
- Environmental organizations collaborate to deliver educational programs in schools.
- A housing organization partners with local corporations and employees to build homes.

Experience suggests that collaboration among organizations can produce significantly better results for everyone involved. Nonprofits can start with a simple "hello" and end up in a merger, moving from cooperation, to coordination, to collaboration in between.

Relationships within Your Organization: How the Various Parts of Your Organization Relate

The relationships within your organization powerfully influence your performance. It's one of those bottom-line things: If your organization doesn't relate well internally, it's likely to be less effective. And organizational effectiveness impacts all your other relationships, including your relationship with donors.

What does this mean? Examine employee interaction, teams, and interdepartmental cooperation. Review Chapter 3, "Key Components of Effective Organizations," including culture of philanthropy, organizational development, and conversation and questions. All of this is about human interaction and connection, and affects how your organization relates internally.

There's another critical internal relationship: how staff enable volunteers to act effectively on behalf of the organization.

This is the looking-in-the-mirror moment. If your volunteers and staff are not as effective as you want them to be, examine yourself first. My theory: Usually they are only as effective as we enable them to be.

So what, exactly, is enabling? It's the process of empowering others. In my theory, enabling means giving people the opportunity and resources to act. Enabling means sharing power.

Enabling functions include respecting and using the skills, expertise, experience, and insights of volunteers and staff. Enabling means engaging people in process, not just tasks, thus building understanding and ownership. When you enable others well, you anticipate conflicts and facilitate resolution. You model behavior. You coach people to succeed. You encourage others to use their power, practice their authority, and accept their responsibility. See Appendix A for a list of the enabling functions and the skills and attitudes of enablers.[2]

Advocacy and Public Policy Relationships: How Your Organization Promotes Public Policy that Fosters Healthy Communities

Some of us believe that ensuring democracy and freedom is the ultimate role of the nonprofit/NGO sector. Here's Alexis de Tocqueville again: "[The] liberty of association has become a necessary guarantee against the tyranny of the majority."

He goes on to say:

> [T]he unrestrained liberty of association for political purposes is the privilege which a people is longest in learning how to exercise. . . . [C]itizens who form the minority associate in order, first, to show their numerical strength and so to diminish the moral power of the majority; and, secondly, to stimulate competition and thus to discover those arguments that are most fitted to act upon the majority.[3]

Acting collectively, the nonprofit sector builds relationships to "ensure that the principles we wish to see enacted are heard and acted upon. This requires association. This is the core job of the sector," says Roger Lohman.[4]

Worldwide, the nonprofit/NGO sector serves as the conscience and strategy to secure "the inherent dignity and the equal and inalienable rights of all members of the human family," as cited in the United Nations Universal Declaration of Human Rights, adopted in December 1948.

Bold and uncowed, the sector speaks out, and organizes its constituents to do the same. The sector challenges the public conscience, whether citizens, government, public institutions, or corporations. For example, NGOs worked together to bring down the Berlin Wall. Cancer and lung associations fight tobacco companies and obtain judgments. Nonprofit legal battles protect voting rights and racial and gender bias. And that's just the tip of the iceberg.[5] We would live in a very different world without nonprofit/NGOs. And it would be a more dangerous world than it already is.

RELATIONSHIPS ARE DEFINITELY NOT TRANSACTIONS

Relationships differ from transactions. Transactions typically are described as negotiating something or carrying out a business deal. In contrast, relationships refer to a bond, a form of "kinship." Relationships depend on interest and rapport to form connection and loyalty.

According to Adrian Sargeant and Elaine Jay, until the early 1980s marketing usually focused on transactions.[6] The marketing process identified needs, designed products to meet those needs, and developed communications programs that facilitated the transaction.

In contrast, contemporary marketing focuses on building a relationship with the customer rather than fostering a series of one-time transactions. Nowadays people don't buy products and services; they buy relationships. Relational marketing recognizes and reflects customer interests and nurtures the bond between customer and organization.

> *Do your donors feel like automatic teller machines? Do you stop by regularly to withdraw some money?*

Fund development has followed the same path as marketing, but trails a few years behind. Fundraising techniques sound like a series of transactions. Even after identifying the basis for a donor relationship, too many fundraisers turn too quickly to technical expertise. The demand for quick financial return produces appeals that may not connect sufficiently with donor and prospect interests.

The emphasis on the immediacy of a specific appeal focuses on donations, not donors.

But is this our intent? Especially when we know that relationships differ from transactions?

Ken Burnett introduced relationship fundraising in his 1992 book of that name. He says:

> Relationship fundraising is an approach to the marketing of a cause that centres on the unique and special relationship between a nonprofit and each supporter. Its overriding consideration is to care for and develop that bond and to do nothing that might damage or jeopardize it. Each activity is therefore geared toward making sure donors know they are important, valued and considered, which has the effect of maximizing funds per donor in the long term.[7]

Yet despite Ken, relationship fund development is still struggling for broad acceptance and broader practice. There's work to be done in order to put the donor at the center.

DO DONORS REALLY WANT RELATIONSHIPS?

Now that's a big question. Do donors really want relationships with organizations? Some say yes. But I can hear Richard Radcliffe, U.K. legacy consultant, whispering no rather loudly in my ear!

Here's my answer: In *their* terms and according to *their* definition, I think many (if not most) donors want relationships with organizations. It's a personal thing, as usual.

Giving (time or money) is one of the most personal acts in any society.

I suspect most volunteers want a relationship. They expect fairly regular connection with representatives of an organization. Some volunteers actually use volunteering as a way to create human connection in their lives. Others prefer isolated tasks with little human connection, but I'll bet not many. Volunteering seems to be, in general, an activity that brings people together to do something.

But do donors of money want a relationship with the organization? We know some donors often give out of habit. We know there's trouble with donor retention rates. We hear donors complain, "You only contact me when you want money." And we know that many donors stop giving because they don't feel adequately connected to the organization and its results. Surely that "connection" refers to some form of relationship.

The point is, an organization needs to find out what donors want. What does a donor mean by "relationship"? What kind of relationship does a donor want? The successful organization develops relationships accordingly.

WATCH A GOOD RELATIONSHIP BUILDER

Watch a star relationship builder at work. You'll observe good listening skills. You'll hear interest in the voice and watch curiosity flit across her face.

Her sensibility helps others verbalize their thoughts and feelings. Her quick and ready insights, as well as self-disclosure, build connections.

The star relationship builder readily distinguishes among facts, judgment, and inference, reinforcing her trustworthiness. Here's how that works while nurturing a relationship with "José."

- Fact: He's a 30-something man with one child. José works for the government.
- Inference: José appears to be interested in the arts because he talks about theater and music during the conversation with the relationship builder.
- Judgment: A good way to cultivate José would be to offer complimentary tickets to the organization's upcoming matinee production and invite him to bring his child.

Good relationship builders are perceptive and intuitive. Their empathetic behavior builds trust and deepens bonds. Don't we all aspire to this?

KEY CONCEPTS IN RELATIONSHIP BUILDING

You want to build profitable relationships that last. Everyone else does, too. Be careful. The phrase "profitable relationships" refers to mutually beneficial exchanges. It's not just about you; it's about the others in the relationship, as well. And for Tom and me, it's more about the others, as Dale Carnegie says. For us, "profitable" means "meaningful," not financially lucrative!

Fundamentally, relationship building is about respect: Your courteous regard for others, their feelings, their opinions, their experiences. With respect as your overarching principle, ground yourself (and your organization) in these five key concepts:

1. Sincerity
2. Closeness and boundaries
3. Diversity and cultural competency
4. Values
5. Dynamic and changing

Sincerity

Sincerity "requires us to act and really be the way that we present ourselves to others," says American literary critic, author, and teacher Lionel Trilling.[8] Sincerity is in the eye of the beholder, of course. The goal: Others see you as genuine, honest and trustworthy. Neither you nor your organization is perceived as superficial or phony.

Orlando Patterson provides a critical benchmark for sincerity when he says: "The criteria of sincerity are unambiguous: Will they keep their promises? Will they honor the meanings and understandings we tacitly negotiate? Are their gestures of cordiality offered in conscious good faith?"[9]

For me, here's the first promise in philanthropic relationships: sincere belief that philanthropy refers to all gifts of time and money, no matter the size. To behave this way honors definitions of philanthropy. To believe this respects the tacit assumption any donor or volunteer makes: that his or her gift is meaningful to the organization.

Second promise: There is a clear distinction between the relationship with the organization and a personal friendship. Treat me as a donor or volunteer rather than a personal friend. Respect these boundaries.

Yet I hear stories and witness acts that make me cringe. Worse, donors and volunteers experience these situations and notice the insincere behavior. For example:

- **Fundraisers who see relationship building as a strategy to get larger gifts.** These fundraisers are not genuinely interested in their donors. Instead, they go through the motions of donor contact, anxious that the proscribed recipe produces a bigger gift in a timely fashion.

- **Fundraisers who do not actually value all donors equally.** These fundraisers stop what they're doing to talk with a big donor but barely have time to speak with the man who gave $25. Or my recent client who proposed to make thank-you calls to large donors only, because they're the most important. (I easily convinced them otherwise, but "large donors only" was the first reaction.)

- **Fundraisers who abruptly finish a conversation with the volunteer receptionist in order to spend significant time with a board member.**

- **Fundraisers and volunteers who trespass on personal and professional connections to garner gifts.**

- **Fundraisers who develop personal friendship with donors and volunteers, and don't differentiate the personal relationship and the "business" relationship with the organization.**

Frankly, I'm uncomfortable with titles like "major gifts officer." This suggests that there are minor gifts. Do you expect donors to call asking for the "minor gifts officer"? Like my rant about annual funds, I think "major gifts" and "major gifts officer" are terms that inappropriately migrated out of the organization's privacy into the public sphere. And to our detriment.

The relationships in this book are between your organization and its volunteers, donors, elected officials, organizations, and so forth. The nature of the relationships depends on your organization and its mission.

I call these "business" relationships because your organization is the business that does the relating. These relationships with your organization are not personal friendships.

Part of sincerity is ensuring that everyone understands the nature of the relationship. I think of my relationship with Marcia, the executive director of the Women's Fund. When we are together doing the business of the Women's Fund, this is a "business" relationship. We are interacting as executive director (her) and board member and donor (me). Certainly we are cordial, even friendly. Marcia and I also, however, have become personal friends. So in any interaction, we make clear what the relationship is. Are we interacting as personal friends, or is this Simone in relationship with the Women's Fund? It's an important distinction.

> There's lore about how managers and baristas make an effort to remember the customers' names and their preferred drinks. As a result, consumers don't simply go to a Starbucks, they go to their Starbucks.
>
> —DANIEL GROSS, "ROMANCING US WITH COFFEE"

Now that's a relationship: welcoming, considerate, personal.

Closeness and Boundaries

There is no relationship without some degree of closeness. You develop a relationship based on some knowledge of each other. You develop a closer relationship through increasing familiarity.

The best relationships depend on enough closeness to create an enduring bond, but not so much to cause discomfort. An organization's relationship-building program focuses on nurturing the appropriate closeness.

For example, what does closeness mean in a donor relationship? It's two-way. The organization respects donor interests, experience, and background. It understands the donor's emotions and aspirations as much as possible.

At the same time, the donor feels sufficiently connected to the organization and has an adequate understanding of the organization's vision. Donor dreams align with the organization's dreams.

If you're going to ask Tom and me for what we consider to be a large gift, you better make sure you know what we're interested in. You have to know how we feel about the cause and what kind of difference we want to make. We have to feel that you respect our interests and emotions. And we have to feel sufficiently connected to and bonded with your organization. Then your relationship building can be effective. Only then could your solicitation succeed.

Comfort with closeness likely depends on personality, life experience, generational attitudes, and cultural background. For example, a few years ago I discussed closeness in donor relationships with my French cousin Fabienne and her husband, Jean-Claude. I tested ideas for a relationship-building workshop I was to present at the annual conference of l'Association Française des Fundraisers (www.fundraisers.fr).

Fab and Jean-Claude are from a society that values privacy more than U.S. culture does, and their reactions showed it. They were not sure my proposed relationship-building strategies would work in France. For example, Fab wasn't sure that she would attend a cultivation gathering hosted by an NGO, although she is a donor to several French charities.

Managing various levels of closeness requires sensitivity and insight. You must recognize, anticipate, and respect the boundaries preferred by those within the relationship. And the boundaries may be fairly fluid, dependent on a particular issue, the evolution of the relationship itself, changes within the relationship partners, or something else altogether.

Your Own Boundaries   Your organization has boundaries, too. So do you. Even with the relationship at the center, you do not compromise your own values, vision, and mission. Either you find sufficient commonality to develop some form of a relationship with benefits accruing to all participants, or you don't pursue a relationship.

Also keep this in mind: In any relationship, the larger the request you wish to make, the more intimate the relationship must be. It doesn't matter if you seek a financial contribution or board membership, collaboration with another organization or a public policy vote. And remember, the size of the request depends on the view of who you are asking, not your organization's view.

Diversity and Cultural Competence

Sometimes it's called pluralism or inclusion. No matter the label, diversity describes differences that significantly affect the way each of us experiences our own self and the way each of us is treated by others.

> *The most banal of human fault – a failure to imagine the life of another.*
>
> —RICHARD NORTH PATTERSON, *EXILE*

As my friend Sarah quipped, "Diversity is here today and here to stay." Look around. What is the composition of your community today? How has it changed? How might it change again? Who are you clients today, and who might they be in the future? Who do you think will be your future employees, donors, and volunteers?

It's curious that anyone thinks they can steer around issues of diversity. Yet I see organizations, their boards and fundraisers do just that. They claim "our community is predominately Caucasian so race doesn't matter for our board or staff." Or they note "We're looking for specific skills so we don't need to discuss diversity."

Think about your own life. What's influenced you because of your gender or ethnicity, age or socioeconomic status?

Ask a Black man how he's experienced life differently because of race. Ask a woman or a lesbian colleague. Ask someone in a wheelchair or ask a teenager. Ask a Muslim or Jew. Or think about the last time you were ignored or criticized because you held a very different opinion. All this is about experiencing life differently.

Differences seem "troublesome and difficult because we are more comfortable with sameness. We are socialized to look for similarities."[10] But there are very negative implications for society's socialization around differences like gender, ethnicity, and sexual orientation. Even worse, as Mary Ellen Capek and Molly Mead note, social constructs often depend on a particular society and a specific era.[11] Ironically, it's our differences that "provide us with our individuality and the unique perspectives and talents we bring into any relationship or situation."[12]

> *Honoring the simple reality of another person's experience is an instant link to the bigger world outside of one's self. It's the seed of empathy, and it's free.*
>
> —GROUP OF 33, *THE BIG MOO*

What a shame: People may want to help your organization. But because of differing life experiences, they'll come with a different perspective. And you won't connect with them unless you recognize and respect their diversity.

Organizational Effectiveness through Diversity The twenty-first century demands more culturally competent individuals and organizations. In fact, cultural competency is a key component of effective organizations. With cultural competence, you can nurture the full scope of relationships that are indispensable for a viable organization. Only in this way can you and your organization help sustain and renew healthy communities.

As key players in creating healthy communities, nonprofits should be leaders in pluralism and cultural competency. Yes, I think "should" is the right word.

Exploring the different cultures, beliefs, and values of others allows us to reach out with sensitivity. Then we can find mutual interests and act respectfully and responsively. We're able to design culturally sensitive cultivation and communications strategies that connect with diverse audiences.

Effective relationship builders understand, respect, and manage diversity. *Excellent* relationship builders actually welcome and seek pluralism. These professionals acquire information and tools, develop their own skills, and expand their own insights. This is not about stereotyping, tokenism, or quotas. There's no manipulation, only sincerity, integrity, and respect.

> *We assume that our readers have the moral sense to try earnestly not to use this information to stereotype people, but rather to become better listeners, better observers of the human condition, better bosses, and better friends. Our goal is not to put people in a box, but to open up the box so that we can all get a better glimpse of who and what is inside.*
>
> —Lynne Lancaster and David Stilman, *When Generations Collide: Who They Are, Why They Clash*

Values

What are your personal values? What beliefs are so enduring that they guide your thinking and decision making, direct your actions and judgments?

These values are nonnegotiable and unconditional, forming your own personal philosophy of life. You consciously chose these values, knowing full well the consequences. You cherish these tenets, affirming them publicly and holding yourself accountable to act accordingly.

Organizations have values, too. Values define the enduring character of an organization, precede its mission, and last even as priorities, programs, and strategies change.

So the first question is: Have you defined your personal values? Are you prepared to fight for them? How do your personal values fit with your organization's values?

Next, has your organization articulated its values? Was the process participatory, engaging staff and board members? How well does your organization live its values? Every organization needs to articulate its values. Everyone within the organization has to be on the same page to function effectively. And donors need to know our values to find their way in, or not.

Now think about the relationships that your organization develops. How do your organization's values affect its diverse relationships? Does your organization speak its values loud and clear, even at the risk of losing donors and volunteers?

Readily apparent value conflicts typically stop the start-up of a relationship. Before working closely with other organizations, it's useful to evaluate the alignment of values. Doing this helps each organization determine the desirability of initiating the relationship. For example, many proposed mergers have fallen apart due to values conflicts.

Sometimes value conflicts appear within an existing relationship. Then the participants determine if and how the relationship can continue. If the relationship continues, participants usually agree to avoid the conflicted area. For example, a donor learns more about an organization's advocacy activities and is uncomfortable. The donor continues giving to direct service and you don't discuss advocacy. Or the donor stops giving because the conflict is too great in her opinion. That's her choice.

Typically, the closer the value match, the closer the relationship. You can see this in your personal and professional life. You witness this values alignment in particularly successful collaborations between organizations. And you certainly see value matches with your most engaged donors and volunteers.

Keep in mind: Values don't change much. They are relatively permanent frameworks that shape and influence the behavior of individuals and organizations. Values define what individuals and groups stand for. You and your organization embrace and live these values daily.

See sample values statements in Exhibits 4.2 and 4.3. See also Appendix 4A.

Dynamism and Change

Who doesn't want long-term relationships that deepen and grow more complex over time? Wouldn't it be wonderful if all your organization's relationships were truly synergistic, producing mutual enhancement? Don't we all seek transformation through relationships with others?

But relationships are dynamic, not static. Relationships may grow or diminish in intensity. This ebb and flow responds to multiple variables affecting the involved parties. Your partners in the relationship constantly evolve and will likely expect the relationship to evolve, too. And sometimes the relationship is no longer valuable to some of the partners and they move on.

Professional fundraisers devise systems and strategies to manage the relationship-building program, described in subsequent chapters. The system includes regular connection and feedback from parties in the relationship. With that, your understanding of them remains contemporary and responsive, as far as your organization is able.

In Conclusion

Nurturing relationships is *not* about finding people just like you. It's about finding people who share your interests and emotions.

EXHIBIT 4.2   **VALUES OF THE AUDUBON SOCIETY OF RHODE ISLAND**

Our values describe the way we treat people and the way we do business. These values guide our decisions and actions. These values belong to everyone in the organization.

Natural World
Nature contains a web of complex relationships. We value the integrity and connectedness of the natural world, and appreciate its biodiversity. We recognize that preservation of the natural world is essential for human life.

Good Science and Sound Knowledge
Objective empirical science sets the standard for the preservation of natural systems. We promote good science and sound knowledge. We believe that people deserve to be fully informed.

Civic Engagement, Community, and Action
Civic engagement—acting individually and collectively—is essential to sustainable development and global stewardship of the earth's resources and the environment. We recognize human responsibility to the global environment. We believe in collaborative action in order to live in harmony with nature.

Excellence and Permanence
Integrity, trustworthiness, and quality are essential to permanence. We pursue excellence in every area of our work. We successfully adapt due to our external focus, network connectedness, inquisitiveness, and innovation. We are committed to future generations, passing on a strong organization and a sustainable environment.

Respect, Diversity, and Access
The earth and all living organisms deserve respect. Our world and its people are rich in diversity. We embrace inclusion and access regardless of race, ethnicity, culture, language, gender, age, socioeconomics, physical challenges, sexual orientation, or any other difference. We embrace inclusion and access regardless of differences in background or life experience. We welcome ideas and provide opportunities to our guests, donors, volunteers, and employees.

Tradition and Accomplishments
The past provides important perspective and insight for today and tomorrow. We respect our history, honor our accomplishments, and embrace change for the future.

Source: Used with permission. Courtesy of the Audubon Society of Rhode Island, www
.asri.org.

Nurturing relationships bridges gaps. That's how we create a sustainable world, foster healthy communities, build successful NGOs and businesses, and create personal bonds of friendship and collegiality.

Effective organizations and professionals build genuine relationships that last.

The best relationships create sources of energy and produce a synergy that helps the entire organization thrive.

EXHIBIT 4.3	VALUES AND MISSION OF THE WOMENS FUND OF RHODE ISLAND

These values define the enduring character of the Women's Fund of Rhode Island (WFRI). As individuals and as a group, we nurture these values because they serve as our foundation, framework, and guide.

Access:
We believe in social justice, that women and girls must have equal access to all opportunity, whether social, cultural, economic, educational, or political.

Collaboration:
We know that the greatest results come from the combined efforts of diverse organizations and individuals. We reach out to work cooperatively with others, in order to make meaningful and long lasting change.

Empowerment:
Power shared is power multiplied. We believe in helping women and girls acquire the wherewithal, opportunity, and adequate power to realize their own potential and life goals.

Equity:
We believe that all people deserve fairness, impartiality, justice, and opportunity.

Inclusion:
We embrace diversity including race, ethnicity, religion, economics, age, education, sexual orientation, and other differences. We celebrate the richness of our community and build bridges and bonds.

Informed and responsive:
We value knowledge and informed decision-making. We reach out for information and share it with others. We listen to the ideas and advice of others, learning together so that we can respond to the unique needs of women and girls.

Integrity:
We are honest and reliable, open and sincere. We hold ourselves accountable, doing what we say we're going to do. We evaluate our effectiveness and change as necessary.

Leadership:
We foster innovation and encourage the best in ideas and efforts. We're bold and courageous, taking thoughtful and well-planned risks. We're proactive and initiate positive action.

Permanence:
We value intergenerational equity, stewarding endowed resources to meet the unique needs of women and girls, now and in the future.

Respect:
We are committed to dignity for everyone.

Transformation:

Our work is about change. We are change agents, catalysts for positive transformation in the lives of women and girls.

> The mission of the Women's Fund of Rhode Island is to advance equity and social justice for women and girls. The Fund champions fairness, impartiality, opportunity, shared power, and responsibility in all spheres of personal and community life including economic, cultural, educational, social, and public policy.
>
> The Fund serves as a catalyst for persuasive, progressive, and enduring social change for women and girls by:
>
> - Making grants that address unique needs
> - Focusing attention on inequities in status and advocating systemic change
> - Engaging women and girls as active philanthropists and mobilizing them for action
> - Positioning funding for women and girls as an essential investment to build sustainable communities
> - Convening, collaborating, and leveraging leadership and resources
> - Celebrating accomplishments
> - Creating a thoughtful, flexible, and proactive agenda to guide this critical work, in keeping with stated values

Used with permission. Courtesy of the Women's Fund of Rhode Island, www.wfri.org

Quit looking for quick fixes and silver bullets. Help your staff colleagues, your boss, and your board understand this reality.

The work is long and arduous and produces as many challenges as rewards. Professionals share these truths with their organizations and lead them to a deeper understanding of philanthropy and fund development. Professionals promote these ideas within the sector, expanding the framework for this work.

ENDNOTES

1. Tom Kramlinger, Ph.D., Michael Leimbach, Ph.D., Ed Tittel, B.A., M.A., David Yesford, *The Social Styles Handbook: Find Your Comfort Zone and Make People Feel Comfortable With You* (Wilson Learning Library, Nova Vista Publishing, June 25, 2004), p. 14, www.novavistapub.com

2. These functions are described in detail in my book *Strategic Fund Development: Building Profitable Relationships That Last,* 2nd ed. (Sudbury, MA: Jones & Bartlett, 2001). A few years later I added a seventeenth function, thanks to the students in Cohort 14 at Saint Mary's University.

3. Nineteenth-century Frenchman Alexis de Tocqueville talked about "the principle of association" while traveling in the United States. His writings have long inspired the

nonprofit and philanthropic movements in this country and, by extension, to civil society around the world. This quote is from his *Democracy in America,* The Henry Reeve Text as Revised by Francis Bowen and Further Corrected by Phillips Bradley, Abridged with an Introduction by Thomas Bender (New York: The Modern Library, 1945), p. 404.

4. "The Commons: Our Mission If We Choose to Accept It," *Nonprofit Quarterly* (Summer 2003): 9, www.nonprofitquarterly.org.

5. There's some wonderful writing about this relationship. Some of my favorites include: *Robin Hood Was Right,* by Collins and Rogers; *You Can't Be Neutral on a Moving Train* by Howard Zinn; and articles by Scott Harshbarger, Jeff Madrick, and Roger Lohmann in the summer 2003 issue of *Nonprofit Quarterly,* www.nonprofitquarterly.org.

6. Adrian Sargeant and Elaine Jay, *Building Donor Loyalty* (San Francisco: Jossey-Bass, 2004).

7. Ken Burnett, *Relationship Fundraising,* 2nd ed. (San Francisco: Jossey-Bass, 2002), p. 38.

8. Quoted in Orlando Patterson, "Our Overrated Inner Self," *New York Times,* December 26, 2006. Used with permission. Courtesy Orlando Patterson.

9. Ibid.

10. Linda Ellinor and Glenna Gerard, *Dialogue: Rediscover the Transforming Power of Conversation* (New York: John Wiley & Sons, 1998), p. 195.

11. Mary Ellen S. Capek and Molly Mead, *Effective Philanthropy: Organizational Success through Deep Diversity and Gender Equity* (Cambridge, MA: MIT Press).

12. Ellinor and Gerard, *Dialogue.*

Values and Mission of the Equity Action Fund at the Rhode Island Foundation*

EQUITY ACTION: RHODE ISLAND'S FUND FOR SEXUAL ORIENTATION AND GENDER IDENTITY INITIATIVES

Social justice means that each individual is treated fairly, with voice, access, opportunity and responsibility in all areas of personal and community life.

Our community is not yet just. Instead, injustice is an intricate web that weaves together diverse elements including sexual orientation, gender, gender identity, race, ethnicity, nationality, religion, age, disability, and socioeconomics. Injustice is reinforced through social and cultural values, public policy, and institutional systems.

Mission and Philosophy

Equity Action envisions a world that is fair, just and equitable. The Fund is committed to social change in order to achieve justice, recognizing that this struggle requires dedication to progressive policy at all levels and in all areas of community life.

To foster social justice, the Fund will:

1. Strengthen the infrastructure of LGBTQ-led and serving organizations by making grants, providing educational opportunities, and partnering with funders and donors to leverage resources

---

*Drafted by Simone P. Joyaux, ACFRE, as a gift; approved by the Equity Action Steering Committee in September 2003.

2. Raise awareness by highlighting the need for equitable treatment of lesbian, gay, bisexual, transgender, and queer (LGBTQ) individuals.

3. Facilitate an integrated community by convening LGBTQ and mainstream organizations, encouraging networking, and fostering collaboration.

4. Promote social change by encouraging progressive public policy and public debate, and by standing for the protection of human rights.

5. Enhance philanthropy by and for the LGBTQ communities by establishing an endowment fund and actively soliciting gifts.

Values

The values of Equity Action define who we are, what we stand for, and how we do our work. They are principles against which we measure the worthiness of our decisions and actions. We hold ourselves accountable for transforming these values into action.

- *Activism.* We are activists, seeking equity and advocating for social change. We know that equity is about making the invisible visible. We believe in grassroots action, public debate and progressive policy in political, social and institutional arenas.

- *Courage.* We speak our minds while telling our hearts. We defend our convictions. We are risk-takers and catalysts for change.

- *Diversity.* We recognize that diversity describes the differences that significantly affect the way we experience ourselves and are treated by others. We welcome diversity including sexual orientation, gender identity, gender, race, ethnicity, nationality, religion, age, disability, and socioeconomics. We will work to foster respect for the uniqueness of individuals.

- *Justice.* We seek to right the imbalances of an unjust society and an unequal distribution of resources. We challenge the assumption that economic and social inequities are the unavoidable price of progress and prosperity.

- *Power.* Each individual should have power over her/his own life, sharing power with others to build a healthy community for all. Power is not an end but a means, an essential tool for ensuring basic human rights, opportunity and access, and justice and freedom for all.

- *Responsibility.* We accept responsibility—both individually and collectively—to pursue a socially just community. We strive for excellence even when resources are limited.

- *Trustworthy.* Our interactions will be based on openness, sincerity and transparency, and we will strive to do so with the utmost integrity.

Used with permission.
Courtesy of the Equity Action Advisory Council and The Rhode Island Foundation

CHAPTER 5

Five Rather Deadly Sins

WARNINGS ABOUT RELATIONSHIPS AND SOLICITATION

Success in securing philanthropic gifts is not the result of mastering techniques, deploying the latest technology, or enjoying the most hallowed tradition. Simply stated, successful philanthropic fundraising is the product of the intentional, strategic, and consistent building and nurturing of relationships with an ever-expanding pool of stakeholders.

—TIM J. BURCHILL, STRATEGIC FUND DEVELOPMENT

DEAR READER

Before delving deeper into relationships, I'll offer some warnings. You might not like some of these tips. Perhaps mine conflict with those of other professionals. Or maybe you just plain disagree. But think long and hard first. These tips resonate with thousands of donors, staff, board members, and other volunteers at conferences and in client engagements around the word. *Simone*

SIN #1: SEPARATING FUND DEVELOPMENT FROM PHILANTHROPY

You can't have philanthropy without fund development. You know the mantra: "Question: What is the major reason people give contributions?" "Answer: Because they are asked!"

Have you ever heard a board member say "I don't think we should have to ask for money. They should just send it." (Yes, I've heard that!)

But think about it: Do people sit down monthly and ask themselves "To whom shall I send money?" No. People look at their "requests" for money. You know, the bills sent by the gas and telephone companies. Or the requests—written or oral—from charitable organizations. It's the same with volunteers: Ask and you're more likely to recruit volunteers than waiting for their calls.

Obviously, fundraisers and their organizations are in the asking business. It's the asking that helps produce philanthropy.

> *Philanthropy and fund development are inextricably linked. No doubt about it. But sadly, my experience says that both are not equally respected.*

Try this experiment: Ask your board members to define philanthropy. Ask your neighbors, too. Ask your family members and even people on the street.

They all say wonderful, positive things. They smile and you can hear the smile and warmth in their voice.

Now ask those same people to define fund development. Guess what happens?

Voices become tense. Not many smiles. And the words? Negative. Phrases like "begging" and "pushy pitches like used car salespeople."

Hundreds of such discussions produce the same result: Philanthropy generates positive emotions reflected in positive words. Fund development generates terse responses and negative vocabulary. Furthermore, most respondents equate *philanthropy* and *philanthropist* with large gifts and wealthy patrons.

This is not good. Actually, this is very bad.

People—and that includes board members in particular—need to feel positive about fund development. They need to understand that philanthropy depends on fund development.

Philanthropy means voluntary action for the common good. Fund development is the essential partner of philanthropy. Fund development makes philanthropy possible by bringing together a particular cause and the donors and prospects who care about that cause. Through relationship building, fund development nurtures loyalty and lifetime value, thus facilitating philanthropy.

Now here are the big questions: Do you think your board members understand that philanthropy depends on fund development? Do you think your board and staff feel as good about fund development as they do about philanthropy? It's our job as fund development leaders to celebrate the link philanthropy and fund development, and nurture great feelings about both.

SIN #2: TREATING GIVING AS A FINANCIAL TRANSACTION RATHER THAN AN EMOTIONAL ACT

When did fund development become a financial transaction?

What happened?

It's the twenty-first century. Everything moves more quickly. Technology produces ever-faster results. Communication speeds by. Change accelerates. Expectations increase.

Now add to this pace the growth of the nonprofit/NGO sector. The global sector expands with more organizations and a greater demand for charitable gifts. Research, experience, and technology introduce new strategies and tactics.

Immediate funding needs demand immediate return, producing shorter-term thinking. New strategies seduce organizations, allowing them to avoid difficult learning and change. Intense focus on technical expertise and the demand for money causes a disconnect between the why and the how-to.

Combined, this growth and tempo often produce a quick-fix mentality that ignores all the whys. Instead, organizations and professionals focus more and more attention and resources on technical expertise. We focus on the urgent—getting gifts immediately—rather than the important, developing long-term sustainable approaches.

> *We are so busy doing the urgent that we don't have time to do the important.*
>
> —Confucius, 551–479 BCE, Chinese philosopher

Are You Treating Your Donors like Automatic Teller Machines?

Often organizational behavior reinforces the focus on money. For example:

Direct marketing often overwhelms personal contact. Staff-led cultivation and solicitation has long overtaken volunteer participation, yet voluntary action is the definition of philanthropy. Big gifts and their donors may receive preferential treatment.

Listen to the conversation when professional fundraisers get together. Hear the concerns of chief executives the world over. Pay attention to the talk at board meetings. What do you hear?

People talk about the bottom line. By that, most often they mean the money. "Our agency needs money right now to accomplish its mission." "We have so many needy people to serve that we must raise more money quickly." "What strategy can we use right now to produce more donations quickly?" "Which tactic has the best (and quickest) return on investment?" "How can I tweak the direct mail letter to get a better response?" "How many new sponsors can we recruit to support that event?"

It's about the money. More money. More money more quickly. Of course, more money to do good work. But still, money seems to be the theme, leading one donor to say that he felt like an automatic teller machine.

With all this, fund development seems to focus on donations rather than donors. And all this reinforces the message that philanthropy is about money.

It's past time to realize that nonprofits/NGOs are the means by which the donor fulfills his or her own interests and aspirations. Emotions drive everything, including relationships. You'll hear this theme over and over throughout this book—and in every encounter with either Tom or me. Of course, rationale is important in making the case. But rationale is the handmaiden of emotion. Without an emotional basis, your fund development cannot reach its full potential.

SIN #3: TRESPASSING ON PERSONAL AND PROFESSIONAL RELATIONSHIPS. PLEASE PROMISE THAT YOU WON'T!

How many times have you heard a fundraiser ask all board members to share their personal mailing lists with an organization? Of course we've all done this. But let's think about what happens.

The fundraiser explains that the organization needs to find new donors. The fund development committee suggests that each board member bring in his or her personal list of contacts—for example, the people you send holiday cards to or your golf and tennis buddies, or members of your club, or . . .

The organization prepares a letter explaining the importance of its work. The board member is asked to sign the letter—and hopefully write a personal note—to the names on his or her list.

The results: Some board members provide a list and follow through. Some don't. You receive some gifts, but probably not many. The gift sizes may not be as much as you hoped. The gifts are not commensurate with gifts the respondent gives elsewhere. In the future, when your board member is no longer affiliated with your organization, the gifts may well stop.

What happened? Your board members used their friends, family, and colleagues—asking, essentially, for a favor: "Please give a gift to support this charity that means a lot to me."

Sometimes their contacts did a favor and gave a gift; sometimes not. And when someone gives a gift as a favor for a friend or colleague, it is likely that the gift is not as large as would be given to something the donor cared about.

Moreover, a back-and-forth favor exchange often results. How many times have you heard someone say "I just cannot help fundraise any more. I'm all tapped out." In other words, I don't have any other friends or colleagues who owe me a favor. Or I'm not willing to owe anyone else a favor after they respond to my gift request.

What happened here? Your board members were trespassing on personal and professional relationships. And you asked them to do this.

How Do Your Board Members Feel?

Not only is this weak fund development. This is poor treatment of board members.

Have you ever asked your board members how they feel about asking their friends and colleagues to give money simply because they are friends and colleagues?

I've asked thousands of board members: Mostly they feel uncomfortable.

Have you ever asked your board members what they don't like about fund development? Their most frequent complaints are: "I'm uncomfortable asking for favors." And "I feel like I'm pushing people."

Yes, thousands of board members from Joyaux clients and attendees at Joyaux workshops have expressed these concerns for years. When will fundraisers listen?

But Lots of Organizations Do This and We Need the Money!

Yes, lots of organizations ask board members to do this. Undoubtedly you've given gifts in response to pleas from friends, family, and colleagues. I certainly have.

Sometimes this approach can be done very carefully, without great harm. And anyway, you cannot simply give up all these gifts, especially if this is your primary fund development method. But you can start changing. Review Exhibit 5.1 and keep reading this book.

The alternative—identifying those who may care—is so much easier, more productive, and longer lasting! In thousands of conversations, this approach

---

EXHIBIT 5.1   TRESPASSING PRODUCES LESS-THAN-SATISFACTORY RESULTS

Trespassing on personal and professional relationships produces less-than-satisfactory results like these:

- The solicitor often feels like he or she is coercing gifts based on favors. The solicitor feels awkward and uncomfortable and thinks that all fundraising is based on this dynamic.

- The prospect thinks that all fundraising is based on this trespassing and favor exchange, thus perpetuating bad fundraising practice.

- Your organization acquires donations, probably not donors. The gifts are most likely smaller than could be possible with a donor who really cares. Also, the donations are often short term.

- You are not developing a base of loyal donors.

- You are not developing a strong and effective fundraising relationship with your solicitors.

resonates with both staff and volunteers—with rare exceptions. See complete details about this approach in Chapter 7.

Now for that rare exception I just mentioned: a presentation I made in Canada a few years ago. A participant said: "I don't know about you people south of the border, but here everyone knows that joining a board means using your connections to raise money. It's all about getting the right connected people on your board—people with influence and affluence who can get to the right people and produce money and other important favors. That's the political reality. That's just the way things work."

Yes, indeed. Lots of organizations recruit board members because of their affluence, influence, and connections. These organizations expect the board members to use their connections and influence to get gifts, with apparent scant regard for the interests (or disinterests) of those being contacted. I think that is trespassing and I think it's a lousy idea.

That was my point during the presentation, and that is my continual point whether consulting, writing, or presenting. I challenge the status quo, "the way things are done" and "the way things work." There in Canada, I was asking the audience to question the convention of recruiting connected people so they'll use their connections on your behalf.

I also questioned accepting the "political reality." I always challenge "political realities." So here's that challenge to us all: Why do we accept—no, why do we *promote*—political realities that are so troublesome? For example: Since when is a board only about connections, influence, and affluence? Do we equate philanthropy with wealth only? Are we modeling the philanthropic sector after this have and have-not society and government and corporate antics? Do we justify this approach because the end—philanthropic service—is good? (See further exploration of this topic in Chapter 25.)

SIN #4: UNIVERSALIZING YOUR OWN PASSION. INSTEAD, FIND THEIRS—OR LEAVE THEM ALONE AND MOVE ON!

Caution: Do not spend your limited resources (both human and financial) to try to make *them* interested. People express offense and aggravation when cornered by an enthusiastic representative of an organization who is trying to convince them of the organization's value.

The job—with the help of the organization's staff, board members, and other volunteers—is to find those who are interested in the cause and organization. Do *not* try to convince people to be interested. This gambit wastes organizational time and resources—and makes you and your volunteers feel unsuccessful. And this approach offends, annoys, and may well anger those you've decided to target.

There are hundreds, thousands, millions of worthy organizations and important causes. But not everyone is interested in everything—and that includes your cause. In fact, we want diverse donors giving to various causes. That increases social capital and produces healthy communities.

> *Do not try to "educate" people or businesses about how important your cause and organization are. This is patronizing and offensive. Moreover, it's a waste of your resources.*

Also keep in mind: Lots of people give to causes that you do *not* support financially, but you enjoy (and want) the benefits of those causes. Consider that freeloading. You and I benefit from something that is funded by someone else.

For example: Everyone wants clean air to breathe. But how many of us give to environmental organizations that fight for clean air? I'll bet, however, that you are as pleased as I am that some people give to organizations that fight for clean air.

Of course no one wants to die from cancer. But does everyone give to cancer organizations? No. My father died of cancer. But still, I don't give to cancer organizations. I know many others give to the fight against cancer, and I thank them.

Each of us "freeloads" on the gifts of others, whether the freeloading is for clean air or an end to cancer, good public schools or the local hospital, museums or theaters, or some other wonderful cause. I freeload on your gifts and give to my major interests. Then you freeload on my gifts to my major interests, and you give to your major interests.

SIN #5: ASKING PREMATURELY

Sometimes organizations ask for a gift when the prospect is not yet ready to be asked. Be careful! Premature asking could annoy those you ask. Instead, use the relationship-building process described in this book to prepare prospects and donors for your request.

Take a look at the situations described next.

More Visibility Does Not Produce More Gifts

People (and businesses and everything else) pay attention to what interests them. Your agency can be highly visible, but if I'm not interested, it's likely I won't notice. I pay attention to what interests me.

It's okay if someone doesn't know who your agency is or why it matters. Tell them if you think they might be interested. Talk with them. Listen to them. Pay attention to their reactions. You'll find out quickly enough if they're actually interested. And if not, change the subject. Leave them alone when it comes to our organization. Do not try to "educate them!" Remember, Sin #3 and Sin #4.

I can just see your suspicious glances reading this. Some of you are convinced that you can educate me. Others are quite assured that visibility will draw my attention to your organization. And through visibility, you'll educate me.

Stop right now!

Let me tell you the story about me and the NCAA basketball championship; see Exhibit 5.2. (And if you ask "what's the NCAA?" you'll know what I mean!).

EXHIBIT 5.2   SIMONE, THE NCAA BASKETBALL CHAMPIONSHIP, AND THE MYTH OF VISIBILITY

First, here's the backstory.

Every spring in the United States, "March Madness" engulfs sports enthusiasts. This is the month for the annual collegiate basketball playoffs. The actual formal title is the NCAA (National Collegiate Athletic Association) basketball championship.

Board members change board meeting dates to stay home and watch the games on television. Television networks battle with big bucks fighting for the rights to televise. Employees talk about the games at work.

And apparently, all the media participate in March Madness at equally frenzied levels. Headlines, feature stories, newscasts. Evidently this is quite a show.

I, however, don't pay attention. Why? Because I'm not interested.

I don't like sports. I don't watch them—not even the Super Bowl thing. I don't engage in sports chatter. Often I don't know if a sports team is football, basketball, or baseball.

Actually, I had to get a friend to verify that I correctly recited the backstory!

So here's my story about the NCAA basketball championship.

In March a few years ago (see, I don't even remember which year!), my sister Nicole called me. I could tell she was very excited.

"Hey, Simone, I know you don't pay any attention to sports, but guess what?"

"What?" I responded with no enthusiasm whatsoever.

"MSU is one of the teams in the final game of the NCAA basketball championship."

Unless you're familiar with the NCAA basketball championship, you probably wonder what MSU is.

Michigan State University. I'm an alumna and so are most of my siblings.

But it's bigger than that. My dad was a professor at MSU. I grew up in East Lansing, Michigan, home of MSU. The campus dominated the landscape because of its landmass and numbers of students. My family socialized with MSU professors. I visited dad in his office at MSU beginning, I assume, in my infancy.

I'm actually very interested in MSU! I even approach strangers wearing Spartan sweatshirts.

You would think, given my deep attachment to MSU, that I would have noticed its name blaring at me in such a highly promoted activity like the NCAA basketball championship. But I didn't.

What's the moral of this story? Even though I'm very interested in Michigan State University, I didn't even notice its name when it was all over every single form of media for weeks. Because I—along with all other people—pay attention only to what interests me.

Then see Chapter 8—the story of Tom and Simone and the World Cup of Soccer, surely the most visible sporting activity in the world. That story is even more poignant when it comes to visibility.

What's the bottom line? There are two. First, how do you maintain sufficient visibility among your current donors? And second, how can your organization identify those who might be interested. I call that "identifying the predisposed," and it's described at length in Chapter 7. That's the constant job of your staff and board members.

Ensuring Visibility with Your Donors and Prospects

Your organization must be visible to your qualified prospects and current donors. You establish that visibility through your relationship-building program, described in subsequent chapters. You communicate effectively in order to maintain visibility. And you cultivate relationships through various activities in order to maintain your visibility. Read on!

Don't Solicit Unless You Know that the Person Knows Your Organization

Be careful. Don't solicit an individual or a business—or any other entity—unless they are familiar with your organization. And be fairly sure they want to be solicited.

Here's a rather strange story:

One day, I was presenting a fund development workshop in a Midwestern U.S. state. Workshop participants included board members and staff from different types of nonprofits.

The workshop conversation eventually touched on visibility, as fund development conversations invariably do. Participants very much wanted their organizations to be more visible, convinced that this would help them raise money. I kept explaining that there was no direct correlation. I used the NCAA basketball championship story. They laughed because apparently a majority of the attendees knew about the championship. Nonetheless, my self-mockery didn't seem to trigger an understanding of visibility and interest.

With some exasperation, a board member firmly said: "Of course greater visibility would help. Just imagine, I went to solicit a friend of mine for a gift and"—she paused, then went on with great drama— "she didn't even know who the agency is! She would have known about us if we were more visible!"

I tell that story over and over. People titter a bit and then respond: "How can her own friend not know who the agency is? Shame on that board member for not informing her friends about the board she serves on."

That's true. How can your friends not know what interests you? Presumably your board members are sufficiently interested in your organization that they talk about the cause periodically with their friends.

But there's another issue, a larger issue: Why would you solicit anyone unless you knew for sure that the person knew about your organization? If the person is your friend, you know his or her interests, including whether she or he cares about your organization's cause.

(But what about direct mail acquisition? you ask. Direct mail acquisition targets a solid group of the predisposed and then requests a gift. To be productive, direct mail acquisition requires thousands or more names that are clearly predisposed. Lots of organizations cannot afford the financial risk of direct mail acquisition. Instead, these organizations personally identify the predisposed and personally qualify them as prospects—or not. In this scenario, only qualified prospects receive a solicitation.)

And still, this situation doesn't make sense. Surely you don't ask for a gift at the start of the conversation! First you talk a bit about the organization and why its results make a difference. And when you're talking (and watching your friend's face), you'd know she didn't know the organization. So you wouldn't ask for a gift! You only ask once you confirm some level of interest in the cause.

NOT SINS BUT CERTAINLY WORRIES

Some issues grow and grow to fairly gigantic proportions. But are they really real? Perhaps these issues are more myth than reality. Or at least less gigantic and more manageable than all of us suppose.

For example:

Are You Worried about Donor Fatigue?

Is donor fatigue real? Or do we perhaps misunderstand what is happening?

Are you really sure that donors *who care about your cause* are tired of receiving your solicitations? I doubt it. Donors who care about your cause—loyal donors—may not respond to a particular solicitation. But my experience shows these donors are seldom annoyed by receiving the solicitation. They simply choose not to give at this moment. But they will give again.

What's the true cause of donor fatigue? Probably receiving too many solicitations from organizations that are of no interest to you—and then wondering how you got on that list! And getting too many requests from friends and family and colleagues who want a favor, which you give, and then continuing to receive solicitations.

People are most often offended, annoyed—and yes, fatigued—when they receive solicitations from organizations and causes that are of no interest. And then

EXHIBIT 5.3   WHAT DOES *PREDISPOSED* MEAN?

An individual, business, or some other entity whose interests and actions suggest a possible inclination or susceptibility toward your organization's mission. Sound familiar? The fundraising business often uses the term *"suspect."* But think about that. Do you really want to refer to anyone or anything as a suspect? Such an unfortunate term! Please use something else!

these organizations keep sending more newsletters and more solicitations, seemingly not getting the point: "I'm not interested in you!"

Quit trying to convince others to care about your cause. Stop asking your board members to get favors from their connections. Change your paradigm. Start immediately!

Instead, identify the predisposed, as described in Exhibit 5.3 and Chapter 7. The predisposed are less likely to be annoyed with your solicitations. Qualify the predisposed as true prospects, and they won't be angry or fatigued when you ask. They likely will be pleased that you are providing them an opportunity to fulfill their interests and aspirations. In general, these qualified prospects and loyal donors are not distressed by multiple solicitations per year. You just have to do it well, with demonstrable respect and clarity.

For example, I'm a longtime donor to the Planned Parenthood Federation of America. They send me multiple solicitations per year, which they begin by acknowledging my long history of giving. And they state that they're asking me to give another gift. I know they know that I'm a loyal donor. I don't respond to each request, but I surely give more than once per year. And I'm not angry at multiple requests. In fact, I keep the response envelope in my "pay file," which regularly reminds me of my interest and my desire to make a difference in reproductive choice.

Another piece of advice: Monitor your lists carefully. Purge them regularly. When gifts come as a memorial or in honor of someone, or as a favor, the donor may not give again. These donors are probably not interested in your cause. Eventually you must stop soliciting them.

Are You Worried about All that Competition for the Same Donors?

The word "competition" suggests that there is a limited number of donors and that donors neither increase their gifts nor add new causes to their philanthropy. That's contrary to experience and research.

Are you perhaps thinking of a foundation that may give a limited amount of money per year? Are you thinking perhaps of a handful of wealthy philanthropists in your community? Every organization wants gifts from those donors, and so do you. Maybe that's what you consider competition: trying to gain access to those foundations and handful of wealthy donors—because you figure you can convince them of your organization's worthiness and need.

But my first question is: What makes you think these donors might be interested in your cause? These donors have their own interests, and your organization may not fit into their interests. Or do you plan to trespass on someone's relationship and then try to educate these donors—that is, universalize your own passion? If, however, you think they're predisposed, then proceed accordingly.

My focus for fund development is finding those who might be interested. Back to the predisposed. In my experience, those who are interested in your cause may give a gift to you, just as they give to others addressing the same cause. Especially if you nurture the relationship well. I think that's the issue facing most organizations.

> *Stop looking for wealthy donors. Start looking for those interested in your cause.*

In general, I think competition is a myth, a refusal to accept that organizations and their fundraisers cannot educate donors and prospects to care. And sadly, it's a handy myth that easily distracts organizations from confronting the five deadly sins, and facing the inadequacy of their fund development programs.

I do, however, believe there is congestion: lots of requests from lots of different organizations. For efficiency and return on investment, find the predisposed. Introduce your organization, and try to qualify these predisposed as prospects. That narrows your target. And if their interests align with your cause or organization, launch your comprehensive relationship-building program, as discussed in chapters to follow.

In Conclusion

Nothing spreads more quickly and more broadly than a bad reputation. It seems that fund development and fundraisers often acquire ill repute by ignoring interests, trespassing on relationships, and universalizing personal passion. All this displays significant disregard for others. This disrespect—in the name of philanthropy and the good works of charitable organizations—runs counter to genuine relationships and good business sense.

People talk about their bad experiences. People tell stories about disrespect. If your common sense doesn't convince you of this, then consider this: Donors may share their bad experiences with as many as seven other people![1] Let's assume that same reach is true for anyone who has a bad experience, donor or not!

ENDNOTE

1. Sargeant and Jay, *Building Donor Loyalty.*

Direct Mail and Relationship Building

Most nonprofits/NGOs use direct marketing in some manner. Maybe you have 300 donors. You solicit them via direct mail letters sent once or more per year. Perhaps you have 100,000 donors and a top-notch direct mail program that generates all your charitable contributions.

This book assumes you will continue your direct mail program. But even with 100,000 donors, this book encourages you to nurture relationships through a donor-centered approach. The whys and how-tos included here can help you, no matter how many donors you have.

This book also assumes you'll identify selected donors with whom you'll nurture stronger relationships. Eventually, you solicit these donors more personally, meeting them face to face, either actually or virtually.

"Playing for keeps," demands donor-centered organizations, steeped in relationship building. Deep relationships are the basis for donor loyalty.

How do you start? Identify just a few donors to begin. Use profiling to select those with whom you'll nurture these closer relationships. For example, consider these selection criteria:

- Longtime donors
- Donors who've contacted you with questions and comments
- Donors who've participated in your programs
- Those who've given gifts you consider significant

Then launch the steps described throughout this book. Learn more about their interests and emotions. Create opportunities for them to engage more fully. Monitor the relationship-building process. And then ask for gifts, using strategies like direct mail and face to face.

You may well feel overwhelmed by the donor-centered process of relationship building described in this book. Where will you find the staff time in your small organization? How can this work when your donors live all over the country or all over the world?

French fundraiser Jon Duschinsky said it well: Many CEOs and boards see net margins and cost ratios as the bottom line. But good fundraisers express the bottom line as gifts, goodwill, and mission advancement.

CEOs and boards demand proof that relationship building actually produces more money. They seem willing to accept or ignore the sky-high donor-attrition rates that plague large-scale fund development programs. Maybe they assume nothing can be done about their chronic and worsening attrition problem. But something *can* be done: build better relationships with donors.

The bottom line: Closer relationships produce increased support and donor loyalty. Invest now or invest later. Your organization decides.

CHAPTER 6

Eight Steps to Develop and Nurture Relationships

IT'S WHAT I'M BUYING THAT COUNTS

It's not what you're selling that matters. It's what I'm buying that counts.

—SIMONE P. JOYAUX, ACFRE

DEAR READER   This chapter presents an overview of my eight steps for building relationships. These steps work with all kinds of relationships. Subsequent chapters provide detail about selected steps. *Simone*

Nurturing relationships is about creating ways to connect, develop rapport, and build bonds. Relationship building is an ongoing and unending process. Perpetual loyalty is the ultimate goal.

Think about relationships first. It's not time to think about the gift solicitation part. And it may never be time. Some of an organization's relationships don't involve giving time or money. That's okay. Think about the philosophical framework described in Chapter 1.

Remember the key concepts in relationship building described in Chapter 4: sincerity, closeness and boundaries, diversity and cultural competency, values, and dynamism and change. Look back at the five deadly sins in Chapter 5, and review the definitions in Exhibit 6.1.

Think in terms of Dale Carnegie's comment: "You'll have more fun and success when you stop trying to get what you want, and start helping other people get what they want."[1] Exhibit 6.2 presents his strategies for making people like you.

EXHIBIT 6.1   **DEFINITIONS AND APPLICATIONS**

Predisposed   An individual, business, or some other entity whose interests and actions suggest a possible inclination or susceptibility towards your organization's mission. ("Suspect" is more common terminology. But who wants to hear anyone referred to in such a pejorative manner?)

For example: The Women's Fund of Rhode Island is a social justice organization committed to equity for women and girls. Who might be predisposed to this type of cause? Donors to domestic violence shelters and Planned Parenthood. Supporters of progressive political action groups like MoveOn.org and EMILY'S List. Volunteers working in community organizing for civil rights. Parents and grandparents of girls who attend local all-girls schools.

Prospect   An individual, business, or some other entity that has demonstrated an interest in your organization and its mission. Perhaps a prospect for volunteering, for serving on a committee or the board, for lobbying for you, or for giving a financial contribution.

For example: Clients who use your organization's services. (And family members of your clients could be considered predisposed.) Someone who asked to be on your organization's mailing list. Former board members. All of your volunteers. And of course, prospects for future engagement or gifts also include your current donors.

Donor   An individual, business, or some other entity that has given a gift of time or money or service to your organization.

For example: your volunteers. (While they donate time, they are also prospects for giving a financial contribution.) The printer who gives you services at a reduced or rate or at no charge. The restaurant that hosts – with no cost – your annual donor/volunteer thank-you party. And all those who give financial contributions through checks, cash, credit card, and other payment methods.

Now ask yourself: What questions would Dale Carnegie ask of those he reached out to?

- What matters to you?
- What interests you? And if it's this cause or my organization, why are you interested? Why does what we do interest you?
- What are your hopes and dreams?

EXHIBIT 6.2   **DALE CARNEGIE'S SIX WAYS TO MAKE PEOPLE LIKE YOU**

Rule 1: Become genuinely interested in other people.
Rule 2: Smile.
Rule 3: Remember that a [person's] name is to [him/her] the sweetest and most important sound in any language.
Rule 4: Be a good listener. Encourage others to talk about themselves.
Rule 5: Talk in terms of the other [person's] interest.
Rule 6: Make the other person feel important—and do it sincerely.

With this context in mind, now you can develop (or improve) your relationship-building program.

DEVELOPING YOUR RELATIONSHIP-BUILDING PROGRAM

In the ideal world, most of us want strong relationships with as many people and organizations as possible. Wouldn't it be great to have strong connections to each of your donors, with all of your partner organizations, with every elected official?

However, that's not realistic. Organizing your relationship-building program is no small task. Limited resources affect all organizations, no matter their size or finances. Every organization establishes priorities.

STEPS IN RELATIONSHIP BUILDING

Apply the eight steps shown in Exhibit 6.3 to any kind of relationship. Embrace the why behind these steps, and you'll produce a true culture of philanthropy. Combine the why with good implementation of the how-tos, and your organization will produce significantly better results.

EXHIBIT 6.3   **JOYAUX'S EIGHT STEPS IN RELATIONSHIP BUILDING**

All the steps matter. Modify the scope of work depending on your goals and resources.

1. Identify the predisposed.
2. Get to know the predisposed well enough to either qualify them as a prospect, or determine they are not interested and hence not a prospect. If they're not interested, you move on and they move on.
3. Understand their interests and disinterests, their emotions, and their motivations and aspirations.
4. Identify the mutually beneficial exchange, what you have in common and define.
5. Nurture the relationship to develop commitment. This includes communications and cultivation.

   These first five steps apply to any relationship. And the relationship is the result. In some cases, however, you'll want to make a request of some form. Perhaps to join the board or serve on a committee. Maybe to invest financially or to lobby for a particular public policy.

6. Evaluate interest and readiness for the request. If yes, design the request. If the prospect is not ready for this step, continue relationship building.
7. Ask. Thank. And continue nurturing the relationship.
8. Monitor progress, and measure results.

   Step #1 initiates the relationshipp-building process: finding those who might be interested. From a fund development perspective, this begins the acquisition process. Once you have qualified prospects, your process is no longer linear. Steps #3 through #8 become a virtuous circle, "a condition in which a favorable circumstance or result gives rise to another that subsequently supports the first."

What kind of results?

- Connections throughout the community that strengthen your organization.
- Board members and other volunteers who feel "less worse" about fund development. (Hey, most never will like fund development. But that's not your goal. Your goal is to reduce their discomfort and commit to doing the work. The achievable goal is to make fund development less worse!)
- More donors and volunteers who are more loyal.
- Fewer one-time donors and volunteers.
- And probably more charitable gifts and some at higher levels.

Step #1: Identify the Predisposed

I've said it before and I'll say it again: Please let's not use the word "suspect." It's so derogatory. I always imagine people overhearing our discussions about "suspects" and getting turned off. Instead, think of the predisposed.

The predisposed are those who seem to have interests similar to some element of your organization's mission. They are individuals, businesses, or some other entities that have demonstrated interests and actions that suggest a possible inclination toward your organization's mission.

By identifying the predisposed, you avoid two of the five deadly sins described in Chapter 5: trespassing on personal and professional relationships, and universalizing your own passion. See Chapter 7 for details and examples about identifying the predisposed.

Step #2: Get to Know the Predisposed

Get to know the predisposed well enough to either qualify them as a prospect—or determine they are not interested and hence not a prospect. If the predisposed are not interested, move on—because they already have.

So important it bears repetition! Do not spend your limited resources (both human and financial) to try to make others interested. Don't universalize your own passion.

Do not try to educate people or businesses about how important your cause and your organization are. This is patronizing and offensive. And it's a waste of your resources.

Of course, people do change. Those who are not currently predisposed may have a later experience that develops their interest. You'll find that out because these are friends and colleagues with whom you stay in contact.

Remember that a "prospect" means the person (or business) has somehow expressed interest in your organization or your cause. The person raised her hand in some way.

EXHIBIT 6.4	AVOID THE ONE-STEP COLD SELL

One day, my colleague Jon Duschinsky and I were complaining about the concept of cold recruitment. That's when an organization decides I'm predisposed and immediately asks me for a gift. The organization hadn't qualified me as a prospect yet. Instead, it just rushed to solicit.

How about the intermediary step? Qualify me as a prospect after you've identified me as predisposed. Create an opportunity for me to signal I'm a prospect, or signal not.

I know you feel that's a delay of game. But I think it's a smarter strategy.

Here's Jon's example: Amnesty International sends a great solicitation letter about a political prisoner in China. You give. But you're not very likely to give again. That's a fact in today's attrition rates.

Now here's Jon's two-step recruitment process: Amnesty International first sends you a letter requesting that you sign a petition for that same prisoner. You signed up, thereby qualifying yourself as a prospect, and authorizing Amnesty to ask you for a financial gift. This entry-level engagement may be a better start to the relationship-building process and strengthen the probability of retention.

So watch and listen to the predisposed. Make some form of offer—an invitation to an activity, a free subscription to your e-news, and so forth. And if I "sign up," I've raised my hand. Now you can consider me a prospect. Remember, I might be a prospect for different things: to volunteer time, to give advice, to help you connect to a particular neighborhood in the community, to sign a petition, or to invest financially. Keep the options open. This is about relationships, not about money.

And if the person doesn't raise her hand indicating some kind of interest, leave her alone. Drop her from your list of "people to go after." You need to move on because she already has. (See Exhibit 6.4.)

Step #3: Understand Their Interests and Disinterests, Their Emotions, and Their Motivations and Aspirations

After Step #2, focus on those you have qualified as prospects. Now get to know these prospects better. Also, keep in mind that the process of getting to know prospects (and donors) better is a great cultivation strategy.

Learn about their interests and disinterests. Find out their motivations and aspirations. Understand their emotions. This is the fundamental concept of a genuine relationship. This makes life interesting—your personal life and your professional life and your organization's life!

Some of this you learn through research; for example, read the various studies in the field. Then you ask your own questions of your own donors and prospects. The most effective development programs include both primary and secondary research.

The term "primary research" refers to that which you initiate yourself. For example, launch a donor survey. Host conversations with prospects and donors. "Secondary research" refers to existing information in the marketplace. Search the

Internet and read sector publications. Chapter 10 provides more detail about the use of primary and secondary research.

> ... *stay relevant by remembering to continually ask, listen, and act.*
>
> —GROUP OF 33, *THE BIG MOO*

Step #4: Identify What You Have in Common and Define the Mutually Beneficial Exchange

What are the shared interests between the donor or prospect and your organization? Where do the values match or conflict? Where is the greatest affinity and the biggest disconnect? This step helps you decide how to nurture the relationship and which topics to avoid.

Remember that the mutually beneficial exchange may change over the course of the relationship. Document the changes. But more important, make sure you understand the donor's why(s). Ask. Ask the same question in different ways to get more detail.

Review the donor questions in Chapter 17. Examine and modify the questions located throughout this book.

Step #5: Nurture the Relationship to Develop Commitment

Ah, commitment and loyalty. That's what we all aspire to.

> *Through relationship building, organizations help their donors and volunteers feel, experience, and witness mission.*

This step includes three key elements. You consistently move among the three. They reinforce each other throughout the duration of the relationship. Keep thinking about that virtuous circle.

Specifically:

1. Getting to know each other better and better
2. Communicating regularly
3. Cultivating the relationship through various activities, such as programs, fundraising events, and the like

Any organization needs a variety of activities (or offers) that your prospects/donors/predisposed can participate in. These activities are typically available to multiple affinity groups at any time.

Step #6: Evaluate Interest and Readiness for the Request

At this point, I imagine you may be ready to throw up your hands in despair. I can hear you now: "Oh hell, this is insane. No way am I doing all this for small gifts or a couple of volunteers."

But wait. I warned you at the start of this section: This is a framework that you modify as necessary. By understanding the framework, you are better able to personalize for your own use.

These eight steps provide a critical framework for the work of fund development. In the ideal world, I think we should know all this about everyone with whom we are trying to create a meaningful relationship. While that's neither realistic nor practical, at least keep the vision in your mind and heart. Then, with this vision, decide what your organization can do. How can it best nurture relationships, given your resources? How can you maximize your return on investment in your relationship-building program?

Preliminary Tips from a Fund Development Angle   Here's how I approach this process when I'm thinking about donors. But keep in mind: You can modify this for any relationship building.

1. Learn as much as possible about prospects and donors, based on the various steps outlined in this chapter. For example:
   - What might the demographics suggest, based on your review of secondary research in the sector?

2. Design relationship-building strategies and solicitation strategies based on available information, personalized to particular affinity groups or to particular individuals. For example:
   - If the prospects/donors provided an e-mail address, maybe they would be receptive to an e-newsletter.

3. Monitor the patterns of response. Take additional action as suggested by the response patterns. For example:
   - Who gives most frequently? Should we invite them to a cultivation gathering?
   - Which solicitation letters produced the greatest response? How can we use that theme to learn more about or engage our donors better?
   - What kinds of offers can we produce for which groups of donors?
   - Given the patterns, which prospects and donors should be approached through face-to-face solicitation, a regular part of our annual fund development program? (Obviously, for each face-to-face solicitation, I probe more deeply. I'm not willing to send out volunteers or staff to ask personally for a gift unless we've prepared sufficiently.)

- Given the potential return on investment, how will our organization spend its resources?

> *Personalize these tips to fit your organization. You decide the depth of exploration in this and all other steps. On some level, you execute all these steps—just in different ways—for any prospect and all donors and for any gift size.*

Designing the Solicitation   Compile everything that you've learned about the prospects. Reflect on any conversations and other connections. Appendix 6A presents a tool that can help you with this work.

With whatever information in hand, answer the following three questions:

- What have you learned about the prospect's interests and disinterests?
- What are the intersections between the prospect and your cause/organization?
- How do you define the mutually beneficial exchange between the prospect and your organization?

If you decide that the prospect is ready to be asked, then design the request. And if the prospect is not yet ready to be asked, renew your relationship-building strategies and tactics.

If you are designing the request, consider these two steps:

1. Review everything you've learned, including the results from the evaluation questions in Step #6. Define what you think you should request from the prospect. Carefully outline why you picked that. You might have to evaluate, eliminate, or fine-tune multiple ideas to create the optimum opportunity at this time.

2. Now explore these questions:

    - What are the emotions that you think most resonate with the prospect?
    - What stories does the prospect tell that reflect these emotions?
    - Which stories from your organization reflect the prospect's emotions?
    - What level of support do you think is appropriate and why? (And remember, this may not be money but position on the board, leading a campaign, serving as a mentor, or something else altogether.)
    - What are the barriers that the prospect might raise? Why? How will you answer these without being asked?
    - What is the best solicitation approach: in person, by telephone, with a letter? Why do you think so?
    - Who is the best solicitor or solicitors? Why do you think so?

- How should the conversation with the prospect evolve?
- What questions will you ask to stimulate conversation?
- Which stories will you tell, when, and why?
- Who will ask for the gift, and how will the request be structured?
- How will you close the conversation?

One more tip: Remember the bigger the gift request, the greater the level of knowledge and intimacy required. This level of knowledge and intimacy is two-way. The prospect or donor must see herself as intimately connected with and comfortable about the organization – in whatever way she deems appropriate to consider what she feels is a major request. And the organization must know her well enough to be able to design a request that she feels is appropriate.

Step #7: Ask and Thank

Just some quick thoughts, even though asking is not a big part of this book.

Segment by Solicitation Strategy   Before you solicit, segment your database by solicitation strategy. Which prospects and donors will be solicited in person? Which prospects and donors will receive mail solicitations?

Often the individuals and businesses solicited face to face receive only one solicitation per year to support core services. The requests are sufficiently significant that additional requests are not appropriate. Donors pay the pledge within the fiscal year, but possibly in multiple payments.

Those solicited through direct mail, however, should receive multiple requests per year, each with a different theme. Not so many requests that you anger them, but certainly three, if not four, per year. Even once the person gives, send the next themed solicitation letter.

Many will actually give to all of the solicitations because each is a different story, all helping support your core services. Some will give to more than one. And those who give to only one are still not angered. In each letter, you acknowledge the donor's previous gift—if the person gave to one of the other themed letters—and explain that you wanted to share another story in case he or she might be interested. Really. It works!

It's a bit like restricted giving, but not exactly. Each theme is part of your core services. The donors may well be aligning with that particular topic, and that's great.

Annual Fund or Annual Appeal: One of My Pet Peeves   Don't use the term "annual fund" or "annual appeal" ... not in writing, not on a gift envelope—nowhere, never at any time. These are internal management terms that fundraisers have allowed to migrate out to donors and prospects.

I used these terms myself. But not anymore. Purge them from your vocabulary. The words are neither interesting nor motivating. Talk about your results. Tell stories. Reserve the right to ask more than once per year, which is difficult when you talk about an "annual fund or appeal." It's all about themed solicitations.

Soliciting Is a Conversation, Not a Presentation   A solicitation should be a conversation, not a presentation. Without conversation, even when soliciting— or perhaps especially while soliciting—how can you understand what is happening in the prospect's heart? How can you explain the connections to the prospect and build on those connections?

Asking for the Gift   The solicitor actually has to ask for the gift, whether face to face, or if the request is a letter or telephone or some other means. You must actually ask. For example:

- Would you consider serving on our board?
- Would you consider a gift of $1,000 to support the children's initiative that meant so much to your own child?
- Would you testify at the government hearing next week, and help us change this bad law?

An announcement at a board meeting—"We are kicking off our fund development and would like all board members to make their gifts before the end of the month"— is just an announcement. It is not a request. Each board member should be personally contacted (in person, via telephone, or by letter), and specifically asked for his or her gift.

The article in your newsletter about how donor gifts saved lives—with a gift envelope enclosed—is not a request. It's a great newsletter article. And maybe the readers will send in a gift, which is wonderful. And definitely enclose a gift envelope with your newsletter. But still, this is not a solicitation; it's a passive suggestion.

Thanking   Always thank the prospect or donor for his or her time. Even if the answer was no, extend your gratitude. And if the answer is no, do your best to find out why. Graciously ask questions that allow the prospect to give you more information. This is your chance to learn.

Debriefing   Debrief from the solicitation experience. Bring together the volunteers and staff who were involved. Analyze what transpired. Identify what worked well and what didn't work as well. Outline how you can improve the next solicitation.

For more information, read the great books about solicitation. Check booklists from CFRE International, and the various fundraising professional associations like AFP. Ask your colleagues for their favorite titles.

Step #8: Monitor Progress and Measure Results

Confucius said that people need to focus on the important rather than the urgent. So what will you measure in your relationship-building program? What is most important for you to know? And rest assured, the most important will likely be the hardest to measure. We are talking about human connection and interdependence. Chapter 24 explains how to monitor progress and measure results.

In Conclusion

It's the quality of relationships that matter, whether the relationship is between your organization and its donors and volunteers, between collaborating organizations, or any other relationship. Creating these relationships for your organization requires intentional effort. But it's worth it.

The poets offer inspiration. Professional development provides the why and how-tos.

Antoine de Saint-Exupéry (1900–1944, French author) observed, "We forget that there is no hope of joy except in human relationships."

Anne Morrow Lindbergh (1906–2001, American author) said:

> A good relationship has a pattern like a dance and is built on some of the same rules. The partners do not need to hold on tightly, because they move confidently in the same pattern, intricate but gay and swift and free. . . . To touch heavily would be to arrest the pattern and freeze the movement, to check the endlessly changing beauty of its unfolding. . . . They know they are partners moving to the same rhythm, creating a pattern together, and being invisibly nourished by it.[2]

▪ ENDNOTES

1. Dale Carnegie, *How to Win Friends and Influence People* (New York: Simon and Schuster, 1936).
2. Anne Morrow Lindbergh, *Gift from the Sea* (Vintage Books, 1955).

Evaluating Prospect Interest, Readiness, and Capacity to Give and Designing the Ask

The optimum combination of interest, readiness, and capacity produces the best ask. The best ask is the right project, the right amount, at the right time, with right solicitor and the right manner of asking. Try using a 20-point scale with 20 being the best.

Begin with interest. Determine the point rating for the prospect. Make anecdotal remarks about why you have selected that rating. Indicate what has to be done to improve the rating.

Proceed with readiness and do the same.

Interest + readiness = 20. Great! Design the right ask and go for it.

Interest + readiness ≤ 15. You need to cultivate more.

Interest + readiness = 16 to 18. Talk a lot. Would more cultivation be better?

INTEREST

The term "interest" refers to the prospect's feeling of curiosity or attentiveness. Interested people are involved and concerned about your cause and your organization's response to the cause.

Interest also signifies that something is of advantage or benefit to the individual. (It's not what your organization is selling, it's what the prospect is buying that counts.)

Estimate level of interest and note the date, as the level of interest may change over time. Add remarks.

READINESS

The term "readiness" means beings prepared for action or likely or liable to act in a particular manner. Readiness means that the prospect is prepared in his or her mind and heart and likely to act in the manner that you seek. Prospects see how giving will benefit themselves by meeting their needs and fulfilling their aspirations.

> Estimate level of readiness and note date as this may change over time.
> Add remarks.

Total interest + readiness _____

NOT YET READY OR SUFFICIENTLY INTERESTED

If you determine that the prospect is not yet ready or sufficiently interested, what will you do to move the prospect along the relationship continuum to be more interested and/or more ready to be asked? Add pages with your cultivation strategy.

IF THE PROSPECT IS READY TO BE SOLICITED, THEN DESIGN THE ASK

If the prospect is ready to be solicited, then follow these six steps to begin designing the ask:

1. Describe the prospect's interests in some detail.
2. Determine the intersection of prospect interest's with your organization's interests.
3. Identify potential barriers for the prospect and figure out the responses.
4. Decide who the right solicitor is, and why.
5. Decide what the right project is, and why.
6. Decide what the right timing is, and why.

CAPACITY

The term "capacity" refers to the ability or aptitude to do something. It also means the maximum output or production, as in the prospect's wherewithal to do what you ask.

If useful, develop a gift table to help focus on potential capacity.

Consider these six points:

1. To what extent does the prospect have personal, family, and other obligations that affect his or her giving capacity?

2. Does the prospect have sufficient cash to give, and to what extent?

3. Might securities be an option?

4. Is there some other tangible property the prospect has that your organization would want?

5. Would the prospect benefit from life income? If yes, what might you want to offer to the prospect as giving strategies? Consider life insurance, pooled income fund, and various trusts.

6. Would a combination of giving strategies be helpful to the prospect—for example, a combination of life insurance and cash, bequest and cash, bequest and pooled income fund, and so on? How would you suggest this?

Now fine-tune your thinking.

- Bring interest, readiness, and capacity together.
- Go back and fine-tune your responses to the questions located under "designing the ask."
- Then go for it!

For further information, see Simone Joyaux, *Strategic Fund Development: Building Profitable Relationships That Last*, 2nd ed. (Sudbury, MA: Jones & Bartlett, 2001), chap. 4, pp. 197–200.

CHAPTER 7

Identify the Predisposed

FINDING NEW PROSPECTS FOR YOUR ORGANIZATION

People are generally better persuaded by the reasons which they have themselves discovered than by those which have come into the minds of others.

—BLAISE PASCAL, 1623–1662, FRENCH MATHEMATICIAN AND PHILOSOPHER

DEAR READER   Let's start at the beginning: identifying those who might be interested in your particular cause. (Remember, I don't use the word "suspect!")
Simone

WHO ARE THE PREDISPOSED?

The predisposed are those whose interests or connections suggest they might find your mission attractive. By identifying the predisposed, you avoid three of the five deadly sins described in Chapter 5:

- Trespassing on personal and professional relationships
- Universalizing your own passion
- Asking prematurely

For many organizations, identifying the predisposed is a new way of doing business. And they love it! Hopefully you will too.

Introducing the Concept

First, tell your board members and other fund development volunteers that your organization does not endorse trespassing on personal and professional relationships. Also stress that your organization does not believe in premature asking. In fact, tell them that premature asking is a sin!

Now explain your organization's caring and careful approach to fund development. Specifically: Your organization identifies those who might be predisposed, qualifies them as prospects (or not), nurtures the relationship, and evaluates when the qualified prospect is ready to be asked and for what. Then you recruit the solicitor, design the ask, and ask.

Explain that you want board members and friends of the organization to think about their personal and professional relationships and identify those who might be predisposed to the organization and its mission. Tell your board members: "Our organization will not trespass on your personal and professional relationships."

Make it clear that you are not talking about asking for money at this time. Nor is anyone making a presentation about the organization. Identifying the predisposed is about listening and figuring out people's interests.

> Board members identify the predisposed from people they know. By sharing a common interest, board members are connecting with these people, not imposing on them.
>
> —STEPHEN G. SLATEN, EXECUTIVE DIRECTOR, JEWISH FAMILY SERVICE OF WORCESTER, MASSACHUSETTS

Spend time talking about the concept of the predisposed. Remind your board members that they know the interests (and disinterests!) of their friends and many of their colleagues. Help your board members and fund development volunteers feel comfortable about talking with others to screen their possible interest in your organization.

Ask board members to keep you informed about what they learn. Ask them and other fund development volunteers to identify at least one person per month who is predisposed. Then work with board members and volunteers to qualify the predisposed as a true prospect or to halt the process of relationship building.

But What If They Are Reluctant?

Of course, people may tell you that they don't know anyone who might be predisposed. That is not an acceptable response. Identifying the predisposed is at the heart of a culture of philanthropy. You, your board members and volunteers, and staff must listen always. Your organization should be sufficiently important to board and staff that these leaders are sensitive to nuances in any situations that might suggest interest.

Be prepared for board and staff members to suggest that increased visibility will allow those who are predisposed to your cause to find your organization. Be careful. The visibility issue is a perilous path, and part of the five deadly sins. Read all about it in Chapters 5 and 8.

Fund Development Professionals Help Organizations Identify the Predisposed

Fund development professionals must help others operationalize the process of identifying the predisposed.

Collect and Analyze Public Lists

Facilitate a conversation with staff, the board, and the fund development committee to identify which types of organizations might have similarities with your organization.

For example, the Women's Fund of Rhode Island collects annual reports — which list donors—from such organizations as the American Civil Liberties Union, Planned Parenthood of Rhode Island, domestic violence shelters, LGBTQ (lesbian, gay, bisexual, transgender, queer, and questioning) organizations, all-girls schools in the state, and others. We check the Federal Elections Commission Web site to find out who contributed to progressive candidates.

Here's another example: Your organization provides counseling services to troubled youth. Collect the annual reports and public donor listings from other youth development organizations. Use these lists to stimulate thinking. Have board members review the lists and identify those whom they know. Then ask them to think about those people and decide whether they might be predisposed to your organization. You do not solicit people or businesses on these lists. The purpose of the list review is to identify those you think might be predisposed. Then you go about the process of determining whether they can be qualified as prospects.

Be careful as you identify the predisposed and try to qualify them as prospects. Listen to this caution:

> *It would be a fatal mistake to assume that because they share a common connection, all share a common experience or feel the same affection for you.*
>
> —Diana Miller, Cohort 16, Master's Program, Philanthropy and Development, Saint Mary's University

Where was Diana when I needed her? Just look at my sad story in Exhibit 7.1.

EXHIBIT 7.1   **THE SAD STORY OF SIMONE AND HER POOR JUDGMENT**

Twenty years ago, I was the chief development officer at Trinity Repertory Company in Rhode Island, one of the nation's top regional theaters. I remember vividly one attempt to identify new prospects.

I obtained a program book from the Rhode Island Philharmonic. You know, the program distributed to all audience members at a performance. And there was that spiffy list of Philharmonic donors, recognized by gift size.

My theory: Donors to the Philharmonic were committed to the arts. And theater was art, too. I figured that these music donors would be predisposed to Trinity Rep.

One of my staff searched for the donor addresses in the telephone book. I wrote a nifty letter. And we enclosed a designer-designed brochure talking about the importance of the annual fund.

We sent 407 letters and received two responses. Yes, I remember this vividly. Mistakes are such a great way to learn!

I did exactly what Diana Miller refers to as a "fatal mistake." I assumed that the donors' connection to music would transfer to theater. And while I knew that not everyone would respond, receiving only two replies shocked me. I had figured it was time well spent to look up all those addresses.

What should I have done instead? Shared the list of Philharmonic donors with my board. Asked the board members whom they knew on the Philharmonic donor list. Then learned more about the interests of those Philharmonic donors known by my board members before doing any solicitation.

Listen to Your Friends and Colleagues

You talk with these people regularly. In all your conversations everyday, you learn about people's interests and disinterests, their passions and aspirations.

Pay attention! You can easily find out if they are predisposed. Actually, you probably already have a good idea—just probe a bit more.

Don't ask them if they want to give! First, you figure out if they are predisposed. Then you cultivate a bit and determine if they qualify as a prospect. Then you cultivate again. And finally you ask.

Sadly, too many people—board members and staff included—claim, "I don't know what 'they' are interested in." So it's your job to help them understand that they *do* know lots of information. For example: Do you know which of your colleagues want to have lunch at the little Parisian bistro or grab a sandwich at McDonald's? Of course you know! Do you know which of your friends to invite over for your *Lord of the Rings* movie marathon, watching all three extended DVD versions? Tom and I would ask our nephew David. Or Kris and Ari.

You have to help your board members practice this work. See Appendix 7A, "Learning about People through Conversation." I use this with clients and in workshops, to great success. Modify it for your community. Then use it with your own staff and board members. And check out Exhibit 7.2.

EXHIBIT 7.2   **WHAT I LEARNED ONE DAY AT THE EYE DOCTOR**

It might have been winter or spring. G. W. Bush was president of the United States. And I was visiting the eye doctor.

I read a book while waiting for my appointment. I plugged my ears, trying to ignore the television and President Bush's speech.

Of course I took a finger out of my ear regularly in order to turn the page. Soon I noticed murmurings in the reception area. Murmurings loud enough to drown out the television and president. Slightly annoyed murmurings.

I unplugged both ears and forgot my book. The three other people in the reception area were all commenting on the president's speech. Clearly, these women neither respected nor supported President Bush. I joined the conversation and learned more.

Now imagine that I was on the board of the local Democratic Party. Or a staff person with EMILY's List, the PAC that supports the election of pro-choice Democratic women. Or volunteering with an organization that trained individuals to run for office.

I had just identified three people who were predisposed. I could have introduced myself. Invited them to check out information on our Web site. Invited them to attend an upcoming program.

Host Cultivation Gatherings

Assign board members to host cultivation gatherings in their homes or places of business. And invite some of your donors to do this, too.

There are three qualifying opportunities in this scenario.

First board members invite friends and colleagues who may be predisposed to the organization's work to attend a cultivation gathering. The invitation clearly states that this is *not* a fundraising gathering. Guests will learn about the organization's work but will *not* be asked to give a gift. See the sample invitation in "Building Relationships with Your Constituents ," Appendix 10A.

Sometimes you might include selected qualified prospects and current donors along with the predisposed. This expanded cultivation gathering readies prospects for solicitation and nurtures relationships with current donors. Also, the stories attending donors share reinforce positive messages with the predisposed and prospects.

First qualifying opportunity: If the individual responds no to the invitation, the host asks if the person would like to be invited to a future gathering. If the individual says no again, find out if the person might be interested in the cause but just doesn't like gatherings. Perhaps he or she would like to receive some background information (but not a solicitation!)

Second qualifying opportunity: The individual attends the informal gathering. Guests mingle and enjoy talking with each other. A representative of your organization makes some remarks and tells some stories. Guests ask questions and engage in conversation. You pay attention to those who seem most interested. Personal follow-up might be appropriate.

Third qualifying opportunity: Invite people to sign up to get on the mailing list and receive further information. See the Women's Fund Promise Form in Appendix 10A.

Some organizations add people to the mailing list if they attend cultivation gatherings. Others decide that their organization and its mission are sufficiently challenging that guests should have another opportunity to opt in or out. This is accomplished by signing up or not. For example, as a social justice organization with a very progressive agenda, the Women's Fund of Rhode Island adds guests to the mailing list only if they express specific interest by completing the Promise Form.

Make sure that no one receives a solicitation from you (by virtue of signing up to be on the mailing list) until he or she receives at least one nonsolicitation communication.

> *Most of us know how to form a relationship. But we are attending to whether they are interested in us. This is different. I need to find out if they are interested in my cause. I do this by listening to their interests and identifying any links to my cause. If they're talking about their children, that's a natural link to Jewish Family Service, my organization. I can introduce my cause into the conversation when the person asks about where I work. Then I can watch their behaviors to see if my work interests them. We have to train people to attend to detail and analyze their conversations to an extent they probably only do if they are in sales or are a therapist or trying to get someone romantically interested.*
>
> —Stephen G Slaten
> Executive Director, Jewish Family Service of Worchester, Massachusetts

Creating Opportunities for People to Self-Identify as Predisposed

Right now some of you are thinking: If my organization were more visible, then those who might be predisposed would find us and self-identify.

But you'll never have enough money to be sufficiently visible through various media reaching diverse audiences on a continuing basis. The only visibility you should worry about is with your prospects and donors.

I've enjoyed many wonderful visits to Tucson, presenting workshops, connecting with colleagues, and hiking. I always remember one occasion when talking about building relationships: Brian Bateman, MA, CFRE, said, "Fundraisers need to create opportunities for people to self-identify as predisposed."

So if general visibility is not the answer, what is?

Try to be visible within your target audiences. And control your own visibility. Don't rely on the media. (Sure, it's nice to be featured in the media. But recycling the coverage is probably the best benefit. You copy the article and send it out to donors, prospects, or those who seem predisposed. Don't count on people reading the article in the media.)

Try these four steps to create opportunities for the predisposed to self-identify:

1. Describe the general interests and qualities of those who are most likely to be predisposed to you.

2. Identify where they congregate and affiliate.

3. Define ways to connect with them.

4. Connect with them and provide vehicles for them to signal their interest.

How the Women's Fund Uses These Four Steps

The Women's Fund of Rhode Island (WFRI) is a very small young organization, which I founded as a field-of-interest fund within The Rhode Island Foundation, the state's community foundation. The foundation's extraordinary support allowed WFRI to implement programs and build endowment immediately. In spring 2005, with the encouragement and support of The Rhode Island Foundation, WFRI became an independent organization designated 501c3 by the U.S. Internal Revenue Service.

Nonetheless, WFRI is very small. Resources are limited, with an annual budget of $310,000 in 2007, and only two staff people.

Here's how WFRI applies these four steps.

Step #1: Describe the General Interests and Qualities of Those Who Are Most Likely to Be Predisposed   As a social justice organization, the mission says, "the Women's Fund champions fairness, impartiality, opportunity, shared power, and responsibility in all spheres of personal and community life including economic, cultural, educational, social, and public policy." WFRI is known as a very progressive organization, speaking out against sexism, racism, homophobia, and other inequities.

The Women's Fund resonates with progressive women and men and social justice activists. In addition, it often engages those who are concerned about women's issues, such as economic autonomy, educational attainment, political participation, reproductive choice, and domestic violence.

We recognize that some people prefer selected areas of our work and may not be as comfortable with our progressive stances in certain areas. But these individuals still engage with some WFRI activities and contribute financially.

Other people are sufficiently bothered by some areas of our work that these individuals or businesses do not choose to be involved at all. And we don't bother them. We don't add them to our mailing list. We don't keep trying to convince or "educate" them.

And then there are the devotees to WFRI. These fans embrace our work and our progressive stances. Their values align with the values of WFRI. These devotees participate in our activities, welcome our communications, want to serve on our committees, and give gifts—often multiple times per year.

Step #2: Identify Where They Congregate and Affiliate   We collect public lists (e.g., annual reports and newsletters) from organizations that address these issues. We use these lists to identify people to invite to our cultivation gatherings and our programs.

We contact organizations whose missions link to our mission. We ask these organizations if we can make a presentation to their members and boards and staff regarding the mission and work of WFRI.

Step #3 and #4: Define Ways to Connect with Them. Then Connect with Them and Provide Vehicles for Them to Signal Their Interest   The Women's Fund hosts at least six cultivation gatherings each year, hosted by board members, other volunteers, and donors. Also, we try to make four to six presentations to organizations whose members appear to have some predisposition to WFRI. We use these organizations to reach their members, anticipating that some people within the membership may be interested. We demonstrate to these organizations and their members that WFRI can help them in some ways.

We invented "Conversations with the Women's Fund" to nurture relationships with donors and volunteers. We encourage recipients of conversation invitations to forward the e-mail to those they think might be interested, so these conversations also help identify the predisposed.

Conversations are just that. We invite people to come together to discuss various topics and identify strategies for change, collaboration, and action. We provide some brief background information and then facilitate discussion with the guests.

Annually, we host one of the largest gatherings in the state. This dinner with a guest speaker is *not* a fundraising event but a mobilizing event. And it isn't a sedate event. Instead, a social justice activist challenges the guests to examine inequity and promote change. Sometimes we even use the word "revolution." The program book for the event recognizes all our donors and volunteers.

I wish you could hear the chanting and cheering. That's engagement!

Women and men attend year after year. They tell us that this is the place to be if one cares about women's rights and human rights. Our guests count on us to tell the truth about leveling the playing field for women and girls.

We do not have the resources—nor do we choose to spend the time—to do a traditional newsletter. Instead, we send a quarterly "newsy" letter to our donors and volunteers. We produce a monthly e-news, distributed to everyone on our mailing list, if we have his or her address. In each case, we invite people to contact either the executive director or the board chair, and provide telephone numbers and e-mail addresses.

We're introducing an annual report, short and not fancy. It will recognize all our donors and volunteers. And at every program or activity, the Women's Fund provides a mechanism for people to sign up.

Each year, WFRI takes great care to identify volunteer opportunities. We always have more people who want to volunteer than available positions. We use volunteer opportunities as a cultivation strategy and as a way to groom people for board membership.

We solicit gifts three times per year for the direct mail segment of our list. Each letter focuses on a different theme. That means a person has three chances to give. And we have donors who give to multiple solicitations per year. Our personal solicitation program connects board members with specific donors and prospects. We ask these individuals and corporations for a major gift once per year.

One last note:

Early on, the Women's Fund learned that our devotees want the chance to talk about women's issues and social justice. We realized that we have to accommodate this personal conversation time at our committee and board meetings.

Our supporters tell us there are too few chances to talk in depth about vitally important issues. So the Women's Fund continually experiments with different opportunities. For example, this year, we're thinking about launching WFRI book clubs.

Building Relationships (and Identifying the Predisposed) at the Apple Store

Visit an Apple store. Yes. Right now! Sit down at the Genius Bar and you'll enjoy technical support for free. Now that's customer service!

We visited Providence's new Apple store a few weeks after it opened. Finally, our own Apple haven nearby. (Yes, we're confirmed and adoring Macintosh users.)

The store was wonderfully crowded with people trying out gorgeous, user-friendly products. And then I saw the Genius Bar—with a neon sign saying I could get help for free. I could bring my list of questions and have someone show me right there, in front of me.

> *Apple creates intimate, powerful conversations at their stores. What do you do? How do you do that?*

A month later, I read *The Big Moo*, which discussed the then new Apple stores. In 2005, the book's publication date, the authors noted that more than 1 million people a week were visiting Apple stores. Most of the visitors didn't even own a Mac or an iPod, and iPhones didn't exist.

But as *The Big Moo* says, "instead of focusing only on barraging wary strangers with expensive advertising, Apple creates the chance for an intimate, powerful conversation. The stores are not just profitable, they are extraordinarily effective ambassadors..."[1] Apple's successful reemergence as a consumer technology firm is, in part, due to the relationship building at these stores.

In Conclusion

It's up to you. Change the culture in your organization so that everyone understands and accepts the concept of the predisposed. Enable all your board members and other volunteers to help identify the predisposed. Engage your staff in the same process.

Create mechanisms for people and businesses to self-identify as predisposed. Then qualify those who are prospects. And leave the others alone!

ENDNOTE

1. *Group of 33, The Big Moo.* Edited by Seth Godin. (New York: Portfolio) (Penguin Group, 2005) p. 88.

Learning About People Through Conversation

EVERY DAY

Every day, you learn about colleagues, neighbors, friends, and even people sitting next to you in an airplane!

You talk with your colleagues on Monday morning and share stories about weekend activities. You talk with clients and customers about their work or worries or responsibilities.

If you're a good conversationalist, these are *conversations*, not mini lectures or presentations. You are sharing and listening and learning.

All of these conversations provide you with information. You learn about the interests and disinterests, motivations and aspirations, and values of those you are speaking with.

Conversations help you build relationships—professional and collegial relationships, family and friend relationships.

PHILANTHROPY

The process of building relationships [for anything, including philanthropy] is all about finding out the interests of the other person.

Building relationships is *not* about trespassing on your personal and professional relationships. From a philanthropic perspective, you should *not* be expected to raise money by coercing gifts from those who feel an obligation to you. No! That's trespassing and it's unnecessary and certainly inappropriate.

Instead, you find out interests through conversations. Yes. Conversations. You find out if your personal and professional contacts are interested in the cause that you espouse.

Think about the conversations that you had this morning or yesterday. What did you learn? Do you think that any of these individuals are predisposed to your favorite cause?

YOUR RESPONSIBILITY

Unfortunately, too many board members say "I don't know who might be interested in this cause." How can you say that? If you're carrying on conversations, then you know people's interests and disinterests and they know yours.

Ask yourself: How many of your friends and colleagues know which boards you serve on and where you volunteer? Why don't they know? Do you know where they volunteer and what they care about?

All this will help you determine who may be predisposed to your cause; who actually might already be a prospect; and how to cultivate relationships and solicit gifts.

So carry on these conversations. Do it more. Do it intentionally. Remember that it's an informal conversation – not an interview or a presentation about your favorite cause!

SO LET'S PRACTICE!

This activity is designed either for pairs of people or groups of three people. If you do this with groups of three, two people can carry on the conversation and one person can act as the observer to comment and critique. Or, you could carry on the conversation with three people.

The situation

Imagine that you are: At a small gathering or a dinner party. Perhaps meeting the new life partner of one of your relatives. Or, it's Monday morning at work. Wherever. It's one of those conversational moments you encounter regularly in your life.

Things to think about (if you are the observer or if you are one of the two or even three conversationalists)

- Nature of the conversation
- Natural not artificial
- Sharing and listening
- Coherency

ASSIGNMENT

Each conversationalist in the group selects one of the three numbered lists below. Your job is to get answers to the questions in your list. Remember this is a conversation, not an interrogation or an interview.

Do *not* tell the people you are speaking with which of the lists you took! (And if you wish, develop your own list from the items on this list. Or add to these lists.)

If there is an observer, s/he gets a copy of each conversationalist's list in order to monitor the process.

Set a time limit. At the end, determine how much you found out.

Get ready. Get set. Go!

Find out the interests and disinterests, values and motivations of someone else!

Conversationalist #1

1. What are the person's hobbies?
2. What is the person's profession?
3. What does the person think of the *DaVinci Code* – movie or book?
4. Does the person have children?
5. Is the person involved in his / her church, mosque or synagogue?
6. Is the person pro- or anti-Bush?
7. Is the person a *Friends* television show fan?
8. What kind of music does the individual like?

Conversationalist #2

1. What is the person's profession?
2. Did the person see *Angels in America*?
3. Did the person see *Lord of the Rings*?
4. Is the person a *West Wing* fan?
5. Has the person traveled in Europe?
6. What kind of vacations does the person prefer to take?
7. Is the person a wine aficionado?
8. Is the person a sports fan, and if yes, what kinds of sports?

Conversationalist #3

1. Does the person like live theater?
2. Is the individual interested in environmental issues?

3. What kind of music does the individual like?

4. Is the person a fan of the television show *The Sopranos*?

5. Does the individual play sports and if yes, which ones?

6. Is the person a political junkie?

7. Does the person like to garden?

8. Did the person see *Lord of the Rings*?

CHAPTER 8

Understanding the Fundamentals of Marketing and Communications

THE RIGHT MESSAGE TO THE RIGHT PERSON AT THE RIGHT TIME

In Marketing I've seen only one strategy that can't miss—and that is to market to your best customers first, your best prospects second and the rest of the world last.

——JOHN ROMERO, LEGANDARY CASINO MARKETER

DEAR READER I entered fund development from a marketing background. For five throbbing years I ran what's called a "marcomm" (marketing communications) shop inside a world-striding international technology firm. The company sometimes spent years chasing a sale. Since each sale was worth tens of millions of dollars, it was well worth any amount of effort. And I learned, among other things, the value of long-term relationship building. Now, true, fund development differs from technology marketing. But not as much as you might imagine. Both must pay attention to the special interests of various target audiences. And, bottom line, it's still *not* what you're selling that matters, it's what they are *buying*. *Tom*

COMMUNICATIONS: FOR MANY, IT'S ALL THEY KNOW OF YOU

Donors, prospects, and the predisposed have very little to go on. They know your organization mostly through what you tell and show them in your communications, through your words and images.

You know the *real* you. They know the *paper* you: a fundraising appeal, a newsletter, or an annual report. Or the *electronic* you: your Web site and e-mails. And that's all they know: words and images.

That's why fund development communications are so vital. Much of the time, they *are* your reality. They:

- Remind people that you exist and matter
- Build trust in your organization
- Deliver proof of what you've accomplished with gifts
- Declare your organization's urgent need for additional donor investment
- Unveil your organization's inspiring plans
- Offer readers useful information
- Answer typical questions and objections
- Talk about sustainability and "tomorrow dollars" (bequests and other planned gifts)
- Make the ask, either in a leading (appeal letters) or supporting (newsletters) role

Even an unforgettable personal experience of your organization—the kind alumni have with their schools or the healed have with their hospitals—won't by itself produce a gift. People give because they are asked. You have communicated with them somehow—in person, by phone or letter, by a combination of methods—and asked for their help. You cannot consistently and predictably raise money any other way than through some form of oral or written communication. Donors cannot guess your needs.[1] Your communications have to express those needs.

You have two methods: oral communications and written communications.

Time-pressed fundraisers have to prioritize. They tend to restrict their "face time" to people with large-dollar potential. Small gifts rarely merit a personal call or visit. (But be aware of recent research: Making personal contact with small donors can significantly improve your donor retention.)

Your written fund development communications, however, let you effectively and efficiently reach out to an unlimited number of donors and prospects: hundreds, thousands, even millions if you're a national charity.

FUND DEVELOPMENT IS A TYPE OF MARKETING, AND USES THE SAME METHODS

The dictionary defines the term "marketing" as "the business activity of presenting products or services to potential customers in such a way as to make them eager to buy."

Fund development is just marketing under a different name. Some might sniff in disapproval, thinking the comparison crass and commercial. But substitute "mission or vision" for "products or services," "donors" for "customers," and "give" for "buy." The result? A reasonable definition of fund development: the business activity of presenting mission or vision to potential donors in such a way as to make them eager to give.

Marketers find potential customers and persuade them to buy. Fundraisers find potential donors and persuade them to make a gift. And we use the same three basic methods:

1. **Advertising.** You buy access to a targeted audience for your message. Messages can be delivered via media such as newspapers, magazines, radio, TV, bus ads, billboards, or the Internet. But direct mail is also a form of advertising, as are other so-called direct marketing techniques such as e-mail solicitations and telemarketing. Direct marketers sometimes call their methods "addressable" (capable of being sent to specific addresses) to distinguish them from "mass" marketing methods.

2. **Promotions.** Here you offer incentives to increase response. In retail, promotions include coupons, "50 percent off" sales, refunds, and such. In fund development, common promotions include:

   a. The "challenge," where, say, every new dollar given is matched one-for-one by a major donor
   b. Membership, where benefits, such as unlimited visits or discounts, are exchanged for cash
   c. Fundraising events, such as golf tournaments, which promise fun in exchange for cash
   d. Premiums, such as self-sticking return address labels included in direct mail appeals

3. **Public relations.** You "encourage the media to say good things about whatever you want to promote so that more people will buy your product, use your services, or think you're great," as one no-nonsense definition said. In some minds, PR is merely "free advertising," a way to get exposure without paying for it. Good press relations are certainly part of PR's role. Press releases, press conferences, meetings with editors, letters to the editor, having a spokesperson a reporter can speak with—these all relate to public relations. But public relations also embraces any activity that fosters goodwill, acceptance, understanding, and a positive image among your key constituents. For fundraisers, this latter category of PR activities includes Web sites, donor newsletters, blogs, annual reports, case statements, face-to-face meetings with gift prospects, and cultivation events.

MYTH OF "MORE VISIBILITY"

Many a board member, nervously attempting to fundraise, soon returns with this lament: "I told my friend about our organization, and he said he'd never heard of us. If only we had more visibility in the community, it would be so much easier to raise money!"

And now this false notion is on the table: that "increased community awareness" (the other name for a visibility boost) will raise more money. Their solution: Send out press releases. Get some stories written about our work. We could produce Public Service Announcements for radio and TV, too. Maybe even put some posters up on buses. Then everyone will know who we are. Even better, to know us is to love us, and love us generously. Gifts will spontaneously erupt! That's what the "visibility" gambit implies. The subtext is this: We deserve support, and once people know we exist, that support will flow.

It makes perfect sense . . . to novices.

But it's about as likely as expecting a magic fish to grant your wishes.

People pay attention to what interests them, and little else. If sports don't matter to you, the NCAA "March Madness" basketball playoffs or World Cup football, among the world's most heavily publicized events, simply disappear. We can prove this from personal experience. We own a house in France. In 2006 the French team was in the World Cup finals. We wondered why everyone in town seemed to be hanging around an outdoor movie screen in the village. So we asked a neighbor. He looked at us strangely. *"Mais madame, c'est le Coupe du Monde ce soir. Et l'équipe de France joue."* Ah, the French team is playing for the World Cup. Perfectly wonderful. But we didn't care about sports, so we never noticed.

If the test is "I can call anyone in town, and that person will recognize our organization's name and what we do," your organization will simply never pass. It's an unrealistic goal.

The only organizations known to almost everyone in a community are those that touch every life in an important way, such as a volunteer fire department in a rural town, or familiar brand names, such as the Boys and Girls Clubs, the Red Cross, and the YMCA. But just because most people know the name doesn't mean they give to it!

And if you're an agency that helps, say, deeply troubled teens, you'll *never* be sharply visible to more than a relative handful of people: school guidance counselors, ministers or rabbis, the families you help, probably the police. In most households, your agency will never be personally relevant. A newspaper article that lasts for a day, has no particular call to action, and is not required reading will not change that.

Burn this into your brain: People give because they are asked to give (and that goes for bequests, too, not just annual gifts). When there is no ask, nothing much happens. The fantasy that someone out there will read about your organization and spontaneously write you a large check is just that, a fantasy... at least, statistically speaking. Miracles happen, of course. But well-managed fund development programs don't count on them.

The good news is that a lack of visibility will *not* hurt your chances for donor support. "Invisible" organizations, ones that neither you nor your friends have ever heard of, attract outstanding, passionate philanthropic support, while ones that have been around forever in a community, with an instantly familiar brand name, struggle to find a next generation of donors. Ask any Boys and Girls Club director, for instance, if bearing a familiar name guarantees gifts. The answer will be a flat no.

Increased community awareness, so-called, will not reduce the real labors of fund development: creating a case for support, identifying those most likely to be predisposed, marketing your organization, training your solicitors, making the ask, cultivating donors through communications.

When you consider the vast outpouring of charitable support that followed the 9/11 attacks or the South Asian tsunami, you might reasonably conclude that increased media attention is the secret to fund development.

But those were major news events: The earth moved, literally and emotionally. And the media attention never quit. Nor should we discount the role of the Internet, which made giving easy and quick through secure online sites. Many of those gifts were, in effect, impulse purchases, spur-of-the-moment decisions. And experience shows that relatively few impulse givers ever make a second gift.

On a local level, things are different. And there are no shortcuts to fund development success.

It's Not What You're Selling, It's What They're Buying

One of the most profitable truths in marketing is this: It's not what you're selling that matters. What matters is what your customers are buying.

Consider the American auto industry's high-profile example.

A sales strategy called "planned obsolescence" was among the industry's great business innovations. Just about the time your car started to look dowdy to your neighbors, it fell apart in your driveway. That's what Detroit got rich on selling. The plan worked fine while there was no choice.

Then along came Honda, Toyota, Subaru, and other Asian car manufacturers. They offered the U.S. consumer something new: quality-built, fuel-efficient vehicles that would last 200,000 miles. Exactly what a huge share of the market wanted to buy, as it turned out. America's vast home-grown auto industry is still trying to recover.

Or as fundraisers might say it: Donors give for their own reasons, not yours. It's vital to understand this distinction.

Dale Carnegie, author of the influential "people skills" book *How to Win Friends and Influence People* (still a best-seller a half-century after publication), offered pretty much the same insight to his readers (or so it's said): "You'll have more fun and success when you stop trying to get what you want and start helping other people get what they want."

Translation for fundraisers: "You'll have more fun and success when you stop trying to get what you want"—a donation—"and start helping other people get what they want"— a feeling of having accomplished something, of being important because they have made a gift to your organization. You will end up in the same place—with money—but the two viewpoints are entirely different.

When you focus on getting what *you* want, you tend to treat the donor as a bystander whose role (let's be honest) is to produce cash on demand. Like an ATM: You drive up, press a few buttons, and cash slides into your hand.

But when you focus on helping other people—prospects and donors—get what *they* want—a feeling of importance, say—you tend to refer to them automatically as the heroes who make achieving your mission possible.

This is what we call being "donor-centric": treating your donors as heroes. Donors never tire of hearing that kind of praise (assuming you sound sincere, of course). And a relentlessly donor-centric tone in your oral and written communications brings financial rewards.

Not only will a donor-centric voice tend to raise more money in any single appeal, it will also allow you to send more appeals in a year, with less risk of offense. When you speak in an earnest donor-centric voice, you clearly respect the donor's contribution and sacrifice. And when you're respectful in that way, you'll trigger fewer complaints that "you people are always asking for money." See Chapter 14 for more details about donor-centrism.

WHEN DONORS LAPSE . . .

You probably won't know why people stop giving. (Unless you ask, of course. Fundraisers at the top of their game call donors personally to talk about a gift change, bigger, smaller, lapsed.)

Maybe something changed on their end.

They might have less disposable income to give away. This can happen when people retire to live on fixed incomes.

Or a donor's interest in your mission might have reached some perfectly normal expiration date. Parents who gave to scouting when their kids were young and involved often call it quits when the kids grow up.

Or maybe they've fallen out of love. That could be a symptom of a serious problem on your end. When donors lapse, often the real culprit is a mediocre communications effort that delivers little emotional bang for the buck or in other ways fails to engage donors' real interests. Lackluster retention rates are directly linked to lackluster donor communications.

TARGETING: HOW YOU FIND NEEDLES IN A HAYSTACK

A basic problem in fund development is how to break the mass known as everyone or the general public down into smaller, more manageable groups. After all, you know it intuitively: The same message will not work with every audience. At a minimum, you need to sort out from the faceless mass those who are most likely to respond with a gift. There is no such thing as "the general public."

"Targeting" (as marketers term it) helps you solve the problem of finding needles in a haystack.

When one of your board members invites 10 friends and colleagues into her living room to learn more about a cause, that's a type of targeting. When you send an appeal letter to a purchased list, hoping to acquire new donors, that's targeting, too. You've chosen (targeted) a group you believe will be responsive for one reason or another. In the board member's case, she asked the people first if they were interested enough to listen to a brief presentation. In the case of the list purchase, everyone shares certain revealing characteristics.

What kinds of revealing characteristics?

There are two: demographic characteristics and behavioral characteristics.

Demographers use statistical evidence to study changes and trends in human populations. Demographic characteristics include essentials such as age, education, gender, income, place of residence, and the like. Demographic characteristics are not conjectural. They are basic, observable facts.

Fundraisers often target groups that share certain demographic characteristics.

A development officer at a community foundation, for example, spotted a demographic trend: Most bequests in recent years had come from childless households. She decided to find other childless couples in her area and ask them if they were interested in local philanthropy. She figured she could nurture a relationship with those who said yes and eventually broach the subject of charitable bequests.

So she phoned a direct mail list broker. She asked for the names and addresses of all "DINK" (dual-income, no kids) couples in her community. "Oh, and one more thing," she added. "Make sure those couples are all at least 50 years old." Why? Because by the age of 50, a couple's childbearing potential is at or near zero. Their DINK status won't change.

Demographics are the facts of life. Behavioral characteristics, however, try to peek inside the mind. They can help you predict whether certain people will respond to your appeal.

Behavioral characteristics (also known as psychographic or lifestyle characteristics) include indicators such as purchase decisions (hybrid vehicle versus SUV), tastes (symphonic music versus hip-hop), brand preferences (Apple versus Dell), magazine subscriptions that imply special interests (travel, food, exercise, investments, etc.), and philanthropic habits (liberal versus conservative causes).

The next case is a simple, real-life example of applied psychographics.

In this case, a nonprofit planned an "acquisition mailing," a mailing intended to find new donors. This particular agency teaches refugees from troubled countries how to speak English and adjust to life in America. After much deliberation, the agency decided to rent a mailing list of subscribers to a U.S. newsmagazine, *Newsweek*. The reasoning went like this. A subscription to a newsmagazine might imply a mind that is curious about the world. *Newsweek* reports on crisis spots around the world, the same sad places our refugees escape from. Maybe our work will strike a chord. Not a bad guess, as it turned out. The *Newsweek* list outperformed a list of people with a history of charitable giving, and the agency increased its donor base by 50 percent.

Let's review. What is a target market? It is a group of people who all share at least one particular characteristic. That characteristic suggests they might be sympathetic to your cause. A few examples of target markets:

- Alumni, for universities. Alumni know the institution intimately. They might even be grateful for their education. The desire "to give something back" strongly motivates many donors.

- Former patients, for a hospital (minus anyone who sued for malpractice).

- Baby boomers, for hospices. Many baby boomers have become caregivers for aging parents. Caregivers long for pain-free endings. Hospice offers the gold standard in end-of-life care.

- Pet owners, for animal rights organizations.

- "The philanthropically inclined who live within our service area," for a community foundation.

- Military veterans, for an armory museum. They have a deeper-than-average appreciation for the tools of warfare.

- Congregation members in the same faith, for a seminary.

- Families of residents, for a nonprofit elderly housing complex.

- Parents, for a zoo, a children's museum, a science museum, or an aquarium. Most visitors have kids in tow. Parents see special value in these attractions as places to entertain and educate a growing family.

When you target, you choose one group to focus on and (for the moment, anyway) ignore the rest of the world. The "ignoring" part is just as critical as the "choosing" part.

Targeting forces you to prioritize. You often have a dizzying number of targets under consideration. But one will always be more promising than the rest. Start there.

Targeting also guides you away from individuals who won't share your enthusiasms. Extreme example: You can't raise money for gun control from members of the National Rifle Association. Fundraisers talk about "making our case" as if we're arguing in front of a neutral jury. But that's not really true. The jury isn't neutral at all. No matter how well you argue your case, if individuals aren't emotionally predisposed to favor your cause, they're not likely to make a gift.

WHAT DIFFERENT TARGET AUDIENCES WANT

This list of target audiences was prepared for the Connecticut Community for Addiction Recovery and is reprinted with permission. Two targets are very specific to the CCAR cause: "families" and "people in recovery." Most of their targets, though, are typical for any nonprofit.

- Individual donors want to change the world (or a piece of it). They want to matter. They're intensely interested in what your organization has achieved (or will achieve) with their money. If you can present with authority a vision worth attaining, you will find donors.

- Foundations want to "move the issue." They hope to be strategic. They like model programs. They're investment-minded. They want to seed a program and then get out, once the program has established its value.

- Businesses want to be seen as "good corporate citizens." This can positively affect their hiring, their stock prices (if they're publicly traded), how regulators see them. A reputation for social responsibility can be a competitive advantage, attracting consumers to a brand.

- Successful entrepreneurs who donate want to see results. They view their charitable giving as an investment. They respond to big, bold ideas.

- Families want healing, help, comfort, hope, advice, understanding, referrals, and an end to pain. They don't want to feel guilty, helpless, ashamed, or alone.

- People in recovery want to stay in recovery. Recovery feels good. Recovery means the disease is properly managed. Recovery means they can regain their self-respect. And they want others who are still addicted to recover, as well. There is strength in numbers. Every person who recovers long term helps to dilute the stigma of addiction.

- Politicians want to win. They want power and status. They want allies. They want people to like them. They want good, clear, well-reasoned answers that take into account their constituencies. They want to make smart policy. They want to spend wisely. They want to be able to say they've saved the taxpayer money. They don't want to look foolish or stupid or cruel to the public, because negative perceptions cost them votes.

- Clergy and faith-based groups seek salvation by serving the desperate.

- Reporters want a good story. They want a fresh story (i.e., "news" is not old). They want sound bites, which are important to "selling" the story. They depend on astounding new facts to surprise and hold their readers and listeners.

SEGMENTATION: HOW YOU INCREASE PENETRATION OF A TARGET MARKET

Hidden inside any database are opportunities to raise more money, if only you could dig them out. "Segmentation" is your pick and shovel.

Segmentation looks at an existing database and asks: Are there any distinctions among these people that are worth taking a closer look at?

The goal is to isolate from the database at large a smaller group (a segment) that might respond to some kind of special message or relationship-building strategy.

Call it microtargeting, if you will. Find the right message for the right set of people at the right time, and money will flow in your direction. It is axiomatic to marketers: The more you can segment a target market, making special pitches to special interests, the more thoroughly you will penetrate that market overall.

One venerable form of segmentation are donor categories such as LYBUNTs (gave "last year but unfortunately not this") and SYBUNTs (gave "some year but . . ."). Colleges, hospitals, and other institutions that make multiple appeals in a year use LYBUNTs and SYBUNTs to segment out donors who have made a gift in the past but not to any appeal in the last 12 months. A recent lack of responsiveness worries fundraisers. They fear loyalty could be waning. So current donors (those who *have* given in the last 12 months) get one sort of appeal letter. But LYBUNTs and SYBUNTs might get something entirely different, perhaps a letter that references their lapsed status: "As president, I've been asked to write you to make a personal plea: We can't afford to lose you." Written with enough urgency and emotion, a special letter, it's hoped, could trigger a renewed gift.

Segmenting donors by "recency" (how long it has been since someone last gave) pays dividends. Consider it "defensive segmentation." It helps you spot donors as they're going stale, so you can intervene and try to revive their interest. It will also help you trim costs by highlighting those no longer worth the postage.

Then, too, in fund development, as elsewhere, some version of the 80/20 rule usually holds sway: 20 percent of your donors produce 80 percent of your income. Segmentation can raise the profile of that 20 percent, if you'd care to give them special attention.

Maybe the most exciting promise of segmentation, though, is this: It offers you the chance to find new money among your existing donors. Best: You don't need a big database to make this kind of "exploratory segmentation" work in your favor.

Say you want to encourage more people to leave you charitable bequests. You've done your homework. Here's what you've learned, from researchers like the U.K.'s Richard Radcliffe.

- You know that most charitable bequests come from women (because they live longer, on average, than men).

- You know that the majority of charitable bequests come from people who are not wealthy.

- But most important, you know that it's the loyal donors, those with a long history of giving to your organization, who are most likely to write a gift into their wills.

> *Fund development is one of the toughest types of marketing. You're not selling tangible products or services that people can use and benefit from. You're asking people to trust you with their money in exchange for some fairly elusive feelings and the occasional bit of information.*

There's your segment: loyal donors. You can ignore gender. It's an actuarial curiosity that women end up with the assets, not an indicator of generosity. You can ignore average gift size. Wealth is no indicator of a person's likelihood to leave a legacy. What you focus on instead is the easiest data you can track: how often has a person has given a gift. Segment out anyone who has given your organization gifts for, say, five years straight, and you'll have a highly qualified list of bequest prospects in your hand.

FREQUENCY AND REACH

Success in sales, advertising, *and* fundraising depend heavily on two things: frequency and reach.

- **Frequency** means this: How *often* can we reach a single, specific, well-qualified mind with our message? How many times can we knock on one particular door, knowing that the person *behind* that door is a good candidate for our product, service, or, in the case of fundraising, mission? How many times can we say the same thing to the same person?

  A national charity might know from experience, for instance, that it takes up to 10 mailings a year, of solicitations, premiums, and newsletters, to dislodge a new gift from a previous donor. In that case, your frequency is how many times you mail to the same person.

- **Reach** means this: How *many* of these well-qualified brains will our message potentially reach? How many of the right doors can we knock on?

  An international child development charity, for instance, might prospect for new donors by sending mailings to people who have already proven responsive to another charity with a similar child-related mission. In that case, your reach is how many qualified people you mail to.

Discovering your total potential for getting a single message across requires nothing more than a simple math calculation: your frequency times your reach. Let's do the math based on a real advertising campaign.

Since 2004, the Rhode Island Foundation has placed large ads on the op-ed pages of the state's paper of record, the *Providence Journal*.[2] Each time the ad runs, the foundation reaches a quarter million potential readers (the average readership). These ads appear four times a month, year round. So: multiply 250,000 potential readers (the reach) times four insertions a month times 12 months (the frequency). Result: The foundation has purchased 12 million chances annually to get a message across.

What is the message? That the foundation is a good neighbor, active in making Rhode Island a better place to live, and a trusted partner for those interested in philanthropy.

Are the minds receiving this message well qualified? Well enough. They won't all care, of course. But some will, because the foundation benefits the very community that the newspaper's readers live in.

What are the advantages to the foundation of its advertising program? For an investment of something like $150,000 annually, it now attracts gifts in the millions each year that are traceable in some way to ad-generated awareness of the foundation's existence, mission, quality, and services.

(You might be thinking "And where am I going to come up with $150,000?" There's no need. We're just explaining how marketing works. That $150,000 advertising investment brings in, through raised awareness of the foundation, sums worth 10, 20, 30 times as much. In your particular case, maybe a $150 investment in phone calls would yield the same multiplier effect, bringing in sums worth 10, 20, 30 times as much.)

Frequency and reach are key factors in the decisions you make regarding matters such as:

- How many solicitations to mail in a year
- How many donor newsletters to produce
- How much advertising (if any) to do
- What kinds of content to place on the Web site
- When to send out e-mail alerts
- And so on

Bottom line: You need to stay in touch with your donor base. Absence does *not* make the heart grow fonder. Instead: out of sight, out of mind. (If we've said it once, we've said it a dozen times.) Which is a vast missed opportunity, since your best prospects for more and bigger gifts are (please carve this into the surface of your desk) *your existing donors*. But everything can't be a solicitation; you're building relationships, not picking pockets. You need a varied annual schedule of communications activities that report and inspire, as well as raise cash.

ALTERNATIVE MARKETING: SOME QUICK OVERVIEWS

Blog Marketing

A web log (blog) allows you to interact with your customers easily and frequently. You post items. They post comments on your items. A blog can be the online equivalent of a combination focus group, suggestion box, and community bulletin board. For marketers, blogs have become important channels for direct customer feedback.

Customer Evangelism

Customer evangelism is based on the idea that a consumer who has a good experience will tell others who might need the same product or service. Needless to say, only firms that are "customer-centric" (or donor-centric, in fund development) can succeed with this type of marketing. You need to intensely focus on your customers' needs, interests, and emotions, forever seeking ways to increase the value of your product and service. That behavior will in turn inspire loyalty and evangelism.

Guerrilla Marketing

When Jay Conrad Levinson published his best seller, *Guerrilla Marketing*, in 1983, he wanted to help small businesses promote themselves on very

(Continued)

low budgets. Instead of cash, guerrilla marketing relies on time, energy, and imagination. Viral marketing can be an Internet-enabled form of guerrilla marketing, for instance. Guerrilla marketing counts customer loyalty among its foremost goals, because it's cheaper to sell to an existing customer than to acquire a new customer. Levinson writes in a follow-up volume, *Guerrilla Marketing Weapons*: "Savvy marketers spend 10 percent of their marketing budgets talking to the universe in general; they spend 30 percent talking to prospects; they spend 60 percent of it talking to satisfied customers. [Treat] your satisfied customers"—fundraisers can substitute *repeat donors* here—"with love, loyalty, devotion, consideration, and professionalism."[3] Aim for more referrals, more transactions with existing customers, and larger transactions, Levinson advises.

Social Networking

Social networking sites like MySpace.com, which boasts millions of users, let strangers with common interests connect easily and in large numbers. Social networks segment by age, geography, and interests. In theory, social networks are ideal for promoting products and services among the like-minded. "Part of the popularity of these things is that they are more credible and not explicitly commercial," says Wharton marketing professor David Bell. "If somebody on the Mac fanatic site tells me about iPod, it's more credible than Mac advertising."

Viral Marketing

Viral marketing is based on the idea that people will pass on interesting or entertaining content. Advertisers hope to spread their message in this way to large groups, "infecting" those who are "susceptible," as viruses might, at relatively low cost (compared to more traditional methods such as direct mail). The term appeared in connection with early e-mail campaigns and is an Internet phenomenon. Think of it as an online form of word-of-mouth campaigning.

WHAT IS BRANDING?

There is a rumor among nonprofit fundraisers that branding is somehow very good for an organization. And that, more important, branding can cure ills in the income department. At major conferences, you won't look hard to find a seminar on branding. People are desperate to know the secret, because branding promises to increase revenues. *Somebody's doing branding, and it's very good for them, we've heard. Shouldn't we do branding, too?*

Yes. But branding might not be what you think it is.

It's clear from many conversations that the concept is mostly misunderstood. One common confusion: that branding has something to do with a logo or a look, a misunderstanding often abetted by graphic designers. But that's a different kind of branding. That kind goes on cattle. Branding your organization is something else.

Your brand is not your logo. That's your trademark.

Nor is your brand what's called a "corporate identity," which refers to the consistent use, for instance, of visual elements like trademarks, on everything from stationery to vehicles.

Nor is your brand your product or service. Animal exhibits are not the brand of a zoo. Music is not the brand of a symphony. Hiking trails are not the brand of a nature organization. Donor-advised funds are not the brand of a community foundation. Hot meal programs are not the brand of an inner-city youth development agency.

These things *contribute* to branding, because people experience a nonprofit by using its products or services. But the products and services themselves are not the brand.

Your brand is this and only this: how a target audience feels about you.

"A brand," writes Marty Neumeier in *The Brand Gap*, his definitive book on the subject, "is a person's gut feeling about a product, service, or company." Neumeier is among the world's top authorities on brand building. His San Francisco–based firm coaches the branding strategies of powerhouses like Hewlett-Packard and Sun Microsystems. He writes:

> [A brand is] a GUT FEELING, because we're all emotional, intuitive beings, despite our best efforts to be rational. [And] in the end the brand is defined by individuals, not by companies. . . . Each person creates his or her own version of [your brand]. . . . When enough individuals arrive at the same gut feeling, a company can be said to have a brand. In other words, a brand is not what YOU say it is. It's what THEY say it is.[4]

Some of this you can control, by what you choose to communicate.

For instance, if your newsletters, brochures, annual reports, Web site, direct mail, conversations, thank-you notes, case statements, press releases, and signage are fervently donor-centric—saying, in essence, "With your help we can do all these wonderful things. And without your help we can't"—then, over time, drop by drop, you will instill in your audience a sense that you need and value donors.

If, for instance, on your Web site you anticipate the *real* "frequently asked questions" of your target audience and supply frank, believable answers, then your organization will seem authentic, open, and trustworthy. Consider this statement on a research hospital's Web site: "Do our methods always work? No, sadly.

But failure can be a great teacher. Some of our biggest breakthroughs in treatment began when things didn't turn out as we'd hoped."

There are other aspects of brand building in your control—if you care to bother. Every contact between your organization and your target audience has the potential to brand you, either positively or negatively. Relationships can start or end based on how we treat the public. One community foundation gave its receptionist a new title, "Director of First Impressions." It's profoundly true. An organization's entire brand can hang by a single thread: on the voice, training, and helpful attitude of the person who answers the phone.

In Conclusion

Marketing is anything but manipulation. The same is true of fund development. Oh, we'd *like* to manipulate, if it would raise more money for our worthy causes. We'd be mad *not* to. It would be vastly easier than how *real* money is *really* raised.

But the truth is, *we're* the manipulated ones. Sad us.

In order to raise funds, in billowing amounts, we are completely at the mercy of prospects and donors. They determine what we say, when we say it, how we say it, and to whom. Because if we don't say it the right way, nothing happens. The person doesn't respond.

Unless you are fully funded by just a few people, fund development always becomes in part a volume business. Successful fund development is essentially about delivering the right message to the right person at the right time, over and over, as often as you need to, to get results.

The surprising part is, it's not all that complicated a thing to do. It might be a bit different from what you're already doing for marketing, communications, and relationship building. But it doesn't take more time. And it *does* raise more money.

ENDNOTES

1. One delightful exception: the windfall bequest that arrives unexpectedly from someone your organization doesn't know.
2. A newspaper is a medium. A medium is any means for communicating with an audience. It derives from the Latin word meaning "middle." A medium is in the middle, linking you and your audience. Lumped together, all these means become "the media."
3. *Guerrilla Marketing Weapons,* Jay Conrad Levinson, (New York: Plume, 1990), p. 174.
4. Marty Neumeier, *The Brand Gap,* rev. ed. (Berkeley, CA: New Riders, 2006), p. 2.

CHAPTER 9

Emotions

THE DECISION MAKERS

On ne voit bien qu'avec le coeur. (We only see well with the heart.)

— Antoine de Saint-Exupéry, *Le Petit Prince*

Emotion needs no translation

— From a *New York Times* movie review headline

There can be no transforming . . . of apathy into movement without emotion.

— Carl Gustav Jung

DEAR READER: Coming into advertising early in my career, I soon learned to respect the dominant role emotions play in purchase decisions. But I had no idea how vital that role really is until I began to research modern neuroscience and apply its findings to fund development.

Tom

INTRODUCTION

Fund development seems simple enough. One brain (yours) tries to convince another brain (the prospect's) to take action and make a gift.

But there *is* a catch. (Well, more than one. But let's keep it simple for the moment.)

On the fundraiser's end, where the message originates, respect for rationality rules.

Instinct and training tell us to argue our case logically. Proceed from fact to fact. Build toward some undeniable and (we hope) inescapable conclusion. Presented with the right information, in the right order, prospects can't help but be persuaded, we assume. And cash blooms to support our cause.

In the world according to Spock (the *Star Trek* character), this would all be true. Logic would guide our decision-making processes.

However, among humans, that's not really how decision-making works much of the time. Emotion plays a far more dominant role in decision making than the average person suspects. And where is reason in all this? A bit player at best. Reason enters the credit card numbers online or, in the case of a check, tells the heart what it can afford. Science reporter Dennis Overbye sums up the emerging view on rationality's inflated sense of self: "A bevy of experiments in recent years suggest that the conscious mind is like a monkey riding a tiger of subconscious decisions and actions in progress, frantically making up stories about being in control."[1]

ORBITOFRONTAL DAMAGE AND ITS IMPLICATIONS FOR FUNDRAISERS

In 2006 neuroscientist Dr. Antoine Bechara, a leading authority on the mental processes behind decision making, published this abstract summarizing a decade of research:

> It is assumed that humans decide as if they were equipped with unlimited knowledge, time, and information-processing power. The influence of emotions on decision-making is largely ignored. Indeed, there is a popular notion, which most of us learn from early on in life, that logical, rational calculation forms the basis of sound decisions. Many people say, "emotion has no IQ"; emotion can only cloud the mind and interfere with good judgment. But what if these notions were wrong and had no scientific basis? What if sound, rational decision-making in fact depended on . . . emotional processing? The studies of decision-making in neurological patients who can no longer process emotional information normally suggest just that . . . I will make the case that decision-making is a process guided by emotions.[2]

Dr. Bechara's subjects were people uniquely suited to prove a point. They had all suffered damage to the brain's emotional headquarters, the orbitofrontal cortex. Otherwise, their brains worked just fine. Reason was intact. Intelligence remained as it had been. Only the ability to feel emotions was gone. And the oddest thing happened as a result: Without emotions in the mental mix, even simple decisions, like what to choose for dinner, proved nearly impossible. Our feelings, in some fundamental, physiological way, make decisions occur.

A Bechara colleague, Dr. Antonio Damasio, has delved even deeper.[3] Dr. Damasio is the author of several influential books on brain science (*The Feeling of What Happens; Descartes' Error: Emotion, Reason, and the Human Brain; Looking for Spinoza: Joy, Sorrow, and the Feeling Brain*), a researcher so profound and original he's taken seriously as Nobel Prize material. On the Web site ChangingMinds.org, editor David Straker sums up Dr. Damasio's and other scientists' discoveries:

> at the point of decision, emotions are very important for choosing. In fact even with what we believe are logical decisions, the very point of choice is arguably always based on emotion ... we are living an illusion of conscious choice.

DID PHILANTHROPY START AS AN EVOLUTIONARY ADVANTAGE?

We talk about human nature and the "philanthropic impulse." What if philanthropy were really a genetic adaptation that improved our species' chances of survival? Geneticists now think that could be part of the truth, that our DNA actually programs us to help others. A hormone called oxytocin operates on the brain. It wasn't always part of our makeup. It appeared during human brain evolution about 1.7 million years ago. In the brain, *Newsweek* magazine reports, "[oxycotin] promotes trust during interactions with other people, and thus the cooperative behavior that lets groups of people live together for the common good."

Sharon Begley, "Beyond Stones & Bones," *Newsweek*, March 19, 2007, p. 57.

EMOTIONAL TRIGGERS: AN INTRODUCTION

Presented with stunning neurological evidence that debunks conventional wisdom about reason and decision making, marketers can be forgiven for muttering "Tell us something we *don't* know."

In 2006, U.S. marketers spent an estimated $615 billion to convince other people to buy goods, services, and ideas.[4] In 2006, U.S. marketers far outspent even our nation's Defense Department, which had an official budget of just $419.3 billion. Direct mail alone accounted for about $60 billion of the 2006 U.S. marketing outlay.[5]

The direct mail industry lives and dies by one credo: Test everything, assume nothing. Revenue depends on a never-ending, trial-and-error search for improvements in copy, package formats, and lists. Thanks to this prevailing industry attitude, direct mail has long ranked as the world's most thoroughly poked and prodded communications medium. No one knows more about effective persuasion and applied psychology than the professionals in the direct mail industry.

And here's what they believe: Emotions move cash. Mountains of cash, as vast as the Himalayas.

Over the decades, direct mail copywriters have isolated seven emotional triggers that lead to higher response rates in fundraising appeals:

1. Anger ("This is wrong! Do something!")
2. Exclusivity ("Me? You want me to join your circle of friends?")
3. Fear ("This scares me. Is the problem hopeless?")
4. Flattery ("You're absolutely right. I *am* one in a thousand.")
5. Greed ("You want to give me something? Bring it on!")
6. Guilt ("Wish I hadn't done that. Want to feel better.")
7. Salvation ("There's hope for me.")

The exact number goes up and down a bit, depending on the expert. The legendary ad man Herschell Gordon Lewis listed only four emotional triggers in his 1984 hardball classic, *Direct Mail Copy That Sells!* "Of the four," he writes, "Fear is the most potent. In a skilled surgeon's hands, Fear cuts through the layers of fat around a reader's brain, jabbing and needling until, trembling with the unquenchable desire built on frustration, the recipient of your Fear message grabs his pen or his phone to soothe his fever."[6]

The use of emotional triggers to engage the predisposed and to nudge them toward supporting your organization is not restricted to direct mail. On the contrary, actually. Emotional triggers work in every kind of relationship-building communication, from board recruitment, to personal solicitations, to writing a letter of intent to a foundation, to speeches.

The Economist magazine, reporting on the theories of Todd L. Pittinsky, a social psychologist at Harvard University studying allophilia (liking for other groups), concludes that "people's choices in charitable giving, study, voluntary work and travel are guided ... by the sort of groups that make them *feel good*."[7] In other words: Successfully stroke the emotions of your prospects and donors, and they become more likely to support you. (Exhibit 9.1 shows how a community foundation benefited from responding to a donor's emotions.)

UP TO 135 TRIGGERS TO CHOOSE FROM

How many emotional triggers exist? More than the seven listed above, surely.

Mal Warwick, an extraordinarily experienced fundraiser, has proposed adding six other (and sunnier) triggers to the fundraiser's toolbox: caring, compassion,

EXHIBIT 9.1   THE EMOTIONS BEHIND A VOLUNTEER'S ACTION

In spring 2000, I approached the Rhode Island Foundation about initiating a women's fund. In fall 2000, the Women's Fund of Rhode Island (WFRI) was launched as a field-of-interest fund within the community foundation. Because of the foundation's extraordinary support, the Women's Fund flourished. By March 2005, endorsed by the Rhode Island Foundation, the Women's Fund began operation as an independent 501c3 corporation.

The founding of the Women's Fund is one of my proudest and most rewarding experiences. And a reflection of my most fundamental values and deepest feelings.

The seven emotional triggers resonate with me: anger, fear, greed, guilt, flattery, exclusivity, and salvation. I wear a bracelet engraved with these emotions.

So here's my story.

In the late 1990s, my anger and frustration about the social and political fabric in the United States seemed overwhelming. (Little did I know that beginning in 2000, and continuing as I write this book, my anger would be even greater.)

I was raised in an international household, taught to welcome pluralism. I learned to respect the different life experiences of people. My French father[i] always reminded his family and students: "The most important thing is to step out of your linguistic ghetto and become aware that there are people who live, eat, learn, and make love in a medium which is not English."[ii]

Over the years, I modified my dad's statement and use it all the time. When I shared the statement with Tom, he proclaimed, "that's our family slogan!"

The word "slogan" comes from the Gaelic term "sluaghghairm," used by Scottish clans. It means "war cry." An inspiring thought from Tom: Your organization's tagline or positioning statement could be considered your slogan. Shout it at the top of your lungs and charge into — not battle but relationship building, surely.

So here it is, Tom and Simone's family slogan:

> "People eat, sleep and make love in languages other than English, in colors other than white, and in pairings other than opposite sex. We are committed to giving voice to and fighting for that beauty."

Now back to the 1990s and my anger. I felt I wasn't doing enough, investing sufficiently in progressive change. Then I began consulting with the Women's Foundation of Southern Arizona. Inspired by the women's funding movement, I wanted to start a women's fund in Rhode Island. I hoped this could help me manage my feelings.

I believe in social justice and equity for everyone, where all rights and opportunities apply to all justly. But that is not our truth. The United States — and indeed the world — is unjust in heartbreaking ways. The power of privilege — racial and ethnic, gender and gender identity, sexual orientation and more — has flawed the United States since its founding. Our dream has never been realized. But I continue to hope we can do better.

So I am *angry* because social injustice still reigns here in my country. I'm *afraid* of living in a community and a world where so many people are excluded, where their voices are not heard. We lose so much.

I am *greedy* to live in a world that embraces differences, and welcomes *all* voices at the table. I seek *more* people committed to social justice and change.

I feel *guilty*, because while I'm disadvantaged having been born female, at least I'm a white, well-educated, affluent, heterosexual female. I enjoy enormous unearned privilege.

The Women's Fund of Rhode Island is respected and admired. I'm *flattered* to be part of this *exclusive* group of women and men who fight for social justice. I'm proud to be known as the founder of the Women's Fund.

And I believe that my work in philanthropy – as a volunteer and as a professional – is the reason why I exist. For me, this all-consuming passion for philanthropy is my *salvation* – not a god or goddess salvation – but my salvation as a human being.

(Continued)

Each of these seven emotions motivates me. These emotions are not negative – they are simply emotions. Betty Freidan, Simone de Beauvoir, and Susan B. Anthony were angry. Surely Gandhi was angry. And I believe that Martin Luther King Jr. was angry, too.

But as Saint Augustine said: "Hope has two daughters, anger and courage. They are both lovely."[iii]

[i] My father, Georges J. Joyaux, moved to the United States as an adult after World War II. He was noted for his work in advancing the study of foreign language and for his scholarship in twentieth-century French literature, French culture and society, and the French literatures in Africa, West Indies, and Canada. In addition to receiving the Croix de Guerre twice, the highest medal awarded for wartime valor, he received the highest nonwartime medal from the French government, Chevalier and Officier des Palmes Académiques, for disseminating French language and culture.

[ii] "Linguist cites nation's loss," Sharon Bertsch, Staff Writer, *The State Journal* (Lansing, MI), 1979.

[iii] Quoted by Studs Terkel, *Hope Dies Last: Keeping the Faith in Troubled Times* (New York: The New Press, 2003)

---

duty, faith, hope, and love. Mal's half dozen raises the count to 13 triggers, and we haven't begun to exhaust the topic. In fact, there are dozens of emotions you might trigger.

In 2001, one eminent authority, Georgetown University psychology professor W. Gerrod Parrott, attempted a roll call. He published his list of 135 emotional states (see Appendix 9A). Sad states, ranging from agony to sympathy, comprise the largest grouping. Types of joy form the second largest, ranging from amusement to relief. Anger comes third, ranging from grumpiness to torment.

As with peanuts, you'll find that one emotional trigger is rarely enough.

Professionally written fundraising materials are like minefields: You can't step anywhere without encountering an emotional trigger. Consider this example from the John F. Kennedy Center for the Performing Arts in Washington, DC. This invitation pulled spectacularly well:

> You are hereby invited to become a Member of the Kennedy Center at a full 20% discount and gain the special privilege to purchase advance tickets before the general public to the finest Kennedy Center presentations.

A single sentence, yet it's packed with seven emotional triggers, by our count:

> You are hereby invited **[flattery]** to become a Member **[exclusivity]** of the Kennedy Center at a full 20% discount **[greed]** and gain **[greed]** the special privilege **[exclusivity]** to purchase advance tickets before the general public **[greed]** to the finest **[exclusivity]** Kennedy Center presentations.

Once you learn to recognize the signs, you'll find that many emotional triggers are obvious.

Any time you make an offer that seems to save people money or give them something—a 20 percent discount, half off, three for the price of two, free parking, free DVD, discounts at participating merchants, the list is endless; listen carefully to any National Public Radio fundraising drive—you're adding a greed trigger.

Any time you ask someone to join a membership organization, you're including an exclusivity trigger. Any time you point out to people that they receive some benefit, whether they contribute or not (again, National Public Radio take a bow), you're hoping a feeling of guilt will trigger response.

> *The essential difference between emotion and reason is that emotion leads to action, while reason leads to conclusions.*
>
> —Neurologist and author Donald B. Calne

Any time you speak to a symphony-going audience about the gap between income (ticket prices) and expenses (the cost of first-rate musicians), you're hoping to pull two triggers when you ask for a gift: greed and fear. Greed for the musical experience; fear that it will no longer be available.

Incidentally, if you *do* happen to make someone feel guilty for a moment, there's no lasting damage done. Yes, emotional triggers *are* powerful motivators. But their influence doesn't last long on most donors.[8]

Many, if not most, gifts are the philanthropic equivalent of what retailers call an "impulse purchase." The American Marketing Association defines this as "an unplanned purchase by a customer." Peek inside the donor's mind: "I wasn't thinking about you people today. But you sent me this solicitation, so presumably you need money. I like what you've told me in your newsletter about your accomplishments. You seem to make a real difference. My bills are paid. I can afford $25. I'll write you a check. It makes me feel good to help out."

People give from disposable income for the most part, from money they feel they don't really need. Your use of emotional triggers can encourage that gift but not command it.

EMOTIONAL TWINSETS: RAISE THE PROBLEM, BE THE SOLUTION

In advertising, the most common messaging formula goes like this:

> If you have a particular problem, we have a great solution.

"Do you have dirty bathroom tiles? We have a foaming, easy-to-use, nontoxic spray in an unbreakable plastic bottle that will make your embarrassing tiles"—that's a trigger; embarrassment is among Dr. Parrott's 135 emotions—"look like new."

Problem/solution: It's the most prevalent logic in ads. The logic works in fund development, too. First you talk about a problem that exists. Then you offer your organization's mission or vision as a remedy to that problem. Woven into every inch of the discussion are emotional triggers.

There are negative-leaning emotions (anger, sadness, fear). There are positive-leaning emotions (caring, joy, hope). People seek relief from the negative. They desire the positive. When you talk about a problem, use negative emotional triggers. When you talk about the solution (i.e., your organization's mission), use positive emotional triggers. Somewhere between the two emotions, the negative and the positive, the predisposed mind decides to act. "The community has a problem. Your organization has a solution. I, as a donor, can help."

Two emotions, negative and positive, working together to kindle giving: We call such a pairing an "emotional twinset." It's a name (blithely) borrowed from women's fashion. Two sweaters designed to be worn together are a twinset. Similarly, two emotions working together to raise money are a twinset.

Call it what you like, the twinset notion has intrinsic power. Using negative and positive emotions in combination mimics a dualistic view of the world that is already common in most brains: good versus evil, right versus wrong. When you match a preexisting mental outlook, people will understand your argument intuitively. There's less you'll need to explain.

Putting twinsets to work is easy. You can use the next basic sequence of three messages in any type of fundraising solicitation, written or oral. The sequence derives from advertising's dependable problem/solution formula and always includes a call to action:

1. Brew emotional unease with negative emotions.

2. Relieve that unease with positive emotions.

3. Ask the donor for help.

Some examples of how this problem/solution sequence works follow. You'll encounter disturbing emotions like fear and anger. You'll encounter reassuring emotions like hope, pride, and exclusivity. Note one other detail. In each instance, the case for support is time-stamped: It talks about the situation as it exists *right now*. Donors give because the need is urgent (see Exhibit 9.2).

• For a tutoring program

"Four out of five inmates have no high school diploma, and that's no coincidence. If you're a taxpayer, you're right to worry about our city's appalling graduation rates, because you're paying twice: once to send our children to school, a second time to deal with the aftermath when they fail. But it doesn't have to be that way. Our tutoring programs have proven effective in keeping kids in schools and successful all the way to graduation. We're ready to grow. Are you ready to help?"

EXHIBIT 9.2	USING EMOTIONS IN A PERSONAL SOLICITATION

Tom and I knew that Equity Action, the LGBTQ (the lesbian, gay, bisexual, transgender, queer, and questioning) fund at the Rhode Island Foundation, would ask us for a gift. We told them to ask us, and we planned to give. There were only two questions left really: Would Equity Action follow the tips we had shared with them as volunteers? How much would we pledge?

Here's what happened:

One morning a representative from Equity Action called to set up an appointment. The caller thanked me for our volunteer support and requested a time to meet with Tom and me. The caller also asked, "Since you are our friends, can we send someone who is inexperienced in soliciting, because you are safe and will give?"

My response: "Yes, that is fine. But send the right person, and we will give a larger gift." I figured it was their job to figure out who the right person was.

We met up for the solicitation. In the room: Simone; Tom wasn't able to join us. Kris and Peter from Equity Action. Peter was the co-chair of the fund's advisory council at that time. Kris was a program officer from the Rhode Island Foundation.

I'd never met Peter. But given the request they made, he was an appropriate person by virtue of position.

And then there was Kris: the right person.

I'd met Kris a couple years earlier when I founded the Women's Fund. The Rhode Island Foundation assigned Kris as one of two program officers to help with the Women's Fund, then a field-of-interest fund within the foundation.

Kris and I worked together for several years. Oh, how angry we both were—and still are—about the social injustice in Rhode Island, in the United States, and worldwide. Sexism. Racism. Homophobia. Classism. Kris and I got to know each other's interests and values. During meals and countless meetings, Kris and I talked about social injustice and how to build boards and how to raise charitable contributions. Kris even asked me, as a volunteer, to help draft the values and mission of Equity Action. I was elated. (See Appendix 4A for the Equity Action materials.)

So Kris was absolutely the right person to make this ask. Remember those seven emotions from the direct mail industry? Remember Mal Warwick's five emotions? Remember Tom's twinsets? Kris knew my feelings, and she honored those in the solicitation.

In fact, it was the best solicitation I've ever experienced as a donor.

Kris and Peter acknowledged my **anger** about social justice. They complimented me for my work as the founder of the Women's Fund. The three of us shared stories about social justice, and you could hear the anger vibrating in the room.

You could hear the **fear** we shared, that so many people are excluded—women, our friends who are not white, gays and lesbians, those who are not affluent. We talked about how each community is less than it could be because the playing fields aren't even close to level.

And then Kris said: "You and Tom are the first straight people we are asking to give to Equity Action. We ask you first because we know you two care so much and fight hard for justice."

I was **flattered.**

Then she said, "We ask you first because you are well known in several circles in this community. And people know you are straight. Your support will show that heterosexuals care about social justice for the LBGTQ community. Your gift will help leverage gifts from others."

I was even more **flattered.** I felt part of an **exclusive** group of people who care about social justice. And if a gift from Tom and me will help others to give, I'm thrilled. (I'm **greedy** for more donors to social justice.)

And of course, the whole conversation was about **salvation**—what Tom and I believe is our life's work and our salvation as human beings. And the commitment of Kris and Peter and everyone involved in Equity Action and the Women's Fund and social justice.

Then Kris said, "We're asking you and Tom to become founders to Equity Action. You will be recognized in perpetuity as a founding donor."

Okay. The money piece. Tom and I had already decided to give about $2,500. (A note to Kris when you read this book: Did I tell you that Tom and I had already picked a figure?)

Then I think Peter may have said, "Being a founder of Equity Action, recognized in perpetuity, is a minimum gift of $5,000."

And I responded, "This gift will be from Tom and me together. He wants to help make the decision. I will speak with him and let you know."

As I left the building, I called Tom on my cell phone. I told him every single detail. He kept saying "Yes, Kris heard all the things we told her about fund development. Good for her!"

Of course we became founders, giving twice as much as we expected to give. And two years later, when George W. Bush was reelected President of the United States—and states around the country adopted antigay legislation—we sent another gift (large for us) to the Equity Action endowment fund.

What did this mean for us? A gift for all our friends gay and straight, women and men, of different ethnicities and cultures, poor or affluent. For social justice. For our own salvation.

P.S.: As of this writing, Kris works for the National Center for Lesbian Rights. She's still fighting the battle for social justice. Kris asked us to give a gift to NCLR. She didn't ask us because we're her friends. She wouldn't do that. She asked because she knew our interests and values. And we gladly gave.

- For a family planning center

"These are dark days nationally in the struggle to keep theology out of women's healthcare. But here, in our state, we continue to win our battles, day after day (those picketers never quit), year after year (certain legislators never quit), thanks to your continued support. Now we need you more than ever."

- For a college embarking on an endowed chairs campaign among alumni

"Competition for the leading minds of our time has never been fiercer. Comparable schools have hundreds of endowed chairs, attracting top scholars and ambitious students who want to study under them. We're vulnerable. We have just 15 endowed chairs right now. But within two years, I promise you, we can change all that . . . if you're ready to reach for the stars."

In Conclusion

Thanks to amazing new imaging technologies, neuroscientists are finally penetrating one of humanity's most enduring enigmas, the brain.

And what are they discovering? One of marketing's oldest assumptions: that emotions rule decision making. Including, we now must conclude, the decision to make a gift of time or money to a charity.

In one way, using emotions effectively in fund development is simple. You just have to do it. Many charities don't. They try, instead, to *reason* money out of people. That's like serving your dinner guest raw ingredients, a recipe, and a plate, instead of a prepared meal. Emotions cook and sauce your facts into something tasty (see Exhibit 9.3).

| EXHIBIT 9.3 | YOU KNOW YOUR IQ. DO YOU KNOW YOUR EQ? |

You're born with a certain mental capacity, a general intelligence that allows you to plan, solve problems, think abstractly, learn quickly; so many useful things.

But your brain also comes equipped with other forms of intelligence, researchers say, including something psychologists term "emotional intelligence." You have an EQ (emotional intelligence quotient) as well as an IQ.

A common definition (from Wikipedia) of emotional intelligence is the "ability, capacity, or skill to perceive, assess, and manage the emotions of one's self, of others, and of groups." It's an evolving area of cognitive study. But practical applications in business appeared quickly once Harvard Ph.D. Daniel Goleman, published his bestseller, *Emotional Intelligence*, in 1995. Emotional awareness in leaders helps them develop high-performance teams, for instance.

It's easy to imagine how a high EQ can help a fundraiser succeed, say, in cultivation or during face-to-face solicitations. Unlike your IQ, which is fairly stable over time, your EQ, some theorists believe, can increase. And even if your native-born EQ can't improve, your emotional skills can, with training.

Maybe a good place to start would be an EQ self-assessment. You can measure your EQ online in 10 minutes, using the trademarked Emotional Intelligence Appraisal offered by TalentSmart and based on the model popularized by Daniel Goleman.

ENDNOTES

1. Dennis Overbye, "Free Will: Now You Have It, Now You Don't," *New York Times*, January 2, 2007.

2. Dr. Bechara's abstract appears in the informational materials for the 3rd multi-disciplinary **symposium** organized by the **NWO (**Netherlands Organization for Scientific Research) **Cognition** Programme: How **rational are we**, June 2005.

3. In this book, we use the terms "feelings" and "emotions" interchangeably. But you might be interested to learn how scientists such as Dr. Damasio distinguish between the two terms. Emotions are public: external and observable body states; tears of grief, for instance. Feelings are private: internal, mental states observable only to the person having them.

4. Blackfriars.

5. Universal McCann.

6. *Direct Mail Copy That Sells,* (New York: Prentice Hall, 1984), p. 15. A no-holds-barred sort of entrepreneur, Herschell Gordon Lewis made an early reputation as a prolific creator of cheap "exploitation" films, meant to make a quick buck off some controversial topic. In 1963 he introduced screaming audiences to a subspecialty, the "gore" film. He made buckets of money from buckets of fake blood. Lewis's success as the "father of gore" might account for his fondness for fear as an emotional trigger.

7. "Really Loving Your Neighbor," *The Economist*, March 17, 2007, p. 66. Emphasis added.

8. The topic of emotional triggers strikes a predictable tiny fraction of neophyte fundraisers as somehow manipulative or "mean," as if an understanding of emotional triggers has shoved what should be a purely altruistic impulse into the gutter. But philanthropy is a complex impulse. Altruism isn't the whole story. Nor are emotions. There is evidence, for example, that philanthropy is hard-wired into the human brain, as part of some obscure self-preservation scheme.

W. Gerrod Parrott's List of Emotions

Key

Primary emotion

Secondary emotion

Tertiary emotions

Love

Affection

Adoration, affection, love, fondness, liking, attraction, caring, tenderness, compassion, sentimentality

Lust

Arousal, desire, lust, passion, infatuation

Longing

Longing

Joy

Cheerfulness

Amusement, bliss, cheerfulness, gaiety, glee, jolliness, joviality, joy, delight, enjoyment, gladness, happiness, jubilation, elation, satisfaction, ecstasy, euphoria

Zest

Enthusiasm, zeal, zest, excitement, thrill, exhilaration

---

www.changingminds.org, which cited for the list a book edited by Parrott called *Emotions in Social Psychology,* (Philadelphia: Psychology Press, 2000).

Contentment

Contentment, pleasure

Pride

Pride, triumph

Optimism

Eagerness, hope, optimism

Enthrallment

Enthrallment, rapture

Relief

Relief

Surprise

Surprise

Amazement, surprise, astonishment

Anger

Irritation

Aggravation, irritation, agitation, annoyance, grouchiness, grumpiness

Exasperation

Exasperation, frustration

Rage

Anger, rage, outrage, fury, wrath, hostility, ferocity, bitterness, hate, loathing, scorn, spite, vengefulness, dislike, resentment

Disgust

Disgust, revulsion, contempt

Envy

Envy, jealousy

Torment

Torment

Sadness

Suffering

Agony, suffering, hurt, anguish

Sadness

Depression, despair, hopelessness, gloom, glumness, sadness, unhappiness, grief, sorrow, woe, misery, melancholy

Disappointment

Dismay, disappointment, displeasure

Shame

Guilt, shame, regret, remorse

Neglect

Alienation, isolation, neglect, loneliness, rejection, homesickness, defeat, dejection, insecurity, embarrassment, humiliation, insult

Sympathy

Pity, sympathy

Fear

Horror

Alarm, shock, fear, fright, horror, terror, panic, hysteria, mortification

Nervousness

Anxiety, nervousness, tenseness, uneasiness, apprehension, worry, distress, dread

CHAPTER 10

Relationship Building: Details about Steps #3 and #5

GETTING TO KNOW YOU

Getting to know you,
Getting to know all about you.

—*"GETTING TO KNOW YOU," LYRICS BY OSCAR HAMMERSTEIN*

DEAR READER: Here's more detail about two critical steps in the relationship-building process, which can apply to donors of time or money. You can personalize this to your organization, considering your resources and your capacity. My goal is to challenge your assumptions, stimulate your thinking, and give you a framework for valuing the work of relationship building.
Simone

STEP #3 IN THE RELATIONSHIP-BUILDING PROCESS

As noted in Chapter 6, the aim of Step #3 is to gain the necessary depth of understanding regarding prospect and donor interests and disinterests, their emotions, and their motivations and aspirations. You learn this in order to nurture the relationship.

In the ideal world, you would know all this about every single prospect and donor. But that's impractical. Do this work to the extent that is possible in your organization. Look at the suggestions throughout this book. Examine your organization closely. You may be able to do more than you do now, so be tough on yourself. Or you may be doing all that you can do now, so be patient and add more as you have the capacity.

In the real world, you choose which prospects and which donors to focus on. You look at groups of prospects and donors based on various criteria or affinities: for example, gender and generation, ethnicity and culture, and so forth.

But be cautious.

- **Treat everyone with the same authenticity and respect.** Sadly, too many prospects and donors know what it's like to be ignored when a more important donor comes along.

- **Avoid choices based solely on money.** How foolish to ignore 20 years of a donor's loyalty, no matter the gift size, in order to focus on a prospect with big bucks.

- **Don't be a premature asker.** You judge when to ask, and please judge carefully. You decide how much you need to know before you ask, whether for money, time, or anything else. As you move through the relationship-building process, you regularly evaluate prospect interest in your cause. You determine people's readiness to be asked and judge their capacity to give whatever you plan to ask for.

The process of asking is also part of relationship building. As Tony Myers says, "If I get a no, it's okay. I'll find out the reason for the no, which gives me the chance to deal with the no portion, and then move forward. If I don't ask then how will I know where the no comes from?"

> *Quit going after the same old "important people and big donors," trying to convince them to give to you. Find those who care and nurture the relationship.*

Getting Started

First, think about how you get to know your own colleagues and friends. Lots of this is common sense. You do this every day.

Now think about this as an intentional, well-planned business process. Focus on three key elements. The first two, primary and secondary research, help prepare you to personally reach out and connect to others. And the third, conversation, is just that: talking with people and listening to what the say and, just as important, what they don't say.

Secondary Research   First, acquire information from secondary research, which is already available. Doing this helps sensitize you to the different ways people experience life. For example, lifestyle and demographic differences, including gender and generation, ethnicity and education, and so much more.

- **Collect research results.** Collect surveys and focus group questions from colleagues.

- **Search the Internet for relevant reports and research results.** Don't just focus on the nonprofit/NGO sector.

- **Examine the population census in a particular country or local community.**

- **Check out organizations that regularly conduct research.** Some are unique to a particular country or profession. Others are global. Visit my Web site for some interesting links: www.simonejoyaux.com.

- **Read demographic materials.**

- **Read original research results about donors.** Don't just read media reports about the research.

- Visit the Web sites of various centers on philanthropy worldwide.
  - Review trade publications from around the world to find reports on research. Then go to the original source for further information.
  - Visit the Web sites of key nonprofits/NGOs, including professional associations, and monitor their research activity.
  - Check the various links on philanthropy Web sites to identify useful information sources.
  - Visit www.simonejoyaux.com. Click on Resources. You will find dozens of Web sites around the world, and some provide research information. The site also connects you to the research theses and literature reviews of students in the Philanthropy and Development Program at Saint Mary's University in Winona, Minnesota.

Primary Research   Second, conduct your own research. You might use focus groups, surveys, and interviews. See details later in this chapter.

Use secondary research results to help guide your own research. For example, modify questions used by others. For example, see the Audubon Society's member survey in Appendix 10B.

Use Conversation to Learn   Third, talk, listen, and observe. Learn to be a good conversationalist. Reach out. Be with people. Connect and share. This topic is discussed more fully in Chapter 17. See also Appendix A.

Keep Going!

Gaining understanding happens over months and years as you nurture and deepen the relationship. Use every opportunity to connect and deepen the relationship as you move through the steps of the relationship-building process.

Make sure you document interactions within the relationship. Collect information about interests and disinterests, motivations and aspirations. Record contacts and anecdotes.

What Kind of Information Do You Want to Know?

What would you want to know? Why do you want to know this? How will the information help you nurture a meaningful relationship?

Be careful. Ask yourself: Why do I want to know that? How can I use the information? And as Bob Harris, my marketing research guru, also says: "Will the results—for example, the information you get—be actionable?!" (Sometimes I'm so enamored of a particular question that Bob actually has to argue with me before I either explain how the organization could use the results or, more likely, acknowledge that he's right.)

Given your organization's resources, how much information can you gather and manage? What is the minimal information you need, and why? What additional information do you need when you plan to ask for a gift that the prospect or donor would consider significant? (Remember, larger requests require greater intimacy between your organization and the prospect or donor. And greater intimacy depends on more information, more interaction, and deeper bonds.

You know the basic information you have to collect about donors and prospects: for example, name and contact information, general personal information, and history with your organization.

But building profitable relationships that last requires more information. Each organization decides what it can collect. Here are some more ideas:

1. Demographics that might affect the person: for example, generational attitudes, gender, sexual orientation, and so on

2. Personal relationships: in particular, family of origin, life partner, and children

3. Personal interests including hobbies, reading interests, and so forth

4. Job or professional interests and commitments, and their importance to the individual

5. Nature of the donor or prospect's interest in your organization, your cause, your results, your leadership, and the like

6. Emotions and feelings about key issues, including, of course, your particular cause and probably related causes

7. Philanthropic commitments to other organizations, whether volunteering time or giving money

8. Other meaningful relationships in their lives

9. Cultural upbringing and life experience

10. How they perceive that they experience life differently, how important this is or isn't, and how this affects their feelings, choices, and actions

11. Their values and how these align or not with your organization

If possible, learn these points about those with whom you wish to develop the deepest relationships:

1. Their communications style, including social styles

2. Their preferred mode of communications—and what they don't like

3. Their preferred mode of recognition—and what they don't like

4. Their preferred cultivation activities—and what they don't like

5. Whom they would be comfortable speaking with in your organization— and those who would make them uncomfortable

Make sure you record what they don't like and who makes them uncomfortable. Avoid these when possible.

By the way, donors have a right to see their records. That means the records must be judiciously written, and they should probably include the date donors reviewed them.

A Few Strategies for Getting to Know Your Donors and Prospects

Of course, the best way to get the information is to ask. You can ask the specific individual or group. You also can ask others about the individual or group—but be careful about privacy and confidentiality. Sharing information about others refers to "public" information only. Here are a few examples:

- **Private and confidential information.** Information you as a best friend know about a pending divorce.

- **Public information.** Knowing that Simone and Tom are interested in social justice is public information; lots of people know that.

Remember that asking questions is part of ongoing conversation. Conversation serves two simultaneous purposes: learning more about your donors and prospects, and nurturing the relationship.

> *Truly remarkable businesses never lose touch with their customers.... Remarkable companies create [communication] that strikes an emotional chord in the hearts of their customers.... [Remarkable companies] stay relevant by remembering to continually ask, listen, and act.*
>
> —GROUP OF 33, *THE BIG MOO*

But how, exactly, do you ask? Here are my favorites. Use and modify them, depending on the geographic reach and resources of your organization.

Conduct Focus Groups   Conduct focus groups with donors every year. If you wish, consider different donor groupings based on donor affinities: gender and generation, interests within your organization, lifestyle, and so on. How about trying focus groups with lapsed donors? See Chapter 17 for lots of questions to ask prospects and donors. How would you modify those questions for use in focus groups? Don't incur a lot of expense. Conduct these focus groups yourself. How about modifying the traditional focus group approach by using an Internet strategy?

Conduct a Survey   Conduct an anonymous written donor survey at regular intervals, perhaps every two to three years. (But if you have the resources, do a survey every year!) Compare results over the years. See Appendix 10B for the Audubon Society of Rhode Island donor/member survey, which was part of a strategic planning process. Many of the questions were modified from sector research collected over the past decades.

Meet One on One   Meet one on one with selected donors and ask them some of the questions proposed throughout this book. But you're only one person. And your development office may be small. Involve your organization's chief executive officer and other key staff. Engage board members to help do this work.

Call Donors   Conduct donor thank-you calls regularly. In addition to the genuine and heartfelt thanks, ask a couple important questions. (Note: These are *not* solicitation calls. Do not request a gift. A formal thank-you call program is an important part of your cultivation activities.)

Quick tip: Tell donors at the start of the call that you will not ask for a gift. You just want to thank them and ask them a question about why they give. Tell them this quickly, at the start of the conversation. Most likely, their experience is a solicitation call, which begins with a thank you. Never underestimate the power of being different and behaving in a different way than expected.

I usually recommend an annual thank-you call campaign, carried out by board members. Find a logical time to call; for example, if your country celebrates some form of "Thanksgiving," this might be a good time to call.

On the other hand, check out Penelope Burk's research about thank-you calls. No surprise, her study shows that a call—by a board member—within a day or two of gift receipt, is highly valued by donors. More importantly, such a call can increase the likelihood of a subsequent gift from individuals by 85%.

Sadly, donors don't experience personal thank-you calls from volunteers very often. Burk asked donors "what would you think if a board member called to thank you within a day or two of receiving your gift?" Donors responded with words like: *fabulous, wow, surprised, dumbfounded,* and *shocked.* And consider these specific responses:

"I would think that they really cared about my gift."

"It would be great . . . but it never happens."

"I'd be more impressed if they said, 'Do you have anything you want to say about our work or how we're doing it?'"[1]

Engage People in Conversation   Your organization likely hosts various programs, cultivation gatherings, or fundraising events each year. Assign board members and staff to engage attendees in conversation. Train your colleagues about how to conduct conversations. Make sure that your board members and staff mingle and reach out to people rather than chat with their friends. Collect the information immediately following the event.

One final note: Use information carefully. Keep in mind appropriate intimacy without crossing boundaries that cause discomfort and awkwardness. See the story in Exhibit 10.1.

EXHIBIT 10.1   OOPS. THE SOLICITOR CROSSED A BOUNDARY AND THE PROSPECTIVE DONOR WAS OFFENDED

A fundraising colleague told this story about one of her solicitors:

The development office provided the volunteer solicitor with background information on the donor. The prospect sheet included gift history and previous connections with the organization, including board and committee service. The prospect sheet also included family information and birthday.

The well-prepared solicitor met the prospect at a local café. The conversation was comfortable and cordial—until the solicitor wished the prospect "happy birthday."

The prospect was quite disconcerted that the solicitor had this information. And then the prospect asked what other kind of information was in the file back at the agency's office.

A gracious gesture crossed the intimacy boundary. The prospect was suspicious about what kind of information the organization collected, and both the solicitor and prospect felt awkward and uncomfortable.

The caution: Don't presume an intimacy within a relationship unless the other person demonstrates that desire through his or her behaviors.

A Reminder about Step #4

While you learn more (Step #3 in the relationship-building process) and nurture relationships (Step #5), you also identify the mutually beneficial exchange within the relationship (Step #4).

Over and over you articulate the mutually beneficial exchange and commonalities within the relationship. Relationships are dynamic and changing—and will require you to be the same.

You identify the shared interests between the donor or prospect and your organization. You identify where interests diverge. You notice the values match and values conflicts. You pay particular attention to the greatest affinities and the biggest disconnects. All this helps you decide how to nurture the relationship and what to avoid.

Step #5: Nurture the Relationship to Develop Commitment

Here's where all the steps come together, nurturing the relationship. Nurturing relationships includes things like customer service, communications, and cultivation.

The parties in the relationship get to know each other better and better. Regular contact and connection nurtures the relationship and maintains its contemporaneity. Communications speaks emotionally to interests and aspirations. Various cultivation activities reinforce bonds.

Always remember, as my friend Doris says, "Absence does *not* make the heart grow fonder." Quite the contrary, responded one of my workshop participants. "Out of sight, out of mind" is more likely.

> *94% of study donors say that charities they support never or hardly ever call them up without asking for another gift. 98% say that charities never or hardly ever pay them a visit without asking for money.*
>
> —Penelope Burk, *Donor-Centered Fundraising*

Role of Customer Service

How do you define customer service? How do your various customers define quality service: for example, your donors, your volunteers, and your clients?

Christopher Meyer and Andre Schwager note that customer satisfaction is "the culmination of a series of customer experiences or, one could say, the net result of the good ones minus the bad ones."[2] They go on to explain that customer experience is "the internal and subjective response customers have to any direct or indirect contact" with the organization. In the nonprofit/NGO sector, customers include donors, volunteers, clients, partner organizations, and more.

Think about your own customer service experiences, as client, volunteer, and donor. Imagine these:

- You're caught in voice mail hell trying to reach the development office or any other office. You're increasingly frustrated. Maybe you even give up. That's not good customer service.

- You slip on the ice visiting one of your favorite charities where you volunteer time and give money. This wasn't very good cultivation, was it?

- A 20-year donor has trouble at your theater's box office. Of course she keeps giving; it's been 20 years, after all! But the box office is regularly a challenging experience and leaves her out of sorts with the theater. Do you think she'll give another gift right away? Maybe not.

When was the last time you talked about customer service within your organization? When did you last speak with your various customers about their perception of quality service? How would you rate the customer service in your organization? How do you think your customers would rate your service?

What would you include in your list of criteria for customer service? Consider these few ideas:

- Good first impressions: receptionist, telephone system, Web site home page
- Timely response to donor inquiries, complaints, ideas, and gifts
- Respect and demonstrated caring
- Efficiency and transparency
- Effective communication skills including good listening
- Gracious apology and quick repair

> *My favorite definition of customer service: meeting the expectations of each customer. And how about adding this: treating each customer as an individual.*

Some Preliminary Thoughts about Cultivation

The term "cultivation" refers to activities (or offers) that your organization provides to the predisposed, your prospects, and your donors. Any organization needs a variety of cultivation activities. You devise some cultivation activities for targeted groups: for example, families with young children or retired elders. You offer other cultivation activities to everyone.

Characteristics of Effective Cultivation Activities   Effective cultivation activities share certain characteristics. Consider these. What would you add?

- **Cultivation concentrates on those you are cultivating, not on your organization.** Cultivation is mostly about listening to them, not overwhelming them with your information. Beware. Too many board members and staff think cultivation is about promoting your organization.

- **Cultivation activities do not include gift solicitation.** Since this is counter to the experience of many of your guests, tell them in the invitation that no gift is expected. Be different! Surprise them. The Women's Fund invitations to cultivation gatherings often say "Please do *not* bring your checkbook!"

- **Cultivation activities should be culturally sensitive.** For example, if many of your invitees are Muslim, don't serve alcohol.

- **The cultivation activity should provide some—preferably lots!— of personal connection and contact for those who are being cultivated.**
  - For example, the Women's Fund of Rhode Island annual gathering includes a reception and dinner where people mingle and connect with friends. WFRI board members intentionally mingle with guests.
  - Many individuals host tables and facilitate conversations with their table guests. The executive director and board chair of WFRI circulate and try to visit each table to personally thank people for attending.

- **The cultivation activity should—as often as possible—provide opportunities for representatives of the organization to get to know more about their prospects and donors.** You have to make good conversation happen as often as possible!

- **The cultivation activity should—as often as possible—connect with the mission of the organization.**
  - What about those golf tournaments? You know the golfers are talking about golf. Lots of them care only about golf and couldn't care less about your mission. How effective is a golf tournament for cultivating relationships? Don't do too many events like this because you lose the opportunity for effective cultivation (see Exhibit 10.2).

- **The best cultivation activities are clearly identified with your organization, its values and mission.**

EXHIBIT 10.2   SIMONE AND GOLF TOURNAMENTS

Just about anyone who has ever heard me speak, listens to my complaints about golf tournaments!

Part of my problem is I don't golf. I realize that's a disadvantage in this situation. But here are my other problems:

- Organizations think that fundraising events—unrelated to mission—"help get the word out."
- Organizations think events and activities—unrelated to mission—provide good public relations.
- I cannot envision the kind of cultivation happening at a golf event. I don't think the golfers are paying much attention to your mission speech at the dinner after the tournament. And what could you possibly do at each tee to share your stories?
- One of my clients received the following angry telephone: "Who are you people? Why is there a charge on my credit card from you?" It turns out the man had golfed in the organization's golf tournament. He sure didn't remember—or care—what the organization was.

Yet I know an organization that nets $125,000 per year on a golf tournament. Enjoy the money, I say. But don't mistake these kinds of events for cultivation opportunities.

By the way, when Tom read this list, he asked, "Where's the food?" And then he stipulated, "Always have scrumptious food!" Tony Myers added, "And drink!"

Think about the concept of "breaking bread together" and "families and friends gathered together over a meal." There's some meaning there.

Tony got into the food and drink scenario and began talking about traveling together and journeying. "When we travel, the ultimate gift is food, drink, a comfortable place to rest, and real conversation. Cultivation is like this, as well. It's about welcoming. Cultivation is a journey. How we journey together and build trust on the journey will have a profound influence on the outcome."

Creating Opportunities for Connection

Let's expand the concept of cultivation. Let's talk, instead, about creating opportunities for those in the relationship to connect and act on their connection. The more deeply your supporters feel your mission in their heart and soul, the stronger the relationship.

And let's remember the big why. People need to connect. Remember Peter Senge's web of connectedness and Robert Putnam's social capital. Revisit the words that define relationship: for example: concern, interest, interdependence, affinity, bond, and attachment.

Your job is to invite those you are cultivating to share their experiences and ideas. Your job is to help them transform their feelings into action by volunteering, by giving money, by providing advice, by helping to plan...the list goes on indefinitely.

Part of your relationship-building program will be generic, that is, common to all donors. For example, all donors might receive your newsletter. You may also customize some opportunities for particular affinity groups or a particular individual or entity.

> *They get to dream together with us and have the opportunity to join with us in making our shared dream a reality.*
>
> —DIANA MILLER, COHORT 16, MASTER'S PROGRAM,
> PHILANTHROPY AND DEVELOPMENT, SAINT MARY'S UNIVERSITY

Ways of Making Emotions Tangible and Expressing Feelings

Try to be different. Try to be unique. Try to be remarkable, as *The Big Moo* says. People remember what is different, unique, and remarkable.

Burk's research found that 53 percent of the donors in her study remembered "an instance when a charity did something unexpected or out of the ordinary to acknowledge their philanthropy."[3] That could definitely affect your retention rates!

You decide which strategies suggested here might work for your organization, its prospects and donors. Think about what your organization does now. Assess what works well and why. Figure out what doesn't work well and why. And as a donor yourself, think about how you like to be cultivated.

Cultivation as a Community-Building Process

But before the list of strategies, here's a thought: How about distinguishing between cultivation activities that focus primarily on the individuals and those that try to build a network?

What do I mean? Some volunteers and donors want to be part of a network. They want to create a safe place to discuss their thoughts and feelings with others who share common interests and feelings. This is about building a network of shared concern and commitment.

The Women's Fund of Rhode Island discovered this when our board members, other volunteers, and donors would stick around after programs and meetings—often long after! These women weren't talking about WFRI per se. Now they were talking about the cause of women's rights and their own experiences. These women wanted a place to ask the toughest questions and explore the deepest conflicts with others who shared the same commitment and need. It's like coming in from the cold and finding a sense of belonging.

I suspect that nurturing relationships by building this network may work better for certain causes and organizations. For example, perhaps some donors to activist and advocacy organizations do want a safe place to talk about the issues. I'm thinking about organizations like Planned Parenthood, women's funds, and other social justice organizations. I'm imagining community organizing and advocacy work, rallies and protest marches. If you think nurturing relationships through this networking would work with your organization, explore the research and publications on grassroots community organizing and public policy and advocacy work.

Ideas for Nurturing Relationships

Here are 21 ideas for nurturing relationships with donors and volunteers.

1. **Create networking/community-building opportunities where people can talk about the cause and spend time with others who share their interests and concerns.**
    a. Don't underestimate the power of the Internet for building community.[4] For example:
       - You might host a listserv where your supporters can talk with each other about the issues.
       - You can use e-mail to distribute information and invite feedback.
       - You can foster conversation via e-mail—with multiple parties—if you ask that everyone hit "reply all."
       - For all things Internet, visit the ePhilanthropyFoundation.org. This nonprofit/NGO provides resources, training, and guidelines for using the Internet to support philanthropy. Check out all the social networking information out there.
    b. Host book clubs where participants read books about the cause.
       This could work well for the Women's Fund of Rhode Island. We've already identified dozens of books and articles about social justice, women's rights, human rights, and so forth. We plan to recommend books and eventually might start book clubs around the state.
       For WFRI, this would expand understanding of the dimensions of the issue, engage women in our mission, increase visibility within target audiences through word of mouth, build our base of supporters including donors, and identify prospective board and committee members.

2. **Connect donors and prospects with the ultimate beneficiaries of your work.**
   a. At WRFI, we invite beneficiaries to speak at our annual gathering, which brings together one of the largest audiences in the state. We also share donor testimonials at this gathering. Next year donors might speak from the podium.
   b. Invite beneficiaries to speak and mingle at cultivation gatherings.

3. **Give donors and prospects genuine choices.** Make offers available regularly, according to your resources and your plan. For example:
   a. Invite people to decide how to spend their gift. That's quite powerful. Offer choices about how your organization could use their gift.

   This is not about restricting gifts. Instead, you make tangible what you do and let them pick. For example, WFRI may offer endowment, grantmaking, and political participation initiatives. We need money in all three areas. And grantmaking and political participation initiatives are both core programs.
   b. Planned Parenthood of Rhode Island asks me how I want to be solicited: by mail or in person. It asks me when I want to pay my pledge and which publications I want to receive.
   c. Ask people what information is of greatest interest to them, and make sure they receive that. Ask them how they want to receive information, and behave accordingly.
   d. Of course, ask them how they want to be recognized.
   e. What other choices can you offer?

4. **Invite honest feedback.**
   a. Test ideas with focus groups. For example:
      - How to recognize donors of time and money
      - An idea for a new fundraising event or ways to improve a current fundraising event
      - Quality of customer service and ways to improve
      - Brainstorming and/or testing the case for support
      - Identifying powerful key messages and/or evaluating your current messages
   b. Include bounce-back cards in all your publications, inviting readers' comments on articles and suggesting new articles.
   c. Regularly conduct donor and volunteer surveys and focus groups. And report on the results.
      - How about sending out a question a month to all those on e-mail? Just one question about something.

5. **Invite donors and prospects to share their stories about why the organization matters to them.**
   a. Collect and publish their stories in your newsletter and annual report, and on your Web site. For example, CFRE International included a blog to celebrate the twenty-fifth anniversary of voluntary certification for fundraisers. See www.cfre.org.
   b. Use testimonials and personal stories in your publications and in your solicitations.
   c. Invite donors and volunteers to share their stories at some of your programs, fundraising events, and cultivation activities. For example, host an annual volunteer/donor thank-you party and ask a donor of time and a donor of money to speak briefly.
   d. Tell your donors how you use their money. Really tell them—with detail about results, activities, and cost. And tell volunteers what a difference their gifts made; too often we forget this.

6. **Invite your donors and volunteers to share what they are trying to accomplish in their lives by giving.** This isn't as much about your organization as it is about their emotions and their aspirations. Keep asking these questions: If you could change the world, what would you do? How does your giving reflect your values, your feelings, and your aspirations? Feature their stories in your publications and on your Web site.

7. **Make sure your Web site is rich in information and resources.** Regularly add new information. Create interactive opportunities, such as blogs for ongoing dialogue. To encourage repeat visits, find out what people want on your site.

8. **Communicate regularly and often enough.**
   Use an e-news or print newsletter or just newsyletters. For example, the Women's Fund of Rhode Island doesn't have the capacity to do a traditional newsletter. So we do a monthly e-news for those who enjoy electronic communication. And we send out a quarterly, personalized, friendly letter to update our donors and volunteers. Our *newsy* letter does not include a solicitation or a gift response device. See samples of the Women's Fund newsyletter in Appendices 19B and 19C.

9. **Maximize the cultivation opportunities at your fundraising events.** For example:
   a. Have greeters/hosts meet your guests at the door. (Yes, like Wal-Mart!)
   b. Make sure your board members mingle and schmooze and engage in conversation. At your events, your board members and staff shouldn't hang out with each other and their own personal friends. Board

members and staff are the hosts and the schmoozers and the conversationalists.

10. **Invite donors and prospects to share their ideas, perspective, and expertise.** If you cannot do this honestly, then don't do it! You actually have to want their input. You must explain how you used their input or why you didn't. For example:
    a. Ask for their advice on a specific topic.
    b. Ask them to evaluate your performance including your relevancy, your programs and products, your fund development, your customer service, and so forth.
    c. Regularly conduct focus groups, and launch anonymous self-administered written surveys.

11. **Mark milestones with your donors and volunteers.**
    a. Recognize milestones that are important to them and that you are privy to without crossing intimacy boundaries.
    b. Recognize things of importance in their lives, even those unrelated to your organization: for example, send them articles and information, and the like.
    c. Invite them to mark milestones with you (see Appendix 10D).

12. **Engage them in one-off or longer-term volunteer opportunities:** For example, a short-term task force, a committee assignment, direct service experience, planning cultivation activities, and the like. We all know the connection between giving money and volunteering time. Burk's research notes, "93% of individual donors in the study serve as volunteers and 95% give to organizations for which they volunteer."[5]

13. **Devise cultivation-only activities.** That means no solicitation! Make sure you diversify these activities See Exhibit 10.3 and Appendix 10A.
    a. Host updates and provide tours. Whenever possible, invite your clients—the actual beneficiaries of your service—to speak personally with your prospects and donors.
    b. Visit them personally. Think of all those development officers traveling around the country to visit donors. And if you cannot afford that (I never could!), consider these ideas:
       • Tea by telephone. Schedule a telephone conversation and send tea leaves and cookies as refreshments.
       • Use e-mail as effectively as possible.

14. **Tell your prospects and donors how you use their money.** This is the communications part of nurturing relationships.
    a. Be specific. For example: The GAIA Vaccine Foundation sent me a handwritten note thanking me for a gift. GAIA is the Global Alliance

EXHIBIT 10.3	TOM AND SIMONE DON'T LIKE PARTIES. HOW WILL YOU CULTIVATE A RELATIONSHIP WITH US?

In the late 1980s, when Tom and I were in our thirties, we made our first will. It's changed since that first version: Now 100 percent of our estate goes to charity, and 80 percent goes to the Rhode Island Foundation.

Naturally, we hope to live another few decades. By the time we die, the Rhode Island Foundation (RIF) will have known about this bequest for almost 50 years. Imagine cultivating a relationship for that long! Foundation staff members have already changed. Our interests have changed, too. But the bequest remains.

RIF communicates effectively. There's an annual report and a quarterly newsletter and a weekly e-mail update. The annual thank-you party always has an interesting angle. And our name is recognized on a big wall in the lobby.

But still, it's easy to change a will. And RIF staff know how much Tom and I dislike parties. We went the first time—especially since RIF took my suggestion to host an annual thank-you party! We'll go again, but not often.

So how do they cultivate us—on purpose? The chief, philanthropy officer Carol visits us at our home. We've known Carol for years. What do we talk about? Tom's new gardens and what's happening in Carol's gardens. A new painting or mask on our wall. Past vacations and upcoming ones. Carol and I usually share book titles.

Sometimes we talk about what's happening at the foundation. But sometimes we don't. I know that she knows that I know that she represents the Rhode Island Foundation. She knows that I know that she is cultivating Tom and me as donors.

She could wish me happy birthday and I could do the same to her. She asks my opinion and perspective about various issues related to philanthropy. And I do the same with her.

How do we maintain our connection outside of that cultivation visit? Throughout the year, we e-mail about various items—related or unrelated to the foundation. We see each other in different venues under various circumstances.

---

to Immunize against AIDS. Here's what Annie de Groot, the founder, said in her note: "Your contribution will support one of our peer educators for 6 months! Imagine—2 families per day × 6 months will learn how to prevent AIDS because of you."

b. Be transparent. Tell people how much you spend on what and why.

c. Tell them in your thank-you letter. Tell them in your updates or your newsletters or your newsyletters.

d. Tell them in your annual report and at cultivation gatherings.

15. **Keep cards on hand to send quick notes.** For example: Use a note to thank someone for attending a meeting or providing advice. Enclose an article of interest to them. Share your own idea or perspective on something. Invite them to respond with their perspective.

16. **Mark some particular holiday—for example, the turn of the year— with a special greeting.** The Audubon Society of Rhode Island sent out a wonderful e-mail at the turn of the year 2006 (see Appendix 10C).

17. **Do mini questionnaires in your newsletters, through your e-news, via email, and on your Web site.** (See Appendix 10B for a survey sent by the Audubon Society of Rhode Island).

18. **Call donors and volunteers just to say hi.** Share an idea and get their reaction.

19. **Create a recognition program that's meaningful to your donors and volunteers.**

    a. In Rhode Island, our National Philanthropy Program provides every nonprofit in the state the opportunity to recognize one or two donors or volunteers. This statewide gathering celebrates philanthropy with some 700 or more people together applauding. Can your organization participate in such a celebration?

    b. Host your own annual donor and volunteer thank-you party.

    c. Find the right mementos for your organization. Or don't use them!

    • For example, the Women's Fund of Rhode Island buys books about social justice to give its retiring board members. We created note cards with social justice quotations to give to donors. The cards were part of a single print job, using paper left over from reprinting our brochure. So the only cost was for stock envelopes from the office supply store.

    • According to Burk, 86 percent of individual donors "expressed negative views about token gifts such as address labels or fridge magnets." Twenty-eight percent of all donors in the study (individuals and corporations) felt that gifts were "inappropriate under any circumstances; 21% felt they were appropriate in cases of exceptional giving; 17% said that gifts are acceptable if they are obviously inexpensive."[6]

    d. Think about how you recognize your donors of time and money in your publications.

    • Do you list your volunteers, too? Philanthropy values both giving time and money.

    • Do you list donors by gift size? As a social justice organization, the WFRI lists donors in alphabetic order, not by gift size.

    • Consider including icons after donor and volunteer names that indicate such things as years of giving time and money, type of gifts (e.g., annual, capital, legacy), and so forth.

20. **Thank you, thank you, thank you, thank ...** Yes, lots of thank-yous. More than the obligatory traditional letter and gift receipt. Try personal calls. Host an annual thank-you phone-a-thon. Assign thank-you calls to board members. Handwrite personal notes. Acknowledge gifts in ways meaningful to your donors and volunteers. Ask them what they would like.

Burk has done some wonderful research about saying thank you. She talks about what makes a great thank-you, based on what donors say. For example, 51 percent of her survey respondents said "personalize the letter in some way." Burk identifies 20 attributes that make a great thank-you letter. One of my favorites is mentioning, in the letter, when the donor might expect an update on the program for which the gift was given. And here's a shocker: 85 percent of Burk's study donors said that a personal call from a board member—within a couple days of gift receipt—would influence future giving. How can any fundraiser ignore that finding?[7]

21. **Invite them to give money.** Yes, this is intentionally the last item on the relationship-building list. Genuine relationship building focuses on the relationship, not the ask. But a good solicitation can help nurture relationships.

Using Incentives to Nurture Relationships

I feel a bit uncomfortable with the strategy of using incentives to nurture relationships. And I'm a novice at it.

I realize that gift clubs and exclusive activities may make a difference with some donors. But I've heard colleagues urge caution. Beware of donors who expect excessive attention and expensive incentives. Be careful of offending donors who want their gifts used for mission rather than recognition. Think carefully about your organization's values. And furthermore, take a look at Burk's research, just cited.

Using an Individual to Cultivate a Particular Relationship

Often organizations assign a particular individual (e.g., a staff person or board member) to take on the cultivation of a particular relationship. Sometimes staff and volunteers cultivate multiple relationships for an organization over the course of a year or more. Particularly in higher education, this process may be called "moves management."[8]

Whether you call it relationship building or moves management—or something else entirely—the label doesn't matter. It's the strategic thinking, stewardship, and commitment that matter. The individual is working on behalf of the organization. The organization nurtures the relationship with prospects/donors by using volunteers and staff in the organization. The goal is to engage prospects and donors with their passion, as reflected in your organization.

You assign people—volunteers and/or staff—to cultivate relationships on behalf of the organization. This is no casual exercise but rather a formal assignment with a multitude of formal and informal interactions, carefully managed over a period of time.

Make sure you recruit an individual who best meets the personality and interests of those you are cultivating. Also consider social styles, described in Chapter 16.

Be careful when you use individuals to nurture relationships. The individual serves as the conduit for the relationship with the organization. The individual cultivator is representing the organization, not him- or herself. As board chair Patty Dowling said, "This is a grounding principle. The organization is the common thread and binder, not the cultivator." The cultivation process focuses on reinforcing the bond with the organization, not with a single individual or representative of the organization.

Sadly, some people abuse relationship building for personal gain. Others do not understand the business nature of the relationship. They develop a personal relationship and have difficulty focusing on their role as a representative of the organization. It's up to the organization to reinforce the relationship as a bond with the organization, not a particular representative of the organization.

And one final note; here's a great tip from Karla Williams, ACFRE: Make sure that a number of people from the organization know every donor. Relying on one person to nurture a relationship limits a donor's connection to the organization. And what happens when that person leaves?

Also make sure that donors know a number of people within the organization. Donors need the comfort and connection deeper into the organization.

Debrief after Cultivation

Cultivation and its partner, communications, are two critical elements of your relationship-building program. And your relationship-building program is an integral part of your written fund development plan.

Naturally, you must debrief after cultivation activities. You must document any information gathered. You must evaluate the success of the cultivation and decide how to continue the process. And eventually, you determine if the prospect or donor is ready to be asked.

In Conclusion

Her name was Nancy. She was a university development officer.

One day Nancy reported to her vice president about a delightful lunch with a major donor. "Mrs. Jones and I sat in her garden under the shade tree, eating lettuce and tomatoes from her garden. Can you imagine, she's still out there weeding and watering! We talked about hardy fall plants and her next trip."

(The Widow Jones was elderly but still had lots of energy. She traveled extensively and was curious about everything.)

Nancy's VP interrupted and asked, "What else did you talk about?!"

"Well, I recommended some books for her trip. I plan to send her one, along with an article about Barcelona, where she—"

The VP interrupted again. "Did you talk about the new building campaign?"

"No. We just chatted about gardens, books, and travel."

And the VP responded, "If you ever visit a donor again without mentioning the university and our activities, I will fire you."

Please tell me that's not your organization.

ENDNOTES

1. Penelope Burk, *Donor-Centered Fundraising: How to Hold on to Your Donors and Raise Much More Money* (Hamilton Ontario: Cygnus Applied Research, 2005), p. 76.

2. "Understanding Customer Experience," *Harvard Business Review* (February 2007): 118. The article talks about "Customer Experience Management—CEM" and "Customer Relationship Management—CRM," and provides useful information.

3. Burk, *Donor-Centered Fundraising*, p. 19.

4. See, for example, Ted Hart, Jim Greenfield, and Sheeraz Haji, *People to People Fundraising: Social Networking and Web 2.0 for Charities*. The authors talk about leveraging the Internet to build relationships.

5. Burk, *Donor-Centered Fundraising*, p. 15.

6. Ibid., p. 117.

7. Ibid., p. 32.

8. G. T. (Buck) Smith developed this concept to measure the progress of major gift fundraising. Smith talked about a series of initiatives (aka moves) that would build donor relationships. In "CommonWork," the newsletter of Johnson, Grossnickle and Associates, Inc., interviewee Paul Pribbenow defines move management as a process "designed to honor the relationship a donor has with an institution or organization by ensuring that the institution recognizes and documents the 'history' of the relationship. [A moves management program] encourages strategic thinking on behalf of the institution to further donor relationships and appropriate cultivation practices." See www.jgacounsel .com.

Building Relationships With Your Constituents

Read this appendix over and over until it's second (or first!) nature to you.

RELATIONSHIPS RULE!

Developing stronger relationships with your constituents is critical to effective and productive fund development. The success of your organization depends on your ability to build relationships.

Your constituents are at the center of this relationship, not your organization. To be effective, you must focus on them. Remember, it's not what you're selling but what the constituent is buying that counts.

The process of building relationships for philanthropy is all about finding out if *your* personal and professional contacts are interested in the cause that you espouse.

Building relationships is *not* about trespassing on your personal and professional relationships. You are *not* expected to raise money by coercing gifts from those who feel an obligation to you. No! That's trespassing, and it's unnecessary and certainly inappropriate.

FOUR STEPS IN RELATIONSHIP BUILDING

1. **Respect and understand the needs and motivations of your constituents.** (This means you have to get to know them, keep the information on file, and use it appropriately.)

2. **Meet their needs if they are in keeping with your organization's values, mission, and vision.**

3. **Communicate your programs and activities and their value to the constituents.** (Strengthen your written communications. Remember to communicate without asking for money all the time.)

4. **Follow up and nurture the relationship.** (Cultivation activities include donor recognition, personal meetings, and events where you hang out with them and talk with them.)

UNDERSTANDING TERMINOLOGY

Constituent: Someone (or some group, e.g., business) that has somehow raised its hand, signaling its interest in your organization. For example: clients, donors, and volunteers.

Predisposed: Refers to someone (or some group) that you suspect might be interested but the interest has not yet been confirmed.

Prospect: Shorthand for *prospective donoror volunteer.* For example, the term "prospect" could refer to a legislator who might help you develop public policy, a prospective board member, or any other mutually beneficial exchange that you are trying to negotiation. The key point: Use the term "prospect" when you have confirmed their interest, no matter the nature of that interest.

WHAT *YOU* HAVE TO DO

- Identify the predisposed. Find out if they are actually prospects. (Or you might find out that someone you've classified as predisposed is not actually a prospect so don't add the person to your list. Move on!)

- Then move them into cultivation, asking, and cultivating again to maintain loyalty.

- For those who are already donors, nurture the relationship to retain their loyalty.

Who does all this? Every single board member and every single staff person. And the "development office" facilitates and coordinates the effort. Be intentional and well planned.

GETTING TO KNOW THEIR INTERESTS, DISINTERESTS, MOTIVATIONS, AND ASPIRATIONS

You can find out about people's interests through surveys, focus groups, and personal dialogue. You listen to what people tell you. Remember: Getting to know them is *not* telling them about your organization!

Use conversation! Everyday you learn about colleagues, neighbors, friends, and even people sitting next to you in an airplane.

You talk with your colleagues on Monday morning and share stories about weekend activities. You talk with clients and customers about their work or worries or responsibilities.

If you're a good conversationalist, these are *conversations*, not mini-lectures or presentations. You ask engaging questions and share and listen and learn.

You try to keep the conversation going. We could say that each exchange is "the purchase of more time" to continue the dialogue, thus nurturing a relationship.

All of these conversations provide you with information. You learn about the interests and disinterests, motivations and aspirations, and values of those you are speaking with. (And then you tell the office so the information is kept on file!)

CULTIVATION GATHERINGS: NURTURING DONOR LOYALTY AND INTRODUCING THE PREDISPOSED

Gatherings are a great way to nurture donor loyalty. Ask a donor to lunch and tell him about your successes and invite his comments. Invite several donors to meet with you and conduct a mini-focus group. Meet with some lapsed donors (they gave before but aren't giving now). Ask them why they stopped—and maybe you can help them start giving again.

Or have a big party and ask lots of people: current and prospective donors and the predisposed. (And by the way, the gathering doesn't have to be a big party. Have a small party. Or ask these donors, prospects, and the predisposed to attend a seminar or other event that you are hosting.

But make sure that you mingle with these special guests. Board members and staff should *not* hang out with each other. They should mingle and connect and carry on conversations. That's how you learn and cultivate relationships!

P.S.: Do not ask for money at a cultivation gathering. And tell your guests before-hand you will *not* be asking for a gift at the gathering.

HOST YOUR OWN CULTIVATION GATHERING

Every single year, people from your organization should host cultivation gatherings. It is best to host these gatherings in homes or offices of the host. Hosting the gathering at the nonprofit/NGO is not that effective because it isn't particularly personal.

By the way, if you don't want to host a cultivation gathering by yourself, cohost it with someone else from the organization. This can reduce the stress, increase the invitation list, and share the workload.

Ask some of your donors to host a cultivation gathering for their colleagues and friends. Sometimes attendees at a cultivation gathering offer to host another one.

Purpose of Your Cultivation Gathering

There are two purposes for your cultivation gathering:

1. Introduce the predisposed and prospects to the organization, its mission and services.

2. Nurture the relationship with current donors and volunteers and strengthen their loyalty.

Potential Invitees

- Current and lapsed donors to your organization. And volunteers too!
  - Get the list from the office.
  - Start by inviting those who will know your name or know you personally.
  - Then invite people you don't know/who don't know your name but are donors and do know the organization. (They are not as likely to attend, but you can still try.)
- Prospective donors
  - Get the list from the office. These are people, businesses, or civic groups that the organization has qualified as prospects; these are *not* the predisposed (those you suspect will donate/volunteer but are not sure).
- The predisposed
  - Now you have to identify the predisposed. Yup, you. Think about your professional colleagues and friends and neighbors. What do you know about their interests? Does anything you know suggest that they might be predisposed to some part of your organization?
  - Will they come? Who knows, but you sure can try! Focus on their interests and what your organization can do for them.
- Current donors
  - Use this opportunity to cultivate your current donors. Invite them to attend. And ask them to share why they give. Mingling your current donors with those who are predisposed and are prospects is a wonderful strategy.

Invitation

You develop and send the invitation. (See the sample invitation at the end of this appendix.) Don't ask the staff to do it; this is your gathering. Don't use the organization's letterhead; use your own. Or buy some interesting stationery or cards. For the right audience, you can also use e-mail.

Compose an invitation and print it from your computer. Or hand-write the invitations.

Make sure you ask for an RSVP. Give an RSVP due date, and provide an e-mail address and telephone number for RSVPs.

Send out the invitation at least one month in advance, given people's complex schedules. You should estimate that about 25 percent of the invitees will say yes. Some of those may not actually attend. And sometimes people who didn't RSVP do attend.

P.S.: You should contact each invitee who does not RSVP and get their answer. This is a qualifying action. The person may be unable to attend and may wish to be invited again. Or he or she may simply not be interested. You have to find this out.

P.P.S.: Put in the invitation that this is *not* a fundraising event and the invitee will *not* be asked for a gift at this gathering.

Attendance

Your gathering is a success no matter how many people attend. Five to 10 people is comfy sitting around the living room, and attendees ask lots of questions. Twenty to 30 people is *big*! Any more than that and it's hard to ask questions and have conversations.

Who Attends the Cultivation Gathering?

- The host or cohosts, of course, and the invitees
- If appropriate, a staff person from the organization who can talk firsthand about services and answer questions
- Perhaps a couple of board members who haven't hosted a cultivation gathering yet and want to have a personal experience first

WHAT HAPPENS AT THE CULTIVATION GATHERING?

Cultivation gatherings usually follow a specific sequence.

1. Mingling. Refreshments. Meeting new people and current colleagues and friends.
2. As people arrive, offer refreshments and engage them in conversation.
3. After 20–30 minutes or so of mingling, convene the group. Ask everyone to take a seat.

4. The host welcomes and thanks people for attending. The host explains why he or she is involved in the organization and thinks it is important. Then the host introduces the guest speaker.

5. The guest speaker speaks for 15 minutes or so, then invites questions and engages people in dialogue.

The gathering usually lasts at least one hour and typically lasts one and a half hours or so. The more questions asked, the longer the gathering lasts.

Here's another idea for your cultivation gathering: Conduct a mini-focus group. You ask questions of the invitees instead of them asking you questions. For example, a human service agency might ask:

> We are thinking about developing a seminar series. Experts would talk about issues that might be of interest to you and your family. A modest fee would be charged to pay for refreshments. Might you be interested in such a series? If yes, what kinds of topics would be of interest to you?

Guest Speaker

There are different ways to approach this. For example:

- The executive director can talk about people in need and the service response: why the organization does what it does and why is the results matter —not just what the organization does.

- A staff or volunteer expert can talk about a specific topic of potential interest for the invitees.

- One of the speakers can include a few remarks about how your organization's services are funded.

Handouts

Handouts are acceptable, but don't get carried away. Don't overwhelm attendees with paper. Bring the organization's capabilities brochure for everyone. If you have multiple services (with a different brochure for each one), just bring a few— or those targeted to the invitees.

Closing Your Cultivation Gathering: The Sign-Up Sheet

The host thanks people for coming and invites people to sign up if they would like further information/to be on the mailing list. Pass the list around. Make sure a pen is available. Don't watch as people sign up or not; that's off-putting. (Develop a sheet that provides space for name, snail mail address, e-mail address, and telephone number.

See also the sample sign-up form at the end of this appendix.

Remember, some people will not sign up. After listening, they simply won't be interested. But typically, if people attend the gathering, a significant number of them will sign up.

Who Pays for the Cultivation Gathering?

Often the host(s) do, *not* the organization. You pay for the refreshments and invitations and postage. This shouldn't be expensive.

SAMPLE INVITATION

Lots of exciting things are happening at the Women's Fund. We'd like to share our vision and accomplishments with you and hear your thoughts.

Bring your questions and please join us for an informal gathering to learn more.

Wednesday, January 9, 2008, at 5:15 p.m.

10 Johnson Road, Foster, Rhode Island

Your hosts: Mary Jones and Simone Joyaux

P.S. This gathering is for information only. Do **not** bring your checkbook.

Please RSVP by January 5 to Simone at 397–2534 or spjoyaux@aol . com

---

SAMPLE SIGN-UP FORM

(Note: This is for a social justice organization, the Women's Fund of Rhode Island. How can you modify this sample for your organization? What might be your choices?)

YOUR *PERSONAL PROMISE* FORM · YOUR ACTION MAKES A DIFFERENCE

Please complete this form. Turn in your *Promise* and we'll keep in touch. Keep a copy for yourself.

☐ I will be a voice. I will speak out for the rights of women and girls.

☐ I want to be counted. Make sure I'm on the Women's Fund mailing list and e-mail alert list.

☐ I want to help. Send me information about volunteer opportunities.

☐ I want to fuel the fires of change. I'm sending in my financial gift to help the Women's Fund do its important work.

☐ I want to be part of a social change community. Invite me to gatherings where we talk about the issues facing women and girls, and figure out how to work together for progressive change.

I am a social change agent. I know I can make a difference.
I'm turning in my *Personal Promise*.

Please print clearly.
Name_____
Address—Telephone numbers
E-mail_____

Member Survey of the Audubon Society of Rhode Island

YOU CAN HELP THE AUDUBON SOCIETY OF RI PLAN FOR THE FUTURE!

Your opinion is critical

Your responses are anonymous. Please complete only one copy of this survey.

RETURN YOUR COMPLETED SURVEY NO LATER THAN APRIL 1

Deliver or send to ASRI, 12 Sanderson Road, Smithfield RI 02917–2600. Thank you.

1. **How satisfied are you with the following aspects of the Audubon Society of RI (ASRI)?**

	Very satisfied	Satisfied	Dissatisfied	Very dissatisfied	No experience
a. Membership benefits	☐	☐	☐	☐	☐
b. Programs in general	☐	☐	☐	☐	☐
c. Activities and attractions compared to other environmental groups and wildlife sanctuaries	☐	☐	☐	☐	☐
d. Membership cost	☐	☐	☐	☐	☐
e. Program fees	☐	☐	☐	☐	☐
f. Preservation of natural habitats	☐	☐	☐	☐	☐
g. Environmental advocacy	☐	☐	☐	☐	☐
h. Information about what's happening at ASRI	☐	☐	☐	☐	☐

Used with permission

Courtesy of the Audubon Society of Rhode Island, www.asri.org

2. **How recently have you or a member of your family done the following?**

	Within the last year	Within the last two to three years	More than three years ago
a. Visited the Environmental Education Center in Bristol	☐	☐	☐
b. Visited any ASRI wildlife refuge	☐	☐	☐
c. Attended an ASRI program	☐	☐	☐
d. Shopped at an ASRI gift shop	☐	☐	☐

3. **Which of the following do you think are the TWO most important environmental issues facing Rhode Island? Please check only two.**

☐ Water quality including drinking water
☐ Air quality
☐ Loss of habitat and biodiversity
☐ Urban sprawl and loss of open space
☐ Global warming

☐ Renewable energy
☐ Invasive plant and animal species
☐ Waste management
☐ Quality of Narragansett Bay and coastal waters
☐ Other

4. **Do you agree or disagree with the following statements?**

	Strongly agree	Agree	Disagree	Strongly disagree
a. ASRI staff give me confidence in the organization.	☐	☐	☐	☐
b. ASRI staff are always pleasant and courteous.	☐	☐	☐	☐
c. ASRI staff are competent and knowledgeable.	☐	☐	☐	☐
d. ASRI gives me individual attention.	☐	☐	☐	☐
e. ASRI understands my specific needs.	☐	☐	☐	☐
f. When I have a problem related to ASRI, ASRI shows an interest in solving it.	☐	☐	☐	☐

5. **Which descriptions do you think best apply to ASRI? Please check all that apply.**

a. Innovative organization... ☐
b. Well-endowed financially.. ☐
c. Friendly... ☐
d. Opposes development of any type... ☐
e. Educational organization... ☐
f. Environmental advocacy organization... ☐
g. More interested in birds than people... ☐
h. Old-fashioned organization .... ☐
i. One of the best environmental groups in RI .... ☐
j. Needs to raise significant charitable contributions to operate .... ☐
k. Rehabilitates injured wildlife.. ☐
l. Major player in helping to protect RI's environment........................ ☐

6. **In your opinion, if ASRI discontinued operations tomorrow, what impact would that have on the following?**

	Very negative	Moderately negative	No impact
a. Land conservation	☐	☐	☐
b. Environmental education	☐	☐	☐
c. State environmental policy	☐	☐	☐

7. **In your opinion, are the following statements true or false?**

	True	False	Don't know
a. ASRI offers more environmental education programs for the public than any other organization in Rhode Island.	☐	☐	☐
b. ASRI is the second largest landholder in RI after the State of RI itself.	☐	☐	☐
c. ASRI's primary focus is creating a healthy habitat for birds.	☐	☐	☐
d. A percentage of ASRI's money goes to the National Audubon Society.	☐	☐	☐
e. ASRI offers more environmental education programs for school groups than any other organization in Rhode Island.	☐	☐	☐

8. **Are you a member of ASRI?**

☐ Yes, I am currently a member.   ☐ Yes. previously but not currently.   ☐ No.

9. **Do you volunteer for ASRI?**

☐ Yes. I currently volunteer.   ☐ Yes, previously but not currently.   ☐ No.
If you checked "yes," please skip to question #11.

10. **Which of the following best describes why you do not volunteer.**
a. I didn't know that I could volunteer with ASRI.   ☐
b. I've never been asked.   ☐
c. I prefer to volunteer for other causes.   ☐
d. I don't volunteer for any organizations.   ☐
e. I have volunteered for ASRI in the past but did   ☐
   not find the experience satisfactory

11. **Have you ever given a contribution to ASRI in addition to BUYING a membership?**

☐ Yes.   ☐ Yes, previously but not currently.   ☐ No.
If you answered "yes," please skip to question #13.

12. **Which of the following describes why you do not give a contribution to ASRI? Please check ALL that apply.**
a. I cannot afford to contribute.   ☐
b. Other causes are more important to me.   ☐
c. I am dissatisfied with ASRI's performance.   ☐
d. I have not been asked.   ☐
e. I used to give but now I think another environmental   ☐
   organization is more effective.
f. ASRI does not keep me sufficiently informed.   ☐

If you are not currently or have never given a contribution to ASRI (this is different than buying a membership), please skip to question #21.

13. **Which of the following is the single most important reason you give to ASRI? Please check ONE only.**
a. To support environmental education   ☐
b. To support land conservation   ☐
c. To support advocacy and public policy activities   ☐
d. Because I like nature and wildlife.   ☐

14. **As a donor, please indicate the extent to which you agree or disagree with the following statements.**

	Strongly agree	Agree	Disagree	Strongly disagree
a. ASRI keeps me informed about how my money is used.	☐	☐	☐	☐
b. ASRI always responds promptly to my requests for information.	☐	☐	☐	☐
c. ASRI cares about the needs of its donors.	☐	☐	☐	☐
d. ASRI doesn't ask me for funds too often.	☐	☐	☐	☐

e. ASRI asks for appropriate amounts
when soliciting me.   ☐   ☐   ☐   ☐

f. ASRI appropriately recognizes my
charitable contributions.   ☐   ☐   ☐   ☐

15. **Why did you give to ASRI? Please check all that apply.**

a. ASRI communicates an urgent need.   ☐
b. I attended an ASRI sponsored activity and was impressed.   ☐
c. ASRI is very effective in carrying out its mission.   ☐
d. ASRI has a great reputation.   ☐
e. I believe in ASRI's mission and the results it achieves.   ☐
f. I was pressured into giving.   ☐
g. A friend or colleague asked me to give.   ☐

16. **Are you or your family a regular contributor to charitable organizations other than religious congregations?** ☐ Yes ☐ No
If you answered "no," please skip to question #21.

17. **If you are a regular contributor to charitable organizations, how important to you are your gifts to ASRI compared to your other giving?**

☐ More important   ☐ Of equal importance   ☐ Not as important

18. **Do you have a will or estate plan?** ☐ Yes ☐ No ☐ Don't know

19. **What was the total amount you donated to charitable organizations in the past year, excluding religious congregations?**

☐ Less than $1,000   ☐ $2,500 to $4,999   ☐ $10,000 to $24,999   ☐ $50,000 +
☐ $1,000 to $2,499   ☐ $5,000 to $9,999   ☐ $25,000 to $49,999

20. **As a donor, what one piece of advice would you give the Audubon Society about nurturing relationships with donors?**

About you

21. **Where do you live?**

☐ East Bay   ☐ South County   ☐ Northern RI
☐ West Bay   ☐ Providence Metro   ☐ Nearby Massachusetts

22. **Do you have a bird feeder in your yard?** ☐ Yes ☐ No

23. **What is the primary language spoken in your home?**

☐ English   ☐ Spanish   ☐ French   ☐ Asian   ☐ Other

24. **If English is not the primary language spoken in your home, do most people in your household also speak and read English?**
☐ Yes   ☐ No

25. **Do children under age 16 live in your household?** ☐ Yes ☐ No

26. **What is your gender?** ☐ Male ☐ Female

27. **What is your age?**

☐ 16 to 19 years   ☐ 25 to 34 years   ☐ 45 to 54 years   ☐ 65 to 74 years
☐ 20 to 24 years   ☐ 35 to 44 years   ☐ 55 to 64 years   ☐ 75 years or older

28. **What is the highest level of education completed by a member of your household?**

☐ High school   ☐ 2-year college   ☐ 4-year college   ☐ Graduate school

29. **In what range is your total annual household income?**

☐ Under $25,000   ☐ $75,000 to $99,000   ☐ $500,000 to $999,999
☐ $25,000 to $49,000   ☐ $100,000 to $199,999   ☐ $1,000,000 or more
☐ $50,000 to $74,999   ☐ $200,000 to $499,999

30. **What one piece of advice would you give to the Audubon Society of RI?**

Thank you for sharing your opinion. Please return your completed survey to the Audubon Society office no later than April 1. ASRI, 12 Sanderson Road, Smithfield RI 02917–2600

E-Mail Survey from The Audubon Society of Rhode Island*

*H*ere is a year-end e-mail from the Audubon Society of Rhode Island. How could you develop something like this for your organization?

Greetings as we approach the doorway to the new calendar year and the month of January. January is named for Janus, the god of gateways, portals, and thresholds—whose image faces two directions.

For the new year, the Audubon Society invites you to add, "acquire greater knowledge of the environment" to your resolutions.

First, start by quizzing your 2006 self. Just hit reply to send your answers back.

You can win prizes! If you get 100% correct, cross the threshold into the ASRI headquarters gift shop. Your reward: a 25% discount!

Good luck!

- The **last native flowering plan to bloom in our area** is _____, which generally flowers in October. **First to appear in the new year** is _____, whose spathe absorbs sunlight and melts snow around it.

- A common blue violet will bloom earlier in Jamestown than in Burrillville. True or False this happens due to the influence of Narragansett Bay. True or False

- Looking ahead to 2007, **temperatures will decrease** due to (1) distance to sun, (2) polar axis angle, (3) elliptical orbit around sun, (4) land mass versus ocean mass in the northern hemisphere. Select the correct answer(s).

---

*Used with permission
Courtesy of the Audubon Society of Rhode Island, www.asri.org

- Looking back to 2006, **how much carbon did you add?** Go to www.bp.com. Click on "Environment and Society" then look for "Get Interactive" on the right side of the screen and click "Carbon Calculator." Looking ahead to 2007, name 3 ways you will reduce your carbon footprint: _____, _____, and _____.

Very best wishes for your health and good efforts for restoring our environment in the coming year.

Women's Fund of Rhode Island
Marking Milestones Brochure

Why your gift to the Women's Fund matters so much to Rhode Island's women and girls...

Something wonderful is happening here in Rhode Island... with your help. Since our first grants in 2002, the playing field for women and girls here in the Ocean State has leveled just a little bit more each year. You can almost hear the earth creak.

Still, we wouldn't be surprised if you're wondering: "Does a gift to the Women's Fund of Rhode Island really make that much difference?" Yes! Here's how.

For one thing (and it's important), when you give to the Women's Fund, you invest in ideas that no one else is likely to fund.

Not because they're bad ideas. On the contrary: your gift supports ideas that are well conceived, innovative, passionate, desperately needed by women and girls. We get a lot more grant applications than we can afford to fund. So the ideas we do fund are standouts.

But they can be controversial. And sometimes they're dreamt up by grassroots organizations so small and new they can't get on the radar of the state's major grant makers.

At the Women's Fund of Rhode Island, those ideas are the very ideas we want. We encourage controversial, innovative solutions from unheard-of sources.

These ideas all have one thing in common. Every idea we fund aims to fix some problem that has severe negative consequences for women and girls in Rhode Island.

What kinds of ideas get funded? Well, there's not space to get into it here. But visit our Website: www.wfri.org. You'll find our grants and other initiatives explained in detail.

And thank you so for your support!

 the Women's Fund OF RHODE ISLAND

One Union Station, Providence, RI 02903
Phone: 401-274-4564
www.wfri.org

 the Women's Fund OF RHODE ISLAND

Introducing the
MARKING MILESTONES GIFT PROGRAM

Now you can mark important occasions in a unique and memorable way.

...while helping level the playing field for Rhode Island's women and girls

"I'm looking for a gift that's different... and really matters."

When you want to do something memorable for....

- Birthdays
- Weddings
- Anniversaries
- Graduations
- Bar and bat mitzvahs

- Holidays
- Mother's Day and Father's Day
- A thank you
- A memorial gift in lieu of flowers
- Your very own special occasion

How it works (it's oh so easy)

Step 1 (Relax, you're done)

You fill out the Marking Milestones form and send it in to the Women's Fund of Rhode Island. Your Marking Milestone gift can be any size.

Step 2 (Acknowledging your gift)

You're officially thanked by the Women's Fund (including a record for your tax files).

Step 3 ("What a wonderful surprise!")

The person you've honored with your Marking Milestones gift (or her/his family) receives a special, distinctively designed card from us. The card says that you have made a special gift and explains what it's for. We do not reveal the amount of your gift.

Step 4 (Taking a bow)

Both your honoree and you, as the donor, are recognized by the Women's Fund of Rhode Island, at our big annual celebration...in our printed materials...and on our Website. For example:

- Alice Weibel in honor of Hazel McKay's 60th birthday
- Cynthia Johnston in honor of her daughter Wendi's Bat Mitzvah
- James Patterson in honor of his beloved aunt, Mary Cole (1923-2005)

CHAPTER 11

Creating Your Relationship-Building Plan

WRITE IT DOWN

If I had an hour to save the world, I'd spend 55 minutes defining the problem.

—ALBERT EINSTEIN, 1879–1955, NOBEL PRIZE–WINNING PHYSICIST

It will not do to leave a live dragon out of your plan if you live near one.

—J.R.R. TOLKIEN, *THE HOBBIT*

DEAR READER This mini chapter provides some tips about the written relationship-building plan. You'll find a more detailed description of creating a fund development plan in my book *Strategic Fund Development: Building Profitable Relationships That Last.*
Simone

To start, I believe in written plans. The relationship-building plan describes your relationship-building program. The plan outlines results for the year and defines ways to measure performance.

Your relationship-building plan is a critical part of your overall fund development plan. And your communications plan is part of your relationship building.

In this scenario, relationship building serves fund development. Relationship building secures gifts of time and money. This book describes all that, chapter by chapter.

Good Process Produces the Best Results

Like any plan, the process used to create the plan is as important as the resulting plan.

Good process engages stakeholders (or constituents, whichever word you use). Your stakeholders include board members, staff, donors, volunteers, partner organizations, and other relationships in your community. Participation builds stakeholder understanding and ownership of the decisions planners make.

Yes, I expect staff beyond the development office to discuss relationship building. I expect the board to engage in the conversation, too. And in my world, the board approves the fund development plan when it approves the budget.

Good process depends on quality information translated into trends and implications. Only then can planners make good decisions. Throughout this book, Tom and I suggest valuable information to gather.

The best decision making requires great conversations stimulated by cage-rattling questions. Disagreement is welcome and dysfunctional politeness is avoided.

Finally, as with anything in your organization, your relationship-building program and plan reflect your values. The soul of your organization comes through in the way you talk about relationships and the way you nurture those relationships.

Plan Practicalities

Like any plan, the relationship-building plan includes these elements:

- Goals
- Strategies and tactics
- Performance measures
- Projected performance results (or benchmarks) for the period: for example, fiscal year
- Assignments of accountability
- Timetable
- Resources
- Process for monitoring progress and evaluating results

The plan includes strategies and tactics for donor cultivation and communication. In summary, relationship building describes how you operate as a donor-centered organization. And the plan's ultimate purpose is to nurture donor loyalty.

A DIFFERENT APPROACH

As I write this, I'm just back from presenting at the April 2007 Kaiser Institute.[1] I'm mindful of conversations with Reg Wagle, the chief philanthropy officer for Memorial Hospital of South Bend, Indiana, and Scott Adams, the CEO of Pullman Regional Hospital in Pullman, Washington, in particular, and remarks from Lee Kaiser.

Now here's what I'm thinking:

What if your relationship-building program and plan were *not* in service to fund development? What if relationship building was the driving force to support your mission?

In this different approach, meaningful relationships are the goal. I don't mean just donor relationships; I mean all relationships that advance your mission and help your community.

When we start the relationship journey, we don't know where we will end up. We have neither ulterior purpose nor expectation.

It's the journey together that will disclose the nature of the relationship. Perhaps a trusted advisor for our organization. Or a gadfly who connects us to others. Perhaps a candid critique. Or a vital informant on community issues. Perhaps an ambassador or an advocate. Maybe a volunteer or donor.

Yes, Scott, we'd keep nurturing the relationships, without expectation of money ever! That's what you and I discussed. And Reg, the development operation would function like yours: all about developing the community, not just the institution. Then philanthropy serves as the think tank and change engine for the institution and the community.

Sure, a relationship-building plan could be this expansive. And one portion of the plan would focus on donor relationships. In this scenario, the relationship-building plan is not a part of the fund development plan. Instead, the relationship-building plan is the institution's driving force, after the strategic plan. The fund development plan is a subset of the relationship-building plan.

In this broader concept, the plan focuses on building relationships with:

- Your clients
- Your board members and other volunteers
- Your organization's neighbors
- Policymakers
- Advocates and grassroots activists
- Collaborating organizations
- And, yes, your financial donors

The relationship-building program and plan take on new significance.

In Conclusion

Why this different approach? Because relationships matter. They matter on their own, without any defined "productivity." Imagine the genuineness, the relief, the freedom, and the joy of reaching out without expectation or exploitation. Of valuing a relationship just because.

What do you think?

P.S.: What's your dragon?

■ ENDNOTE

1. A special learning opportunity designed by Kaiser Consulting: Lee, Leanne, Kevin, and Betty. Their institute brings together leadership teams from healthcare systems. These CEOs, development officers, and board members discuss how to strengthen philanthropy at their institutions. For more information, go to: www.kaiserconsulting.net.

CHAPTER 12

Planning Donor Communications

STAYING IN TOUCH

It takes as much energy to wish as it does to plan.

—ELEANOR ROOSEVELT

By failing to prepare, you are preparing to fail.

—BENJAMIN FRANKLIN

Plan your work for today and every day, then work your plan.

—DR. NORMAN VINCENT PEALE

DEAR READER If I correctly interpret the guilty groans that escape when I raise this topic at workshops, communicating with donors on a regular basis is an unpleasant chore for many fundraisers. You can almost hear the silent prayer: *There must be another way. Maybe if I ignore it, the need for regular communications will go away.*

Regular communication with donors, though, is a *guarantee* of fund development success. And there *is* no better way. Planning at least removes the uncertainties of when, what, and to whom.

Tom ▪

INTRODUCTION

Which came first, the communications or the fund development? It's hardly a chicken-or-egg puzzler. Without some form of communications, written or verbal, most gifts won't happen. (Let's ignore bequests that arrive out of thin air, or other spontaneous combustions; they're the exception, not the rule.)

We might even argue that so-called fundraisers labor under a somewhat misleading job title. That, in fact, healthy philanthropy is a by-product *primarily* of communications activities, not fund development activities. Consider the workhorse of many fund development programs: the appeal letter. Is it an attempt to communicate or an attempt to fundraise?

These distinctions might seem trivial. They're not. When you see yourself as a fundraiser, you tend to focus on meeting cash goals. When you see yourself as a communicator, you tend to focus on the donor.

Q & A

E-MAILED QUESTION:

With regard to solicitation letters to individuals, what's your position on handwritten notes at the bottom of the letter: "Mary—Your gift will really make a difference"? —Michelle

ANSWER:

Hello, Michelle! This one I'm REAL sure of (I think): Handwritten notes like that always make a positive difference. Now, that said, if it's a clearly fake handwritten note on a mailing of thousands, maybe not so much.

But I'd be willing to wager that even then, it works its wiles. The handwritten aspect is personalization, which usually improves response. It's conversational, which is the right voice to take. It's in a blue ink that stands out, so visually it will be read first, before the body of the letter.

I think there is probably an art to these things, too.

In e-mail appeals, for instance, the thing that makes the biggest difference are the 58 characters or less that appear in the subject line. In handwritten notes, using something ordinary will not work (I'm guessing) as well as something a bit not so ordinary. "Mary, I see the results of your generosity every day. Trust me: Your gift will put a smile on these kids' faces, some for the first time. —Jim."

You know, add a dash of the anecdotal. Take a personal risk. Bland won't work as well as bold. Hope that helps! —Tom

---

WRITING A PLAN

Communicating successfully with donors takes more than desire; it requires a plan. A written "donor communications plan" is essential, not optional. Communications planning is characteristic of high-yield, predictable, and efficient fund development programs, and distinguishes them from hit-or-miss programs.

A good plan will likely be more than the sum of the things you already do. Mailing an annual appeal, holding a fundraising event or two, and grudgingly putting out an unfocused newsletter a couple of times a year is *not* a fully functioning donor communications plan.

Planning forces you to consider seriously vital aspects such as:

- The segments within your donor base
- The frequency with which you'll contact each segment
- The types of communication you'll send to each
- The costs and goals of each communication effort

An annual donor communications plan is essentially a schedule of contacts. The table in Exhibit 12.1 shows a year's worth of contacts by Planned Parenthood of Maryland. The agency informally calls it the "who should receive what mailing" schedule. It's a master list, covering both donors and prospects. These are the *scheduled* contacts. Missing from the schedule are informal phone calls to donors and thank-yous, which are contingent on responses to the various appeals.

A donor communications plan is as much about retention (donor loyalty to the mission) as it is about near-term cash flow; probably more, actually. The plan makes sure you're regularly nourishing your relationship with your donors: reporting on the accomplishments they've invested in, sincerely thanking them for their support, inviting them inside your grand vision. Your aim? To give donors a full measure of emotional satisfaction and plenty of chances to participate in the work.

Can you *over*communicate?

Yes, if your communications program fails to "give good weight" and doesn't deliver sufficient emotional value for the money. You want donors to think "They need my help, and they're accomplishing good things." You do *not* want donors to think "I only hear from them when they want some more money."

What do *your* donors think? It's an excellent question to pose in a donor survey. They'll love you for asking.

Building an Annual Donor/Media Communications Calendar on the Schwartz Plan

Rick Schwartz, an accomplished public relations practitioner specializing in nonprofits, bluntly tells clients, "If you don't plan it, it won't happen." He's developed an easy-to-adopt method for compiling a calendar of press and donor communications. *In Rick's own words:*

EXHIBIT 12.1   ANNUAL COMMUNICATIONS SCHEDULE, 2006, PLANNED PARENTHOOD OF MARYLAND, SHOWING WHICH TARGETS RECEIVE WHICH MAILINGS

Audience	Newsltrs	Cult. EV	DMFA	EOY	Jan AP	Spring AP	CEO Ltrs	Ann Rep	Spcl AP	Fund. EV	E-news	Winter Rec.	Phonathn
Prospects	x	x	x	x		x			x	x	x		
Lapsed Donors	x			x					x	x	x		x
One gift/yr (under $999)	x	x	x	x	x	x	x		x	x	x		x
Multiple gifts/yr	x	x	x	x		x	x		x	x	x		
Choice partners	x	x					x	x	x	x			
Former Board	x	x					x	x	x	x	x	x	
Current Board	x	x	x	x		x	x			x	x	x	
Staff	x	x					x		x	x	x	x	
MGs	x	x					x	x			x	x	
MLs	x	x					x	x			x	x	x
Event attendees	x	x		x			x			x	x	x	
Foundations	x	x					x	x		x			
PPFA imports	x			x					x	x	x		x
VIP	x	x								x	x	x	
Workplace Dnrs	x								x–x				
Get Active				x							x		

Key:

- Newsltrs: quarterly newsletter
- Cult EV: invitation to cultivation event
- DMFA: direct mail appeal from national
- EOY: end of year appeal

- Jan AP: January appeal
- Spring AP: Spring appeal
- CEO ltrs: letters signed by CEO
- Ann Rep: annual report
- Spcl AP: special appeal
- Fund. EV: invitation to fundraising event
- E-news: emailed Newsletter
- Winter Rec.: Winter recognition event for major donors
- Phonathn: Phone-a-thon
- Prospects: never given, review annually in July.
- Lapsed donor: has not given in 18 mos.
- One gift/yr: give one gift a year of under $999
- Multiple gifts/yr: give more than one gift totaling $999
- "Choice" partners: continuous monthly deductions
- MG: flagged prospects for gifts of over $2500 and current donors over $2500
- ML: flagged prospects for gifts of over $1000 and current donors between $1000–$2499
- Phone-a-thon recipients: people who are called during one of our phone-a-thons
- Foundations that give small gifts: those that give over $1000 or are prospected ML/MG are not included here.
- PPFA imports: names imported from the national database, 18 months since import date to PPM database
- VIP: influential community members
- Workplace dnrs: 2 appeals—give through work (e.g., United Way) and then directly
- Get Active: 18 months since import date to PPM database

Too many nonprofits foolishly believe that word of their good works will mysteriously make it out into the real world without much effort on their parts. That it will magically fall upon the ears of certain important people—let's call them 'donors'—is even more improbable.

"It's a superhighway of messages out there, and your organization must take to the road with powerful content, continual effort, and an overall plan to get where you need to go.

"You start with the basics: a 'crowd-pleasing' publication every quarter. Start planning *newsletters* one month before, *annual reports* two months before. Thus:

January	February	March	April
	Prepare newsletter	Mail newsletter	Prepare annual report
May	**June**	**July**	**August**
Prepare annual report	Mail annual report		Prepare newsletter
September	**October**	**November**	**December**
Mail newsletter		Prepare newsletter	Mail newsletter

"The newsletter can be two sides of a page, four pages, or a mini-magazine. That depends on the size of your organization and the 'news' you create. But newsletters are the glue that keeps an organization's members and/or friends in close contact.

"An annual report is your turn to awe your audiences with what you've achieved in a mere 12 months . . . and to show how brilliantly and wisely you've used their contributions. Again, an annual report is as long as it needs to be.

"Two more essential items for your calendar. You get the media to speak on your behalf by sending *press releases* on notable achievements. Even the quietest nonprofit has one piece of news per month: a new board member, a new program, a major gift, an open house, etc.

"Almost nonexistent 10 years ago, *e-mailed news* is almost automatic for the smart nonprofit today. Don't hope and pray that the local newspaper will pick up your story; send it yourself to everyone on your list with an e-mail address.

"And as long as we're talking about cyberspace, you should give your *Web site* a good tune-up every month by updating calendars, deadlines, your list of press releases, new staff, etc. Build that into your contract with your website developer, or make sure you set aside enough time to make the changes yourself.

"Your calendar now looks like this:

January	February	March	April
Issue e-news	Prepare newsletter	Mail newsletter	Prepare annual
Issue press release	Issue e-news	Issue e-news Issue	report
Web updates	Issue press release	press release	Issue e-news
	Web updates	Web updates	Issue press release
			Web updates

May	June	July	August
Prepare annual	Mail annual report	Issue e-news	Prepare newsletter
report	Issue e-news	Issue press release	Issue e-news
Issue e-news	Issue press release	Web updates	Issue press release
Issue press release	Web updates		Web updates
Web updates			

September	October	November	December
Mail newsletter	Issue e-news	Prepare newsletter	Mail newsletter
Issue e-news	Issue press release	Issue e-news	Issue e-news
Issue press release	Web updates	Issue press release	Issue press release
Web updates		Web updates	Web updates

"These are just the basics that nonprofits from Little Leagues and community churches to the hospital and university should have.

"Let's add to the list for the community-leading institutions. How about just two *editorial meetings*: one with the major daily newspaper, the other with the business weekly... or arts quarterly, or minority publication, or public radio station. Your choice.

"And just two *public presentations*, say to the Chamber of Commerce and the local Rotary. Or to the bar association and medical association. Don't do them in the summer or near Christmas; no one will come.

"Yes, your calendar looks crowded, but only the annual report should take a lot of time, and we've spread it out over three months. And the tasks should be divided among multiple people.

January	February	March	April
Issue e-news	Prepare newsletter	Mail newsletter	Prepare annual
Issue press release	Issue e-news	Issue e-news	report
Web updates	Issue press release	Issue press release	Issue e-news
	Web updates	Web updates	Issue press release
	Presentation		Web updates
			Editorial meeting

May	June	July	August
Prepare annual	Mail annual report	Issue e-news	Prepare newsletter
report	Issue e-news	Issue press release	Issue e-news
Issue e-news	Issue press release	Web updates	Issue press release
Issue press release	Web updates		Web updates
Web updates			

September	October	November	December
Mail newsletter	Issue e-news	Prepare newsletter	Mail newsletter
Issue e-news	Issue press release	Issue e-news	Issue e-news
Issue press release	Web updates	Issue press release	Issue press release
Web updates	Editorial meeting	Web updates	Web updates
Presentation			

"Now, let's talk donors and prospective donors (they're very different, of course)!

"You have a number of different options that should be fit into your year's calendar. *Donor programs* is one, namely opportunities for your donors to see what you do, via panel discussions, site visits, lectures, and the like. They can be small and cozy for 10 to 25 donors and prospective donors (excellent to have a mix), or you can fill a lecture hall with a well-known speaker. Let's say a smaller venue event in the spring and fall.

"We like *board cocktail parties*, where a board member invites 5 to 20 couples among his or her friends to hear a "no solicitation" presentation about the organization by the organization's CEO. The organization hires the caterer and cleanup crew.

"If you're a larger organization with lots of donors, you should consider an annual *donor appreciation event* where the message is 'thank you, thank you, thank you.' It could be tied in with one of your donor programs above.

"Donors are, of course, on your mailing list for publications and e-mails. If you have a unique niche in the world, you can somewhat straightforwardly conduct a *direct mail campaign* three times a year to a highly targeted audience. Yes, results are in the single digits, but a compelling piece will get stored in the mind of even the nonresponder for future outreach. Figure testing the same mailing list three times in 12 months.

January	February	March	April
Issue e-news	Prepare newsletter	Mail newsletter	Prepare annual report
Issue press release	Issue e-news	Issue e-news	
Web updates	Issue press release	Issue press release	Issue e-news
	Web updates	Web updates	Issue press release
	Presentation	Board cocktail party	Web updates
		Direct mail 1	Editorial meeting
			Donor program

May	June	July	August
Prepare annual report	Mail annual reportIssue e-news	Issue e-news	Prepare newsletter
Issue e-news		Issue press release	Issue e-news
Issue press release	Issue press release	Web updates	Issue press release
Web updates	Web updates	Board cocktail party	Web updates
Donor appreciation			

September	October	November	December
Mail newsletter	Issue e-news	Prepare newsletter	Mail newsletter
Issue e-news	Issue press release	Issue e-news	Issue e-news
Issue press release	Web updates	Issue press release	Issue press release
Web updates	Editorial meeting	Web updates	Web updates
Presentation	Donor program	Direct mail 3	
Direct mail 2			

"That's a generic but full-fledged communications calendar for talking with donors and other influential people who can make a mighty difference to your organization. Mix and match, subtract a few, move the dates around. That's not the point. Having a plan is!"

So Says Rick Schwartz

In Conclusion

Communicating well and frequently with donors is the foundation for a thriving fund development program. It can't be done efficiently or effectively on an ad hoc basis, though. An annual plan is essential.

Characteristics of Effective Communications

HOW THE SAUSAGE GETS MADE

The product is what the customer thinks it is, and what I think has little to do with that. I can only learn from the customer what they expect ... a product isn't for everyone, it's for someone.

—Group of 33, *The Big Moo*

DEAR READER   Can you legitimately call something a "communication" if, in the end, it produces no results? I wonder. Without any results, it seems you *are* sending, but they are *not* receiving. Maybe it was merely a "cast," as in broadcast, narrowcast, newscast, and casting for fish. This chapter is about turning your *attempted* communications, your casts, into *real* communications.

Tom

ACTION IS THE OBJECTIVE. READING IS OPTIONAL

We put words on a page, printed or electronic. It's reasonable to assume, therefore, that reading is our objective.

It's not, though. The purpose of fund development (and other marketing) communications is not to cause reading; reading is merely a means to your end.

The real purpose of your communications is to cause people to act, sooner or later. Sooner, if you're sending an appeal letter. Someday, if you're sending a reminder about charitable bequests.

It's a distinction that makes a difference.

If you think reading is your objective, you will tend to write more than you really need to. You will tend to argue your cause as a scientist might, with lots of statistics and little reliance on anecdotal evidence. You will view your presumed reader as judicious, thoughtful, and attentive.

The truth is this: Once you've left school, where teachers were *paid* to be judicious, thoughtful, and attentive readers of your writing, everything changes. No longer is someone paid to read you. Donors and prospects owe you nothing. They are under no obligation to spend their precious "discretionary attention span" on your newsletters, direct mail, or Web site. Writing that is not entertaining, informative, or useful is quickly dismissed. Those long articles you've labored over never had an audience to begin with.

INERTIA IS A POWERFUL ENEMY

Even on your best day, most people will ignore you, even your loyal donors. That's just the way it is in our busy, overmessaged, and oversolicited world.

Let's look at the case of direct mail.

Response rates to acquisition campaigns are in the cellar. They are now predictably below 1 percent—and falling.

There is one way you *might* be able to improve a dismal acquisition response, though: through repeat mailings of the same appeal.

Inertia is a powerful enemy. When people don't respond, it's often because they've simply ignored you, for one of a thousand different personal reasons. Maybe next time they won't. Here's a case to consider.

The Rhode Island Foundation uses direct mail to invite philanthropically minded millionaires in its region to join its mailing list. The assumption is that once a person comes on board, he or she can be cultivated. And cultivation pays off handsomely. In 2005, the foundation received $26.5 million in gifts, a sum that increases pretty much every year.

The first time the foundation mailed its invitation package to 3,340 households, 100 signed up: a 3 percent response rate.

Assuming that many households hadn't responded because they'd simply ignored the mailing, the foundation waited a couple of months, then sent the very same package to the very same list, deleting only those who had responded first time. This time, another 2.5 percent responded.

Again, the foundation waited a few months, then once more mailed the very same package to the very same list, deleting only those names who'd responded to the first and second mailings. And another 1.3 percent responded.

Total accumulated response rate: 6.8 percent. Had the Rhode Island Foundation stopped with a single mailing, more than half the millionaires who ultimately responded would never have come on board.

AN HONEST-TO-GOODNESS SECRET TO SUCCESS: WRITE A CREATIVE BRIEF FIRST

In the advertising world, they have a handy little tool called the "creative brief" or "strategy statement." This written strategy answers critical questions, such as: Who is the target? Why does this product matter? What makes it unique? What is the "personality" of the brand? (Fun, sexy, serious, elite?) Why are we doing this? Why are we spending this ridiculous amount of money? What are we trying to accomplish with this ad? What will the ad cause the target audience to think, feel, or do?

The purpose of a written strategy is to get everyone on the same page. Literally so. Writers, designers, clients: You want everyone involved in this expensive process to be headed in the same direction. A written strategy avoids conflicts. It helps reduce (you'll never eliminate) dumb ideas and guesswork.

The nonprofit world does not orbit a different sun from advertising.

To succeed in fund development, you need a strategy, too. You need to know your destination—where you wish to end up—before you try to attempt any sort of communications (speech, grant, article in your newsletter, solicitation letter, annual report, letter to the editor, presentation to a prospect). Your "strategy brief" (feel free to call it anything you want, as long as you do it) answers essential questions. It gets you straight in the head. What are you trying to accomplish with this communication effort? What's your worthy goal?

Work it out in your head, if you care to. You don't actually have to write your communications strategy down (though it helps if you do, because then you can share it). But you cannot skip this step and expect good to great results.

Here's a simple form that automatically produces a strategy brief once you've plugged in your information:

> This [insert item name; say, article in your donor newsletter] will convince [insert specific target audience; say, those with wills] that [insert action you want reader to take; say, request your informative brochure about bequests] will result in [insert benefit reader will value; say, giving your organization a strong future by building its endowment].

If you *do* skip this step, good luck. You'll need it.

THERE'S AN ONSLAUGHT, AND YOU'RE PART OF THE PROBLEM

People are busy. They receive far more appeals for their attention than they know what to do with. Most of the time they respond by ignoring you. Don't take it personally. It's not because they hate you. It's because they're paying no attention to you at the moment your communications presents itself for consideration.

Witness your own behavior. Most of us have a domestic ritual: standing over the trash basket while we sort the mail. We sort mail and other messages into three piles:

1. "Stuff I can*not* ignore, or something bad will happen to me." Bills go into that pile.

2. "Stuff I can *safely* ignore, and *nothing* bad will happen to me." That's everything else, pretty much. That pile goes straight to trash, except for . . .

3. "Stuff I could be interested in. I'll save that for a second look." Very few things end up here. Most that do relate to our material comfort and status, such as catalogs of home furnishings, electronics, and clothes. Your donor newsletter and other communications can, if they work hard at being interesting, find a place in this pile; but not every time, and not with everyone.

YOU'RE SELLING FEELINGS, ESPECIALLY HOPE

What do you have that's so wonderful, to compete with luxurious sheets, gadgets, and the new fall line?

Nonprofits sell a *feeling*. It's the warm feeling that a donor has done something beneficial, useful, important, good, and proper by engaging in a philanthropic act.

Fund development is a great business. Unlike commercial operations, you carry no inventory. You can store a universe of hope inside a #10 envelope.

And hope is what gets you into the third pile. Selling the feeling of hope. Hope is a narcotic. Hope is an anti-aging drug. Hope lifts everything, including a sagging spirit. It restores diminished expectations. Hope can repair a broken heart. You'll never go broke selling hope.

YOU'RE SELLING A FEELING OF IMPORTANCE, TOO

"No one starts the day," writes George Smith, one of the United Kingdom's most successful fundraising direct mailers, "with the intention of making a charity donation. And no one says to their partner, 'Honey, the appeal mailings have arrived.' A routine charity appeal has to fight its way through torpor."[1]

Which you can do, he goes on to say, if you create the sense that giving to you will make someone feel they've done something important. "Fundraisers cannot presume on this perceived importance," he cautions. "They have to create it."

You can't let up on this job. Every communication with donors is a chance to reemphasize their vital importance in achieving the mission. And note: It's *the* mission, not *your* mission. Donors (assuming you can't live without them) own the mission, too. Good donor-centric materials shift the burden of achieving the organization's mission onto the donors' shoulders.

In 1936, Dale Carnegie published the book that would make him a household name, *How to Win Friends and Influence People.* In it, he put to everyday use the ideas of Dr. Sigmund Freud and philosophers like John Dewey and William James. Carnegie lists eight things that "almost every normal adult wants," among them sexual gratification and health. "But there is one longing," Carnegie wrote, "almost as deep, almost as imperious, as the desire for food or sleep which is seldom gratified. It is what Freud calls 'the desire to be great.' It is what Dewey calls the 'desire to be important.' Here is a gnawing and unfaltering human hunger; and the rare individual who honestly satisfies this heart-hunger will hold people in the palm of his hand."[2]

You, fundraiser, can be that "rare individual." Make your donors feel important, and you will hold them in the palm of your hand.

INTEREST ME (OR ELSE)

Advertising Copywriters Hall of Famer Howard Luck Gossage (d. 1969), uttered this oft-quoted truth of effective communications: "The real fact of the matter is that nobody reads ads. People read what interests them, and sometimes it's an ad."

And sometimes it's your solicitation letter. And sometimes it's the headline on the front page of your donor newsletter. And sometimes it's your e-mail's subject line.

In each case, interest, as Mr. Gossage pointed out, is key.

When you interest people, they give you their attention. If you don't interest them, they don't. Your donors and prospects are in no way obliged to read your stuff, as we noted earlier. To gain a place in pile #3, that treasured "I'll take a second look" pile, you absolutely *must* interest your readers. Somehow.

A personal story by Simone Joyaux that illustrates the key principle: It's not what you're selling; it's what I'm buying. In 1990, my father died suddenly of cancer. We discovered he was sick, and he was dead six weeks later. He died in Michigan, before I could get there.

I arrived in East Lansing a few hours after his death. That afternoon I phoned Michigan State University (MSU) and set up a scholarship fund

(Continued)

for travel in a French-speaking country. The fund was named for my father, Georges Jules Joyaux. He had not yet been dead 10 hours.

Within a few weeks of my father's death, I received solicitation letters from the national and local cancer societies. Timely and appropriate letters. Good fundraising efforts triggered by my father's death.

And I threw each of those letters away.

Why?

Too soon? No. Too impersonal? No. (Although a personal call probably would have generated a nominal, one-time gift from me.) On paper, I looked like a prospect. But as it happened, I wasn't. The cancer societies sold certain worthwhile things. But my interests were elsewhere.

The cancer societies were selling freedom from pain, health, a cure for cancer so others would not suffer, as had my father and family. Protection so I might not die from this dreaded disease. Protection for my husband, mother, my brothers and sisters, and my friends.

But what was I buying?

Not health. I rarely give to health organizations. Certainly I want everyone to be healthy, myself and loved ones included. But I'm not buying health.

Not freedom from cancer. I am sorry my father died from cancer. It was ugly, as so much of death is. But I'm not buying an end to cancer.

What did I buy that afternoon when I called MSU from the living room of my parents' home?

- My French heritage. Love and respect for different cultures, taught by my father. Joy of travel to other countries. Commitment to education as I look at all the teachers in our family.
- A warmth toward MSU. My father came to the university as a young man from war-torn France. There he met my mother and taught for 41 years. All six of us kids went to school there.
- Love and admiration for my father, his vision of a world where pluralism is honored, his wit and sarcasm, his intelligence and eloquence, his strengths and weaknesses, his love for teaching and his students.

Cancer took him. But it did not define him.

So, my mother and the six Joyaux kids set up a scholarship fund in Georges' name. Each year, an MSU student receives funds to study in a French-speaking country. The country doesn't have to be France, only French-speaking. An academic curriculum isn't necessary. Traveling and experiencing are what count. My father always reminded everyone: "The most important thing is to step out of your linguistic ghetto and become aware that there are people who live, eat, learn, and make love in a medium which is not English."

It amuses me to think of Georges' reaction to his fund. He would laugh and make a smart remark. But he would remember the students. I think he would be pleased.

With the scholarship, the students receive a description of my father and what he accomplished in his lifetime. I trust they read it.

I tell this story around the country when I teach and consult. I ask people what they think the cancer society is selling. People are so gracious. They use polite words and euphemisms. It takes a while before anyone gets to the nitty gritty—protection from death. Better yet, protecting me personally from dying and protecting others that I care about.

People are just as gracious when they talk about what I'm buying. They always emphasize the honoring of my heritage, my father, and his beliefs. Sure, that's a part of it. But then I laugh. Irreverently, I proclaim: "Just honoring my father and my heritage? I bought a house in France, and that's sure not for my dead father! This gift is about me and my interests. I love France, and I'm committed to pluralism."

You have to look deep. Get down to the essential, not just the surface.

— *Simone Joyaux*

How to Interest Donors and Prospects: The Big Four

So, what will interest donors and prospects?

Four things figure prominently on many experts' lists.

1. **Your organization's accomplishments.** How are you changing the world? Why does your organization matter? Why is your mission worth supporting? For the donor, it all comes down to one frank query: What did you do with my money?

2. **Your organization's vision.** What are your plans? Where are you headed? What do your dreams look like? Why is your vision worth supporting? For the donor: Why should I give you more of my money?

3. **Your organization's degree of donor-centricity.** "Donor-centricity" is "donor recognition" by another name. Actually, it's more like a "new and improved" donor recognition. A donor's need for recognition is widely misunderstood to be met when an organization publishes a list of names, next to a word of thanks. True enough: Donors probably expect you to list their names in some publication. It is a well-established fund development convention, often grouped into monetary categories: "Gifts below $100," "Gifts of $100–249," and so on. Donor-centric recognition is a different thing altogether: It treats donors universally as heroes. It lays the credit for achieving the organization's mission and vision on the donors'

doorstep. When you are engaged in donor-centric recognition, you drive home two messages at every opportunity:

a. "With your help, we accomplished these wonderful things."

b. "Without your help, we cannot achieve much at all."

4. **Your organization's efficiency as a business entity.** Skepticism is intrinsic. It is part of human nature. You can safely assume that prospects and donors, being human, are skeptical. If that native skepticism boils over, you will lose their charity. To calm skepticism, you must repeatedly remind people that you're "business minded" (i.e., not a bunch of flaky do-gooders) and that you spend a *minimum* on overhead and a *maximum* on your programs. Don't be lax on that last point. One piece of research in the United Kingdom found that donors assumed the worst: that 65 percent of their charitable dollar went to administration and fundraising, not to program costs.

Many, maybe most, donors don't really give to you. They give *through* you; to change something in the world they care about, some need that moves them somehow, enough at least to write a small check. (Anything above that, and the work gets harder.) They give through you to (among other reasons):

- **Fix a problem that tugs at them.** ("These days, people need a high school diploma to have any shot at all. Dropout rates of 60 percent in some cities? That's just awful." The emotional triggers involved? Some degree of anger or fear.)

- **Get more of something they like.** ("I wish there were more art shows at the museum." The emotional trigger? A type of greed.)

- **Feel that they are contributing to society.** ("My gift goes right into research that is already helping save the bay." The emotional triggers? Salvation and hope.)

- **Give back.** ("Mentors were very good for me. They helped me see the light." The emotional triggers? Duty, love, compassion, gratitude.)

- **Halt the loss of something they value.** ("They tell me my school is losing its reputation as a great place for research in the biological sciences." The emotional triggers? Fear, greed, hope.)

Donors don't really give to the Memphis Child Advocacy Center, for instance. That's just a name. What they *really* give to is the *promise* of the center, expressed in its tagline: "Helping victims become children again." It sounds like a miracle. But it's a *credible* miracle. (The center is very good at its work). That's what donors want to buy from you: a credible miracle.

Donors see little enough evidence, though. "A recent study by Foundation-works documented that the news media has produced 38,000 articles about philanthropy in the past 15 years yet only 1 percent of them discuss the results of a gift," reported Mark Kramer, a senior fellow at Harvard's John F. Kennedy School of Government. "We have created a black hole in philanthropy, capable of absorbing endless amounts of money without demonstrating impact. Until they see results, however, donors don't shift from giving away modest sums to reaching deep and engaging personally in solving social problems." Kramer redefines what charities have to do to educate donors. "It is about how nonprofit groups ... perform, and the opportunities they provide their major donors to experience the problems and see the solutions they have financed firsthand."[3]

In other words, accomplishment reporting.

See Exhibits 13.1, 13.2, and 13.3 to see how a donor newsletter reports on accomplishment, donor recognition, efficiency, and vision (reprinted courtesy of Planned Parenthood of Rhode Island).

HOW TO INTEREST ANYONE: FOUR CHANCES TO WIN

Imagine that each person you're attempting to communicate with has four sets of ears and eyes. And each set responds to a different sort of signal. You have your ...

- **Amiable ears and eyes.** This set responds to intimacy, warmth, human interest. Favorite visual: authentic faces, not all of them smiling. Favorite

Recognition   Accomplishment

Thank you, donors! You funded this health promotion...and we're seeing great results.

Number of Latinas coming to PPRI for reproductive health care jumps 40%

Salud Entre Amigas (Health Among Friends) campaign makes major headway in hard-to-convince Latina market. New ads working.

SOME OF THE STATISTICS REGARDING reproductive health care for Rhode Island's rapidly growing Latina population have been less than rosy.

But PPRI's bilingual public health campaign, Salud Entre Amigas, paid for with gifts from the Partnership Foundation

Efficiency

EXHIBIT 13.1   **Article on increased visits by latinas emphasizes donors' starring role**

Recognition → 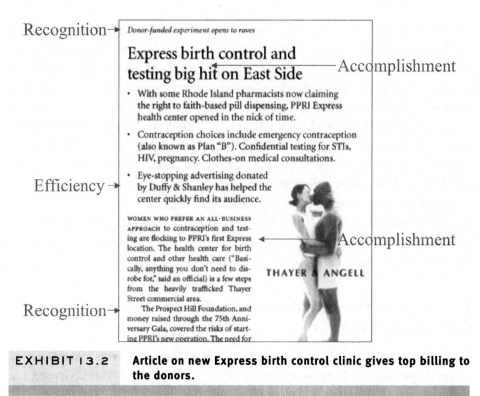 ← Accomplishment

Efficiency →

Accomplishment

Recognition →

EXHIBIT 13.2   Article on new Express birth control clinic gives top billing to the donors.

tone: conversational, even intimate, with honest warmth. Favorite story: an anecdote where (often tragic) conflict turns to some form of triumph. Favorite word (because it makes everything sound personal and closes the distance): you.

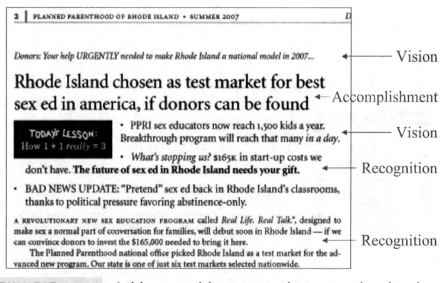 ← Vision

Accomplishment

Vision

Recognition

Recognition

EXHIBIT 13.3   Article on promising new sex ed program makes clear donors are essential.

- **Expressive ears and eyes.** This set responds to drama, excitement, anything new. Favorite visual: anything that's new. "Tell me or show me something I don't know, please, I'm begging you!" Shock me. Surprise me. Frighten me. I'll pay you for the sensation. Favorite tone: dramatic, telegraphic, colorful, sharp, smart, provocative, controversial, unanticipated, with flair. Favorite words: new, secret, inside, special, revealing, unique, for the first time, unexpected.

- **Analytical ears and eyes.** This set is skeptical, slow to respond, demands more facts. If you must write long pieces (because of some genetic disorder, perhaps, or your inerasable self-image as an essayist), know you are writing for this set of ears *only*. Favorite visual: charts, tables and graphs. Favorite tone: clear. Favorite words: credible evidence (testimonials, e.g.) that prove what a good job your organization does.

- **Driver ears and eyes.** "Driver" as in "driven." This set makes quick decisions and wants to act quickly, too. Favorite visual: the reply envelope. Favorite tone: simple, easy, fast, convenient, straightforward. Favorite words: as few as possible.

Dividing people into four personality types has an old pedigree, Roy H. Williams (a.k.a., the Wizard of Ads) notes.[4] He traced the four-part model back to observations made by the ancient Greek physician Hippocrates; revived in the twentieth century via the psychologist Carl Jung, whose theories then inspired Isabel Myers (of Myers-Briggs personality inventory fame); and onward into modern sales training. The model appears again in Chapter 1, talking about "social styles."

I've adapted the same four-part model to help you choose *which* stories are worth telling and *which* words are good to use. These will improve your chances of speaking to all four sides, not just one or two.

Nonprofit organizations are intuitively pretty good at introducing amiable content into their communications. We've all heard the truism: "People give to people." So our donor newsletters feature plenty of smiling faces, either folks we've served or donors enjoying themselves at a fundraising event.

But missed opportunities abound. The most common? You leave ...

- **Expressive eyes and ears unprovoked.** Your executive director (or, worse, that bunch of second-guessers ironically called a "communications committee") believes "bland is beautiful" ... so your communications never dare anything. See Exhibit 13.4 for an example of a short article with many expressive touches, reprinted from a donor newsletter (courtesy of Planned Parenthood of Rhode Island).

- **Analytical eyes and ears still wondering.** You assume everyone trusts you (or *should* trust you) ... so your communications fail to reassure donors and

Expressive verb — **Dare to wear the T-shirt**

Fun visualization — Make your liberal friends cheer. Make your very proper friends feel faint.

Expressive adjective — It's yours as a cheeky *thank you* when you make a $250 or more gift online...

News announcement — COMING SOON TO OUR WEBSITE: the healthful adventures of PPRI's very own cartoon mas-

Taboo words — cots, Beaver and Cock. And, heck, they've already started

A non-journalistic voice — their own line of signature apparel, available online exclu-sively through PPRI. Get this

Two expressive adjectives — cheeky (or shocking, depend-ing on your audience) T-shirt as PPRI's thank you — when you make your next gift of $250 or more online. Quantities are limited. Order today.

The new critters —

KEEP 'EM HEALTHY,
KEEP 'EM HAPPY.

EXHIBIT 13.4   ADDING NEWS VALUE IS EASY. EXPRESSIVE CONTENT MAKES THIS BRIEF ITEM MORE EXCITING.

prospects repeatedly. No small oversight. In a 2006 Cone study,[5] donors said "I trust the charity" was the most important factor influencing their decision to give. Reassurance doesn't require all that much time or energy, either. The International Fund for Animal Welfare brilliantly reassures its donors in just four words with this tagline, updated annually: "37 Years of Action."

- **Driver eyes and ears frustrated.** You fail to make your calls to action big, bold, obvious, and frequent. And convenience is an afterthought. There's no fast, easy way to make a gift (a reply envelope in your newsletter, say, or an online giving option) . . . so your communications program yields disappointing results.

SELF-INTEREST: WHY GREED IS GOOD (FOR YOUR ORGANIZATION)

There's another kind of interest we can tap in our efforts to acquire donors: self-interest. Not all giving derives from unalloyed altruism. In some cases "what's in it for me" is a deciding factor. For instance:

- Prospects who crave a certain social ranking might find your charity of interest because the "right people" give to it.

- Young professionals who long to furnish a bare resume might find your charity of interest because they know that employers value volunteerism.

- Newcomers to a community might find your charity of interest because they desire fellowship and connections in a strange new place.

MAKE OFFERS

An offer promises something in exchange for a response. *Time-limited* offers ("offer ends ... ") give readers a reason to respond *right now!* Offers are essential. They motivate people to act. Without offers, response to your communications sinks to nothing.

Typical fund development offers include:

- Any ask, oral or written (You're basically saying "If you make a gift, we'll make the world a better place in exchange." In direct mail, fundraisers sometimes sweeten the offer and make it a bit more tangible by slipping in premiums like address labels.)
- "For more information"
- An invitation to join an exclusive society, such as a President's Circle
- An invitation to an event
- A free, informative brochure
- Free membership
- Discounted membership ("Your family membership entitles you to unlimited visits ... ")
- A member card
- A free subscription to your electronic or printed newsletter
- Special, timely updates from the president
- A free calendar of upcoming events and shows
- Discounts for advance purchase of tickets
- Reduced fees for particular programs or events
- Special member-only previews
- Matching gift campaigns
- Challenge grants
- The ease and convenience of giving online

- A naming opportunity
- A behind-the-scenes tour

PASSING THE "YOU" TEST

Get yourself a red pen. Then get out a copy of your donor newsletter, your latest direct mail appeal, your annual report, your event invitations, and definitely a printout of your Web site's home page—any communication that you hope will attract the support of prospects and donors.

Here's the test: Each time the word "you" appears on the page, in any of its forms (you, your, you're, yours, yourself, you'll . . .), circle it.

To earn a passing grade in this test:

- Your donor newsletter will have red circles in the headlines, the decks (nonjournalists call them subheads), the lead paragraphs, every offer, many captions, and throughout the articles.

- Your appeal letter will have red circles in first or second sentence, last sentence, P.S., and thickly sprinkled throughout the rest of the text.

- Your home page will have red circles in the headlines, in the banners, in the clickable teasers ("You can learn more . . . click here").

Pass the "you test," and your newsletter, appeal letter, annual report, invitations, and home page can succeed. Fail the "you test," and they will probably be dead on arrival. Using this one word is *that* critical. In fact, there's every reason to call the pronoun "you" the most profitable word in fund development, capable by itself of raising lots of cash.

There are a couple of reasons why.

First, your brain is a creature of habit. You're addressed as "you" countless times from the day you're born—by family, friends, teachers, doctors, strangers, and eventually by the nothing-if-not-persistent world of advertising. "You are such a beautiful baby. Do you need to go potty? Would you like more to eat? Honey, would you please stop teasing the cat? Yes, sweetie, mommy loves you." Your brain quickly learns to respond to this simple stimulus. You—involuntarily and automatically—pay a bit more attention whenever "you" is uttered or written. "You" becomes glue. And *for the rest of your life*, that one brief word keeps you interested and reading.

Second, the word "you" is a great little personalizer. We know that personalization (using real names instead of "Dear Friend") improves response in direct mail. "All well and good for direct mail letters," you say, "but how do I personalize a newsletter, annual report, or website?" Problem solved: Use the word "you" early and often. Frequent use of the word "you" *instantly* makes your organization sound more conversational, natural, warm, and approachable—rather than stiff, self-absorbed, and distant.

DON'T TALK SO MUCH ABOUT WHAT YOU DO. TALK ABOUT WHY IT MATTERS

Shelve the desire to explain how your programs work. *How* you do what you do is (take a deep breath, please) not all that important to your readers. If you could achieve your goals with a wave of your magic wand, that would be fine.

Donors are really interested in other things: your results, why you matter, what you *have* accomplished, and what you *hope* to accomplish. The details of your working day hold nothing more than modest interest for outsiders . . . unless you're doing things that are shockingly unusual such as, say, artificially inseminating an elephant: "Our story begins with a long rubber glove . . ."

HAVE THEMES

Themes help guide your choice of which stories to tell and which angles to emphasize—in your direct mail appeals, your Web site, your cases, your annual reports, your newsletters, and when you're speaking personally with prospects and donors. When people talk about "staying on message," they're talking about sticking to themes.

A theme is something along these lines:

> ***Donors make it all possible.***   *Three*-quarters of our income comes from charity of some kind, whether from individuals, corporations, or foundations. Without charity, *we don't exist. And without even larger gifts, we cannot extend our successful problem-solving programs to more people.*

This is an example of a *core* theme. Core themes deal with basic issues, such as your sustainability over the long haul or, in this instance, your dependence on donors. Core themes stay valid for years.

Reassurance themes are also important. Reassurance themes persuade people that your organization is a good place to invest their charity. Like core themes, reassurance themes rarely change, and include messages such as:

- Ours is a well-run business.
- You can trust us with your money.
- We spend the minimum on administrative costs and the maximum on delivering services.

And then there are *mission-related* themes, themes that talk about why your work matters, what your beliefs are, and what you hope to accomplish. While core themes and reassurance themes change little and are often somewhat generic (i.e., they could apply to many nonprofits), your mission themes are unique to your time, place, and activities.

Mission-related themes for an environmental advocacy group, for instance, might include:

- Environmental education is as important as the 1-2-3s and A-B-Cs, if we expect to raise the next generation of environmentalists.

- Nature can't lobby for itself, so we step in.

- A healthy environment is vital to the state's reputation as a good place to live and raise a family.

A tagline is a form of mission-related theme. One of the best-known and longest serving is this one used by the United Negro College Fund and introduced in 1972: "A mind is a terrible thing to waste."

See Appendix 18D, the Audubon Society of Rhode Island's Internal Case for Donor Support, for examples of using themes and emotions in fund development messages.

You've Heard of "Values Voters"? Meet "Values Givers"

Linguist George Lakoff became a much-quoted political commentator by analyzing how words, carefully chosen to frame issues in a certain light, helped conservatives win huge political victories in the United States. What Lakoff calls frames are probably not all that different from what we call themes, at least not in intent. The intention is to stir response from the predisposed, by speaking to their values.

Substitute the word "give" for the word "vote" in this passage from Lakoff, and you'll see what we mean.

"People do not necessarily vote in their self-interest," Lakoff cautions in his influential study, *Don't Think of an Elephant!* Nor do people *give* in their own best interests. This insight helps answer a very basic question in fund development: namely, since we can all die from cancer, why don't we all rush to support cancer research? "They vote their identity," Lakoff warns. *Identity* is how they see themselves or *wish* to see themselves. "They vote their values. They vote for who they identify with.... It is not that people never care about their self-interest. But they vote their identity. It is a serious mistake to assume that people are simply always voting in their self-interest." And that goes for giving, too.[6]

Indeed, one of the peculiar paradoxes of fund development is why U.S. environmental causes have historically had such a tough time raising money. After all, polls show that Americans place a high value on the environment. Yet giving to environmental causes is one of the thinnest slivers on the pie chart of annual giving.[7]

Environmental causes, especially at the grassrootsier regional and local levels, tend to wage their arguments not through values but through self-interest. The underlying premise seems to be: "When we tell you how bad it is, you will want to support us." Followed by a seven-course meal of statistical evidence. Reams of statistical evidence *will* keep scientists awake at night. Yet the same evidence often misses the mark emotionally for the average person, because it frames the issue rationally but without appealing to heartfelt values. (And who has time to read all that evidence, anyway?)

Trying to reason someone into supporting your cause is a low-yield, slow-growth proposition, Lakoff would argue (and we agree).

"There is [a] myth that . . . comes from the Enlightenment," he notes, "and it goes like this. It is irrational to go against your self-interest, and therefore a normal person, who is rational, reasons on the basis of self-interest."

Unfortunately, the Enlightenment got it wrong. "The myth has been challenged by cognitive scientists . . . who have shown that people do not really think that way." People *will* act in ways that are counter to their own best interests. Economists and political scientists have plenty of proof. What people *won't* act counter to is their own values.

When *your* themes reflect *their* values, you pluck a responsive chord on the heartstrings of prospects and donors. If you ask for help at the very same time as you pluck that chord, giving feels right and good, almost inevitable.

Let's bring it down to earth. Madeline Stanionis, among the world's top authorities in the specialty of e-mail–spurred giving, writes in her how-to guide, "If you take no other lesson from this book, remember this one: To be successful with email fundraising, you must send the *right* message to the *right* person at the *right* time."[8] Part of that is database management. Part of that is having a crisis worth responding to. But part of it is plucking a responsive chord on the heartstrings of people who share your organization's values.

In Conclusion

Flattery is a good thing. Greed is a good thing. Action is all that matters. Fund development obviously isn't always Caesar's irreproachable wife. It's complex; pragmatic and philosophical at the same time; loving and ruthless, too.

Does fund development have lofty goals? Absolutely: from feeding world hunger on down.

But fund development is marketing, too, and marketing is about two things: emotional satisfaction and shopping convenience. When those two things harmonize, money flows.

No matter how it sounds, the wonderful thing about fund development is that it works best when it's authentic, honest, ethical, values-oriented, human, involving, intimate, surprising, delightful, heartwarming, invigorating, ennobling, grateful, and entertaining.

You do not trick people into giving you money. They give you money because you give them something they want, a feeling of mattering.

ENDNOTES

1. George Smith, *Tiny Essentials of Writing for Fundraising* (Kermarguer, Melrand France: The White Lion Press, 2003), p. 21.
2. Dale Carnegie, *How to Win Friends and Influence People* (New York: Pocket Books, 75th printing, 1965), p. 30.
3. Mark Kramer, "Donors Learn How to Be Effective by Seeing a Charity's Real Challenges," *Chronicle of Philanthropy*, November 23, 2006.
4. Roy H. Williams, *Magical Worlds of the Wizard of Ads* (Marietta, GA: Bard Press, 2001), p. 63.
5. "2006 Cone Nonprofit Research," www.coneinc.com
6. George Lakoff, *Don't Think of an Elephant!* (White River Junction, VT: Chelsea Green Publishing, 2004), pp. 18–19.
7. *Giving USA 2006* (Glenview, IL: Giving USA Foundation,) pp. 16 and 173, reports that contributions to "environment and animals" was 3.4 percent of the total for 2005. Leaders were religion at 35.8 percent, education at 14.8 percent, human services at 9.7 percent, and health at 8.7 percent. Still, giving to the environment is beginning to rise noticeably. Persistent news of a pending global environmental catastrophe could be stirring a stronger emotional response.
8. Madeline Stanionis, *Everything You Need to Know to Raise Money with Email* (Medfield, MA: Emerson & Church, 2006), p. 29.

What's the Role of a Fundraiser?

Let me tell you a secret: I don't care if the donor gives a gift to my organization or to another organization. It's all philanthropy. And philanthropy is about the donor. Philanthropy is bigger than any single organization.

I believe "a rising tide raises all boats." I believe that relationships are an end in themselves, not merely a strategy to secure gifts of time, advice and money.

One of the problems I think we face in fund development: Fundraisers and their organizations are not sufficiently connected to philanthropy and the larger community. No surprise that I say that, given what you've read thus far.

Here's a wild suggestion. How about this threefold role for a fundraiser:

Role #1. Nurture philanthropy as a community-building process, in Gardner's sense of place or mission (See Chapter 1) or anything else. Specifically: Increase social capital and promote civic engagement. Build civil society and civic capacity.

Role #2. Nurture relationships to foster philanthropy and strengthen community. Specifically: Help the community build relationships. Help the fundraiser's organization develop all four types of relationships proposed in this book.

Role #3. Increase and diversify philanthropy for the fundraiser's employing organization. Specifically: Act as an organizational development specialist, assuring an effective organization. Operate a donor-centered fund development program that nurtures relationships and effectively communicates. Then you'll build donor loyalty.

As you would expect, I don't think that the third role happens well without the first two. Furthermore, I think that excessive focus on the third role can harm the first two. I think that's dangerous for all organizations and all communities.

Philanthropy and fund development are not about getting your organization's fair share. Philanthropy and fund development are about finding those who might be interested and then nurturing relationships and loyalty. And not just for money!

CHAPTER 14

Are You Really Donor—Centered? Are Your Donors Truly Loyal?

WHY BUILDING A BETTER MOUSETRAP DOESN'T WORK UNLESS YOUR DONORS ARE MICE

Anyone can bring in a first gift. But good fundraisers can keep those donors.

—JENNIE THOMPSON, INDEPENDENT CONSULTANT, SPEAKING
AT THE 25TH INTERNATIONAL FUNDRAISING CONGRESS

Remarkable isn't up to you. Remarkable is in the eye of the customer. If your customer decides something you do is worth remarking on, then, by definition, it's remarkable.

—GROUP OF 33, *THE BIG MOO*

DEAR READER   Call it a struggle between two ideologies. Whispering at one ear is the siren call of donor-centrism. *Build better relationships,* it coaxes. *Make them last. Trust us, you won't regret it. You'll make far more money in the long run. And it's the honorable thing to do.*

Shouting in the other ear, though, are the hard-nosed, number-crunching demands of cash-driven pragmatism. *Fundraising above the local level is a mass-market venture,* they point out. *You don't need relationships to make it work. And who has the time? You want a relationship for a $25 gift? Get serious. We have salaries to meet.*

Donor-centrism sees the fundraising industry's low retention rates as symptoms of a curable disease.

Pragmatism sees low retention rates as a fact of life in a mass-market business. Regrettable, yes. But unavoidable. And accounted for in the cost structure.

Which ideology will prevail? Does either *need* to prevail? Or can they coexist?

Let's see.

Simone ▪

Some Facts about Donor Retention

Researchers Adrian Sargeant and Elaine Jay have both good and bad news about donor retention.[1] The bad news includes:

1. **Retention is an increasing problem in fund development.** Most organizations lose as much as 50 percent of their donors between the first and second gifts. And then organizations "tend to lose 30% of the remaining donors each year."

2. **Direct marketing by itself is ineffective as a retention strategy.** Organizations "typically lose a high proportion of their donors each year, especially if the organizations use direct-marketing fundraising."

3. **Keeping current donors is cheap. Adding new donors is expensive.** It "costs up to 10 times more to reach a new donor than to successfully communicate with a current donor." Hence, organizations that routinely fail to retain donors could be seen as financially irresponsible, open to charges of waste and mismanagement.

Yet Sargeant and Jay also offer some very good news.

Just a small increase in donor loyalty, for instance, can produce a major increase in lifetime value. Their research shows that reducing the attrition rate from 20 to 10 percent can produce a 50 percent improvement in profitability.

Loyal donors are also much more likely to participate in the organization in other ways, too. They're willing to pitch in with advocacy and lobbying. They tend to increase their gift size when asked. They will even help fundraise and promote the organization to friends and colleagues. Last but not least, loyal donors are the best prospects for a bequest or other planned gift—as research and experience both prove.

Volunteerism and generosity have long been linked. Studies show that volunteers who are also donors tend to give at significantly higher rates than donors who do not volunteer.

For U.S. charities it is worrying, then, that volunteer rates recently declined sharply. According to a 2007 report, the number of American adults volunteering dipped by a third between 2005 and 2006. "Our failure to retain more volunteers from one year to the next is cause for concern and should serve as a wake-up call ..." concluded the Corporation for National & Community Service.[2]

DONOR-CENTRISM: THE NEW OLD THING

Sometimes we forget why we end up with new donors.

In our business-minded struggle to "raise funds" for our operations, we forget that donors respond to our appeals for their own reasons, not ours.

They hope to heal wounds, fix problems, and make a difference. They hope to change the world, a lot or just a little, for the better. They don't give *to* us. They give *through* us, to make something happen.

> It's easy to be remarkable when you can truly connect with your customers; it's hard when you can only relate to the person in the mirror.
>
> —GROUP OF 33, *THE BIG MOO*

Often people give simply because they're charitably inclined; and we ask them at the right time, in the right way.

The day your direct mail appeal happened to arrive, the donor felt her bank account could afford a little generosity. The day your solicitor engaged her on the street, she happened to be in a trusting mood. The night your advertorial for needy children ran on television, she was moved enough to phone your toll-free number. The day your crisis e-mail popped into her in-box, a shocking news report about the disaster still rang in her head.

Sending that first check is the first step in what fundraisers hope will be a journey of many miles. But donors don't necessarily see it that way. Donors aren't necessarily looking for a "relationship" (whatever that is) with a charity. That first gift might be simply an everyday example of "stimulus-response." You asked. They reacted.

Still, while it might not be much, it *is* a start. You've acquired new donors. They've joined your world for a moment.

Now it's up to you to keep them.

Acquisition Is Easy. Retention Is Tough

Mass acquisition isn't the hard part.

Building a mousetrap to catch dozens, hundreds, tens of thousands of new donors is not particularly difficult, if you have the cash to hire the best minds. The fundraising industry spends a vast amount of money and cleverness on its traps. It's one of the things the industry does very well.

But buyer beware: These are traps with a difference. They do half a job. In fact, less than half, we would argue. In what way does a single gift really matter? It adds a few coins to your pile of gold, nothing more. The real value of acquisition is in retention, in all the gifts (and other kinds of support) that follow, as Sargeant and Jay's research argues, and any fund development strategist knows.

That's where many fund development programs fail, on the retention side of the trap.

The mice escape. More all the time.

The days of enrolling a huge number of newbies through an appeal, *then* holding on to them for years, are history. Not everywhere, true. Where charities are relatively few, those days may still linger. But where the density of charities per capita is thick, as it is in the United Kingdom, Canada, and the United States, prospective donors feast on unlimited choice.[3] There's a lot of cheese being offered for the mice to sample.

Maybe it's better not to think of donors as mere mice for the trapping.

Thinking about them, instead, as people we'd like to retain as friends for our organization makes good sense. The profitable part of a donor captured through mass trapping, after all, comes only after the catch is made, *if* (not *when*) the donor sticks.

Let's look for a moment at the most conventional means for mass acquisition, direct mail. Direct mail is not a cheap medium. The cost of acquiring a donor through a mailed appeal is high, often exceeding the amount of cash brought in. You can easily end up spending two dollars for every dollar you raise from first-time donors. You only start making a profit from these new donors if they give to future appeals, when your costs are a tenth of what they were for acquisition.

And what keeps new donors giving? Trust, results, familiarity, a desire to be philanthropic, shared values, habit, because they were asked again; all of the above.

"Donor-Centric" Is Another Way of Saying "Building Trust"

Books, research, and continuing education in the fund development field talk about donor-centricity[4] as if it were a recent discovery. It's not. It's a *rediscovery* of something professionals have talked about forever: the fact that donors are central to a charity's mission.

Which seems obvious. Yet despite raging lip service, actual practice often misses the donor-centered mark. How many organizations are truly donor-centered? Far too few in our experience, both in their approach and in their communications work. Most organizations still focus on *their* needs and why *their* good work requires donations.

How do you know if your fund development is insufficiently donor-centric?

There are several symptoms. A poor retention rate is chief: Too many of your new donors leave too soon. Associated symptoms include low average gifts;

individuals who give infrequently, though asked often; and only bequests or gifts considered major by the donor.

Donor-centrism serves a particular purpose in fund development: to build in your donors a high degree of trust in your organization's effectiveness.

Don't be confused by the soft talk. Fundraisers commonly talk about "relationship building" as a fundamental principle of comprehensive fund development. But imprecise words like "relationship" can mislead.

A donor relationship is not all that intimate. Your donors won't be showing up for family dinner (although annual donor meetings do serve somewhat the same purpose, as a gathering of the clan). This is a "business" relationship, as previously noted. However, a donor's relationship with your organization deepens or frays mostly based on how much trust you can create in three areas:

1. Trust that donors play an essential, vital, *central* role in your mission's success.

2. Trust that your organization does worthwhile things with the donor's money

3. Trust that your organization conducts its operations efficiently, with a minimum of waste and a maximum of impact

Why *Donor*-Centered? Shouldn't *Mission* Be at the Center?

Answer this question bluntly: Is donor money necessary to achieve your mission?

If so, then donors need to be included in your inner circle.

Not every nonprofit/NGO operative believes that is the case. Many act as if donors are merely a necessary nuisance. These organizations give those they serve pride of place. Donors become bystanders, tossing cash onto the field, but not part of the winning team.

And there is some infinitesimal potential for harm, if you always do what a donor wants. Every fundraiser knows at least one story of a donor run amok.

A donor who threatens to change her will when you displease her (maybe these *are* a bit like family relationships, after all). Or someone who insists that his money be used in some way that is not a priority for your organization: a gift with strings prominently attached. A typical, real-life example: a wealthy parent who will immediately pay for a new sports team (which you *don't* need, but his daughter will play on) but won't contribute toward a school's new library (which you *do* need for all your students). Nothing you say changes his mind, either. So you're left with only undesirable options: Refuse the gift and lose the money; or compromise your organizational priorities, maybe even mission.

But those are exceptions, not rules.

By and large, being mission-centered and being donor-centered are essentially the same thing. The simple truth is, a charity cannot achieve its mission without a team effort. Donors are critical, contributing members of that team, as important as staff to the final outcome.

> *The purpose of fund development is to find donors, not donations. And then the organization must nurture the relationship.*

Nonprofits that depend on charitable gifts for their existence sooner or later learn that it is profitable to view donors and their emotional needs as a top priority. They learn that talking to donors, valuing their opinions, asking questions of them, and listening to the answers leads to unexpected riches. Above all, through communications, verbal and written, these nonprofits urge donors to see themselves as central to the organization's mission.

Simple Demands of Donor-Centricity

Penelope Burk's research showed that donors aren't very demanding. They feel satisfied when they know just three things:

1. Your organization received the gift and was happy to get it.
2. You put the gift to work in the manner that the donor intended.
3. The project or program funded by the donor is producing the desired results.[5]

Straightforward. Just three fairly obvious things.

But Burk's research showed that behavior that runs counter to these simple donor desires is disturbingly commonplace among charities.

Only 34 percent of the donors, for instance, said they "always or most of the time receive information about what their gift is expected to achieve."[6]

Fundraising firm Merkle | Domain calls this sort of information "accomplishment reporting." Accomplishment reporting is the top priority of an effective fund development communications program. Nothing matters more. Yet Burk's findings show that the *majority* of nonprofits (66 percent), in donors' opinions (and do other opinions really matter in fund development?), do an indifferent to bad job of accomplishment reporting.

This is a severe communications failure; and, we think, unarguably a major cause of donor disillusionment. Burk also found that donor thank- you letters had much room for improvement. Charities claim they care. But donors often find the thank-you letters mechanical and rudely pushy about a next gift (see Exhibit 14.1).

Donor Loyalty and Donor-Centrism: Inextricably Linked

But if you improve your thanking and informing skills, you can renew donors more readily, Penelope Burk found.

EXHIBIT 14.1   BRIAN'S WARNING

- What is the most serious complaint you have heard from donors or prospects? "I made my gift and have never heard anything back from the organization."
- What is the most surprising comment you have ever heard from a donor or prospect?" "I made my gift and have never heard anything back from the organization."
- What keeps you awake at night? "The knowledge that a donor has not learned how his or her gift enriched the lives of others."
- What do you wish you could do better than you do now? "Listen. While I learn more every day about how I can more actively participate in a dynamic conversation, I have a long way to go in mastering the art of listening."

Ninety-three percent of the individuals Burk studied said they would "definitely or probably give again the next time they were asked to a charity that thanked them promptly and in a personal way for their gift, and followed up later with a meaningful report on the program they had funded. Under these circumstances, 64% would give a larger gift and 74% would continue to give indefinitely."[7]

Is your organization donor-centric? Here are some hallmarks:

- Donor-centric organizations are loyal to their donors. This loyalty is articulated in professional codes of ethics and the Donor Bill of Rights. A published donor privacy policy is a sign of donor- centricity. The existence of this policy is one of the few things other than numbers that Charity Navigator, which evaluates charities for donors, considers worth noting in its profiles of charities. (See www.charitynavigator.org.)

- Donor-centric organizations make donors feel as if they are an integral part of the organization. The organization's stories focus on the donors' role. The messages align with donor interests and reflect donor emotions.

- Donor-centric organizations hold themselves accountable to donors. These organizations steward both the donors and the gifts. Donor-centered organizations are transparent in their communications, telling donors the truth about challenges and opportunities.

- Donor-centered organizations link the donor's engagement with the results of the organization. You make it clear that without the donor, your mission would not go forward and people's lives would not change.

Which kind of organization are you? (See Exhibit 14.2.)

EXHIBIT 14.2   WHICH KIND OF ORGANIZATION ARE YOU?

In newer fundraising markets, cash-driven pragmatism seems to be all that matters. In older fundraising markets, donor-centrism is all the rage. But pragmatism and donor-centrism are not really in conflict. Fundraisers pressured by relentless goals might heartily disagree.

Donor-centrism views the donor's customer-service experience as its top priority. Donor-centrics talk about "relationship building." Cash-driven pragmatism views cash flow as its top priority. Pragmatists talk about "return on investment."

Donor-centrism views everyone as potentially a major donor, given sufficient time and communication. Cash-based pragmatism views everyone as a category: lapsed, current, LYBUNTs, SYBUNTs.

It's tempting to say that donor-centrism sees donors as people while pragmatism sees donors as labels, percentages, averages, and integers. Pragmatism isn't "donor be damned," but it's close enough to fool an observer. What it really is, though, is the difference between sales and marketing. In sales, customers are interchangeable and valued for their immediate cash value. In marketing, customers are unique and valued for their product loyalty.

What is Loyalty?

Loyalty is an odd word, and not especially donor-friendly in all its connotations. Its opposite, "disloyalty," carries a distinctly admonishing moral overtone, for instance.

"Loyalty," though, has a technical definition, swiped by fund development from the world of marketing.

In marketing, loyalty reflects the customer's acceptance of a brand's promise.

Both sides gain from brand loyalty, by the way. The company makes more sales; that's the obvious advantage. But the customer benefits, too: Purchase decisions become quick and easy. Laundry soap marketers long ago realized that consumers don't want to waste time weighing the merits of a dozen similar products. Consumers just want to make a quick, assured decision every time. That's what brand loyalty is all about: customer confidence in a product's ability to deliver satisfactory results.

In fund development, similarly, loyalty reflects acceptance that a charity has earned (or at least not abused) a donor's trust.

Sargeant and Jay observed two types of loyalty in their 20,000-donor sample, what they termed "passive" loyalty and "active" loyalty.

Passive Loyalty

Passive loyalty is one phrase. Perhaps *easygoing giving* is just as good.

According to the research, passively loyal donors feel comfortable with an organization. They respond periodically to solicitations and give modest sums. However, these donors would not be described as committed to the organization.

They'll take a small risk on you. But they remain unconvinced. It's up to you to convince them.

Consider the implications of these *easygoing donors*. For example:

- They may be searching for that which provides them with the most meaning. Perhaps some angle of your mission caught their eye. Maybe, with good relationship building, you can show them that you could fulfill their aspirations. But maybe not.

- Maybe these donors are very interested in your cause but your relationship-building program is so inconsequential that they will eventually give to another organization that addresses the same cause.

- Some donors choose to spread their philanthropy around. They give fairly regular gifts to multiple organizations that meet various community needs. These donors have no deep commitment to any single cause. But maybe with good relationship building on your part ... who knows?

Now think about the *favor donors*, another type of passive loyalty. Favor donors give in response to requests from friends and colleagues. That's Sin #3, trespassing on personal and professional relationships. How committed are they to your mission?

Take into account this finding from Sargeant's research: "Donors who feel obligated or pressured to give ... are among the most likely to lapse. ... Pressuring donors into giving may yield immediate return, but the subsequent attrition rate will be high. Worse still, we know that donors who have a bad experience with giving will share that experience with up to seven other people."[8]

And certainly pressure and obligation are bad experiences!

Active Loyalty

Sargeant and Jay describe active donors as passionate believers in your cause.[9] Their values align with your organization's values. (See Chapter 4 for a discussion of values.)

These donors "regard their support as an essential component of their personal and household budgets."[10] That's real commitment!

The challenge with truly loyal donors is to retain that level of loyalty and perhaps strengthen it. You want to create the virtuous circle, where they give something of value to you, and you give something of value to them. On and on, through the years.

Of course, there is no guarantee that active loyalists will be actively loyal forever. Let's be realistic. Relationships change, despite attempts to the contrary. We fall in love. We fall out of love.

Lifetime Value

For Sargeant and Jay, lifetime value is "a measure of how much a donor will be worth to an organization over the duration of the relationship."[11] You can calculate lifetime value by considering the costs and revenues related to maintaining the relationship with a particular donor or donor segment. Sargeant and Jay explain all this in their book.

However, here Tom and I only ask you to expand your thinking about loyalty. And we ask you to think beyond finances to the broader concept of relationships.

Giving is an act of kindness. It is not a financial transaction. Smart organizations realize that gift size by itself is not much of an indicator.

Imagine what you can miss when you focus primarily on gift size! You could miss individuals and families who have given to your organization for 20 years or more. Each of these donors gave no more than $100 per year. Their lifetime value so far is $2,000 each. Yet these donors are the likeliest prospects for a legacy gift.

Lifetime value is about more than money. It includes the word of mouth these donors provide your organization, the testimonials and stories they tell others. Lifetime value includes their volunteering, serving on your board, and lobbying on behalf of your mission.

Are Donors Loyal to Your Organization or to the Cause You Represent?

Donors might passionately "love" a certain cause (say, animal rights) while merely "liking" the specific charities that work to advance that cause.

The bond to a specific charity is likely to be conditional and dependent on the results that the charity can show. And if a more effective charity comes along? "Cause-loyal" donors are liable to switch.

Many organizations act as if this were not the case, however.

They contact their donors only to ask for money. Maybe they manage a couple of issues of their anemic newsletter in a year. Or excessively worried about donor fatigue and alienation, the organization intentionally maintains a low profile with its donors. A tepid relationship-building program, though, merely provides the opportunity for that terrible cliché, "out of sight, out of mind." I'll say it again. Remember what my friend Doris says, "Absence does *not* make the heart grow fonder!"

Always remember, if you don't keep me engaged so you nurture my commitment, I may well find another organization through which I can fulfill my aspirations (see Exhibit 14.3).

EXHIBIT 14.3   **DONOR-CENTERED AND DONOR LOYALTY: TWO SIDES OF THE SAME COIN**

"Donor-centered" describes how the organization reacts to its donors and how the organization performs in the relationship.

For an organization, loyalty to donors means that the donor is at the center of the relationship. Donors are more important than donations. Donor loyalty is valued more highly than a quick repeat gift in response to a catchy solicitation. The fund development program, centered on relationship building, revolves around donors.

"Donor loyalty" describes how the donor feels and how the donor expresses those feelings.

The donor is actively loyal to the cause or to the organization. The donor reveals his loyalty through commitment. The donor experiences this loyalty as a fulfillment of her interests, a reflection of her emotions, and a way to express her aspirations. And the organization experiences this loyalty as donor retention and stronger commitment.

CURRENT DONORS COME FIRST

Which has the greatest yield on investment: hunting for new donors, or nurturing longer, more loyal relationships with current donors?

Serious marketers don't consider this a subject for debate. Acquiring a new customer is horribly expensive. That's a given. After all, you're finding a proverbial needle in a haystack. Repeat sales to a loyal customer are cheap. That's a given. You already know where all the needles are. If you're a charity, the needles you found are all gathered together in one place, your database.

Cost-effective charities and professionals focus on retaining and upgrading.[12] They restlessly search for ways to nurture relationships. Retention rates matter more than acquisition rates.

But what often happens instead among fundraisers? We focus virtually all our cash and human resources on acquiring new donors. Acquisition mode is our first and foremost concern. Why?

- Many organizations assume that their donors are *actively* loyal rather than passively loyal (or easygoing givers, in my new phrase). With this assumption, organizations give only cursory attention to nurturing relationships, thus losing the easygoing givers, and possibly demoting the active loyalists to easygoers. And the bottom line? Above-average attrition.

- Lots of organizations think that they should diversify their donor base instead of returning to their active loyalists and upgrading their participation. With this assumption, organizations hesitate to nurture relationships that invite greater engagement, thus likely losing opportunities with their true believing donors.

- Always in acquisition mode, some organizations do not analyze how long the newly acquired donors stick around. With this assumption, these organizations are not expanding their donor base. Instead they acquire new donors and lose those same donors within 12 to 24 months.

Don't ignore your true believers because you are distracted by the idea of acquiring new converts. There might not be so many others that you can acquire, at least if you're a local charity with a limited pool of qualified prospects. Keep in mind, there are probably fewer predisposed accessible to you than you imagine.

> *Nurture true believers before seeking new converts.*

Think about the concepts of passive and active loyalty. Make an effort to distinguish which of your donors demonstrates which type of loyalty. Find ways to test whether some of those who are passively loyal might transition to more active loyalty, through volunteering, say, or by joining a monthly giving plan.

HELPING YOUR DONORS DREAM

According to Sargeant and Jay, donor commitment develops through:

- Trust
- Concern
- Exercise of choice
- Involvement (interaction with the cause)
- Provision of benefits
- Respect

Clotaire Rapaille talks about the relationship in terms of the organization's loyalty to the customer—that is, donor-centrism. Criteria include:

- Always there for you
- Face-to-face communications
- Freedom of expression
- Direct involvement[13]

I've reinterpreted these characteristics in Exhibit 14.4.

It's Relationship Building, It's Not Education

You've probably heard more than one board member muse aloud, "If we can only educate people about our mission, they'll give."

Beware: Relationship building is not a matter of "educating the donor."

Think about what the word "educate" means: to provide knowledge to someone. To develop or improve that person's abilities.

Honestly, how does that sound? Your donors are already smart enough to sustain themselves in a complex world. They probably know lots of information,

EXHIBIT 14.4	DONOR LOYALTY AND DONOR CENTRISM: HERE'S HOW THEY LOOK TOGETHER

Donor Loyalty (Relationship from the donor's perspective)		Donor Centrism (Relationship from the organization's perspective)
I feel passionate about the cause ...	Because the organization	Tells me stories that engage my interest and trigger my emotions. Creates diverse opportunities for me to engage—tangibly and emotionally—with the cause.
I trust and respect the organization ...	Because the organization	Is honest and transparent about its values and mission, accomplishments and vision, governance and management, and finances.
I know that I personally make a significant difference to this cause and this community ...	Because the organization	Regularly communicates how it used my gift and how much I matter to the beneficiaries, the cause, and the organization.
I feel comfortable and respected ...	Because the organization	Understands my interests and disinterest, my emotions, and my aspirations. Respects my individuality and differences, asks my opinion and welcomes my candor, and offers me choices in various situations.
I enjoy connecting with this organization ...	Because the organization	Is effective, efficient, courteous, timely, and genuine in its dealings with me.
My bottom line: I feel important, treasured, and powerful. I am transformed.	The Result	The organization's bottom line: Donors are our partners. Together we can transform the community.

even about your organization. Their giving is about their interests, emotions, and aspirations. I think "educate" is code for telling them how important the organization is and pushing hard to convince them to give.

Instead, focus on involving your donors. Develop and continually improve your relationship-building program. Understand and respect where they're coming from. Engage your donors in conversation. Tell them stories. Ask their opinions and advice. Dream together.

This is what dreaming sounds like. "Before this summer, I always thought of this dream I had as a rainbow, something I could see but never grasp," said Becky Love, a volunteer in a Kansas City homeless shelter. "I finally got the chance to journey inside my own rainbow, the colors were more magnificent than I could have every imagined! I discovered I was a lot stronger inside than I ever imagined and found I had talents and abilities I had never discovered before."[14]

"Effective donors are made, not born," says Mark Kramer, cofounder and managing director of FSG Social Impact Advisors. The firm conducted interviews with two dozen wealthy donors, identified by their peers as effective donors.[15]

The research found that these donors began their giving as so many donors do. They responded to inquiries from diverse charities. Communal obligations, social ties, and business relationships often motivated the giving.

But then something happened, something really big and important to the donor. "A cause or an issue came along of great personal significance and urgency. . . . Each of these donors stepped up in a new way, often giving a far larger sum than they had ever imagined. . . . The urgency of the cause and the magnitude of their commitment forced them to roll up their sleeves and take an active hand in solving the problems they had discovered. This insight and commitment produced a new understanding for the donors."

They learned that

> their work and money could produce a genuine impact . . . they stopped thinking about giving away money and started to think about how to solve social problems. These donors became passionately engaged, focusing on one or a few issues about which they could truly become well-informed, and staying with the same issue for years. They used every skill, connection, and resource they possessed and made careful efforts to measure their impact —not just through other dollars raised but on the issue itself. They became highly effective donors and leaders in the nonprofit world. And in return, they found their work profoundly rewarding.[16]

Now apply this same experience to your most loyal and active donors. Don't think about donor affluence. Think instead about gifts of significance to your particular donors. Remember that giving money is about emotions, not wealth. Kramer's words could apply to one of your donors who gave her most significant gift to you, regardless of the gift amount.

Those are the donors you seek: the donors who are transformed by the gifts they give you. Your organization is transformed, too, not because of the gift size but rather because of the donor's commitment and the donor's own transformation.

Kramer observes that we have "created a black hole in philanthropy, capable of absorbing endless amounts of money without demonstrating impact." But donors need to see—more important, to actually experience—the organization's results. Once donors see this, they "reach deep and engage personally."

Kramer closes by saying that it is how your organization performs that convinces the donor. It's how your organization helps the donor "experience the problems and see the solutions they have financed firsthand" that transforms the donor and her giving. Burk emphasizes this same thing in her research. Read on.

Engaging Donors with a Targeted Gift

Burk actually talks about the importance—to the donor—of giving to a particular project or program. How does that sound to you? I start thinking a restricted or designed gift, and that's somewhat disturbing. The bottom line for most of us is "undesignated and unrestricted gifts." Frankly, lots of us are probably concerned about this increasing tendency for donors to want restrictions.

But Burk makes a very interesting point, which I paraphrase here: When a donor first gives, the relationship with your organization is tenuous at best. At worst, the donor may just be trying you out. So now we're back to the hazards of first-time gifts, which so rarely these days turn into donors.

As Burk, and Sargeant and Jay note, trust builds loyalty. But when a donor first gives, loyalty does not yet exist. It's the donor's positive experience with your organization that shows her she can trust you.

And Burk's research shows that donors are testing nonprofit organizations. Sixty-seven percent of her respondents noted that their first gift is always or sometimes smaller than it could be. In order to give a larger gift next time, 68 percent of these donors said they wanted to know measurable results. Nine percent said they wanted personal contact, and another 9 percent said they wanted prompt acknowledgment of their gift.

Burk notes that timely and personal gift acknowledgment helps build trust. But more important, telling donors how their gifts were used—including measurable results—is even more important. And Burk notes that measurable results require that the donor's gift be directed to a specific purpose.

Think more broadly about Burk's point. Link this to the themed solicitations that I discuss in Chapter 6. Translate your "general operating support" into specific programs and services. Surely your organization must track the results, both qualitative and quantitative, of these programs and services. Now let donors pick which program or service is of greatest interest to them. Their gift supports a particular program or service within your core operations. And you can report on the results.

ACQUIRING A NEW DONOR

With a strong program for cultivating loyal donors—*active* loyalists—in place, it's time to seek new converts. (And without a strong retention program, you're wasting your acquisition investment by settling merely for short-term, temporary gains.)

Usually organizations hope to acquire hundreds of new donors through each acquisition activity. Such acquisition typically depends on direct mail. But as a volume business, direct mail requires a financial investment that usually exceeds income in the acquisition phase, thus producing a net loss. This financial loss is compounded because research documents that the sector is having trouble retaining donors in the first place.

You're Invading Their Privacy

Just ask any individual or group of individuals about the solicitation letters they receive. You hear lots of groans. People use words like "begging" and "junk mail." And they talk about throwing away these envelopes, often immediately and usually without opening. Take a look at Tom's three piles of mail in Chapter 13.

> *Nothing says "You haven't interested me" like the absence of a second gift from a first-time donor.*

U.K. direct marketer George Smith comments:

> The hardest truth about fundraising direct mail is less the pitiful number who ever respond but the rising majority who never even considered responding. They never ever noticed what you had to say. It is now probably true that most fundraising direct mail is thrown away unopened. . . . How else can you explain recruitment mailings where more than 99 people in a hundred fail to respond? Or "supporter" mailings where 90 "supporters" in a hundred fail to respond? These are now familiar response statistics and they are about a third of what a charity might have expected 10 or 15 years ago.[17]

Here's a wake-up call if I ever heard one: "Who the hell do you think you are?" asks Smith. As fundraisers, we reach into the privacy of someone's home or business, asking them to give money. This is an intrusion unless we have carefully executed the steps of relationship building described in this book.

In my ideal world, we fundraisers wouldn't solicit the predisposed. We would only solicit those predisposed whom we first qualify as prospects.

However, I realize that my ideal isn't possible. If you have the money and expertise, do great direct mail acquisition and use that first-time solicitation as the qualifying strategy. But at least, please, avoid the favor exchange strategy. That way you can reduce some of the angst on the part of your board members and eliminate that annoyance for those receiving the contact.

Many Nonprofits Cannot Afford Bulk Direct Mail Acquisition Anyway

By the way, for many organizations—like most of my clients—direct mail acquisition isn't a viable choice. These organizations do not have sufficient funds to make the numbers work in direct mail acquisition.

You have to buy qualified lists with thousands of names in order to compensate for typical response rates of 0.5 to 2 percent. Then you have to buy a good letter and pay for printing and postage. The cost will likely exceed the income for a response rate. You will acquire some donors, and then you'll face the attrition rates.

That's why so many of my clients identify the predisposed by the handfuls and pursue relationship-building personally.

Create an Exclusive Program to Bond with First-Time Donors

Make a big deal of first-time donors. If you do, you'll improve your retention rates. Merkle|Domain (www.MerkleDomain.com) recommends this "bonding" program for new donors:

- Thank the donor immediately. And "affirm the excellent choice [the donor] made to support your work." Merkle|Domain calls this the "no gift-ask affirmation letter."

- Provide information about your organization's results and vision. Help new donors understand how your organization uses their gifts.

- Try hard—very hard—to get a second gift quickly. Merkle|Domain notes that "new donors who give a second gift relatively soon after their first gift will continue their support at a rate two or more times greater than those who do not give again right away."

Your Thank-You Letters   The thank-you letter sets the tone for all your subsequent communications with the donor. Will you honor the profession's rule of thumb by sending this letter within 48 hours of gift receipt? Sadly, Penelope Burk's research found that fewer than half the charities followed this rule.

Look at timeliness from the donor's point of view. I send you a gift on March 1. You receive my gift within two to three days, but maybe more time elapses than that. As part of the slow-to-thank group, your organization sends me a thank-you letter in the middle of March. I receive it within two to three days, but maybe more. The bottom line: I receive a thank-you letter some three weeks after sending you my gift. How do you think the donor feels?

You're already familiar with best practice, if you've ever shopped a major Internet retailer like Amazon.com. An e-mail arrives almost instantly once you've placed your order, thanking you and informing you about the status of your order. And then you receive follow-ups on subsequent days to tell you about shipping. This approach honors your decision to purchase.

Memorable Thank-Yous   Make your thanks memorable: It's such an easy way to improve retention and get a higher return on your acquisition investment.

Most organizations have a standard thank-you letter, easily and readily produced. But what if you personalized that letter to each first-time donor? (Even better, what about personalizing every thank-you letter always?)

Personalized means more than the salutation. Make every effort to include something that you have learned about the donor. Or at least refer to something unique to the moment in time for your clients or your organization.

Here's another idea: In addition to the formal thank-you letter sent from the office, is it possible for each new donor to receive a handwritten note from a board member? (Even better, what about a handwritten note for every gift from all donors. Obviously you must consider volume and organizational capacity. But it's amazing how surprised and delighted donors are when they receive a handwritten thank-you note in addition to the formal thank-you letter.)

Do *not* include a gift reply envelope or any other suggestion of a gift request when thanking this new donor. Yes, that's what Merkle|Domain says.

Your Welcome Package   For the second step in your new donor-bonding program, develop a welcome package. Always include a cover letter, personalized. Do *not* just put items in an envelope and mail the envelope!

Make sure that the welcome package features donors and talks about the difference that donors make. Perhaps you'll include your most recent newsletter or annual report. Attach a sticky note on the newsletter referencing a particular article. And circle the article with a bright marker pen. Enclose that great news article, whether current or old. Maybe include an invitation or announcement for an event or program.

Send your welcome package 7 to 10 days after you have sent the thank-you letter. Again, do *not* include a gift reply mechanism.

Asking for the Next Gift   But when do you ask again? You certainly must solicit them before 12 months elapse! You've fully embraced the command: "Work hard to get a second gift as quickly as possible."

Pay particular attention to this new solicitation of your first-time donors. Merkle|Domain says this new solicitation is actually part of the new donor-bonding program.

Try making your second request within three months of receiving the first gift. That's what I'm recommending to my clients. Most prospects and donors usually seem comfortable with that time frame, as do organizations. And if you read other research or get a different recommendation, then do a test. Try different time frames and evaluate your results.

Once you've made the second request, move the donor into your regular solicitation calendar. But be careful. Make sure that new donors are not solicited for a gift until you have completed all steps in the new donor-bonding program. Sometimes when you add new donors to the mailing list, you inadvertently send them a regularly scheduled solicitation letter. However, do include these new donors in your regular relationship-building program.[18]

YOUR ORGANIZATION CAN SPEAK OUT— BUT DOES IT?

While donors are at your center—deep in the core of the organization—your organization is not a reflection of their interests alone. You do not compromise your own values, mission, and vision to gain donors. Being donor-centered means finding those donors who are interested in your organization's mission, or a portion thereof.

You cannot be all things to all people. Your organization decides its values, mission, and vision. You communicate these clearly. In fact, shout them proudly from the rooftops. Yes, you may lose donors—both current and prospective. But that's okay.

> *Understand what you believe in, show that fervor to your supporters. It distinguishes your organization from its peers.*
>
> —KRIS HERMANNS, DIRECTOR OF DEVELOPMENT, NATIONAL CENTER FOR LESBIAN RIGHTS

Understandably, some organizations are afraid. They worry that their values, mission, and vision may not find a wide enough audience. Dominated by this worry, these organizations find the middle of the road. Uncomfortable challenging the status quo, they speak quietly about their true values. Worried about controversy, these organizations avoid contentious issues.

Trying to be all things to all people makes you meaningless to everyone. You thin out your meaning and your message—removing all controversy—and making your organization acceptable to every conceivable audience. The result? No one is very interested or committed.

More important, however: These organizations have compromised their own values. Values: the nonnegotiable tenets that guide your organization's life. Values: the meaning that precedes mission, the meaning that founded the organization.

This is true tragedy. No exaggeration. Without honor and integrity, how do you survive? Without passion for your honor and integrity, why would your donors remain loyal? (See Exhibit 14.5.)

EXHIBIT 14.5 **WHAT LOYALTY LOOKS LIKE**

In late June 2006, we were sitting outside in the Languedoc sunshine. With glasses of wine and five different cheeses, Tom interviewed our dear friend and colleague Kris Hermanns. Kris was talking about the e-mail fundraising program at the National Center for Lesbian Rights.

Kris talked about values and integrity. "Understand what you believe in, show that fervor to your supporters. It distinguishes your organization from *its* peers."

NCLR doesn't worry about losing members, Kris said. She noted that supporters expect NCLR to be very vocal; to stand for something, and to do something about what it stands for. All this reassures NCLR members.

In fact, the perception among supporters is that NCLR hasn't sold out. NCLR has and continues to focus its programs and services on the most marginalized people within the Lesbian Gay Bisexual Transgender (LGBT) community, even when it is not necessarily popular, built power by sacrificing those values.

"NCLR is the only national queer organization that's been led by a woman," Kris notes. "Our supporters believe that NCLR remains true to its feminist values and hasn't built power by sacrificing those values."

By the way, if you think the quiet and safe approach produces effective communications, you're wrong. The greatest advertisers, marketers, and communicators all concur: Bold makes more money than bland. Be bland and no one will pay attention.

There's no conflict between being donor-centered and standing up for your values. Some donors engage in only one element of your mission. These donors are comfortable giving to the one area of alignment, a narrower connection.

Donor-centered organizations are loyal to the interests of their prospects and donors. These organizations steer clear of donor disinterests, without hiding their values or misrepresenting their mission.

Gather up your courage. As the old English definition says, courage means speaking your mind while telling your heart.

And always remember: The most significant gifts from the donor's point of view generally require major alignment of values, mission, and vision. In fact, it's your organization's values—clearly articulated, widely distributed, and frequently discussed—that likely play the biggest role in donors giving what they consider to be a major gift. (see Exhibit 14.6.)

In Conclusion

Building long-term relationships with others is one of the most important and powerful concepts behind philanthropy and fund development. This work takes time. And your organization's timetable is less important than the prospect or donor's timetable.

The most successful organizations are donor-centric. The most genuine organizations are donor-centric. Professionals of highest integrity focus on the donor.

It's up to you. With relationship building, *you* make donors feel as if they are part of your organization and that they're making a difference.

EXHIBIT 14.6   THE DONOR-CENTRIC PLEDGE

We, [fill in the name of your nonprofit organization here], believe...

1. That donors are essential to the success of our mission.
2. That gifts are not "cash transactions." Donors are not merely a bunch of interchangeable, easily replaceable credit cards, checkbooks and wallets.
3. That no one "owes" us a gift just because our mission is worthy.
4. That any person who chooses to become our donor has enormous potential to assist the mission.
5. That having a program for developing a relationship with that donor is how organizations tap that enormous potential.
6. That we waste that potential when donors are not promptly thanked.
7. That "lifetime value of a donor" is the best (though often overlooked) way to evaluate "return on investment" in fundraising.
8. That donors are more important than donations. Those who currently make small gifts are just as interesting to us as those who currently make large gifts.
9. That acquiring first-time donors is easy but keeping those donors is hard.
10. That many first-time gifts are no more than "impulse purchases" or "first dates."
11. That we will have to work harder for the second gift than we did for the first.
12. That a prerequisite for above-average donor retention is a well-planned donor-centric communications program that begins with a welcome.
13. That donors want to have faith in us, and that it's our fault if they don't.
14. That donors want to make a difference in the world—and that our mission is one of many means to that end.
15. That donors are investors. They invest in doing good. They expect their investment to prosper, or they'll invest somewhere else.
16. That we earn the donor's trust by reporting on our accomplishments and efficiency.
17. That individual donors respond to our appeals for personal reasons we can only guess at.
18. That asking a donor why she or he gave a first gift to us will likely lead to an amazingly revealing conversation.
19. That fund development serves the donors' emotional needs as much as it serves the organization's financial needs.
20. That we are in the "feel good" business. Donors feel good when they help make the world a better place.
21. That a prime goal of fundraising communications is to satisfy basic human needs such as the donor's need to feel important and worthwhile.
22. That the donor's perspective defines what is a "major" gift.*
23. That every first gift can open a door to an entirely new world for the donor, through participation in our cause.

---

*A repeat donor of $25 annual gifts who suddenly increases her gift ten-fold to $250, for instance, is making a major commitment that deserves special acknowledgement.

Don't spend your time raising money. Don't look for new solicitation tactics.

Instead, nurture relationships. Effective fund development starts and ends there.

Imagine if all your organization's relationships were truly synergistic, producing mutual enhancement. Then together, in relationship with each other, we could create transformation and live our shared dreams.

■ ENDNOTES

1. Adrian Sargeant and Elaine Jay, *Building Donor Loyalty: The Fundraiser's Guide to Increasing Lifetime Value* (Hoboken, NJ: John Wiley & Sons, 2004), p. 2.
2. "Volunteering in America: 2007 City Trends and Rankings," Corporation for National & Community Service, July 2007, p. 2.
3. Divide the 2007 population of the United States (300 million) by the number of IRS-certified nonprofits (approaching 1.5 million). That's one nonprofit for every 20 people.
4. "Donor-centered" and "donor-centric" are used interchangeably in the sector. To be donor-centric is positive, not negative like "ethnocentric."
5. Penelope Burk, *Donor-Centered Fundraising*, (Hamilton, Ontario: Cygnus Applied Research, Inc., 2003), pp. 31–32.
6. Ibid., p. 86.
7. Ibid., p. 87.
8. Adrian Sargeant and Elaine Jay, *Building Donor Loyalty: The Fundraiser's Guide to Increasing Lifetime Value* (Hoboken, NJ: John Wiley & Sons, 2004), p. 2.
9. Ibid., p. 161.
10. Ibid., p. 6.
11. Ibid., p. 161.
12. Is anyone else worried about the word "upgrade"? I've always used it, but it seems rather crass and too transactional. Synonyms include "improve," "promote," "advance," and "raise." Let's keep in mind that we mean strengthening donors' commitment to us.
13. Clotaire Rapaille, *The 7 Secrets of Marketing in a Multi-Cultural World* (Utah: Executive Excellence Publishing, 2001), pp. 52–55.
14. Quoted by Sister Jean Rosemarynoski, Cohort 16 Master's Program in Philanthropy and Development, Saint Mary's University, Winona MN.
15. "Donors Learn How to Be Effective by Seeing a Charity's Real Challenges, Opinion," *Chronicle of Philanthropy,* November 23, 2006, p. 39. Reprinted with permission of *The Chronicle of Philanthropy,* http://philanthropy.com
16. Ibid.
17. George Smith, *Tiny Essentials of Writing for Fundraising* (Kermarquer, Melrand France: White Lion Press), pp. 5–6.
18. Visit Merkle|Domain online (www.merkledomain.com) to download their orange papers on donor loyalty.

Telling A Story

THEN WHAT HAPPENED?

The universe is made of stories, not atoms.

—MURIEL RUKEYSER, AMERICAN POET AND POLITICAL ACTIVIST

DEAR READER   You don't have to write novels or news articles to tell stories. You just need a few words, like these that appeared as a photo caption in a Canadian United Way newsletter: "Without SOFIA House, my son and I would not be alive today." Donors want to change lives and save lives. Those dozen words tell exactly the kind of story donors hope to hear again and again.

Tom

WHY TELL STORIES?

"Only stories are really readable," Rudolf Flesch concluded.[1] Meaning: Only stories will entice people to start reading; and without stories, readership lags.

Flesch revolutionized writing in America, beginning in 1946 with the publication of his first book, *The Art of Plain Talk*. An Austrian lawyer who emigrated to New York City in 1938 to complete a doctorate in library science at Columbia University, Flesch "advocated an unadorned style, with shorter paragraphs, shorter sentences, fewer prefixes and suffixes, and greater use of colloquial American English. He equated such plain talk with progressive politics, especially with the New Deal policies of Franklin Delano Roosevelt ... ," according to Oxford's *American National Biography*.

Flesch taught the Associated Press how to write for a modern audience; his *Associated Press Writing Manual* appeared in 1951. He toppled educational orthodoxy in 1955 with his pro-phonics bombshell, *Why Johnny Can't Read*. And today he's at your fingertips, if you use Microsoft Word software, which checks grammar using the Flesch Reading Ease scoring system and the Flesch-Kincaid Grade Level evaluator. "To the extent that a single man was responsible for the simplification of printed prose in the post-World War II period, it was Flesch," historian Francis Morrone writes.[2]

The admirable Dr. Flesch also said, "There's nothing on earth that cannot be told through a hero—or heroine—who's trying to solve a problem in spite of a series of obstacles. It's the classic formula; and it's the only one you can rely on to interest the average reader."

That's one reason why you tell stories. Here's another. Stories linger longest in the donors' minds. "Studies show," wrote Jim Grote, director development for Father Maloney's Boys' Haven, "that we tend to forget abstract information because we cannot identify with 'information.' We can, however, identify with 'characters' and so are inclined to store information in story form."[3]

What Is a Story?

You are already an experienced storyteller. Telling stories is how most of us communicate much of the time. You've done it all your life: to update people on friends and family; to justify the decisions you've made; to explain why you're late to an appointment, for that matter. What makes a good story? We ask this question in our workshops all the time. People always say the same things: conflict and resolution.

A story is an account of an event: something happened to somebody. And telling a story couldn't be easier.

1. The story starts by introducing someone in a situation. Something (usually bad) has happened to them. It's often an ordinary person in an extraordinary situation.

2. The story continues by showing how that person works through the situation, often with great difficulty.

3. The story ends when the situation is resolved, with a change for the better—or failure.

The story starts, the story continues, the story ends. Beginning, middle, and end, usually in chronological order. This three-part story structure is simple, obvious, and easy to use. Hollywood has become especially adept at this; it is the formula behind nearly every American movie. You learn about the situation as the film opens. The guts of the film show the heroes—men, women, sometimes animals—struggling with the situation. Then there's a quick wrap-up to show how it all turned out.

But stories don't have to last two hours. Many last just a few seconds. Successful fundraising stories can be very brief. Here's a real one:

> When she entered our third grade, she couldn't spell "cat." And at the end of the year, she could spell "Tchaikovsky."

With a mere 21 words, a charter school that uses music *somehow* to teach the A-B-Cs and 1-2-3s proves to a prospective donor that the school's exotic methods work remarkably well. Most adults, after all, would need to check the spelling of Tchaikovsky. That a formerly nearly illiterate child has in one grade learned to spell a word that's quite challenging seems almost miraculous.

P.S.: Stay alert to reactions. If you tell someone a story like this and the person responds with an exclamation of delight (e.g., "That's incredible!"), there's a good chance the person is predisposed to your cause and suitable for a solicitation.

FUNDRAISING STORIES REPORT RESULTS, WITHOUT LINGERING ON YOUR INNER WORKINGS

You might have noticed: Something's missing in the Tchaikovsky story.

The story has a beginning: A girl can't spell a one-syllable word in her own language. It has an end: The girl can now spell a multisyllabic foreign name with unusual consonantal sounds.

But where's the middle? How did the child get from point A to point B?

She got there because of the school, of course: what its teachers did; their special methods; and its mission: to revive a student's promise. A year's worth of work happened between the beginning and the end. But it happened offstage.

You can skip briskly past the details of how you do your work—and, surprisingly, donors are still happy. They remain generous. U.K. researcher Richard Radcliffe studies donor behavior and thinking. His considered opinion, after thousands of interviews: "Donors are staggeringly ignorant of the charities they support." And that's not a problem.

Your donors, your prospects, and your predisposed don't require all that much information. They *primarily* want reassurance that their gifts have accomplished, or will accomplish, something worthwhile.

The mundane details of how you do your work are secondary. Consultant Annette Simmons, author of a much-praised business book, *The Story Factor*, warns:

People don't want more information. They are up to their eyeballs in information. They want *faith*—faith in you, your goals, your success, in the story you tell. It is faith that moves mountains, not facts. Facts do not give birth to faith. Faith needs a story to sustain it—a *meaningful* story that inspires belief in you and renews hope that your ideas indeed offer what you promise. . . . Faith can overcome any obstacle, achieve any goal.[4]

ANECDOTES VERSUS STATISTICS: WHICH ARE BETTER?

There are two types of proof you can offer donors and prospects, to persuade them that your organization is effective and worthy of support: (1) anecdotal proof and (2) statistical proof.

Which type of proof is better? Scientists would argue that statistical proof is more conclusive. It is irrefutable, rigorously collected, objective, and factual. It is data, and data have no agenda. *Maybe* no agenda. Mark Twain famously quipped, "There are three kinds of lies: lies, damned lies, and statistics." Still, assuming no distortions, no vital omissions, and no attempts to mislead, statistical proof *should* persuade more convincingly than anecdotal proof. In the analytical world, after all, "anecdotal" is a synonym for "suspicious and inadequate." As in: "A few decades ago we had only anecdotal evidence for global warming."

But this is not the case when you're building relationships. In the battle to awaken interest and emotions, anecdotes have clear advantages. Statistics are:

- Cold, distant, unyielding
- Hard to know: only program pros understand their full significance
- Hard to visualize: they are numbers, abstract quantifications, tell rather than show

In sum, statistics are *exclusive* by nature while anecdotes are:

- Warm, revealing, intimate
- Understood by anyone instantly
- Easy to visualize: they are flush with concrete details, dramatic, show rather than tell

In sum, anecdotes are *inclusive* by nature.

Occasionally you'll hear fundraisers liken their case for donor support to a business proposal. As with a business proposal, the analogy goes, you lay out the problem (or opportunity). Then you lay out your organization's solution. Then you punch in the numbers. And you're done. The donor reads your proposal; weighs her decision; and, best case, persuaded by the facts, agrees to make a gift.

A reasonable enough supposition, when you're applying for grant funding. Funding agencies are inclined to be analytical. Reasonable enough, too, if you're asking an individual for a major gift. If someone's wondering whether to give your organization $1 million, he might indeed want answers to some sharp-edged questions. Why does your organization do what it does? Why does your organization wish to pursue some vision? You need to back up your conclusions and actions with hard data.

But people giving an organization $25, $50, $100 are not engaged in carefully weighed cost-benefit analyses. Donors at that level are making something akin to an impulse purchase. Or a leap of faith. They are momentarily writing themselves, via a check or online transaction, into your story, a story of struggle and triumph, in which they hope to play a role. That, in fact, might be the best reason to tell stories: because stories can expand to include other, supporting characters such as prospects and donors.

When people make gifts to your cause, they expect to hear about your accomplishments. What can a donor possibly make of a statistical avalanche such as this summary from an actual annual report?

> Our Food Pantry welcomed 1,539 visits that received five days of groceries matching the needs of 664 different households; households comprised of 680 children, 843 adults and 38 seniors. Open mornings, five days per week, the pantry experienced an average of better than 6 visits per day.

How much of the problem did you solve? How much of the problem is left to solve? How vital is donor help? The evidence you present to donors must answer those basic questions in a way that is fast and easy to visualize. Here's a hypothetical rewrite, then, that rejects unfathomable statistics in favor of easily imagined scenes, while building a case for increased giving:

> When you chose last year to make a gift to the Food Pantry, you helped make something wonderful happen in this town. For some of our most desperate neighbors, you replaced hunger with a measure of hope.
>
> Thanks to your gift and others like it . . .
>
> • Freddie, 5, now wolfs down a well-balanced breakfast every day, something his mom's minimum-wage job can't always guarantee . . .
>
> • Sean, 39, a jack-of-all-trades come north looking for work, can now feed himself and still have some cash left over to send home to his family . . .
>
> • Hazel, 82, a widow living on a tiny fixed income, can now pay her light bill without skipping meals three times a week . . .
>
> Last year, the average gift to the Food Pantry was $47. That won't be enough this year, though. High housing and utility costs continue to exact a toll on thousands. We see more people at our door every week. What policymakers call "food insecurity" among our town's kids, elderly, and low-paid workers has

risen steeply. We will need to double the average gift this year, to $94, to stay even with the urgent need. Will you help?

HANDLING THE TROPHY STATISTIC

Beware the trophy statistic.

A community foundation trumpets this headline on the front page of its donor newsletter: "Unrestricted Grants Reach $5.7 Million in 20th Year." Is this an awe-inspiring number? In the foundation's view, apparently yes. Will the readers agree? We can't know. What we *do* know is that readers will be puzzled; some will even try dividing $5.7 million by 20 years, thinking the quotient might reveal the true meaning.

But it won't, because those big numbers aren't the real story. The real story is that community foundations, including this one, crave unrestricted funds. Foundations are free to spend unrestricted funds on any problem they deem worth a cash intervention. Yet most donors these days don't cooperate. They set up restricted funds instead, so grants only go to specified charities or causes (pets are a favorite). It's a dilemma, certainly. But it's a dilemma that has little to do with the trophy statistic in the headline.

We humans like big numbers. We admire big numbers. We intuitively feel that size matters; the platitude abounds. But big numbers by themselves either tell no story (as the one just cited) or the wrong story. Left to themselves they are big, fat duds.

Big numbers need context.

In scientific photos you will sometimes see a coin added to an exhibit "to show scale." That's what context does: It shows scale. Here's a simple example of why you need that. The statewide environmental advocacy agency in one of America's biggest states, with 10 million residents, boasts that, in its best year, its outreach staff drove almost 17,000 miles, stirring up trouble. But wait: A consultant we know, one professional in a car, drives 20,000 miles every year to work with her clients, in the smallest state in the union, Rhode Island. By comparison, the environmental advocacy agency's trophy number looks puny . . . to us.

Which is the point: You cannot predict which end of the telescope people will view your trophy statistic through, so you have to set the context yourself. On its "Fundraising and Efficiency Facts" web page, the United Negro College Fund doesn't say "UNCF maintains a cost ratio of 17.6 percent of total revenues." It characterizes that statistic: "UNCF maintains a low cost ratio of only 17.6 percent of total revenues." The words *low* and *only* set the context.

Context does something else that is far more important than acting as scale. Context reveals the secret life of your statistic, the "why it matters" part.

USE STATISTICS LIKE A SPEAR

A scientist talking to advertising students explained how to wield a statistic persuasively. "Treat it like a spear. It has just one point. You stick that point in the reader's stomach, then churn it around."

An Edmonton (Alberta) SPCA brochure offers a bright example of the one-statistic-like-a-spear rule. On the cover it says: "Take that gleam out of his eye. Have your pet spayed or neutered." The next panel says: "They can't read or write . . . but they sure can MULTIPLY!" Beneath that is a pyramid comprised of countless cats. It's a chart, and it bears this warning: "One male and one female cat (and their offspring), when left to breed uncontrolled . . . can produce more than 80,000 cats in 10 years!"

Here's another example of the one-stat rule, from a case statement for a $3 million campaign to build a second woman's shelter at My Sister's Place, a Washington, DC, agency: "Half the violent crime reported to the DC police consists of domestic and sexual violence against women. Clearly, two roofs are better than one." Those two sentences were pretty much the entire case.

But it's hard to resist temptation, especially in science-based or data-driven organizations such as hospitals, environmental defense groups, and education reformers. It's like a box of chocolates; who can eat just one? If one statistic was good, two might be even better, and three could be irresistible. Those afflicted with stats love see nothing but good in abundant statistical evidence. Unfortunately, nonspecialists (i.e., your prospects and donors) would rather you didn't; they're interested in stories, not data. Joanne Edgar, a founding editor of *Ms.* magazine, made the same point in a 2006 *Chronicle of Philanthropy* editorial: "without the stories behind the data, these efforts [to explain what we've accomplished] end up seeming like buying a ticket to the movies and [instead] getting a PowerPoint presentation."

HAVE THEMES, THEN TELL STORIES THAT ILLUSTRATE THOSE THEMES

In this book we've talked about using themes as long-term frames for your messages and stories. If you're a community hospital, for instance, you might (since you've conducted focus groups and now know what people *really* think) have as a recurring theme something along these lines:

> If you think a local hospital can't offer state-of-the-art healthcare, think again. We're much more advanced than you probably know. You can trust us to give you and your family great medical care right here in your own community. You don't have to drive 45 minutes to [big city name goes here], because we're hiring those very same doctors to work here, in [local community name goes here].

You don't utter themes like that out loud, of course. Themes like that serve you as rudders: They're in the water, out of sight, to help you steer your organization through the tides of opinion. Themes are what the little voice in head reminds you of when you're speaking to a person, to see if she is predisposed.

First come the themes. Then come the stories. Stories illustrate your themes.

Example: St. Luke's Hospital in New Bedford, Massachusetts, a community hospital, runs a photo of a strapping young man on the front page of its donor newsletter, with this headline: "I'm Grateful to Be Alive—How Great Medical Care Close to Home Saved Brian DeCosta's Life". With those 16 words and a photo, St. Luke's repeats a core theme: "A great community hospital is worth supporting because it could save your, or a loved one's, life someday." The stories change in every issue of the newsletter. But the themes don't, sometimes for years.

Annette Simmons writes about certain "types of stories that will serve you well in your efforts to influence others." These "types of stories"[5] are really themes by another name. Three are particularly useful for fund development purposes:

1. **"Who I Am" stories.** These stories persuade your audience to trust you by revealing your true nature. An organization's true nature is its values. Let's say you're a free clinic. You tell prospects and donors that "We believe everyone deserves decent healthcare, even when they can't afford it." But declarations are just words. They're not proof. To put down deep roots of trust, you also need to *show* your values at work. You do this through the stories you tell: about the doctors who gave up their holidays to volunteer, about penniless patients whose lives were turned around, about the pioneers of the free clinic movement who inspired your efforts, even about the time you *didn't* succeed. Honesty about our flaws builds trust, Simmons points out, because "self-knowledge demonstrates strength."

2. **"Why I Am Here" stories.** Translation: These stories explain "Why am I here in front of you trying to persuade you to do something on my behalf." Simmons says, "Before you tell someone what's in it for them, they want to know what's in it for *you*." She's talking about a situation where one person seeks to influence others. But there is an analogy for nonprofits. Prospects and donors want to know why you are trying to communicate with them. The answer is obvious: "Because we need your help!" Because your organization simply cannot achieve its goals without volunteers and donors and admirers and advocates. Gifts of "time, talent, and treasure" matter very much to you. Without those acts of generosity, your mission goes nowhere, less far, backward (you choose). Be very frank about that: The mission depends on their support ... and you hope it will blossom into a long relationship, deeply satisfying for both sides.

3. **"The Vision" stories.** These stories reveal the benefits of your organization's mission, activities, goals and dreams. These stories talk about what could be, if only we believe. Simmons says, "To live in this world with purpose and meaning we must tell ourselves some story of vision that gives our struggle meaning." Often people become supporters for exactly that reason, to add a bit more purpose and meaning to their lives by participating in a cause. In 2006, HousingWorks RI, a coalition of nonprofits and business, asked Rhode Island voters to pass a $50 million bond that would fund construction of affordable housing, a controversial issue that had met strong community resistance. As the election neared, the coalition launched a high-visibility public relations campaign called "50 stories in 50 days." In a series of ads, e-mails, press releases, and videotaped interviews on a Web site, 50 different working people who already lived in some form of affordable housing talked about "what home means to me." All 50 were vision stories. Voters passed the bond by an overwhelming majority.

WHAT MAKES A STORY WORK? SENSORY DETAIL

Vision stories help other people literally "see" what you see.

The idea is, once others see your organization's ambitions the way you do (and assuming these others are well qualified and predisposed to care in the first place), then they will be ready for your ask, your clarion call to action: "We want you to join us in this mission!"—by donating money, by volunteering, by becoming members, by protesting, by voting for something, and the like.

But, as Annette Simmons reports, "many people do a lousy job" of telling these critical vision stories. She laments the "linear fact-based description that is as appetizing as saying 'cold raw fish tastes good' when [you] should be telling a story about the sensuality of eating sushi."[6]

Simmons makes a vital point. Stories told *without* sensory details tend to bounce off the heart. It's as if Cupid were lazily shooting rubber bands instead of arrows: Nothing much penetrates, and what *does* penetrate takes forever to push through.

There's a reason. We can't "see" abstractions and ideas in our imaginations. But we readily understand sensory details, the same cues we depend on to assess the world around us: tastes, sounds, sights, textures, odors.

Compare this:

> Our library needs to double in size in the near future, to accommodate the community's population increase and the opportunity represented by new technologies.

To this:

> Ten years ago, the front door would occasionally open; and, for a few moments, disturb the library's customary peace and quiet. But that same front door spins more like a revolving door now, as new families join the community, and we add popular services such as free Internet access. We urgently need to expand the library—a lot.

Which description did you find easier to imagine? We're guessing it was the longer one, with the sprinkling of familiar sensory details.

The noise of a door opening, the whoosh-swish of weather-stripping giving way against a shoulder's determined shove, are easily imagined; and " . . . for a few moments, disturb the library's customary peace and quiet." Verbs that describe common actions are easily imagined: "open," and "spins." Plainspoken, non-numerical measurements are easily imagined: "a lot" versus "double." Physical objects such as "front door" and "revolving door" are easily pictured because you've seen and touched them yourself, thousands of times, compiling profound "sense memories" of how such doors look and feel.

Journalists know they can instantly involve a reader by launching their stories with a few sensory details. They ask themselves:

- **What would someone hear if they were witnessing this story?** ("The sound in the classroom was *so* different from what it had been just a few months earlier. No chalk on blackboard, no lecturer explaining, no dogs barking in the village right outside the window, just the rapid click of electronic keyboards.")

- **What would someone smell?** ("The citrus scent of potpourri rose from her bedside table, between her and the visitor, to mask the other scent, faint and not as pleasant.")

- **What would someone see?** ("In a South Side neighborhood where lost hubcaps wired to fences passed as home decor, a nurse pressed her finger against the bell button. This time she heard a deep bell ring inside. She thanked her guardian angel.")

- **What would they feel?** ("The boards sagged beneath his feet. Nothing special about that. The floors always sagged in homes around here. Termites were a local scourge. But he also noticed that everything that could shine, was shined, dusted down to the molecular level, in case company happened by. Pride, the good kind, spoke from every surface.")

- **What might they taste?** ("It wasn't much. There were no second help-ings. But hunger seasoned the thin soup she ladled from her pot. Everyone in the family smacked their lips in anticipation.")

In Conclusion

Storytelling is essential for effective fund development. *Essential*, not optional, for at least two reasons. One, because stories help people understand your mission on an emotional level, where the decision to give begins. Two, because stories are easy to visualize.

The truth is, without stories, your mission can seem pretty boring, and people soon lose interest. To increase giving and improve retention, get the storytelling habit. Tell stories about how your mission is changing a piece of the world. Tell stories about your mission's urgent needs.

Don't fret that you lack some special storytelling "gift." You're already a seasoned storyteller. You tell stories all the time without thinking twice about it— to your colleagues, friends, and loved ones. Persuasive stories about your mission can be remarkably brief, making a point in just a sentence or two. You won't need the training of a professional journalist to tell a tale that short.

ENDNOTES

1. Rudolf Flesch, *The Art of Readable Writing* (New York: Harper & Row, 1949), p. 59.
2. Writing Oct. 1, 2004 for the 2blowhards website, www.2blowhards.com
3. Planned Giving Today (February 2004).
4. Annette Simmons, *The Story Factor*, rev. ed. (New York: Basic Books, 2006), p. 3.
5. Ibid., p. 4
6. Ibid., p. 15

CHAPTER 16

Communications and Social Styles

DID YOU *SEE* WHAT I MEAN?

Rien n'est vrai que ce qu'on ne dit pas. (Nothing is true except what isn't said.)

—JEAN ANOUILH, 1910–1967, FRENCH PLAYWRIGHT

To influence others successfully, we have to accept that all humans negotiate and relate on the basis of only their own perceptions. And we have to become sensitive about how our own style is perceived by the people we want to influence.

—HANS FENNER, QUOTED IN *THE SOCIAL STYLES HANDBOOK*

DEAR READER   This chapter and the next are dedicated to colleague Susan Rice. She's the one who told me "Please don't just write about print communications. Write about how we talk with our donors." Thanks, Susan, you are so right!
Simone

EVERYTHING BUT THE WORDS

Talking with donors is very important. Talking together (i.e., conversation) is how we nurture relationships.

But talking together is more than words. It's also important to understand how we're behaving and how we're perceived. That, too, is communication.

I first saw the importance of voice tone with our family dog Tippy (Lady Tip de Provence). When we talked sweetly, she'd wag her tail and slobber happily, even if we were actually telling her she was a bad dog. If we used a harsh voice and frowned, she'd put her tail between her legs and slink away in shame, even if our words were nice.

For Tippy and all of us, it's not just the words that communicate. It's our nonverbal cues that most affect the transmission of meaning. Or as Tom says to Simone, "It's not what you said that bothers me, it's how you said it!" (And isn't that the problem, sometimes, with e-mail? We're relying on the words of e-mail shorthand. With no other cues, how many times have you wondered if the sender was annoyed or angry? Or, after you pushed "send," wondered if the reader might think you were angry?)

No surprise. Scientific research actually confirms this: *What* you say is less important than *how* you say it. Things like voice, facial expression, and body language all matter a lot when a speaker tries to express meaning or a listener tries to interpret meaning.

Back in the 1970s, Dr. Albert Mehrabian, professor emeritus of psychology at the University of California at Los Angeles and pioneering researcher in communications, discovered that *spoken* communication depends on three elements to convey meaning, the least of which is words:

- Only 7 percent of meaning derives from the words that are spoken
- 38 percent of meaning derives from the *way* we say the words
- 55 percent of meaning derives from nonverbal cues (e.g., body language).[1]

Mehrabian's oft-quoted pioneering research at the University of California, Los Angeles, still holds true today.

> *The essence of lying is in deception, not in words.*
>
> —JOHN RUSKIN, 1819–1900, ENGLISH CRITIC AND ESSAYIST

What you *see* when you listen to me is actually more convincing than the words I use. Lisa at the Rhode Island Free Clinic sees my frown when she tells me, a potential donor, about the uninsured. I lean forward. My voice gets harsh when I talk about the lack of universal healthcare in the United States.

Lisa correctly interprets my anger. She suspects that I might be interested in advocating for different public policy. Naturally she listens to what I say, but she learns even more from observing my behaviors. She asks me to give a gift and join the advocacy efforts.

How do you improve your awareness of communication? Become acquainted with Social Styles.

WHAT DOES "SOCIAL STYLE" MEAN?

Don't worry. This is not about what to wear to cocktail parties!

This is about "behavioral" styles: the observable behaviors of everyone with whom we interact. Behavioral styles affect how we communicate and how others perceive us, which in turn affect our ability to nurture relationships.

The term "Social Styles," coined by the people at Wilson Learning, a global company that provides research, training, and consulting to improve human performance, refers to observable behavior only.[2] "Perception is reality," goes the adage. Your Social Style is how others see *you. Their* Social Style is how you see them.

If you and I want to develop a relationship, you must earn my trust and confidence, and I have to earn yours. As trust and confidence build, we feel more comfortable with each other. Then we're more willing to develop a relationship. And words alone don't do it. Behaviors, in fact, are more critical.

> *Great fundraisers demonstrate strong interpersonal skills.*

Here's what happens: People observe you, and judge and react to your behaviors. Based on that process, people are either comfortable with you or not. They begin to trust you or not. Their comfort with you affects your ability to nurture a relationship with them.

On your side, you watch and listen to them in order to understand their social style. How they behave provides you with clues about how to make them feel comfortable, to build their trust and confidence. Then you can nurture a relationship.

ASSERTIVENESS AND RESPONSIVENESS COME FIRST

> *The art of human interaction ultimately plays the most critical role in building solid relationships.*
>
> —HANS FENNER, QUOTED IN *THE SOCIAL STYLES HANDBOOK*

According to Wilson Learning research, two aspects of interpersonal action—*assertiveness* and *responsiveness*—best measure our behavior with others.

EXHIBIT 16.1   ASSERTIVENESS BEHAVIORS

Ask-Directed	Tell-Directed
Speaks deliberately, often pausing	Speaks quickly and often firmly
Seldom interrupts others	Often interrupts others
Seldom uses voice for emphasis	Often uses voice for emphasis
Makes many conditional statements	Makes many declarative statements
Tends to lean back	Tends to lean forward

Used with permission
References and charts related to the Social Styles training program and to *The Social Styles Handbook* are made with permission of Nova Vista Publishing.

So here's the guide for our interactions. Stick with me. This is useful information.

"Assertiveness" measures how we influence others. "Responsiveness" measures how we express our feelings when relating to others. Again, perception is reality. What matters is how others perceive *how you try to influence* and *how you express your feelings.*

Assertiveness: Measuring How Others See You as You Try to Influence Their Thoughts and Actions

Wilson Learning defines a horizontal continuum for assertiveness. One end of the continuum is called "ask-directed" and the other end is called "tell-directed." Exhibit 16.1 lists aspects of assertiveness, how others perceive how we try to influence others.

Here's an example: A colleague told me I should quit leaning forward while chairing board meetings because it appeared dominating. Yet I was trying to communicate interest. So now I've modified my behavior. I don't lean forward, hoping this better welcomes board member participation.

My leaning-forward moments and my speaking quickly and often firmly are aspects of "tell-directed" assertiveness. That's not bad. There's no good or bad in Social Styles. The only issue is what is comfortable for those with whom you want to build a relationship.

If you've heard me present at a conference, I think you'd agree I'm tell-directed. I get excited and speak firmly. I definitely use my voice for emphasis! I walk into the audience's space and lean forward to speak with people.

Responsiveness: Measuring How Others See You as You Express Your Feelings

Responsiveness is defined as a vertical continuum. At one end of the continuum is "task-directed" and at the other end, "people-directed." See the list of behaviors in Exhibit 16.2. Exhibit 16.3 shows the horizontal and vertical continua combined.

EXHIBIT 16.2   RESPONSIVENESS BEHAVIORS

Task-Directed	People-Directed
Talks more about tasks and facts	Talks more about people and relationships
Uses minimal body gestures	Uses broad, expansive body gestures
Shows a narrow range of personal feelings to others	Shows a broad range of personal feelings to others
Uses limited facial expressions	Uses varied and open facial expressions and varies voice tones

Used with permission.
References and charts related to the Social Styles training program and to *The Social Styles Handbook* are made with permission of Nova Vista Publishing.

I think I'm more at the "people-directed" end of this continuum. I use many different tones of voice. My facial expressions and body language are active, even dramatic. I also disclose personal feelings in various settings, a sure sign of "people-directedness."

Those who express their feelings through task-directed responsiveness are more reserved. They usually deal with tasks first and then engage interpersonally.

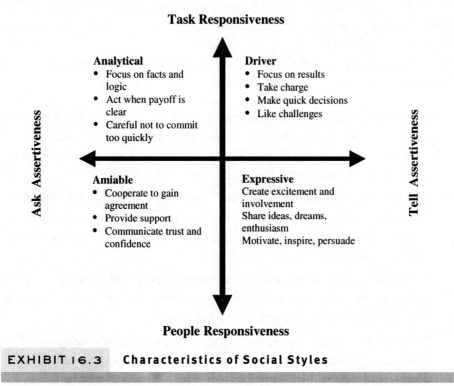

Task Responsiveness

Analytical
- Focus on facts and logic
- Act when payoff is clear
- Careful not to commit too quickly

Driver
- Focus on results
- Take charge
- Make quick decisions
- Like challenges

Ask Assertiveness

Tell Assertiveness

Amiable
- Cooperate to gain agreement
- Provide support
- Communicate trust and confidence

Expressive
Create excitement and involvement
Share ideas, dreams, enthusiasm
Motivate, inspire, persuade

People Responsiveness

EXHIBIT 16.3   Characteristics of Social Styles

Used with permission.
References and charts related to the Social Styles training program and to *The Social Styles Handbook* are made with permission of Nova Vista Publishing.

Remember: No place on either continuum is better or worse. Nothing is good or bad in the discussion of Social Styles. However, when we are nurturing relationships, being versatile by modifying our assertiveness and responsiveness behaviors may be more effective, depending on the style of the person we are connecting with. We want to be very aware and flexible. If we understand where we are perceived on the continuum, we can moderate our behavior to make others more comfortable, by closely matching their behavior.

Examine yourself. Where do you think you fall on the assertiveness and responsiveness scales? Where do your most important relationships fall? A fully functional donor profile catalogs more than the dry facts. It can also note aspects of the donor's ways of interacting and Social Style.

What's Your Social Style?

Wilson Learning has identified four Social Styles: Analyticals, Drivers, Amiables, and Expressives.[3]

Researchers profile people into these four behavioral styles. The styles are equally divided across the population. Of course, this means that your own style will not align with 75 percent of the people you meet! That's why versatility matters so much. If you are versatile, you modify your own style a bit to make others more comfortable.

The minidescriptions of the four Social Styles presented here are just the tip of the iceberg.

- **Analyticals like facts and figures.** They're most comfortable with logic and reason. These individuals are deliberate and thorough, businesslike and methodical, precise and predictable. They may be more reserved in their relationships. Lots of enthusiasm may cause them discomfort.

- **Drivers like to drive the bus.** You know: focus and direction, forcefulness and certainty, intensity, options, quick decisions, and challenge. These individuals may be more formal in their behaviors. They control their emotions and may appear impersonal.

- **Amiables are friendly and warm, supportive, and receptive.** They enjoy personal interaction, shared responsibility, and consensus. They are more likely to tell stories and offer compliments.

- **Expressives are energetic, inspiring, emotional, and engaging.** Expressives are intuitive, enthusiastic, spirited, creative, and visionary. They'll share lots of personal information, along with ideas and needs.

Now take a look at Exhibit 16.3, which shows the horizontal continuum of assertiveness and the vertical continuum of responsiveness combined with key characteristics of Social Styles. Use this snapshot to help you begin thinking about your own behaviors and the behaviors you observe in others.

Let's see. From what others tell me, I think I'm a Driver with some shared behaviors of Expressives and Amiables. I'm mostly not an Analytical. From what I hear, I think that's how others perceive me. Sometimes I can be *ask assertive* for a short period of time, but I'm most comfortable being *tell assertive*. I'm more comfortable with other drivers, expressives, and amiables.

As I write this, I'm thinking about a meeting I have today. I realize that one of the meeting participants is an Analytical. I'm having some trouble communicating with her, and I imagine she's experiencing the same thing. I watch when I respond to her comments and questions. My communication isn't working well. I need to modify my Social Style to improve my communication with her if I want to nurture a relationship. Looking at the matrix in Exhibit 16.3, I think I'll try to:

- Lay out the facts clearly and briefly in writing. Provide these in advance so she can read and absorb.
- Face the fact that she probably needs two meetings to make a decision.
- Carefully construct a rationale that focuses on facts and results.
- Avoid using metaphors or talking about vision.
- Moderate my own enthusiasm and excitement and be more factual.

ARE YOU COMFORTABLE? ARE OTHERS?

Are your donors and board members and solicitors comfortable? Typically, people are most comfortable with those who are most like them. And this certainly holds true for Social Styles. You are most comfortable with someone who shares your Social Style or at least shares some commonality with your style (see Exhibit 16.3).

I remember a workshop about how to solicit gifts personally. Several of the attendees remarked, "We don't have board members who can talk as clearly, enthusiastically, and passionately as you can, Simone!" But wonderful Beth Stafford executive director of the Manchester Area Conference of Churches, said: "I don't want all my solicitors to be like Simone. Some of my donors are quiet and shy. A solicitor like Simone would overwhelm and threaten those donors." Beth fundamentally understood the matching of Social Styles to make people comfortable.

It's not just about matching people based on their Social Styles. It's also about modifying your own Social Style to make others more comfortable. That's versatility.

ARE YOU VERSATILE?

Versatility in Social Styles is critical to nurturing relationships. You modify your own behaviors to help others be more comfortable with you. You focus on others above yourself. You risk your own discomfort to ensure the comfort of others.

> *Using Versatility requires that you recognize which Social Style differences are operating in your relationships and decide to behave differently to make your relationships better.*
>
> —HANS FENNER, QUOTED IN *THE SOCIAL STYLES HANDBOOK*

Versatile people can anticipate the perception problems that cause so many problems in communications and relationships. But only if they remember these three critical points:

1. **Seeing is believing, and perception is reality.** (That's how others will interpret you. How do you appear to your donors and volunteers?)

2. **What we think we see and perceive isn't always what was intended.** Nor is it necessarily true. Maybe we're misreading or maybe we're not paying good enough attention. (Be cautious as you observe and communicate with others. How well do you understand your board members?)

3. **Self-perception doesn't always align with how others perceive us.** And what we think we're projecting may not resonate that way with others. (Remember me leaning forward when chairing those board meetings?)

A FEW CAVEATS

First: Everyone behaves most comfortably in the patterns of their particular Social Style: Analytical, Driver, Amiable, or Expressive. But everyone has the ability to temporarily exhibit some behaviors from other styles. Also, people don't behave consistently in every situation. There's lots of mixing and matching of behaviors out there.

Second: Social Styles focus on observable behaviors only. This concept does not apply to thoughts and feelings, which are internal to each of us. We can learn to better observe and understand people's behavior. But, depending on the intimacy of the relationship, we may or may not understand the thoughts and feelings of those others.

Third: Don't worry about changing your Social Style. That doesn't happen. Instead, focus on temporary modifications in your Social Style to make others more comfortable. With comfort, you can build trust and confidence. And that's how you nurture relationships. You're still you. You're not faking being someone else.

Last: Like any methodology, Social Styles provides generalizations and judgments. Use this tool with great sensitivity and respect for individuals and differences. We all know the value of generalizations; they help us learn and be more sensitive. And we know the risk: stereotyping.

In Conclusion

Fundraisers are often great relationship builders. They're sensitive and insightful, observant and caring. But here's what I'm thinking: If we understood and applied Social Styles, we could improve communication and relationship building more.

Familiarity with Wilson Learning's Social Styles and versatility increases your awareness and sensitivity. Understanding assertiveness and responsiveness helps you modify your behaviors for different people and in different situations. And if you're both willing and able to modify your behavior to put others at ease, that's the versatility part! The most versatile individuals succeed the best at nurturing relationships. Just imagine what more you could accomplish.

▉ ENDNOTES

1. Albert Mehrabian wrote *Silent Messages: Implicit Communication of Emotions and Attitudes,* (Belmont, CA: Wadsworth, 1981) and dozens of other works.
2. See Wilson Learning at www.wilsonlearning.com. Strategic Enhancement Group, a partner of Wilson Learning Worldwide, works with nonprofits as well as for-profits. Maybe your board and development staff would benefit from Strategic Enhancement [Bob Parks] training like the United Way did. See www.strategicenhancement.com.
3. Do these sound familiar? Tom always talks about the four personality types of readers: the amiables, the expressives, the skeptics, and the bottom-liners. See Chapter 13.

CHAPTER 17

Conversation Nurtures Relationships

ASKING QUESTIONS TO LEARN MORE

For enthusiasts conversation is an art, one of the great pleasures of life, even the basis of civilized society.

—"CHATTERING CLASSES," THE ECONOMIST

Conscious leaders have the ability to listen simultaneously to three dimensions of language—the factual, the intentional, and the transformational. They pick up factual details with the precision of the scientist; gain insight into the intention of the speaker with the imagination of a poet, and are willing to be transformed by what they hear with the zeal of a pilgrim.

—DEBASHIS CHATTERJEE, LEADING CONSCIOUSLY: A PILGRIMAGE TOWARD SELF-MASTERY

DEAR READER   Chapter 3 discusses conversation and questions as core business practices. In this chapter, I explore conversation and questions designed to learn about interests, emotions, and aspirations.

This chapter is mainly a compendium of questions. Some absolutely essential questions to ask if an organization wants to develop any kind of relationship. Some great questions that can deepen most relationships. And some possibly awkward questions, applicable in rare (and I hope less rare) situations.

I start with a brief aside about the bottom-line questions you need to explore when asking for a gift. But fair warning: That's not the focus of this chapter.

Simone ▓

A Quick Aside: Questions Related to Solicitation

Before asking for a gift, fundraisers generally have a good idea about the answers to these six questions:

1. What's the right project for this prospect or donor?

2. What's the right request amount, and when would be the right time to ask?

3. Who would be the right person to do the asking?

4. What kinds of stories during the ask would best reflect the prospect's interests and emotions?

5. What might be the barriers to the request, and how will we overcome these barriers?

6. What kind of payment mechanism might be appropriate?

And fundraisers ought to explore these questions with prospects and donors, too:

- Do you have enough money to live on for the rest of your life?

- What do you want to do for your heirs?

Part of nurturing relationships before asking is finding out the answers to these questions.

But neither this book nor this chapter focuses on soliciting. This chapter is all about earlier questions: questions that stimulate conversation and nurture relationships.

I warn you: You might be uncomfortable answering these questions or asking them. Some of these questions may not work for some of the people and organizations you're nurturing relationships with. Use your insights and experience to decide what works for you and for those with whom you are nurturing relationships. It's up to you.

Purpose of This Conversation

I'm describing conversation as a strategy to nurture relationships of all kinds for your organization. I'm promoting relationships as an end, not merely a means to secure gifts of time, advice, and money.

Yes, the questions in my aside are critically important. But this isn't a book about asking for gifts. I'm talking about relationship-building questions: questions to help you learn about interests, emotions, and aspirations. Yes, pursuing asking the questions helps nurture the relationship. But not for a while.

Honoring Conversation

Conversation is at the center of what it means to be human.[1] People connect through conversation. We learn about each other, building trust and understanding. In conversation, we nurture relationships both personal and professional.

Madame De Staël, renowned eighteenth-century hostess of French salons, said that conversation is

> a means of reciprocally and rapidly giving one another pleasure; of speaking just as quickly as one thinks; of spontaneously enjoying one's self; of being applauded without working. . . . [A] sort of electricity that causes sparks to fly, and that relieves some people of the burden of their excess vivacity and awakens others from a state of painful apathy.[2]

That back-and-forth movement engages participants in a sharing process. We often repeat or build on language used by the other conversationalists. When face to face, our body movements actually begin to synchronize one with the other. We clarify what each other said in order to better understand. We validate what each other means and feels, even if we don't agree. As we talk, we may confirm shared values. And in special cases, this conversation is transforming.

These days, conversation is not just oral but also written. Think about how e-mail and instant messaging provide conversational media across space and time, as unique as the telephone in its day.

Naturally, conversation is as much about silence as it is about talking. As my friend Sarah Coviello, CFRE, said to me: "Listen as the desire to learn sincerely, not to give the right answer or get the gift."

> The best relationship builders are good conversationalists. And great fundraisers use conversation to nurture relationships.

Conversation includes listening and observing. "Optimal, active listening is a multisensory act in which you use your eyes, ears and emotions—even the way you sit and look at the person speaking—to perceive feeling and content."[3] Then you think about what's been shared and what it means. This helps nurture relationships.

Think about the best conversations you've experienced. What made them good? Ask others what contributed to their greatest conversations. See

---

EXHIBIT 17.1   TEN TIPS TO CREATE GREAT CONVERSATIONS

1. Body language and eye contact that communicates attention
2. Active listening that communicates respect and caring
3. Genuine curiosity that demonstrates interest
4. Enough self-disclosure to identify common ground
5. Vocabulary and stories that are culturally sensitive and appropriate
6. Requesting clarification for comments made
7. Asking questions to test your own perceptions of others
8. Validating that which is shared by others
9. Responsiveness to the Social Styles, vocabulary, and stories of those with whom you are conversing
10. Taking turns with roles in the conversation, for example, listening and talking

---

Exhibit 17.1: Which of these elements were present in the best conversations? Now do your best to re-create these experiences over and over.

Active Listening

Descartes said, "I think, therefore I am." And Anonymous said, "I have been listened to, therefore I am." That's the power of listening.

If you are truly listening, then you are present and focused. You hear the said and unsaid. But sometimes I catch myself doing e-mail while talking on the phone. Multitasking, sure. Respectful listening, no.

You listen for people's interests. You listen to their language and the messages they communicate. You listen for their emotions. You listen for the *meaning*, not just the words. In fact, you listen mostly for the meaning and not as much for the words.

You try to hear the said and the unsaid. You watch for the nonverbal cues. That means you observe as you listen, if you are face to face. You listen to the tone if you are on the telephone. Finally, you demonstrate that you are listening through your own nonverbal and verbal cues.

> *Celui qui ne sait pas se taire sait rarement bien parler. (He who doesn't know how to be quiet rarely knows how to speak well.)*
>
> —PIERRE CHARRON, 1541–1603, FRENCH PHILOSOPHER

Listening . . . Sort Of

Pay attention to these four "stumbling blocks" to good listening.[4] (And remember, good listening means 100 percent focus. Watch out for the multitasking!)

1. **Rehearsal.** While I'm listening to you, I'm actually figuring out how I will respond to your comments. While rehearsing my response, I cannot devote 100 percent of my focus on you, what you're saying, and how you're saying it.

2. **Selective.** I'm screening what you're saying with my own assumptions. Actually, I'm hoping what you say will reinforce my own thinking. I'm not really hearing you. Instead, I'm choosing what I want to hear.

3. **Sporadic.** I'm in and out with my listening. I'm hearing you, but then my mind wanders. I'm hearing only part of what you say.

4. **Surface.** This sounds a bit like the analyticals in the four personality types discussed in Chapter 13. "I'm listening for the facts and figures. I really like data. I'm not paying attention to your emotions." Now, that's a problem, because psychological research says that human decisions are triggered by emotions.

Imagine a conversation with one of your donors. You're listening, but only somewhat. Actually you suffer from one (or more) of the listening blocks. (Remember, we all suffer from some of them sometimes.) Just imagine what you will miss. Imagine how that will affect your stewardship, your cultivation, and your solicitation. You may pick the wrong approaches. You may offend the donor. You may lose the gift. And worse yet, you could lose the donor.

Listening is relationship building. People want to be heard, and listening is the highest form of respect.

—Diana DiResta, DiResta Communications

Observing

Remember Dr. Albert Mehrabian's research on the greater importance of nonverbal cues when listening to the spoken word discussed in Chapter 16? Observe well. In fact, my colleague Sandra Adams, noted: Good fundraisers must know their subject matter so well that they can pay attention to everything else.

Observe the behaviors of social styles. Watch how people present themselves. Look at their personal or professional environment. What do your observations suggest to you? How can you use what you see to ask questions?

Consider, for example, me, Simone Joyaux. What would you see? People often comment on my jewelry and clothes. Why? Because both are often different and often make bold statements.

That's intentional on my part. And only recently have I realized why: Since I was a child, I have felt different, for all sorts of reasons. (That's a story for another day!) Now I relish being different. I want to communicate that difference. And my appearance is one tool. Nurturing a relationship with me—including a major donor relationship—requires understanding how and why I perceive myself as different. What's one implication of my feeling different? I tend to align with causes and people who are treated inequitably because they are perceived as different.

What do you observe about your donors? How often do you visit them in their personal and professional environments? What do you see?

Genuine Inquisitiveness

The bottom line: Curiosity is vitally important. Genuine inquisitiveness is a hallmark of interesting people. Moreover, curiosity is an important business strategy, fundamental to nurturing relationships and building effective organizations. This quote about Sir Isaac Newton sums it up:

> *Millions saw the apple fall, but Newton asked why.*
>
> —BERNARD BARUCH, 1870–1965, AMERICAN FINANCIER AND PRESIDENTIAL ADVISOR

STARTING A CONVERSATION: WHY TALKING ABOUT THE WEATHER IS GOOD

The Big Moo tells a wonderful story about talking about the weather. The story begins with the usual disclaimer about this topic: It's boring, a waste of time, used when no on can think of anything better. And I suspect that many think, only losers talk about the weather.

But then the author had one of those aha moments: The weather affects everyone. So maybe talking about it wasn't really so inane after all.

The author proposes that perhaps talking about the weather could be a way to reach out and make an initial contact, to find a small way to connect with someone else. Asking about the weather could be the first gambit to start a meaningful conversation.

After all, it's a bit much to begin a conversation with something earth-shattering, such as "What do you think of climate change?" Or perhaps: "What is most important in your life?" Or even: "What is your favorite film, the one novel you'd take to that desert island, and by the way, for whom do you plan to vote?"

According to *The Big Moo,* "honoring the simple reality of another person's experience is an instant link to the bigger world outside one's self. It's the seed of empathy, and it's free." Here's the author's list about why talking about the weather is good:

- Weather is egalitarian in its delivery.
- Weather is fundamentally inoffensive.
- Weather is completely accessible.
- No one is ignorant about the weather.
- Even shy people are willing to share their personal feelings about the weather.
- It's hard not to smile when you ask 'hot enough for you?'[5]

Now customize this for you and your organization. If you don't want to talk about the weather, what could be your opening gambit? What would be nonthreatening, egalitarian, inoffensive, accessible, and sufficiently familiar that no one would feel excluded? Maybe it's something in your community or in your organization. Maybe it's something else entirely. Or maybe it's just the weather. Just think about it.

WHAT IS IMPORTANT TO THOSE IN YOUR RELATIONSHIPS?

Don't presume and don't assume what is important to others. Ask them! The more you know about those with whom you nurture relationships, the stronger those relationships can be. Ask them regularly because things change. Relationships are dynamic, not static.

> *We need to be prepared to care about their response [to our questions]. They will not care about how much we know until they know how much we care.*
>
> —JAMIE CAPPETTA, COHORT 16, MASTER'S PROGRAM, PHILANTHROPY AND DEVELOPMENT, SAINT MARY'S UNIVERSITY

Conversations deepen as relationships deepen. You don't begin a deeper level of conversation unless you receive those signals. Some conversations—just like some relationships—never deepen much. That's fine; whatever is appropriate for those in the relationship. Other conversations may begin at a high level of intimacy. Often these relationships deepen quickly.

Effective relationship builders and great fundraisers figure this all out. Their interpersonal skills and sensitivity leap to the fore for this work.

Here's a Framework That Might Help You Discern What's Important

Take a look at this framework developed by Tracey Biles, Cohort 15, Master's Program in Philanthropy and Development at Saint Mary's University. The framework really resonated with Tom and me so I've made a few minor adjustments. I'd use it as a tool to help volunteers grasp the dimensions of conversation as a relationship-building strategy.

When using the framework, you might or might not actually refer to sand castles, rocks, and pebbles with donors and volunteers. You might only keep those terms in your own mind to help manage the conversation. For some people, you might actually explain the metaphor. It's your decision.

Sand Castle Framework   Tracey uses a sand castle metaphor to explore donor and volunteer motivations. Her sand castle is made up of four building materials:

1. **Big rocks.** What is most important to the volunteer or donor? These "rocks" define the person's individuality and form the foundation of the individual's life. Typically they include the individual's values and belief structure.

2. **Medium-size rocks.** What are the "drivers" in the life of the volunteer or donor? These "rocks" provide impetus and motivation. While not as important as the big rocks, these drivers make life better.

3. **Pebbles.** What are the time-fillers in the life of the donor or volunteer? These "pebbles" are neither important like the big rocks, nor do they make life better, like the medium-size ones. However, individuals still pay significant attention to these areas.

4. **Sand.** What does the volunteer or donor do to feel full? Sand fills in all the spaces between the various size rocks and pebbles. Sometimes these things make people happy, but sometimes they're irritants. These items are squeezed in wherever and whenever. However, in the grand scheme of things, these things are not necessary.

Questions   With this framework in mind, consider the questions that Biles proposes for each element of her sand castle. Think about how you could apply the questions to help identify the predisposed, qualify them as prospects, and nurture relationships with them. Consider using these questions to help your volunteers and donors better understand their engagement with your organization. With increased understanding, they might better articulate what they expect of your organization. Through these conversations, you'll learn more, too.

Big-Rock Questions:

1. What is the most important element in your life?
2. How did you decide this was the most important element in your life? Who and what influenced your decision about the importance of this element?
3. Five years ago, what was the most important element in your life?
4. What do you think your answer will be five years from now?
5. How would someone know that _____ is the most important element in your life?

Medium-Size-Rock Questions:
1. Aside from your "biggest rock," what are you most passionate about?
2. Why are you passionate about these things?
3. When and how did you realize that this is where your passion is?
4. How have you nurtured this passion in your life?
5. How do your "big rocks" fit in with your passion?

Pebble Questions:
1. On your daily list of to-dos, what are the things that must get done?
2. How does your to-do list reflect that which is most important to you (the big rocks)?
3. How does your to-do list affect the pursuit of your passion (your medium-size rocks)?
4. In thinking about your day, where do you spend most of your time, with the big rocks, medium-size ones, pebbles, or sand?
5. What motivates you to spend your time in such a way?
6. If _____ didn't fill up so much of your time, what would you do instead?
7. What part of your everyday life brings you the most joy?
8. Do you feel appreciated for all your pebbles?
9. What's the biggest pebble you'd like to eliminate from your life? Why?
10. What must you do to eliminate that pebble?

Sand Questions:
1. What gets squeezed into your life?
2. Which "sand" item brings you contentment, and which one is an irritant?
3. What motivates you to hang on to the "sand" item that irritates you?

4. What would it take to get rid of the irritating sand?

5. How does the sand interact with your big rocks?

Adjust these questions for use with diverse relationships. Also, consider how you would use these questions to assess your organization. For example, apply these questions to departments, teams, the board, and employees.

YOUR DONORS AND YOUR MISSION

Donors may not fully understand your mission. But that's not a great concern.

Your donors interpret your mission based on their own interests and aspirations. They understand your mission through their own lens, in keeping with their own emotions and life experiences. Donor understanding is rooted in their own life experience.

When you are donor-centered, you want to understand their interpretation of your mission. You nurture a relationship based on their perceptions. But you neither mislead nor misrepresent your values, mission, and vision.

But what if they misinterpret your mission? First, don't expect people to recite your mission statement. That really isn't important. Listen instead for:

- How donors and volunteers explain why you exist
- Why they believe you are important
- Why they believe your results matte.

If they actually think you are another organization, tell them that. Otherwise, you are masquerading, and that's unprofessional and unethical. Yes, you might lose them as donors—but another organization doing equally important work may well gain them.

It's more likely, however, that your donors and volunteers are interpreting your organization in ways that resonate for them personally. And that's just fine. Capture their comments. Use their testimonials.

> *The best fundraisers are philanthropists themselves. Otherwise, how can fundraisers have meaningful conversations with prospects and donors?*

Ask Your Donors Why

Always ask your donors why. Treasure their comments because comments give you important insights. Learn their interests and disinterests so that you can design appropriate relationship-building strategies. Respect their emotions so that you can create aligned solicitation strategies. Use their observations and their questions to develop your various communications and solicitation materials.

Speak with your donors regularly. Remember that people change. Their interests and aspirations evolve. Their answers may be different after time passes. And you need to know this information.

Ask the parties in your relationship "what's new?" For example: What's new in their lives? What do they see as new in the relationship with your organization? What do they see as new in the cause you and they espouse? What most concerns them—why, and why now?

Here are four questions that you can use and modify for the predisposed, your prospects, and your donors and volunteers. You can modify lots of these questions for use with partner organizations. As a donor and volunteer yourself, what are your answers to these questions?

1. I used to give to _____, but now I don't because _____.

2. I am a donor to _____ because _____.

3. I am very loyal to _____ because _____.

4. I used to *not* give to _____, but now I do because _____.

Ask Questions about Your Organization Specifically

I think these five questions are basic. Ask those you've identified as predisposed. Ask your qualified prospects. Most certainly, ask your donors and volunteers these questions. And you can certainly ask these questions of organizations you hope to partner with.

1. What interests you most about this organization? What is less interesting to you?

2. Why do you give to this organization? What does our mission mean to you? How would you describe our mission?

3. What are the most critical results you expect our organization to produce?

4. Why have you given to this organization for so many years?

5. What do you tell others about us? How do you describe this organization to others?

Ask Questions about Your Cause

I think these four questions are basic, too. Don't just ask about your organization. Ask about the cause—because that may well be where the allegiance lies. For example:

1. Why does this cause matter to you? Why now in particular?

2. What do you believe would most transform this particular situation?

3. Which other organizations effectively address this cause?

4. How does our organization compare to other organizations working in this cause?

Ask About Their Giving Habits

1. Where else do you give, and why?

2. What are the common themes and interests that cross your giving and volunteering?

Find Out Their Values and Beliefs

To dig more deeply into donor values, try some of these questions. What would work best for which one of your donors, volunteers, or prospects? How would you modify any of the questions proposed here?

1. If you could change the world, what would you do?

2. What actions do you think would best cause the change you envision?

3. What are the most critical catalysts to produce the change you hope for?

4. What changes do you believe would make the world a better place?

5. What would you like to pass on to future generations?

6. What would you like to pass on to the next generation—for your children, your nieces and nephews, the children of others?

7. How would you like to make a difference in this community? In this world?

8. How do you feel when you make a gift?

9. Would you share with me your life's journey? (Or some variation of this question.)[6]

10. Who have been the leaders and mentors in your life's journey? Why and how they affected you?

11. Share with me your beliefs and values about life, society, and the world.

12. What are your joys and fears, your hopes and worries?

13. What makes you angry and sad? What makes you hopeful and happy? Or another version: What are the deepest desires of your heart?

14. If you had a personal mission statement or slogan, what would it say?

I suspect that volunteers, donors, and prospects are sending messages that answer many of these questions. But are fundraisers and their organizations paying sufficient attention?

> *How do you want to be remembered?*
>
> —CAROL GOLDEN, EXECUTIVE VICE PRESIDENT AND CHIEF PHILANTHROPY OFFICER,
> THE RHODE ISLAND FOUNDATION

CONVERSATION WITH DONORS AT THE RHODE ISLAND FOUNDATION

This story aptly demonstrates two steps in the relationship-building process, specifically gaining deeper understanding (Step #3) and nurturing the relationship (Step #5). Chapter 10 discusses these two steps in detail.

Ten years ago, Carol Golden and Rick Schwartz began interviewing endowment donors to The Rhode Island Foundation, because legacy is implicit in their gifts. Carol is executive vice president and chief philanthropy officer at the foundation. Rick was the vice president for communications.

These interviews reflected their deeply held belief that the act of giving and the ultimate power/use of that gift should never be separate. For example, when scholarships are given, both the recipient and the media receive background about why the donor established the scholarship fund. The foundation's newsletters and annual reports regularly feature donor stories. And donors give testimonials at the annual donor thank-you party.

But these interviews . . . wow. Donors responded incredibly well. As Rick noted, "Most people, even if they deny it, really would like to believe that their gift lives. It's the salvation thing, just like Tom [Ahern] always says! . . . I've seen in their faces their joy that someone—usually the first time ever—is sitting down and asking about their lives!"

What was the benefit to The Rhode Island Foundation? "We learned a lot about charitable giving from these interviews: why people give, the effect of their parents' model, and what happened to them personally that led to a desire to give."

But most important, "the interview has immediately catapulted our relationship to individuals to a very personal space. That distinguishes us in their minds (and ours) from every other 'financial' relationship, and often even their relationships with their favorite nonprofits."

> *Think about the transforming power of conversation.*

Rick and Carol found that their donors share remarkable amounts of information during the interviews. Rick said, "I am continually surprised when I bump into folks I've interviewed at other venues, and they greet me like an old friend. For many, I am their emotional connection to the foundation. And a lot of our repeat business has come from our using the interview to move the relationship deeper and faster."

Rick shared the basic outline of these interviews—but reminds us all: "I listen for unexpected answers, lines of questioning that I should follow instead of marching along with my list of questions."

Interview Outline:

1. **Early chronological questions.** Finding out whether parents were a major factor in the interviewee's decision to "give back." Also finding out if there is a connection to "place," for example, Rhode Island.
   a. Asking about their parents. Their names, what kind of work they did, and how they came to be in Rhode Island.
   b. Asking about their parents' charitable inclinations. Did they volunteer a lot? Was their faith important to them? Did they give money? Did they "model" charitable behavior for the interviewee? What would they think about the interviewee's decision to create an endowment?
   c. Asking about the interviewee's childhood. Was it happy or unhappy? Where did they grow up, and what was it like? If it was Rhode Island, what has changed since they were kids? Where did they attend school, and how did that impact their life?
   d. Asking about first jobs or further education. Why did they choose a particular type of work or a particular major in school? How has their work impacted their life and why?

2. **Learning about their adult lives, work, and family and how they are intertwined.** If Rick is interviewing a couple, he interviews one person first up to the marriage, then he interviews the other person up to the marriage. Then he asks the couple about their life together. If there is a mate, Rick asks how the two met. He notes that this "usually lightens up the conversation since it's almost always a sweet story."

3. **Talking about charity.** When did you decide to make this gift and why? Why did you select the Rhode Island Foundation? What are the particular issues that you care about and why?

4. **And then Carol asks, "How do you want to be remembered?"**

Envision the power of that question: How do you want to be remembered? Ask yourself: "I lived. I will die. In the interval, what difference did I make?"

Rick noted that most of his colleagues who conduct interviews just ask question #3, about the donor's charity. That's probably what most of us do. After all, the questions in this story take a lot of time to ask. And so do so many of the questions throughout this book.

But what a shame to ask only one question. What a loss to cut short the conversation.

That's fine for a testimonial quote or a brief story in a newsletter. But short conversations don't teach you the most. But the charity question alone will not strengthen the relationship between your donors and your organization.

Without the great background questions that Rick and Carol ask, you will not gain any real understanding about the motivations of a donor. Your organization will not understand the donor's emotions, interests, and aspirations.

Pay particular attention to this last thought that Rick shared:

> These questions feel rather cool and superficial. I can only assure you that the interviewer's real curiosity, the sincerity with which Carol and I ask the questions, our sincere interest in the answers, our willingness to listen hard so that we follow strands of thoughts to their logical conclusions, are all essential to the interview and turn this into a fairly emotional experience. I'm always pretty drained by the end, and I think they are too. But it almost always ends with great appreciation on both sides and real warmth. So odd, yet so gratifying.

Surely this is a transformational experience. The donor is transformed by making his or her gift. The recipient organization is transformed by the donor's personal story.

But there was another transformation. We—Tom and Simone—were in that room being interviewed by Carol and Rick. It wasn't an interview. Not really. It was an authentic conversation. We were deepening the relationship between donor and organization and between genuinely caring individuals in the relationship. We disclosed the undisclosed. We shared emotions. It was draining. Tom and Simone were transformed again. We would like to think that Carol and Rick were, too.

In Conclusion

When Rick reviewed this chapter prior to publication, he sent me an e-mail responding to the implied question in my last sentence: "We would like to think that Carol and Rick were, too."

Rick said: "Yes, I was transformed. We had been colleagues until then; now we had shared."

Through authentic questioning and genuine curiosity, we create conversation. With candor and honest disclosure, we create intimacy in a relationship. By careful probing, we demonstrate caring for the interests and aspirations of others.

ENDNOTES

1. Coincidentally, while writing this book, Britain's global magazine *The Economist* published "Chattering Classes: The Rules for Verbal Exchanges are Surprisingly Enduring," December 19, 2006, pages 79–81. Moving from the year 44 BC to contemporary times, this delightful article traces the history of conversation. From Cicero's "rules for ordinary conversation" to the great salons of seventeenth- and eighteenth-century France, from political conversation in eighteenth-century British coffee houses to dinner in restaurants worldwide.
2. Ibid., p. 81.
3. Mary Ellen Collins, "Do You Hear What I Hear?" *Advancing Philanthropy* (November/December 2006): 24.
4. Ibid. Collins also cites Diane DiResta, www.diresta.com, and Jim Pratt, www.listen.org as sources in her article.
5. Group of 33, *The Big Moo: Stop trying to be Perfect and Start Being Remarable,* Ed. Seth Godin, (New York: Portfolio Penguin Group) 2005.
6. Elizabeth Hollander, former president and CEO of Campus Compact, developed questions #9 and #10.

CHAPTER 18

The Case for Support

WHY *SHOULD* ANYONE GIVE YOU MONEY?

The case is the strategy for raising money.

—Karla A. Williams, ACFRE

DEAR READER   These days I'm writing about a case a month. I've realized, on my best days, I'm not writing mere cases, I'm really writing *songs*, songs the organization can sing to a prospective donor. Like songs, good cases are lushly emotional. They tell stories. And every once in a while you slip in a statistic to keep things honest.
Tom

INTRODUCTION

If you're planning a capital campaign, then you likely already know that you will need a case statement.

A case statement is an essential tool for raising large sums, whether your goal is bricks-and-mortar, endowment, or a war chest for some new initiative. The case informs, by describing your project. The case inspires, by showing why the project matters so much. And the case helps your volunteer solicitors succeed, by putting in their hands a clear vision and effective talking points.

"But note this," writes Jerry Panas in his remarkable book, *Making the Case*. "The Case Statement is just as important for ongoing, annual giving. Just as important for planned giving. And for corporate gifts. And foundation grants. If you are interested in raising funds, your institution needs a current Case Statement. Period!"[1]

A good, up-to-date case statement is a key organizational asset. (See Exhibit 18.1 for an award-wining example of a case.) The case explains who you are, why you matter, what you've accomplished, and where you are going. It is your agency's most fundamental communications document. It is the source of all your messaging. It is the blueprint and basis for every effort you make to influence donors and prospects, through your direct mail, your Web site, your newsletters, your annual report and other brochures, your advertising, your public relations, and your events. (See Appendix 18A for Simone Joyaux's seminar handout: "Thoughts about creating a case for support.")

PRELIMINARY STEPS

Before you can craft a successful case for support, take these two preliminary steps:

1.   Collect information about the organization.
2.   Sort that information into categories that answer the donor's three big questions (discussed later in this chapter).

Step #3 will be telling your story. You might be tempted to skip the first two steps, on the reasonable assumption that you already know your organization's story.

It's certain you know *some* story. If someone you've just met asks you what exactly your organization does, you always have an answer. But is it the best answer? Do you know the ideal story to tell, to inspire the predisposed to make that all-important first gift, or to retain a donor's heart?

A GOOD CASE IS, AT HEART, AN INSPIRING TALE

What you *think* you know, and what you *really* know once you start amassing information, might surprise you.

So much information crosses your desk. It's all intriguing for a moment, then consigned to a file, a direct mail appeal, a newsletter, an annual report, or simply forgotten. Every new day brings more data and anecdotes, not to mention countless meetings, e-mails, and phone calls. You'd have to have a brain the size of a stadium to remember it all.

When you live in the tumble of an organization day by day, the real story, *why* you do *what* you do, can slowly fade or be torn into incoherence, told differently by each staff person and volunteer. Making your case is a chance to bring that faded story back to vivid life and make it whole once more.

A well-told case can do more than inspire donors. It can inspire your staff and board, as well. A shared story, powerfully told, can recharge their batteries, sweep away their hidden doubts and fears (why do we do what we do?). A successful case reveals mission and vision from a fresh and profitable perspective: through the donor's eyes.

In *The Big Moo* there is this tale:

> Medtronic, a blue-chip medical-technology company, reports that when their teams need an extra spark, they bring in patients and ask them about how a Medtronic product changed their lives. The results are positively electric. These life-affirming stories leave hardly a dry eye in the house, and the entire Medtronic team returns to work with renewed energy, motivated to do their absolute best.[2]

A good case can have a similarly uplifting effect. We've seen a deeply dispirited board, uncertain they could raise (in this instance) $35 million for new construction, break into spontaneous, relieved applause as their new case was unveiled for the first time. Why? Because they saw their organization anew, the way others would: as a remarkable nonprofit, delivering substantial benefit to the community, and clearly worthy of donor trust and support.

Bear in mind these five points:

1. Most prospects will never see your project the way you see it. You're an insider. They are outsiders.

2. You have your reasons for wanting their gifts. They have their reasons for giving. Your interests are rational. Theirs are emotional.

3. Since they're writing the checks, their reasons matter more than your reasons.

4. A powerful, inspiring case, therefore, describes your project in terms donors understand.

5. You do not argue your case. You reveal your case: dramatically, without jargon, with a good grasp of the emotional triggers behind decision making.

A WORD OF CAUTION ABOUT ACADEMIC-ESE, LOFTY LANGUAGE, AND JARGON

When you make your case, use language easily understood by anyone. As expert Richard Radcliffe advises for legacy marketing, "Write for your mother." (And remember, she still doesn't understand your job.)

Here's an example of actual language lifted from a case that appeared on a university's Web site. It was an early attempt (it got better) to share the institution's vision and raise hundreds of millions of dollars in support. To quote:

XYZ University's strategic plan is designed to amplify the university's academic excellence. The result of a 13-month planning effort, the plan identifies strategies to enhance the university's work for students on three fronts:

- Reinterpreting the liberal arts skills of communication and critical thinking to take into account 21st-century challenges and opportunities
- Multiplying connections between students and faculty members by building on the faculty's record of original research and creativity
- Building on XYZ University's strong sense of community, locally and globally

Let's look at why Mother might not respond.

Verbs of Questionable Repute: *designed, amplify, identifies, enhance, reinterpreting, multiplying.* Verbs such as these come easily to academic lips. They are part of an accepted jargon common to bureaucrats, technocrats, grant applications, and the academy. You rarely hear such talk in daily conversation, though: "My visit to the mechanic this morning was designed to amplify my car's ability to get me to the supermarket."

When you use specialist language (jargon) with nonspecialist audiences (which is pretty much anyone you hope will become a donor), you're risking a lot. You probably sound vague (since no one but other *jargonistas* understand what these words imply); maybe pretentious (never popular with others); possibly even rude. After all, how do *you* like it when people around you intentionally talk in ways you can't understand?

Bottom line: How can you hope to inspire people if they don't really know what you're talking about?

Here's a rewrite of the first paragraph that even Mother would understand:

Within a decade, if all goes according to plan, XYZ University will emerge as the top school in its class, leaving behind our "peer schools" of today. Admittedly, the plan is ambitious. And it won't be cheap: Excellence in education at this level never is. But we will get there, thanks to your vision, your commitment, and your help.

Among the Missing: Any Mention of the Donor. An effective case has as much to do with the donor as it has to do with your plans for one obvious reason: Your plans go nowhere without donor support. And for one not-so-obvious reason: Donors have emotional needs. The more intensely you gratify those needs, the easier it is to raise money.

Most U.S. college graduates didn't attend elite schools. They were good schools, certainly, but not ranked among the best and most competitive. In our hearts, where a teensy-weensy inferiority complex never quite dies, we'd be thrilled if our alma maters gained international reputations.

This longing translates into gifts if you can make a good case that XYZ University will rise in the annual rankings that determine which schools are hot and which are not.

College faculty members profess to despise rankings. Mention, for instance, the influential *U.S. News & World Report*'s annual rankings of top schools at a faculty meeting and watch the contempt fly.

But alumni *do* care about these things. Deeply and generously. In one instance, an MBA program doubled its alumni giving simply by talking openly in its appeal letter about its ambitions for higher rankings.

Don't confuse *your* feelings with your donors' feelings.

Respect their feelings, and you'll raise more money.

In Summary. For goodness' sake, when writing your case, turn off the fog machine. Jargon is forbidden. And respect the potential of the donors' emotions. Judge every statement against two standards:

1. Will the average person know what I'm talking about? (Remember Mother.)
2. Why will a donor care?

What Kinds of Information to Collect? A Checklist

It's not uncommon to start a case by assembling a foot-tall stack of reading material. The kinds of things you might want handy include:

- Your organization's mission.
- Your organization's vision.
- Your organization's values, if you've articulated them.
- Your strategic plan (What are your organization's goals? What are the objectives that will get you to those goals? What are the consequences if funding for your organization, project, or campaign fails to materialize?).
- Your monetary goal for the campaign (if you're campaigning) and what that money will buy.
- Data on those you serve: membership figures, number of clients, program participation; as well as demographic breakdowns regarding age, income, and so on.
- Information on emerging or increasing needs in your community or constituency.
- Every outbound communication from the last few years: donor newsletters, alumni magazines, e-news alerts, invitations, ads, annual reports, direct mail appeals, grant applications, and such.
- All your brochures. (For colleges and universities, your view books and course catalogs are extremely helpful.)

- News clippings about your organization.

- Editorials or letters to the editor originating from your organization.

- Any position papers relevant to the case.

- Descriptions of your programs and services.

- Proof that these programs and services are worth doing: That is, which problems are you trying to solve? What worthwhile things are you bringing to the world (or locally) that, if not for you, would not otherwise exist? Don't limit yourself to statistics. Anecdotal proof is just as useful...and often more compelling than numbers.

- Proof that you're having an impact: statistical evidence of your accomplishments, anecdotes, awards, letters of praise, endorsements, testimonials, and so on.

- Descriptions of your organization's buildings or other physical holdings, if they relate directly to your mission and vision (if, for instance, you're a museum, a youth club, a land trust, or a hospital).

- An overview of your organization's governance: your board, any "friends of" groups, supporting foundations, or advisory groups, with information about how their members are selected.

- Staffing, including biographical information on members of the management team and other key players.

- Financial information (an income and expense statement as published in your latest annual report will suffice for many cases).

- The organization's history, focusing on its accomplishments and service record. (A founding date that goes back decades can, by itself, reassure donors regarding your durability and relevance to the community.)

- Interviews with "key informants." Key informants can be major donors, people whom your organization has served, your executive director, your president, a board chair, a department chair, your founder, your program designers, the front-line staff, a development officer, authorities in your field, the mayor, the governor, the head of a federal agency: anyone, really, whose opinion of your organization's work or knowledge of your special area of expertise might cast a revealing light on your case.

  Interviews are essential ... but time-consuming. Expect to spend at least an hour on each: making the appointment, thinking up revealing questions, conducting the interview, reviewing your notes from the interview. So be judicious. Ask yourself: If I were forced to base my case on conversations with just three people, whom, ideally, would I want to speak with? That's your A list.

EXHIBIT 18.1 **WOMEN'S FUND OF RHODE ISLAND CASE**

EXHIBIT 18.1 (Continued)

The Women's Fund of Rhode Island award-winning case is a four-panel brochure, with a pocket inside for more information. The cover gets right to the point, stating both the problem and donor's role in the solution: "For women and girls in Rhode Island, the playing field isn't level yet. But it could be, with your help."

- Other forms of research, primary and secondary. Primary research is research you conduct yourself, through surveys, focus groups, or key informant interviews. Secondary research is research originated by others. At this point we should silently murmur a prayer of thanks for the invention of the Internet. Secondary research that even into the 1990s was a logistical nightmare, involving travel, introductions, and time frames stretching to months and years, now takes hours and minutes from a chair in front of any computer screen linked to the World Wide Web. In America, many case statements profit from the data and trends reaped through a quick visit to the U.S. Census Web site (for social service agencies), the Centers for Disease Control (for health-related charities), or HUD (the federal Department of Housing and Urban Development, for housing-related issues). Online Wikipedia is like having a bottomless (and only occasionally imperfect) encyclopedia at your fingertips.[3]

YOUR ANNUAL REPORT: A CASE STATEMENT IN DISGUISE

The U.S. Securities and Exchange Commission requires every public company to file an annual report of its finances, for scrutiny by the stockholders. Annual reports tell outsiders who've purchased a piece of the company precisely how the year has gone. Annual reports answer this core question: "Has my investment prospered—or has it not?"

Many nonprofits publish an annual report for the same reason: to show their investors (individual donors, grant makers, volunteers, the community) how the year has gone. No law requires this annual report to donors. But it is a wonderful opportunity to tell your story and make your case. That's what an annual report really is, done well: a type of case statement.

Despite its name, an annual report that has donors and prospects as its primary target audience will be more than a review of the year just past: It should look at the future, as well, particularly at what your upcoming needs will be. Inspire your donors to help you in the adventures ahead. Give them a taste of what's coming.

Of course, your annual report should have a rearview mirror as well as a crystal ball. You have a responsibility: to tell donors what you've accomplished with their investments and to recognize their contribution to the mission. You can't thank donors enough. They deserve a standing ovation.

But spend your money wisely. Robert W. Bly, in his *Advertising Manager's Handbook*, laments: "Many large public companies spend a fortune producing lavish, glossy annual reports—far more than the SEC requires and far more than is usually warranted."[*]

Nonprofits often plead guilty to the same excesses, spending uncomfortable amounts on design and printing. But big-league production values have no relation to effectiveness. Tell a story well, and a simple Microsoft Word document will serve with donors. Tell a story poorly, and no amount of visual fireworks will help.

*Robert W. Bly, *Advertising Manager's Handbook* (Englewood Cliffs, NJ: Prentice Hall, 1993), p. 408.

Much of the information is already at your fingertips. And you probably won't need everything mentioned in the checklist. Writing the Housatonic Youth Service Bureau case, shown in Appendix 18B, required just these items:

- Current fiscal year budget
- Two most recent annual reports
- An organizational profile that covered mission, history, goals, challenges, accomplishments, current programs, and marketplace (competing services)
- Six brief testimonials: from a parent, a school principal, and various teens
- An agency brochure
- One gift-solicitation letter
- Notes from the bureau's strategic planning process, where board members talked about the agency's plans
- About 15 minutes of Internet research

BUILDING A CASE IN A SINGLE MEETING

You *can* build a case statement by committee. See Appendix 18C for an example. Though a professional writer was hired to do a final polish, the hard work of figuring out this case for support was done by staff and board.

A committee of staff and board can do the required spadework for a startling, powerful case in just a few hours . . . if someone asks the right questions. Every great case, some would say, starts with this one simple act: asking the right questions.

A set of questions refined during years of work with various nonprofits follows. Of course, feel free to add questions of your own.

Realize that the most useful, intriguing, and insightful answers will likely lie beneath the surface. They will not come to the surface without your help. You absolutely, positively must probe the answers people give you. Without rancor or accusation in your voice, dig a little deeper: "Why do you say that?" or "Why would a donor care about that?"

Journalists and other professional interviewers learn to probe automatically. They know that the initial answer to any question is often a safe, socially acceptable response. Ask, "Why do people give to our agency?" And someone asserts, as if the answer is obvious: "Because they love children!" Or music. Or nature. Or freedom.

Yes and no, of course. To be human is to generalize from our specific and peculiar beliefs; to assume that the things we believe as individuals (or as organizations), everyone believes. The way around such easy conclusions and false assumptions is to probe. Probe hard (though nicely). Making automatic probing one of your ground rules.

One more tip for this meeting: Shun jargon. Use blunt, plainspoken language even your mother (and, hence, donors) will understand.

Everyone ready? Here are the questions we would ask your case committee.

Why Does Your Organization Do What It Does?

What are you trying to accomplish? What problem(s) do you solve? What trends or opportunities are forcing you to change?

What Have You Accomplished?

What results have you had? How much of the problem have you fixed (assuming you fix problems)? If you went out of business tomorrow, who would miss you dearly? (Be cautious when answering this question. Organizations tend to say "We addressed the problem by setting up the XYZ program." Setting up a program, however, is *not* an accomplishment; it is merely an activity. Yes, it feels like an accomplishment to you, because to you setting up a program is work. But until there are results, a program has accomplished nothing, as far as donors are concerned. You might say instead, "We *hope* to do something about the problem. . . .")

Why Is Your Organization the Best Organization to Do This Work?

What makes you so special? What is distinctive about your work? Are your methods producing unusually good results? Are you particularly capable, trusted, well situated? Is any other organization trying to solve the same problem(s)?

What Do You Do?

What are your key activities? Why do they matter? Push yourselves. Don't just talk about the features of your programs (i.e., how they work). Talk about the benefits, too.

Features talk about what you do. Benefits explain why *what* you do might matter to the rest of us. Benefits are always more important than features, and are too rarely used. These examples for a tutoring program show the difference between the two.

- **Features:** "We provide free tutoring [feature 1] to kids in urban classrooms [feature 2] who are struggling with math, English, and other core subjects [feature 3]."

- **Benefits:** "We tutor because, if we can help kids get back on track academically, they are far more likely to graduate high school. A high school diploma adds a half million dollars in lifetime earnings to a person's income. Which is good for them [benefit 1], good for *their* kids [benefit 2], good for the community [benefit 3], good for the other taxpayers [benefit 4], and good for our economy, too [benefit 5], because these days employers won't look twice at someone without a high school diploma."

How Do You Hold Yourself Accountable?

What would you say to a donor who asked, "How do I know I can trust you?" Do you follow sound business practices? Do you recruit board members using certain criteria? Do you engage in strategic planning or otherwise challenge your own assumptions?

Don't be overconfident in the accountability department. Even your most loyal donors remain skeptical of your business sense, studies show. For the average person, the word "nonprofit" has as many negative connotations as positive ones. "You're a nonprofit? I guess that means you don't care about making money. So you're probably not watching your costs too closely." Studies bear this out: Donors have serious doubts about your management abilities and financial acumen.

Who Are Your Target Audiences?

Who is predisposed to care about your work, do you think? Why are they interested? What links them to you, in heart and mind? What do they share with your cause? Why might they be motivated to give? Where do their aspirations overlap with yours?

Don't worry about how you're going to reach an audience at this point; that's work for another day. Step #1 is to map the universe of potential supporters. Step #2 is to prioritize.

You can't go after everyone, nor will every target audience yield an equal return on your investment of resources. The predisposed come in two flavors: strongly predisposed and mildly predisposed.

Let's pretend you're a local Audubon Society. Birdwatchers in your area are strongly predisposed to become a member, because Audubon has a reputation as "the bird people." But parents of younger children will probably be only mildly predisposed, even though Audubon offers education programs and family fun opportunities.

Brainstorm which audiences are your top prospects and why. Move those audiences to the front of the queue. Move less likely audiences to the rear.

Expect higher response rates from the strongly predisposed and low to almost nonexistent response rates from the mildly predisposed—unless you make them a special segment and target them for custom offers that emphasize tailored benefits. For example: "With your $100 gift to Audubon, your kids all ride free—to any eye-opening, mind-bending, awe-inspiring event Audubon sponsors all year round."

Which Emotional Triggers Would Move Your Target Audience(s) to Act?

Consider each target audience and then ask yourself, "Which emotional triggers will cause the strongest response from this particular group?" (If members of your case committee are not professional fundraisers or marketers, be prepared. They will need a briefing on emotional triggers as well as the concept of emotional twinsets. Refer to Chapter 9 for a full explanation.) Fear and anger are common emotional triggers. "Youth drug use is rising, causing all sorts of problems in the community. Worse, we're afraid there is no solution." If you are the solution to a problem, then you offer hope, an emotional trigger as powerful as any fear.

GOING FROM A TO B: ANSWERING THREE BASIC QUESTIONS

"A case is about moving your organization from point A to point B," Ron Arena observed in 2005. "You talk about where you are, and where you want to go; what you've done, and what you want to do." A former newspaper reporter, now leader of the strategic communications group at international consulting firm Marts & Lundy, Ron asks just three questions when he's tackling a case: "Why us? Why now? Why you?"

Why Us?

Your answer aims to reassure the qualified prospects and donors that point B is (1) within your organization's reach and (2) that you deserve to get there. Ask yourself: "Are we really worth investing in? What is our special promise? What makes us unique?

What opportunities are unfolding? What problem(s) do we solve? What miracle(s) do we deliver? What are we doing to change the world? What have we accomplished that someone other than staff and board would think worthwhile?" (See Exhibit 18.2.)

Why Now?

Your answer adds urgency to the appeal and explains why point B beckons right this minute. Ask yourself: "What's the hurry? Why can't we wait? If funding were to be delayed, what bad things would happen, what opportunities would be lost?" (See Exhibit 18.3.)

Why You?

The "you" in this last question is your target audience. And the answer is simple: "We can't get there without you. If you, the prospect or donor, feel point B is a worthy destination, we need your participation desperately." The donor-centric organization offers something valuable: hero status as a donor. Ask yourself: "How will donors benefit emotionally? Why will this make them feel better? What do they hope for? How is their fear or anger eased? How is something that they care about either healed, preserved, or improved?" (See Exhibit 18.4.)

If the answers to all three questions begin with "Let me tell you a story . . ." that's fine, too. Anecdotes are usually the fastest way to reach an understanding with the greatest number of people. (See Exhibit 18.5.)

TYPES OF CASE STATEMENTS

Case statements talk about why prospects might wish to invest, and donors to reinvest, in your mission and vision. There are three kinds of cases.

Internal Case

The internal case comes first. It is your own, personal compilation of anything that might help you tell a persuasive story: statistics, anecdotes, testimonials, quotes, tidbits from key informant interviews, trends, news items, themes, details on your unique programs, awards, objections (and answers to those objections), frequently asked questions, angles you think might work with various target audiences. You take that foot-tall stack of background stuff mentioned earlier in this chapter. You read it all and extract all the best stuff. That's your internal case.

The internal case is a "database" of information, sorted for your convenience into categories such as "statistical evidence" and "anecdotal evidence." Or categories such as the three whys: why us; why now; why you, the donor. Categories are the equivalent of a rough cut in movie editing. You're breaking the

meet
the kind of patient
you'll be helping

" This man called. He was in his mid 50s. And he was almost in tears. He's been laid off for two years and looking for work. His wife works, but she doesn't have health insurance. After the rent gets paid, the couple has $200 a month left over for everything else they need: food, utilities.

"Here's the thing. This man has had a heart attack before. And he's calling Rhode Island Free Clinic because he's having all the signs of a heart attack again.

"He's afraid if he goes to the emergency room he won't be able to pay his bills, and he'll end up burying them in debt. He's ignored the symptoms as long as he could.

"He's afraid to tell his wife. He's calling us while she's at work, so she doesn't know. He doesn't want to worry her."

Many of the people we see are like this man: desperate, seriously ill, and reluctant to seek treatment because they have no way to pay for it. He was "among the fortunate few to find a solution...at Rhode Island Free Clinic," as the *Providence Phoenix* wrote in 2004.

EXHIBIT 18.2   Why Us?

The case for the Rhode Island Free Clinic opens by putting a face on the issue and inviting the prospect to "meet the kind of patient you'll be helping." By using the word "you" in the headline, the case is already getting personal. Good design made a strong first impression. The clinic looked highly professional, which helped make more credible its message about delivering top-quality health care. Fancy printing, though, isn't always required. Many multi-million-dollar campaigns make their goal without ever publishing more than a Word document.

RHODE ISLAND FREE CLINIC: THE CASE FOR SUPPORT

why
your help is desperately
needed now

A shocking number of working-age Rhode Islanders have no health insurance.

Rhode Island Free Clinic mends that hole in the healthcare safety net.

Being uninsured has dire consequences. "The uninsured have poorer health and shortened lives," the national Institute of Medicine concluded in 2002, after studying a vast body of U.S. research.

These consequences fall disproportionately on the working poor and minorities. The Rhode Island Department of Health reports, "The uninsured rate among people with annual household incomes of $15,000–19,999 is almost four times higher than for people with incomes of $50,000 or higher."

About 85% of our patients are minorities — African American, Hispanic, Asian and Native American. Most suffer from the chronic diseases that hit the poor hardest. Almost half have high blood pressure. And 31% have diabetes, which commonly leads to heart disease, blindness, amputation and a host of other calamities.

The need is urgent. The number of uninsured is rising dramatically in this state. According to the U.S. Census, Rhode Island has the fastest growing rate of uninsured adults in New England. By the latest estimate, roughly 103,000 Rhode Island working-age adults have no health care coverage.

Let's be frank: in our minds, this is as much a social justice issue as it is a health issue. You shouldn't have to beg for healthcare just because you're poor and uninsured.

"I want to thank all the doctors and staff for their wonderful care and understanding. They all make me feel very comfortable when I am here and not embarrassed that I have to come to a free health clinic. I want to thank from my heart everyone here at the clinic."

● J., RIFC patient

EXHIBIT 18.3   Why Now

This page answers one of the three big_questions, "Why now?" The testimonial at the base of the page is a "prethanks" of sorts to the prospective donor.

can
we do more? Yes.
All we need is you.

Rhode Island Free Clinic is ready to take on more patients. Far more.

Right now we are prepared to increase our examining capacity almost 300 percent. Everything is in place except the cash we need to make the leap.

We now have three examination rooms. We have plans for seven. We'll also add five rooms dedicated to counseling and mental health services. We want to add a pharmacy. We want to add a patient and family education room. We want a volunteer conference and teaching room that's bigger than a closet and sometimes has 15 volunteers squeezed in consulting with each other (think telephone stuffing and you're not far off).

We have a waiting list of doctors who want to practice medicine here as it should be practiced: with plenty of time to listen.

We know where to get the donated medicines. We have partnerships with other health care providers, for free services like MRIs, CT scans and diagnostic testing. We have the space.

All we need to get the job finished is your support:
- to pay for the renovations; and
- to set up an endowment.

Twenty-five percent of every dollar contributed to this expansion campaign will be set aside in a professionally managed endowment.

The endowment is not an afterthought. It's our stake in the long run. As you can see from the statistics, the need for health care among the uninsured is going to get much worse before it gets better, assuming it ever gets better.

The endowment eases the frenzy of raising $400,000 every year to cover the clinic's nonvolunteer operating expenses, things like electricity, rent, heat, security and technology, and a skeleton management team.

"I've never been on welfare — raised two children alone and have always worked. I fell between the cracks. But thanks to Rhode Island Free Clinic, I'm in good shape. God bless you all."

● F., former RIFC patient

EXHIBIT 18.4   Why You?

This page moves the donor to center stage. The case makes a promise, "We can do more, far more," then asks the donor to shoulder the responsibility for making this dream come true, "if we have your help."

Rhode Island Free Clinic:
Not what you'd expect

When you hear "free medical care for the poor and uninsured" what comes to mind? Noise, craziness, people rushing in and out, impatience? A TV-inspired image of a city emergency room? (Which is, in fact, the health care option the uninsured most often resort to.)

Surprise. It's just the opposite.

At Rhode Island Free Clinic, all treatment is by appointment. The clinic is clean, friendly, calm, quiet, very organized, running with a professional hum but no apparent hurry. Most of our patients are between 45 and 65 years of age.

One day a month we accept walk-in patients, chosen by lottery. We can take in 10. We turn away 30 or more, all people who are ill and can benefit from our care. But we can dramatically lower the number who are turned away, with your help.

The professionals who volunteer at Rhode Island Free Clinic say our patients "get better care here" than they'd get in the typical doctor's office. Unhurried care. Care that views mental health as an essential part of primary care — an advanced, holistic practice that doctors argue for...but insurers won't pay for. At Rhode Island Free Clinic, doctors, not insurers, decide what's best for your health.

In the works: Plans for statewide expansion We can't go into the details yet. But we know where we're headed. It's all there in our strategic plan. We've shown that our free clinic model can work in Rhode Island. We want to build on that success. We're determined to provide access to high quality healthcare to greater numbers of the uninsured in more corners of Rhode Island. Is this the answer to Rhode Island's ballooning number of impoverished uninsured? It can be an important part of it, if you will help us realize the vision.

EXHIBIT 18.5   News Value

This is the "news value" page, where the case overturns common expectations about how a free clinic really works. It's a behind-the-scenes look that aims to defuse lingering doubts and replace them with pride and trust.

database down and sorting it, so that it becomes quicker to search and easier to work with. (See Appendix 18D for an example of an internal case.)

The internal case is nothing more than a parking lot. Any information that might prove remotely useful ends up there. Because it's unedited, it's a confidential document, not meant for circulation. Only later will you reduce your data heap to a tight, coherent story. The internal case for the Rhode Island Free Clinic stretched to roughly 3,200 words, for example. The published case for the clinic shrunk by almost half, using just 1,800 words to tell its story.

Feasibility, Planning, or Draft Case

Once you've written your internal case, you ready for the next step: writing a case that outsiders will see.

Sometimes this is a feasibility case (also called by some a "planning" or "draft" case). You use a feasibility case *before* your campaign launches, to gauge among your top prospects their interest in your organization's vision. You're asking: "Do you think the project is feasible? Does it deserve support? Here's a document that explains everything."

You're soliciting people's opinions at this stage, not their gifts. Someone's feedback (the theory goes) might persuade you to alter your plans, to add or delete something vital.

Of course, a feasibility case is also a public relations exercise. It introduces your plans to your very best prospects. It might even ignite some positive word of mouth. Still, a feasibility case is a work in progress (until the opinions are all in). It can (and probably should) remain an unpretentious word-processed document, with maybe a few relevant photos, charts, or illustrations added.

It might be that your case isn't meant exclusively for print. It could be meant for voice, as well.

If you set up a speaker's bureau (as HousingWorks RI, an advocacy coalition, did for its successful 2005–2006 bond campaign), you'll need talking points. Talking points keep all your various speakers on message. See Appendix 18E for the talking points that helped a multi-million bond campaign talk its way to victory.

Public Case

The public case is a handy reference during face-to-face solicitations ("Herman, see this laboratory here on the floor plan? We could call it the Jane and Herman J. Smith Laboratory. Just imagine what advances in medicine might begin in that very room"). The public case is also a leave-behind, acting in the valuable role of "silent salesperson" once your solicitor leaves. Exhibit 18.1 shows a typical public case, for the Women's Fund of Rhode Island.

Do you need a pretty, expensively designed brochure? Not necessarily. Your public case might be fine as a simple document. After all, it's the story that matters, not the graphic treatment. The Housatonic Youth Service Bureau, for example, simply printed its case on stationery.

Q & A

E-Mailed Question

I am chair of an adult literacy network with a small staff and no money for—or expertise in—fundraising. What do you suggest we do?—Gordon

Answer

Hello, Gordon . . . Fascinating question, to me anyway. It made me wonder, "What would I do, in their shoes?" Please accept this advice with a few grains of salt because I am *not* an expert in start-up fund development. But I have some opinions.

First, you have to answer the basic question: Do we need to do this? Many nonprofits get by without any fundraising to speak of, because they receive government cash to provide a community service. If, hypothetically, all your bills are paid for from a current income stream such as the government, why bother fundraising, which consumes resources for a while before it yields results. (And, frankly, even the results are uncertain; fundraising is hard to get right.)

But let's say you arrive at one of two answers to Question #1. Either answer or both would be a basis for attempting fundraising.

First answer: We could do so much more if we had a source of discretionary income to spend on our mission. Donor dollars tend to be undesignated (at least the small amounts are; bigger donors sometimes like to specify how their gifts be spent). You can do things with them that government money won't allow.

Second answer: Our government money is uncertain, so we need to develop a second income stream from donors, individual, corporate, and foundation.

Okay, now you have a couple of good reasons for fundraising: to expand your mission, or to ensure the sustainability of a vital community service if the worst case happens.

At this point, I think you want to ask yourself three questions:

1. Why us? (i.e., what makes us so special, so unique, so effective?) Mediocre charities that produce no special value do not succeed, so you don't want to be one of them.

2. Why now? What's the big rush? Donors give to urgency as much as anything, so is your need urgent?

3. Why will this matter to the donor? What are they interested in? Corporations, for instance, might be interested in adult literacy because it has workforce benefits. Individuals might be interested because they know the advantages themselves of being literate and weep inside when they read about how others struggle. You have to give individual donors a way to save or change a life.

Okay, now you've thought through a basic "case for support," so-called. Now I would sit down with your board (boards do some of the work in fundraising) and say: "Let's pick a goal." Make that goal reasonable, achievable with current resources, and worth doing. Attach a dollar figure to that goal. That's the amount you want to raise.

Now get educated. Read a few books. If your board needs a tune-up on fundraising, pass around a copy of Kay Sprinkel Grace's *Ultimate Board* book. (Available on Amazon.) Someone should read a book on grassroots fundraising, from Kim Klein or someone like her (she's the guru). Cruise the Internet. Look hard at what other adult literacy groups are doing. Because probably the best time you'll spend is stealing from other similar groups' experiences. I have leapt tall buildings in a single bound simply by calling a similar group in another location of the country and talking to them about their successes and failures.

I hope all that helps. I run across a lot of adult literacy groups in my travels. And it is a great cause to raise money for; people really get it.

—Tom

In Conclusion

Every organization needs a case for support, and not just for capital campaigns. Your case clarifies why anyone would support you, by answering three big questions: (1) Why does our mission (or vision) matter? (2) Why is it urgent? (3) Why is the donor important?

The last question is the easiest, because the answer's always the same: With your investment of money or time, we can do these amazing things and achieve these worthwhile goals. And without your support, we can't. End of story.

■ **ENDNOTES**

1. Jerold Panas, *Making the Case* (Chicago: Institutions Press, 2003), p. 9.
2. Group of 33, *The Big Moo: Stop Trying to Be Perfect and Start Being Remarkable*, ed. Seth Godin (New York: Portfolio, 2005), p. 115.
3. Items in our list were adapted from, among other sources, a "Case Elements Checklist" written by Kay Sprinkel Grace for the Public Television Major Giving Initiative, funded by the Corporation for Public Broadcasting; *Making the Case* by Jerold Panas; and *Strategic Fund Development* by Simone Joyaux.

Thoughts About Creating a Case for Support

WHAT IS A CASE FOR SUPPORT?

For fund development purposes, a case for support refers to the written document that outlines everything anyone should know about your organization, the community need it serves, and why charitable contributions are necessary.

The case for support is an internal management document that is used by staff and volunteers. This document could be 10 or 15 pages long. It is your guidebook for why you are raising money.

In summary, the case statement answers the six most compelling questions about your organization:

1. Who are you?
2. Why do you exist?
3. What is distinctive about you?
4. What is it that you want to accomplish, and why does that matter?
5. How do you intend to accomplish it?
6. How will you hold yourself accountable?

What Should Be Included in the Comprehensive Case for Support?

Think about writing a proposal to a foundation. What would you include?

08-01-1996© Simone P. Joyaux, ACFRE, Joyaux Associates, Rhode Island, USA, 401-397-2534

See Simone Joyaux, *Strategic Fund Development: Building Profitable Relationships That Last*, 2nd ed. (Sudbury, MA: Jones & Bartlett, 2001).

1. The problem (or opportunity) to be addressed
   • Talk about community need. Talk about the people who need and want your service.

2. Trends affecting the problem (or opportunity)
   • Demonstrate your knowledge and insight. What is happening in the world and your community that has produced this problem, and what is happening now (and what do you anticipate happening in the future)?

3. Your response to the problem (or opportunity)
   • How does/will your organization respond to the community problem or opportunity? How will you respond to the trends? Talk about results! *Why* do you do what you do, and *what* are the results?

4. Your mission
   • Now is the time to weave in your mission. You exist (your mission) because you wish to respond to community situations. Explain how your response to this particular community situation fits in with your overall mission.

5. Your history, track record, and marketplace position
   • Explain why you are the right organization to respond to this community situation. Talk about your track record. Demonstrate why the prospective donor should believe that giving money to your organization is a sound investment. Make sure you position your organization within the marketplace, explaining how you are different from other organizations doing the same or similar work. Talk about collaboration.

6. Goals, strategies, and objectives
   • Provide details about how you will respond to the community situation. What, specifically, are you going to do? Why? When?

7. Organizational resources
   • Justify, prove that you have the resources necessary to address this situation. Describe your staff, professional expertise, volunteer structure, operations, and so forth. Talk about money. How do you currently finance your organization? How do you propose to finance this new activity? What kind of money is necessary? How will you raise the money, and who is helping you raise it?

8. Accountability and evaluation
   • You must assure the prospective donor that you will comply with all relevance regulations and laws and that you are good organization, its programs and finances. Also describe how you evaluate program and institutional health.

9. Future organization plans
   - Present your future organization goals and activities that will continue to help the community address the situation in the future.
10. Role of the prospective donor
    - Engage the prospective donor. Describe how a prospective donor might participate in addressing the community problem or opportunity. Talk about how you can help the prospective donor achieve his or her own goals and dreams. Describe donor acknowledgment and recognition opportunities. Focus on target audiences and the key messages for each audience.

How Do You Translate This Detailed Case into an Effective Public Communications Vehicle?

To translate your detailed case into a public communications vehicle, you write a case statement. You probably write multiple case statements, each targeted to a particular audience

This public communications vehicle expresses the magic of your vision. The case statement informs, inspires, and motivates people and groups to act.

A case statement is a message directed to a particular audience. The message is designed to stimulate a monetary response. How? By establishing your community's needs and your organization's ability to respond and by articulating the benefits to prospective donors.

The case statement is your "brochure." (Although you needn't produce an expensive brochure. Your case statement could be printed on your letterhead.)

What Should Be Included in the Case Statement?

Include everything in the detailed case for support. But be much briefer!

The case must be compelling. Create short and powerful messages. Use short, action-oriented statements. Use emotion and facts. The case statement uses copywriting. The comprehensive case for support does not.

The case statement must describe how a donor's personal gift will solve a specific problem.

The case statement must translate the community problem and your organization's response into compelling benefits to the prospective donor.

Different messages will work for different audiences. You must personalize the message to the audience.

You must consider "packaging." What will the case statement actually look like? (The detailed, comprehensive case for support is simply typed on 8 ½ × 11 sheets of paper.) Your case statement might be designed into a brochure. Or it might be most appropriate for you to use the 8 ½ × 11 paper.

Make sure that the packaging reflects your values. Just because a designer and printer will donate their services, don't get too glitzy. It doesn't matter if the brochure says "donated" all over it. Glitzy might conflict with your values and what you want to transmit to your prospective donors.

How Do You Develop the Case for Support and the Case Statement?

1. Gather together your existing organizational information. Specifically:
    *   Values and vision statements
    *   Mission statement
    *   Strategic plan
    *   Descriptions about your various services
    *   Service statistics and growth patterns
    *   Articles and community information about the problem or opportunity
    *   Organization budget and operational descriptions
    *   Your favorite proposals
    *   Media articles about your organization
2. Look for powerful quotations about your organization and the community problem or situation.
3. Conduct a brainstorming session with staff. (See questions under the next heading.)
4. Conduct a brainstorming session with the board of directors. (See questions under the next heading.)
5. Compile the information from the board and staff brainstorming sessions. Prepare bullet points for each component of the comprehensive case for support.
6. Conduct a brainstorming session with the fund development leadership, using the compiled bullet lists. (See questions under the last heading in this appendix.)
7. Write. Write. Write the detailed case for support.
8. Review the general content of the comprehensive case for support with the board. Do not wordsmith. Secure formal board approval.
9. Compile the key information for the case statement and test with targeted prospects. (Use focus groups, personal meetings. This is a wonderful cultivation strategy.) Adjust as necessary.
10. Draft the case statement "brochure." (You may wish to use a professional copywriter.) The executive director approves the case statement. (She or he may find it useful to show the final copy to the campaign chair(s) and board president

prior to final approval.) The case statement is then provided as a finished/printed document to the fund development leadership, staff, and board.

Suggested Questions for the Brainstorming Sessions with Staff and Board

Remember for questions #1 and #2: You have already made these decisions. You are not doing strategic planning. You are not brainstorming new ways to respond.

You work from your organization's strategic plan and state what you have already decided, clearly, concisely, and with substantiation.

Now ask your board and staff these four questions:

1. How would you describe the community problem/opportunity that our organization wants to address? Describe the facts. Describe the trends affecting the problem. Provide actual figures. Use brief, powerful phrases. Use emotion.

2. Based on our strategic plan (what we have decided we will do), how would you describe how our organization will address this community problem.

3. Describe, with facts and emotions, why we are the best organization to do this work.

4. Briefly and concisely state what the top five messages we want to convey in this fundraising program are? Who are our target audiences for each message? Given our targeted audiences, are there additional messages some of those audiences might want to hear?

Suggested Questions for Brainstorming Sessions with Fund Development Leadership, Donors, Prospects, and Clients

Take a look at the results of the staff and board brainstorming sessions.

Decide what the key messages and the targeted audiences should be. Now test these messages with your new brainstorming group.

- Are these the appropriate messages we need to convey to our target audiences? Do these messages adequately and appropriately represent the organization and what we are trying to achieve? Should we make any modifications to general content?

- Given our target audiences, are there any additional messages that are necessary?

Then ask fund development leadership to comment on the key points gathered together for the case for support.

Housatonic Youth Service Bureau

(ESTABLISHED BY SIX CONCERNED COMMUNITIES IN 1991)

For an agency made necessary by drug and alcohol abuse, teen pregnancy, child depression, youth unemployment, truancy and dropping out, family violence, runaways, homelessness, and petty crime . . . we're remarkably happy.

Must be all the changes we see in the people we help.

> " . . . we in the school community are so very impressed with [HYSB's] unique ability to help children and adults sort through complicated situations without passing any judgment and guaranteeing them 100% confidentiality. . . . From our perspective we see positive growth in the students and parents who work with [HYSB]. We find this growth to be a gift . . . ." —*Karen Manning, principal, Lee H. Kellogg School, Falls Village*

What We Offer Families in the Northwest Corner: Free, Convenient Counseling When Things Threaten to Get Out of Control

- We offer effective, professional counseling to youth who are troubled or in crisis.

- This counseling is "barrier-free." It costs nothing. It's friendly and confidential. And it's convenient—because that makes a difference. Our office is next door to the Housatonic Valley Regional High School. Counseling is available during free periods, after school, and in the evening.

- But HYSB is not just for kids. We also help parents who aren't sure what to do find their way, with crisis intervention, counseling and referrals.

Used with permission

Courtesy of the Housatonic Youth Service Bureau

"Being a single father on a fixed income, having this free service was a blessing. The service scheduled appointments at my convenience. I didn't need to miss any work. [HYSB] was a great help when working with my daughter [and helped] my daughter understand some things that I didn't know how to deal with at home. I would recommend this service to anyone. . . ." —*Trevor Saule*

HOUSATONIC YOUTH SERVICE BUREAU IS NOT JUST ABOUT KIDS IN TROUBLE. IT'S ALSO ABOUT BUILDING STRONGER, MORE SUCCESSFUL KIDS AND FAMILIES

Among our programs . . .

- Our long-running **"Empowering Young Women"** Project (in collaboration with Women's Support Services) offers teen women revealing, new experiences each month: mother-daughter activities (movie discussion night, an all-day retreat); eye-opening trips to Boston and New York City; personal exploration through the "The Way I See It" photography workshop . . . and more.

- Our **Wilderness Club for teenage boys** builds self-confidence and teamwork through monthly outdoor challenges in canoeing, rock climbing, winter survival skills, caving, etc.

- Since 2000, we have taught newly licensed high school seniors how to respond to driving emergencies at our **Defensive Driving Course**, done in conjunction with world-famous Skip Barber Driving School.

- Our regularly scheduled **parent education classes** bring in national and local experts to teach good solutions to tough problems. Topics have included "Strengthening Stepfamilies," "Positive Discipline," "Effective Parenting of Teens," "Raising Resilient Children," single parenting, and substance abuse prevention.

- **Fresh ideas:** In 2005 we launched "F.Y.I.," a series of workshops where parents and kids together learn useful skills and have fun. Topics included yoga, small engine repair, and orienteering. Also in 2005 we premiered our "Battle of the Bands" to showcase and reward the independent work of our area's many talented young adult musicians.

- **Our active community awareness effort:** In 2005 we cosponsored with Region One Special Education Services and the Housatonic Day Care Center the first community-wide forum on Universal Pre-K. Over 70 people participated, with all towns represented. Local radio stations WQQQ and WKZE host our public service announcements on child development issues and raising kids today.

"It taught me that I can be concerned about people I barely know. It also showed me that offering guidance to others can help greatly." —*11th grade boy who served as a mentor to younger kids in the Wilderness Club*

"Empowering Young Women is teaching us how to be independent and to believe in ourselves. And that it's okay to be yourself." —*Freshman at Housatonic Valley Regional*

AND YOU'RE THE HERO. SO MUCH HAPPENS BECAUSE OF YOUR GENEROSITY

Connecticut's 2002–2003 budget crisis and ongoing cuts ransacked HYSB. In just 2004, state cutbacks cost us roughly $30,000, a huge chunk of our budget.

Fortunately we had a Plan B: **you**.

We now survive thanks to charity.

Individuals, local businesses, and foundations have all recognized HYSB's strong contribution to the youth of the Northwest Corner...and invest generously in our services.

In fact, our single biggest source of revenue (36%) is now fundraising. (The remainder comes in from the state's department of education, town grants, and in-kind donations. Thank you, Region One School District, for giving HYSB a home in the "White House," in the perfect location for a youth counseling service, next to the Housatonic Valley Regional High School.)

But we're still in recovery mode.

We've had to trim some useful, new programs because we can't really afford them. We have just one paid counselor. She serves an area the size of Hartford and all of its suburbs. Volunteers handle the rest of the work.

NOW YOU'RE INVITED TO CHANGE MORE LIVES

HYSB knows what to do next: lots more early intervention.

The idea is: Go younger. Stop problems before they get started.

But we need your help to do that. In fact, we need your help simply to survive, so please give generously. Please give as if your community depended on it.

Become a supporter of Housatonic Youth Service Bureau—a public, community-based, volunteer-driven nonprofit organization devoted to providing services to youth and family in the towns of Canaan, Cornwall, Falls Village, Kent, Salisbury and Sharon.

Our motto: "...supporting youth in a changing world."

Now adding: "...with your help."

Volunteers in Providence Schools: Case Statement for Operations

Every year more than 3,000 Providence public school students face some kind of learning crisis that could end their chances of a successful school career.

And then one of our volunteer tutors walks in the door.

I. Why a Child's Failure in the Classroom Matters—To the Adult that Child Will Become, and to You

We're not saying that money buys happiness.

We *are* saying, though, that money can buy a decent home in a good neighborhood, plenty of nutritious food, reliable transportation, excellent health care, clothing for all seasons, a college education for the kids, and lots of other things that contribute to a better quality of life.

Education hasn't changed. It's still the best road to a better life.

Consider the cash value of an education. How much difference *does* a good education make in a person's earnings, her or his ability to afford things (and pay the taxes that build a society)?

In the U.S., right now, if you never finish high school, you'll earn on average $18,874 a year, according to the U.S. Census Bureau. (That's assuming you find work at all. Most jobs require a high school diploma.)

If you *do* graduate high school (or get your GED), your average annual income jumps to $26,104, a 38% boost. If you go on to get your Bachelor's degree, your average annual income soars another 61%, to $42,087.

Used with permission
Courtesy of Volunteers in Providence Schools

On the other hand, drop out of school in Providence, Rhode Island, and you pretty much seal your economic fate. You will live poor. You will be marginalized, starved of resources in an expensive world.

Had you stayed in school, had you found *some* way to succeed in the classroom instead of fail; had a VIPS tutor, for instance, sat at your elbow to help you through the things you couldn't understand the first time, you could have had *so* much more.

How much? Let's do a little math.

In a lifetime of work (47 years, ages 18 to 65), a high school *graduate* earns nearly a half million dollars *more* than the average high school dropout. A college graduate earns nearly $1.2 million more.

That's means not just a better standard of living. That's means a completely different life, furnished with hope instead of fear, deprivation and despair.

In a nutshell . . .

VIPS exists so that Providence public school students who encounter difficulty in the classroom get the tutoring they need to succeed.

There are too many futures at stake not to try.

And if you think kids who fail at school won't cost you money, think again. You're a taxpayer, right?

> "Youth who drop out of school are more likely to rely on public assistance as adults." That's the bottom line, as Rhode Island Kids Count reports in its authoritative 2005 Factbook. Current data reveals, "over half of the people over 25 who did not have a high school diploma or GED reported no earnings."

Burn that into your memory banks: More than half of U.S. adults who do not graduate from high school earn NOTHING. How do they live? Society foots the bill.

Graduation rates and welfare are directly related. If you want to do something to lower the cost of welfare, invest in VIPS, a program that helps kids having difficulty in school stay in school . . . so they get a real shot at a better life.

II. How Do We Achieve What We Achieve? VIPS Uses the Oldest Technique in the Book: One-on-One Attention

Some of the kids we see in early grades come in not even knowing how to hold a book: Which side is up?

We help kids grasp math, the sciences, English reading and writing . . . any subject, when a teacher spots a student who is struggling to learn and needs an unusual amount of personal attention.

What causes a student to leave school?

Several factors, says research from the Annie E. Casey Foundation, which has become, through its Kids Count program, the nation's leading advocate for children's issues.

Most factors have to do with classroom failure: poor grades, being kept back, low achievement on standardized tests.

Teachers welcome VIPS into their classrooms. Teachers desperately want their kids to succeed. But there aren't enough hours in the day for a teacher in a crowded, urban classroom to give every student intense personal attention.

Enter VIPS.

Last year, we gave (it's all free, a welcome relief to inner-city parents) around 3,000 Providence Public School students, mostly in the elementary grades, enough personal attention to overcome academic and social barriers to learning.

But that's not all we do. We teach parents how to read and speak English better in our sold-out adult ESL classes. We've involved 7,000 students in our literacy and free book programs. And we opened a state-of-the-art technology and learning center at the VIPS offices just down the street from Central and Classical high schools, for after-school work.

III. Don't Let Our Name Fool You. VIPS Desperately Needs Your Charity to Survive, Thrive and Try New Things

Yes, we are "volunteers" in Providence schools.

And, yes, the tutoring we offer . . . the tutoring that can turn a kid's problematic school career around . . . costs parents absolutely nothing. (Good thing, too, since 40.5% of Providence children now live in poverty, and every year sets a new record in that dismal category.)

But running and growing an organization this large and entrepreneurial costs money.

Training, placing, managing and evaluating a small army of quality volunteer tutors demand a full-time professional infrastructure. And operating an advanced after-school technology center isn't cheap. (VIPS went into the red for four years on that venture, because we saw that too many kids were failing science. We're proud to say that the results were worth the risk.)

With your help, there's no limit to what VIPS can attempt.

But we can't do it without you.

Well over half of our budget depends on contributions from individuals, foundations, and businesses with vision.

This year, VIPS will train and manage 1,200 volunteer tutors.

Those volunteers augment the learning experience of a crowded city classroom with enough extended one-on-one attention to make a difference for a child who is struggling to make the grade.

A *significant* difference, we're happy to report.

Most VIPS-tutored students (80%) make "significant gains" in their classroom performance, before-and-after assessments show.

What will your dollars buy?

We're organized to oversee 1,200 volunteer tutors now.

But we could double our efforts . . . and the Providence schools would welcome our aid . . . if we have your help.

The proof exists. VIPS kids perform better in the classroom. Imagine what your gift could do to rescue kids from the stunting lifelong consequences of academic failure.

IV. ANSWERS TO A COUPLE OF COMMON QUESTIONS . . .

Q. We hear so much about failing kids. Are the Providence public schools "broken"?

A. Short answer: Not in our well-informed opinion.

We've been intimately involved with the Providence public school system for 43 years now. Okay, we've seen some lows. But over the last 15 years or so we've seen tremendous progress.

So have parents, incidentally. In the latest Brown University poll, only 27% of the general public rated Providence public schools "excellent or good." Parents had a very different opinion. Among respondents with children in a Providence public school, 45% called the schools excellent or good. Public opinion is out of date on this issue.

People have to realize that urban school populations these days are not what they were a generation or two ago. You can't "fix" the schools without "fixing" the world those schools live in.

Sure: Eliminate poverty, addiction, gangs, street violence, parents with little education themselves, substandard housing, low expectations . . . and while you're at it, magically erase the differences in English comprehension among an incredibly diverse population . . . *then* you might have a chance.

Otherwise, no. Otherwise, you have to deal with the consequences of all of the above entering the classroom. And when you find a kid who's beginning to fail for whatever reason, provide enough one-on-one assistance to turn that kid's academic situation around. It's a solution that works. And it's why VIPS exists.

Q. Where *did* VIPS come from anyway?

A. VIPS was formed in 1988 from a merger of two school-based programs: Lippitt Hill Tutorial, around since 1963, and Mt. Pleasant Tutorial, originating in 1975. With the merger, VIPS began offering volunteer tutoring to the Providence public school system citywide.

V. A Few Selected Stats for Your Final Consideration

54

The number of public schools in Providence.

27,900

The number of students in Providence public schools last year.

16,000

The approximate number of Providence public school students who do not speak English as a first language.

49

The combined total of native languages spoken by ESL students in Providence public schools.

3,000 at least

The number of kids tutored by VIPS' 1,200 volunteers in any recent year.

51

The percentage of single-parent families in Providence. This percentage is the highest of any Rhode Island city or town, and has risen steeply in just a decade (in 1996, it was 43.8%).

What this produces is "**not** your father's school system." In 1970, as the Baby Boomers passed through high school, only 12% of the children in Rhode Island lived in single-parent families. And there are consequences.

"Children in single-parent families are at an increased risk for low academic achievement, dropping out of high school and increased levels of depression, stress, anxiety and aggression," recent studies by the Annie E. Casey Foundation show.

Children in single-parent families are more likely to be poor. And the single parent is less likely to have a good education. "Research shows that there are strong links between parental education levels and a child's school readiness . . . and the level of education that the child will ultimately achieve," as Rhode Island Kids Count reports in its 2005 Factbook.

Bottom line: Kids in Providence schools face more obstacles and need more help than any other school district in the state.

Audubon Society of Rhode Island

INTERNAL CASE FOR DONOR SUPPORT

December 2006

Two things are important at this stage, as you chase a larger donor base:

1. Repetition of key messages; and

2. Focusing far more on *why* Audubon matters.

It can take dozens of repetitions for one message to take root in one mind. It's just simple consumer psychology; no organization's exempt; without repetition you cannot succeed. Repeat the key messages recommended below at every opportunity. Any issue of *Report*, for instance, offers a couple of dozen opportunities (every headline, every caption) to repeat key messages in its pages. These repetitions do not have to be verbatim, incidentally; for donors, it's not the words that matter, it's the ideas behind those words.

Focus, focus, focus on *why* Audubon's activities matter. Many organizations get this wrong, particularly environmental groups (an opinion based on having done communications analysis and training with at least a dozen such groups across the country). There is a tendency among enviros to talk about the details of what's being done. We bury the *why* we're bothering to do such things in paragraph ten.

Too bad: Almost no one reads to paragraph ten. But that's minor. The real problem is that people have only a casual interest in *how* you do your business. If you could save the environment with a sweep of your magic Audubon wand, that would be fine, too.

What *does* intrigue people is *why*: why Audubon's activities matter to them, their world, their children, their health, their property values, their lifestyle, and so on. When you get this angle right, the *why* behind your activities will surface in every headline, every caption, every catalog, every refuge sign, every sales slip from the gift shop, every presentation to school kids, every guided tour, every elevator speech, every one-on-one solicitation, every grant proposal, every appeal letter and so on.

I. Key Messages

The boldfaced phrases are the subtexts you need to push, to keep donors intrigued, informed, inspired, and generous.

The messages are broken into three subgroups:

- "Core" messages that donors and prospects must hear over and over, without stint;

- "Reassurance" messages that help (1) keep existing donors loyal and generous; and (2) erase the doubts of prospects;

- "Mission" messages that show why Audubon matters to Rhode Islanders.

Messages from these subgroups should frame and pervade every face-to-face solicitation and every Audubon communication.

(a) Core Messages (essential for every conversation, publication, program, visitor experience; message 1 is by far the most important message Audubon can broadcast)

1. **Donors make it happen.** "With your help, we can do amazing things. And without your help, we can't." It's an honest assessment when 75% of your income is directly tied to some form of charitable gift, as Audubon's is. The education center, for instance, runs at a loss. Without donors, it can't exist. This basic message (*with your help, without your help*), repeated thousands of times in various ways and words, is the raw, beating heart of a donor-centric (i.e., profitable) communications program. When this basic message pops up everywhere, you will make more money, both "today dollars" and "tomorrow dollars" (bequests and such). This basic message should not be sequestered and reserved just for "donor-targeted" communications like appeal letters. It should appear everywhere, all the time. **Your need for donor support is a powerful public message** (just ask National Public Radio). A majority of headlines, captions, and other browser level items in *Report* should convey some form of this basic message. (Bonus: Then you won't *need* a separate "donor newsletter.")

2. **Audubon's need is (permanently) urgent.** Fundraising 101. In the wise words of top Democratic political fundraiser, Hal Malchow:

"... you'll raise far more money with news of a setback that leaves you in desperate need and your mission yet to be accomplished." In other words: "Yes, with your help, Audubon has accomplished these things. But there is still so much more to do." Staff said, "We can't wait for 20 years. We're losing habitat all the time." Don't be afraid to use powerful words like "urgent." The enemy in fundraising is always the same: inertia. You have to get people to act. Without urgency, fewer take the trouble.

3. **We are you.** When speaking or writing to donors, use the phrase "your Audubon" reflexively (as in, "Your Audubon was there, helping decide the fate of the state's rivers . . ."). The phrase builds ownership over time and subtly shifts the burden for your existence onto donor shoulders, where it should be. This, in fact, could well serve as your tagline: "Audubon is you."

4. **Audubon is an important part of the solution to a perceived threat.** Being a good steward is half the battle. The other half is being a bulwark against a relentless problem: environmental degradation. Report on Audubon's accomplishments, but also report on threats to the environment. The threat is real. Development pressures continue unabated. They're not making any more land here in Rhode Island, but they are making more people. Population is forecast to grow: By 2025, Rhode Island will hold another 100,000 people inside its borders. Issues like a water shortage, known to Audubon but unsuspected by the public, can galvanize giving (assuming we're part of the solution). Advocacy fits an ancient and powerful story-telling archetype: the struggle between good and evil, right and wrong. You've got the good, sort of. The evil, though, is missing in action. Recent example: there are six stories teased on the cover of the Sept–Oct 2006 issue of *Report*. "Get out and vote" is the only one that is even remotely about a problem. Headlines for the two big stories are variations on "grandmother turns 100." Stories are about conflict: Look at the front page of any decent newspaper. Those are the stories we pay attention to. Get an edge. Get an angle. Take a side. You are front-line in the struggle to sustain a healthy environment in the face of constant threat. You don't own that story yet. But you should.

(b) Reassurance messages (keep donors loyal and generous; in no particular order)

1. **This is a business.** "Audubon land management" is a good phrase to use often (as in " . . . thanks to Audubon land management . . . "). It sounds important. It sounds business-like. It sounds pretty big. It sounds expensive (welcome, donors). Stick in a "nonprofit" occasionally, too, so they don't forget you're a charity.

2. **Audubon is a professional operation.** To counter the oft-noted attitude that Audubon is volunteer staffed. Staff is trained in the sciences, wildlife and land management. This level of expertise is necessary and expensive.

3. **Audubon plays well with others.** I.e., collaboration. Saving the environment requires many groups working different parts of the problem. Donors want to know that Audubon isn't a stand-alone. They want to feel that they can't go wrong by giving to Audubon, that whatever you accomplish is good for the rest of the environment, too.

4. **Audubon is trustworthy.** "That's why people give us land," staff said. You're trusted because you're responsible land managers. The trust message is always good. Donors and prospects need to hear it. It will make them proud of you and more generous.

5. **Audubon is science-based.** We don't exaggerate threats.

(c) Mission messages (in no particular order; different audiences respond to different messages at different times)

1. **Rhode Island's environment: it's all connected.** In order to save our bay, we have to save our land, which is the bay's watershed. That's Audubon's job. Make it your job, too. Join us in this work.

2. **Environmental education is as important as the 1-2-3s and A-B-Cs.** "Rhode Island is in danger of raising the least environmentally aware kids ever," staff said. Audubon can reverse that and educate the next generation of environmentalists—but we need donor help to do it.

3. **Audubon has local as well as statewide impact.** "Forty-five land trusts have sprung up in Rhode Island. They come to us for guidance and technical assistance," staff said. "We're in everybody's back yard."

4. **Recreation is us.** Audubon provides residents and visitors with major recreational opportunities (thus relieving stress, among other things). Queen River | Wood Pawcatuck is (probably) Rhode Island's cleanest river, a fishy stream much appreciated by discriminating anglers; a calendar-worthy network of first-rate mill-and-woodland canoeing, thanks in good part to Audubon land management. Miles of trails penetrating nature's secrets and wonders. Even Audubon's education programs are a form of recreation, for curious adults, nature lovers, tourists, kids and families.

5. **We manage (well) a big, important portfolio of undeveloped land.** Audubon is Rhode Island's biggest guardian of undeveloped land

outside state government. Audubon manages nearly 9,500 acres, preserving parcels of undeveloped nature in every community. We're good at it, too. When the Nature Conservancy needs land management in Rhode Island, it turns to Audubon.

6. **We play a "larger than you might expect" role in the state's image as a good place to live and raise a family.** Audubon is a major contributor to Rhode Island's quality of life and attractiveness. Audubon is part of the touted "Rhode Island renaissance." Audubon's land management is a factor in the state's economy several ways: by helping sustain our environment's health, here in the nation's Second-most thickly populated state; by helping maintain the state's "curb appeal" as a place that's still picture-book "New England-y" and rural; by contributing considerable assets (a dozen refuges, the environmental education center, nature tours, educational programs) to the state's recreational and tourism mix. Tourism is among the state's top three industries.

7. **Audubon is relevant.** The big environmental news for Rhode Island in November 2006 was the threat posed by deer ticks and Lyme disease. As a prime protector of deer habitat, what is Audubon's take on all this? Are you issuing a release on "Audubon's top 10 ways to avoid Lyme disease"? Given the consequences of Lyme infection (including death and brain damage; it's been called the syphilis of our age); it's not unreasonable for people to start thinking "deer and the woods are dangerous." Engage with current issues. You don't have to have all the answers. You just need to be inside the discussion. (Was Audubon quoted in the *Providence Journal* articles?) If you're seen as irrelevant, your fundraising potential will decline.

8. **Audubon speaks for nature.** "Frogs can't lobby for clean water," staff said. "We can."

9. **Don't overlook the subtler advantages of a strong Audubon.** Audubon is good for property values. A strong Audubon presence helps sustain property values overall in Rhode Island, by preserving the state's undeveloped natural assets and beauty, key reasons why people wish to buy here. You might wonder how important property values really are. To homeowners, "maintaining property value" is a top priority, as we discovered during the research for the affordable housing bond. It is a very deeply felt and emotional issue (and the source of much community resistance to affordable housing projects). Because of the run-up in real estate since 2000, Rhode Islanders have become hugely "property-value aware." The recent slight softening of the market makes people nervous. Now would be a good time to point out how Audubon helps keep Rhode Island an attractive place to live.

10. **Don't drink too much of your own Kool-Aid** (or at least don't spit it on others). You divide the mission into three categories: advocacy, conservation, and education. That's insider-speak. It makes sense to you because it mirrors your org. chart. But what does it mean outside your walls? "Conservation" and "advocacy" suggest everything and nothing. "Education" suggests a classroom. Where are the birds? Where are the butterflies? The clean water? The outsider looks at you through the lens of WIIFM: What's In It For Me. The WIIFM-driven outsider, for instance, would assume recreation is a big part of the Audubon mission. Yet recreation isn't mentioned at all in the headlines of the last annual report, a regrettable omission since 80–90% of the time people only read headlines.

2. THEMES AND STORIES

The bold-faced messages listed above are also called themes. There is an important difference between themes and stories.

"Cases of childhood OCD could be rising because kids don't play enough outside, studies show . . . " is a story. Stories have concrete details. Themes don't. The theme here is "Environmental education is as important as the 1-2-3s and A-B-Cs . . . "

When you start thinking in themes instead of stories, life gets *much* easier. Suddenly you start seeing stories everywhere, because you notice the themes behind the details. Think in themes, and you'll never run out of interesting material.

Now that an attractive, flexible new graphic look has been established in Report, it's time to consecrate the structure to donor-centric content, bow to stern. To achieve that, every major story (and most minor) must be tested against this criterion: *Does this story advance one of our key themes?* If not, rewrite the headline at least.

3. MAKING YOUR CASE FOR SUPPORT

The document you're reading is called an "internal case." An internal case is a database of information and ideas that will interest donors and prospects. The internal case is a "cheat sheet" for staff and volunteer solicitors. Building the internal case is step one.

Step two is making your so-called "case for support." For that, you need to have your prospect clearly in mind. Is it an individual who's given support in the past, a pool of people who have never given, a foundation, a corporation? They all have different interests (environmental education will fascinate some, but not all, for instance). Therefore, your case for support changes from prospect to prospect. You pluck elements from the internal case to create a custom set of messages for each targeted prospect.

When you make a case for support, you're telling a story. A story has a beginning, middle, and end.

- Beginning: You show the problem. You propose Audubon as the solution.

- Middle: You provide supporting evidence, proof that Audubon knows what it's about. This is where you talk about your accomplishments.

- End: You issue a call to action. And you remind the prospect that donors are vital to pursuing Audubon's mission and vision. That reminder subtly and painlessly shifts responsibility for solving the problem onto the donors' shoulders. Which is fine: donors want to feel that their help really matters. And the burden is weightless: it's only money.

4. Communications: Bland Will Not Work

Advertising pioneer David Ogilvy, creator of one of the world's most successful agencies, once observed, "You cannot bore someone into buying your product."

Audubon needs people (prospects and donors) to buy its mission (that's your product). But, frankly, you're bland. Serving up repeated helpings of safe, soft, familiar, predictable, non-controversial news in *Report* and other communications will not (in fact, cannot; there's psychology involved) spur people to buy into your mission.

The formula for inciting a gift is straightforward: (1) you create unease by talking about a problem; (2) you relieve that unease by talking about your solution (your mission); (3) you involve your target audience by asking them to invest in that solution via a gift.

Shock me. Surprise me. Frighten me. I'll pay for the sensation. Cover story ideas:

- **Rhode Islanders: Are you living in America's next desert state?** The bad news: We use drinking water faster than we make it. Inside: What your Audubon is doing about it.

- **Can a walk in the woods cure ADD?** Your mom was right: Go outside and play. New studies underscore nature's role in mental health.

- **When is saving land from development a bad thing?** When you can't afford to manage any more. Without more endowment, another 5,000 acres remain beyond Audubon's grasp.

- **Upscale outsiders flood RI's city housing market.** Among the attractions: A hike through nature's bounty just a short drive away, thanks to Audubon.

- **Land-rich, cash-poor.** Added acreage means added expense. Audubon confronts a stunted future if giving continues to sputter.

- **If frogs can swim in it, you can drink it.** The link between frog deformities and healthy drinking water. Inside: Audubon's role in watershed preservation.

- **Ospreys are back. Bald eagles are back. What's next?** Audubon sees a bright future if donor support improves. Gifts in wills become new focus.

- **The environmental bandwagon: When will state legislators get on?** Lip service abundant, action rare. Audubon's pro-water agenda still in first gear; 3 votes shy on key stream gauge measure.

- **Paying the price: Legacy of poor environmental controls takes a toll on next generations.** Mercury and autism linked? Audubon joins the debate on where state's pollution controls headed.

- **Tomorrow's voting environmentalist is 8 years old today.** Audubon sees need for more environmental education . . . quickly. Donors called to help.

5. NAMING, BRANDING, AND OTHER ASPECTS OF PERSONALITY

Organizations assume their donors are supporting the programs or the mission. True enough, in some cases. Most of the time, though, donors are "staggeringly ignorant" of what an organization does (Richard Radcliffe, UK donor researcher).

So what are they giving to? They're giving to "you," a face that is Audubon in their mind, an image they have in their hearts of your personality and what you do and why it matters.

Marketers call this your "brand." Marty Neumeier, who wrote the book on brand, defines it this way: "A brand is a person's gut feeling about a product, service, or company." This gut feeling might be incomplete ("Audubon? Oh, they're the bird people . . . "), even all wrong. But it *is* what they think you are. It is based on narrow personal experience (a hike, a class, a phone call, an event, a purchase at the gift shop, seeing one of your signs while driving or biking the East Bay bike trail); on an occasional wisp of word-of-mouth (. . . "my kids went to that Audubon nature center yesterday; they liked it . . . "); on your communications, if someone sees them.

You have limited control over this image, since it is locked inside minds, and you don't have that much access. Not to worry, though: People give, and give large amounts, despite staggering ignorance of your activities. (So, is the urge to "educate donors" misplaced energy? No. But don't count on it too much, either. People want to be interested. They want to be surprised. [Keep surprising people in your communications, and you will always have attentive readers.] Most donors don't need or want any great amount of "education," unless it's entertaining.)

Lucky you: You own a truly valuable marketing asset, a great and undented brand name. Mention "Audubon" to almost anyone in Rhode Island, and nothing but good images spring to mind. (By the way, as long as the words "Rhode Island" are somewhere nearby in the text or speech, "Audubon" can be used by itself, without "Society" or "of Rhode Island." The "issue" of confusing local Audubon with national Audubon is a non-issue for fundraising: With small gifts, it's not worth worrying about; with large gifts, the mistake won't be made.)

People give to Audubon, firm in the conviction that they're giving to a good cause. You actually have three things going for you: (1) warm feelings for "Audubon" generally; (2) because you're in "the healthy air and water business" as well as recreation, everyone benefits from Audubon (it's not the symphony, a matter of personal taste); and (3) the fact that people like to give locally. They'll give to the "Rhode Island" in your name simply because they live here, too. They feel they might personally benefit from your mission somehow, some day.

6. Untapped Donor Potential

Because of its near-universal name recognition and positive brand, Audubon might very well be sitting on one of the state's largest unexploited reserves of predisposed donor prospects. The reserve is almost untapped so far.

Membership, as it's now pursued, is "benefits-driven" instead of "mission-driven." The downsides: if they don't want the benefits, they don't want the membership; and the logic falls apart at higher gift levels as the value of the benefits badly trails the value of the gift. Sweetening your offer with a fleece vest seems unlikely to spring many donors from a $100 Defender level to a $250 Advocate level. On the other hand, when you sell mission, the sky's the limit. It's the great outdoors: It can absorb any amount of money.

7. Accomplishments, the Primacy of

Donors care about one thing above all, studies show: an organization's accomplishments. Talk about those: You raise lots of money. Don't talk about those: Your fundraising lags.

But beware, nonprofits: an activity is NOT an accomplishment (yet). Nonprofits often get this wrong. Activities intrigue you (they're your work). But your activities are only mildly interesting to donors. When you *achieve* something with that program, *then* you will be truly interesting.

To donors, accomplishments are why Audubon matters. Accomplishments—or the promise of accomplishment, if a program is especially brilliant or risky—are why they will invest in Audubon's mission.

Note: Being award-winning, as Audubon's urban education program is, is a terrific accomplishment. Shout it from the rooftops.

8. Emotional Triggers

Marketers know empirically that emotions drive decisions. The entire huge American direct mail industry bases its sales on the predictability and profitability of seven emotional triggers.

Think how much money was raised for the 2006 U.S. political campaigns based on anger, fear, and hope. Giving to religious organizations, the largest pie slice of American philanthropy, is purely emotional. The reliable responses to religious cash appeals include guilt, fear, hope, salvation, and duty—all powerful, basic triggers.

Now we have scientific proof: an emotional trigger is actually *required* to detonate a decision–such as the decision to make a gift to Audubon.

Dr. Antoine Bechara is a neuroscience researcher devoted to unraveling the human decision-making process. The subjects of his study were people uniquely suited to prove a point. They had all suffered damage to the brain's emotional headquarters, the orbitofrontal cortex. Otherwise, their brains worked just fine. Reason was intact. Intelligence remained as it had been. Only the ability to feel emotions was gone. And the oddest thing happened as a result: Without emotions in the mental mix, even simple decisions, like what to choose for dinner, proved nearly impossible. Our feelings, in some fundamental, physiological way, make decisions occur.

There are plenty of emotional triggers to choose from: 135 by the count of W. Gerrod Parrott, a Georgetown University psychology professor. He grouped his 135 into six mega-categories: love, joy, surprise, anger, sadness, fear. In the anger category, for instance, emotions included ranged from grumpiness to torment.

Recommended emotional triggers for Audubon:

- Hope (that the purity, the wonder, the diversity, the beauty remain)
- Fear (that the environment we must live in is poisoned and harming us) Note: Global warming and other scary environmental consequences now lead the news. You should talk about these things, so you seem (a) relevant; (b) authoritative (people like to give to authorities and leaders); and (c) pull the fear trigger often. Audubon should be part of this news story. It's a big story. It's a story of good vs. evil, tree-huggers (be proud) vs. polluters.
- Salvation (those who protect nature are on a holy mission)

- Guilt (I drive a car, I'm part of the problem, I want to correct that somehow without changing my lifestyle, so maybe saving a few trees would help [it would, actually])

- Flattery (I'm pleased you know I'm a good person, a capable person, a responsible person, a person of discriminating tastes, a contributor, a true believer, special)

- Greed (this is good greed; a longing for more of the things we enjoy; it also greed for the good things in life like health) Note: Greed for enjoyable things includes events such as the return of Rhode Island's bald eagles. That is a story you have every right to talk about, because it reveals that Audubon has accomplished something (magnificent) by leading the fight against DDT in the 1960s. Jeff brought this up first: The return of the bald eagle would be an excellent story for Audubon to own. It's a successful bird story (and you're the bird people). The bald eagle, once-endangered national symbol and a figure of awe to anyone who has never visited Alaska, is back in Rhode Island . . . in part because Audubon made the state a safe (no-DDT) nesting area (with special thanks to the Providence Water Board). Take a bow.

- Surprise (wow, who knew?) Note: This one is too easy. Neurobiology says that our brains respond to ANYTHING new: significant, insignificant, doesn't matter. The human brain is hard-wired. It will involuntarily respond to the word "new" or things like "Did you know?" Tell me something I don't know, the human mind craves. You folks must know ten thousand secrets about nature right off the top of your heads. Talk about that stuff: The more counter-intuitive, surprising, unexpected, counter to conventional wisdom . . . the better.

- Love (the first robin, the first leaves turning color, the explosive splash of surf against Beavertail, the shadow of a trout in a stream, the taste of my drinking water, the surprise in my child's eye when a butterfly flaps past, the delight of field flowers in a vase, the taste of locally pressed cider . . . these are a few of my favorite things)

- Joy (ditto)

- Exclusivity (on the envelope: Inside—A circle of influential friends awaits the pleasure of your company. That message added more than 500 local millionaires to the cultivation files at the Rhode Island Foundation.)

Emotions tend to work best in pairs. Anger/joy. Fear/hope. Guilt/salvation. Fear and hope, working together, are probably Audubon's default emotional "twinset" (two emotions that, linked, reliably produce charitable gifts). Fear is emotion number one. It's about as primitive as finger paints. Once you know how to use fear, you can graduate to more sophisticated emotional media.

Talking Points: HousingWorks RI 2006

Revised April 17, 2006

Dear speakers: You can use your own words. The facts are important, not the verbatim words.

Topic: The $75 Million General Obligation Bond on November's Ballot

Q. Is $75 million enough to make a real difference?

A. Yes. It's enough to jump-start new affordable housing construction and rehabilitation throughout Rhode Island.

At a minimum the $75 million, and the money it leverages, will make another 950 new affordable rental units and starter homes possible. That reduces Rhode Island's affordable housing shortage by more than 6% at a single stroke (given the estimated gap of 15,000 units required by our low- and moderate-wage workforce).

But that's not all the $75 million can fund.

- Some of the $75 million will be available to help our cities and towns with infrastructure improvements they might need to build affordable homes.

- Some of the $75 million can also be used to reward Rhode Island employers who create housing assistance programs for their employees, an important new trend.

- And $10 million will be set aside as a one-time cash infusion to bankroll the state's long-delayed "Housing and Conservation Trust" fund.

Such trusts are popular with states (15 have them) because they are a win-win for taxpayers. They provide a permanent, non-taxpayer source of revenue that can fund future affordable housing. (Revenue is typically raised through fees on real estate transactions.) And they favor housing that preserves open space.

Woonsocket's Woodridge Estates is a perfect example of how housing and conservation work together. It clusters 26 architect-designed affordable homes for first-time buyers on just three of the site's 10 acres, leaving the rest of the hillside untouched and permanently wooded as natural habitat.

Bear in mind, too, the multiplier effect that $75 million will have.

This $75 million leverages a lot more money, from the feds and private investors. Housing experts say the rule of thumb is a 6-for-1 return. For every dollar the state invests, another $6 enters Rhode Island from private and federal sources. By that measure, our $75 million investment can attract another $450 million, for a total of $525 million applied to the state's affordable housing crisis. Will $525 million make a difference? A *huge* difference. Let's get started.

WHEN TALKING TO LEGISLATORS ABOUT THE BOND

- Consider this a down payment on the state's commitment to fix our well-publicized affordable housing crisis. (A commitment expressed by the house majority leader and the governor at a press conference in November 2005. A commitment applauded by the *Providence Journal* and endorsed by the state's business community, including the EDC, the Greater Providence Chamber of Commerce, and *Providence Business News*.)

- Among other things, this is about "restarting the starter home in Rhode Island."

- This $75 million funds an economic development measure: the construction of workforce housing, as mill housing once was. It is NOT a welfare program. This bond will help eliminate Rhode Island's desperate shortage of affordable rentals and first-time homes for low- and moderate-wage workers and their families. It's not just the right thing to do, it's the smart thing to do—for the economy.

- The cost of housing and the cost of workers are directly linked. This bond is as much an employer incentive as tax breaks are, since it offers relief to rising cost-of-living pressures on the housing end of things.

- This bond jump-starts the solution right now, in 2006. Every year we delay, the problem worsens, raising serious questions (say the EDC and the RI Economic Policy Council) about Rhode Island's economic competitiveness.

- The bond is a one-time investment. It is not a spending program that annually demands replenishment. You see it once.

- It's good for municipalities in your district. The bond legislation is written so any city and town can apply for financial help to defray infrastructure costs associated with building new starter homes and affordable apartments. It can help your cities and towns meet their state affordable housing goals (the 10% rule).

Q. Does the bond replace the Neighborhood Opportunities Program (NOP)?

A. We hope not, given the state's desperate need for affordable rentals and starter homes.

Of course, it would be ungrateful to characterize last year's NOP contribution of $7.5 million in taxpayer money as a "drop in the bucket." But honestly, in real estate terms, $7.5 million (equal to *one-tenth* of 1% of the state's FY2006 budget), won't take us far down the road to fixing the problem.

NOP has a very narrow target. It helps fund housing for very-low-income households. And that was an important first step.

But its limited funds (just $7.5 million in 2005, NOP's fifth year of existence) are spent almost exclusively in the inner cities. The $75 million bond lets us quickly expand the state's investment ten-fold without raising taxes today. The bond extends the range of income-qualified households significantly, to include moderate-wage workers in every Rhode Island city or town.

The bond is a one-time augmentation in a state that until 2004 had invested almost nothing in affordable housing. And now faces the consequences.

Q. Why $75 million? Where did that number come from?

A. Well, it started at $100 million actually. Then the experts whittled it down to the smallest amount they believed would still have a meaningful impact of the state's housing crisis.

The steering committee of HousingWorks RI approved the final $75 million bond proposal. On that committee were representatives from the state's chambers of commerce, major employers, trade organizations, unions, nonprofits, colleges, the state's top charitable funders, and the faith community.

Q. Who is HousingWorks RI?

A. Organizations on the HousingWorks RI steering committee, alphabetically: Brown University, the Corporation for Supportive

Housing, Economic Development Corporation, Fannie Mae, Grow Smart RI, the Housing Network of RI, Johnson & Wales University, LISC, Rhode Island Board of Rabbis, Rhode Island Builders Association, Rhode Island Coalition for the Homeless, Rhode Island Foundation, Rhode Island Housing, Rhode Island Kids Count, Rhode Island Mortgage Bankers Association, Rhode Island State Council of Churches, Statewide Housing Action Coalition, and United Way of Rhode Island.

Q. Can taxpayers handle more bond debt?

A. Yes. Even RIPEC, the state's leading debt hawk, admits that Rhode Island taxpayers carry less bond debt than other taxpayers nationally. This lack of indebtedness feels good superficially. But it also translates into underinvestment in the state's economic well-being.

TOPIC: WORKING-CLASS RHODE ISLANDERS LOSE THEIR SHOT AT THE AMERICAN DREAM OF A DECENT HOME IN A GOOD COMMUNITY

Q. Where did it all go wrong?

A. It's a tale as old as supply and demand.

Since about 1999, Rhode Island has seen demand drive up the price of homeownership and rental with jaw-dropping, double-digit strength.2001: Up 15%. 2002: Up 21%. 2003: Up 22%. 2004: Up 15%.

Finally, in 2006, the price leaps started to lose some of their energy. But prices aren't falling. And even if they did, some national experts predict that a worst-case scenario calls for no more than a 10% retreat from current sales prices.

What happened? Buyers from Massachusetts, New York and New Jersey, willing to pay more, flooded the state's slumbering real estate market and kicked it into overdrive. In 2000, the state's homeless shelters, an early indicator that housing costs are rising, began overflowing all the time. Homeowners watched with amazement as their properties doubled in value in just a few years. For those who owned, these were the happy years.

Not so happy: workers who incomes couldn't handle the higher prices.

The government says, if you spend more than 30% of your income on housing, your place is too expensive. Some other part of your lifestyle has to suffer. You don't save. You stop spending. You go easily into debt. You cut back on your health care. You don't invest in yourself or your family. Above 30%, you probably cannot make ends meet.

Every time there was another year of double-digit appreciation, tens of thousands of working Rhode Islanders without generous incomes were forced past the 30% barrier. For them, these very same "happy years" were the years when their shot at the American Dream disappeared.

The real estate market's gone mad. To afford a starter home in one of Rhode Island's 20 least-expensive cities and towns **requires a household income of $100,000**. Rhode Island's current median household income isn't even half that (our median $45,000). Most Rhode Island workers are in low- to moderate-income jobs.

Q. What's the bottom line?

A. More development, either construction of new single-family starter homes and affordable apartments, or the rehabilitation of existing structures like mills and old schools into housing everyday Rhode Islanders can afford. It's the only solution.

Q. So what's stopping us from just building our way out of this problem?

A. A few things.

FIRST
People are afraid of what affordable housing will look like.

Talk about "affordable housing" in any town in Rhode Island outside the urban core and prepare for the worst. People panic.

Our images of affordable housing have been conditioned by police dramas on TV and commutes past the Hartford Avenue projects.

So when we hear "affordable housing," we switch to the only image we have handy: anonymous brick hive where society warehouses its poor. In focus groups, people frequently link the phrase "affordable housing" to negatives such as "high crime," "run down," "trashy," "ugly." Obviously these have no curb appeal. With these sorts of perceptions common, it's no wonder that "affordable housing" is assumed to be a fast way to lower your property values.

But the truth is, the kind of quality affordable apartments and starter homes we build here in Rhode Island are not like that. At all. Guaranteed. Let me show you . . .

SECOND
People don't realize that most residents of their town's affordable housing will be locals with modest incomes.

People aren't aware of who *really* lives in affordable housing. Again, there is a common image: that inner-city dwellers will pile into a bus and head for Foster. Sort of a large-scale version of the Beverly Hillbillies, only without the oil wells.

It's just wrong.

Affordable apartments and starter homes in places like Foster typically fill with locals, recent surveys show. Statewide the average appears to be about 50 percent local. In far-flung towns like Foster, residents would be almost all locals, experience shows.

These are people who grew up in town, already live in town, or work in town. Maybe they went to college, came back, and now live with their parents once more (yippee). Or seniors on fixed incomes who can no longer afford their rent. Or town employees such as truck drivers or teachers aides. Or divorced moms raising kids on a single income.

The $75 million bond buys Rhode Island "workforce" housing, quality rentals and starter homes, for people who have jobs but can't find anything decent housing they can afford. Nearly 123,000 Rhode Island households—30 percent of our total—earn less than $25,000 per year. Among the first occupations to move into RI's most recent affordable housing development: a firefighter, a teacher's aides, an office clerk, a short order cook, a bookkeeper, a truck driver. Their salaries qualified them for the housing lottery.

If we could raise everyone's wages to $100,000, maybe we'd have the state's housing problem licked. But we can't do that. Just one example: We'd have to close Providence Place Mall. Retailers can't afford $100,000 sales clerks. (Real life: Rhode Island retail clerks earn $23,000 on average.)

In reality, low-income city folk—the proverbial "those people"—don't care to move to towns like Foster. Rural towns are far too inconvenient . . . and, well, just far. Your job is far away. There's no public transportation. You have to drive miles for a carton of milk.

Coincidentally, Foster has gone through the affordable housing trauma—and knows that there's nothing to fear.

Foster's Hemlock Village—a well-maintained, attractive, low-income senior apartment complex hidden among fir trees—met *fierce* resistance when first proposed. Townspeople fought it tooth and nail. And when it opened despite the protests, guess who was first in line for the affordable apartments? That's right: Foster residents. Hemlock Village is filled with this one's mother, and that one's friend, and now is rightly considered a town asset.

THIRD . . .
Restrictive zoning and other devices have slowed residential construction in Rhode Island to a crawl (unless you're building luxury condominiums).

Getting a house built in many Rhode Island communities is like running a hurdles race with one leg. It's painful. You fall a lot. And it's very slow.

Buy land for a housing development in Rhode Island, and it might be three years before you break ground. All that time you're paying interest on your bank loans.

Slow permitting makes it very expensive to build residential units in Rhode Island. (And slow permitting is not the result of due diligence. In New Hampshire, they've found a way to reduce the permitting process down to six weeks, while guaranteeing high quality developments.)

No one except non-profit builders can afford to wait that long. The resistance of Rhode Island towns to development—and particularly affordable housing—is notorious. It got so bad that a few years ago the state had to step in and insist on a 10% goal.

We're creating new jobs. But housing starts haven't had a good year since the 1986, the last peak, when developers built 7,274 units here. In 1989, that number entered a deep slump. By 2004, the number of authorized building permits had fallen to 2,532. Rhode Island added 10,000 households from 2001 to 2003. At the same time, economists reported, we only built 7,800 new homes.

CHAPTER 19

The Donor Newsletter

HOW YOU CULTIVATE (I.E., RETAIN) DONORS

DEAR READER Why have a newsletter, electronic or paper (or both)? It's critical to donor retention. Your newsletter helps you improve relationships with your donors by reporting on all the wonderful, worthwhile things their support has made possible. Yes, your newsletter can spur immediate income, as well as "tomorrow" income in the form of bequests and other planned gifts. But that is not its primary goal. The newsletter's primary goal is to increase donor trust in your organization's effectiveness.

Tom

INTRODUCTION

Does a nonprofit organization *really* need a donor newsletter?

If you *need* donors, the answer is yes.

Done right, your donor newsletter will be your single most valuable communications medium.[1] Why so? The reason goes back to fund development fundamentals. If you *could* speak one-on-one with each donor regularly, that would be an incomparable way to raise funds. But you can't. So a newsletter is the next best thing. A good newsletter is an indispensable "relationship builder." It's a chance for a personal conversation with every donor—four, six, eight, a dozen times a year.

The primary purpose of a donor newsletter is to report on your accomplishments to the people who supplied the money for those accomplishments. A good newsletter earns your organization the donor's trust and loyalty. That's why you publish. And to defuse the reaction "The only time I hear from you is to ask me for money."

A donor newsletter is not a sales brochure in disguise, trying to push this and that giving "opportunity." The newsletter can surely help with tasks like bequest marketing, challenge campaigns, capital campaigns, and appeals; but helping with those tasks is not its primary purpose.

Nor is a donor newsletter simply a clubhouse, a place to flatter donors by running their photos. Yes, your newsletter helps you build community and display all those expensive smiles, but that is not its primary purpose.

Donor newsletters do raise plenty of money in the right hands. But they make a "soft" ask, quietly smiling behind a veil of accomplishment. (See Appendix 19A for an example of an effective donor newsletter.)

A good donor newsletter is a tremendous asset to your organization, well worth doing. Jeff Brooks, who's edited scores of donor newsletters for leading U.S. charities as a creative director at Merkle|Domain, wrote in 2005: "Your newsletter can be one of your best fundraising tools. That's because a newsletter has a unique platform to show donors the impact of their giving—and cement the relationship. And it can do this while earning a fundraising return that rivals (or even beats) appeal letters." In some cases, the newsletters he works on pull in more cash from donors than the charity's appeal letters do. "The key is to make sure your newsletter builds donor loyalty. Loyal donors will give more, stay with you longer, and be your best advocates."[2]

WHAT THE RESEARCH SAYS ABOUT DONOR NEWSLETTERS

The year 1995 had its share of landmarks: DVDs introduced high-quality optical storage; the World Trade Organization formed to promote a global economy (which critics insisted would make the rich richer but do nothing for the poor); the Dow Jones Industrial Average set two millennium records, rising above 4,000 and then 5,000; an apartment fire in Manila exposed an almost-finished al-Qaeda plot to explode 11 airliners over the mid-Pacific; and Amazon.com opened for business, revolutionizing the online retail experience, making obscure books as easy to buy as blockbusters.

It was a notable year for U.S. fundraisers, too. In 1995, The Russ Reid Company in conjunction with George Barna of the Barna Research Group conducted an extraordinary study. The "Heart of the Donor" study asked a nationwide sample of American donors about their preferences and opinions.

Regarding communications, the study asked donors how the nonprofits they supported could best "keep in touch [and] help you feel more closely connected to and interested in the work of the organization."

The study reported, "We identified a single stand-out: newsletters. Almost three-quarters of all donors claimed that receiving a regular newsletter would increase their focus upon and interest in an organization." Donor loyalty, here we come.

And yet . . .

While donors claim they want a newsletter, those newsletters go unread, other research finds. Jerry Panas, one of the industry's busiest campaign consultants and author of several fundraising classics, has remarked, "Every time we survey, donors tell us they don't read the newsletters."

What might sound like contradictory research isn't really.

We've reviewed hundreds of donor newsletters, from nonprofits of all sorts and sizes. Most failed to ignite. Judged against normal journalistic standards, as well as donor expectations, they were fatally riddled with flaws. (Mystery solved!) Strictly speaking, few were donor newsletters at all, since they carried little news of interest to that particular, and quite demanding, reader.

WHAT DO DONORS WANT FROM YOUR NEWSLETTER?

As you might guess, high on the donor's wish list is an answer to this question: *What did you do with my money?*

Penelope Burk found in her research that an overwhelming majority, 93 percent of individual donors,

> would definitely or probably give again the next the time they were asked to a charity that thanked them promptly and in a personal way for their gift, and followed up later with a meaningful report on the program they had funded. Under these circumstances, 64% would give a larger gift and 74% would continue to give indefinitely.[3]

That suggests that a sequential rotating program of appeals, thank-yous, and newsletters would be a big-time winner.

The donor isn't asking for a precise accounting, understand: "Well, you sent us a check for $25. So we rushed out to the store and bought that case of light bulbs we needed." The donor is merely asking, reasonably enough: "What have you accomplished since I gave you my gift?"

Donors don't give *to* your organization as much as they give *through* your organization. Their aim: to change a corner of the world they care about. For donors, your organization is a "change agent," and they're investing in your promise. Sure, the check reads: "Pay to the order of Memphis Child Advocacy Center." But what the donor is *really* giving to is the promise in that organization's tagline: "Helping victims become children again."

Stories in a donor newsletter should stir a warm, satisfied response in readers; a proud, little mental whisper: "I helped make that happen." Ask yourself then: "What do our donors want to make happen? What do they want to change?"

- Do your donors long to fix a problem that breaks their heart, like homelessness?

Family's last address: a junked car. Mom and kids homeless no more.

I was so terrified for my two girls.

- Do your donors believe that certain programs you do, like sex education, make an important contribution to the community?

Early-intervention Sex Ed arrives "in nick of time," teachers say.

It shocked me, how many risks these kids were ready to engage in.

- Do your donors want more of something they already enjoy, like hiking?

Newly opened "deep woods" experience wows walkers.

We saw orchids you wouldn't believe if we didn't have the photos.

You need to report on only five general topics in your newsletter, to convince donors that their money is, and will continue to be, well spent. These topics are, ranked from vitally important to reassuring:

- **Your organization's accomplishments.** *Vital.* The donor wants to know: "What did you do with my money? What are your results? Are you effective? How's the mission going?" Be careful. Understand that things insiders consider important accomplishments often matter little to the donor. The donor's bottom line is this: "Are you achieving the mission I've invested in?" Test every story idea against this standard: Why would a donor care? A new program, for instance, is not an accomplishment . . . yet. Programs come and go. Many never yield results. A new one is, at best, a *hope* that you'll accomplish more of your mission. Same goes for new hires. News to you, but to the donor? You've hired a new executive director. Frankly, my dear, big deal; *somebody* has to run the place. What does it mean to the mission?

- **Threats to achieving your mission.** *Vital.* Jeff Brooks notes, "Many nonprofits shy away from the 'negative.' This is a mistake."[4] Hal Malchow, president of MSHC Partners, a top DC-based "persuasion direct mail firm" helping political candidates and national causes, observed: "You'll raise far more money with news of a setback that leaves you in desperate need and your mission yet to be accomplished." We've witnessed the same phenomenon. In one issue of a client's donor newsletter, we highlighted a story of pressing need on the front page. There was accomplishment reported, too, but not as prominently. Gifts poured in. In the next issue of the newsletter, the front page went into reverse: It featured a story of accomplishment, but no need. Gifts fell off steeply. In the next issue we once again featured desperate need on the front page. Giving poured in again. We learned our lesson. Bad news can be good news in fund development.

- **Recognition of the donor's importance to your cause.** *Vital.* The donor wants to know, "Do I matter? Is my help important to your mission? Is charity essential?" Donors need to feel that charity makes a crucial difference. Your newsletters must say, over and over, "With your help, we accomplished this wonderful thing. And without your help, it wouldn't be possible." Says Jeff Brooks, "The 'star' is your donor. Not you."

- **Your organization's efficiency as a business.** *Reassuring.* The donor wants to know "Do you run a lean operation, reserving most of your income for mission?" And the default assumption is "no, you don't," as we've said before. Perhaps it's not surprising that donor retention is a disgrace. If you're labeled a "nonprofit" (rather than NGO), you're twice cursed. The average person has to wonder, "What does 'nonprofit' mean exactly? Obviously you don't care about profit. Which probably means you're not very businesslike. Which is fine. I understand. Business isn't your first priority. You're doing good work, I'm sure. But you won't mind if I limit my losses, by keeping my gifts small." If you meet or exceed the standards of watchdogs (like the U.S. Better Business Bureau's Wise Giving Alliance, which stipulates that a charity "spend at least 65% of its total expenses on program activities"), make sure you tell your donors. Not once, but in every issue of your newsletter (a simple pie chart does the trick). Do not leave your donors guessing about your overhead costs. They will guess wrong . . . and likely not in your favor.

- **Your organization's vision.** *Reassuring.* The donor wants to know "What would you do if I gave you more money? Flatter me. Inspire me. Make me feel special. Show me how I can change the world. Show me you, too, that you have a plan, ambitions, and a future." That last item (having a future) is key if you're campaigning for bequests.

THE DIFFERENCE BETWEEN AN ACCOMPLISHMENT AND AN ACTIVITY

Because, in any good donor newsletter, you will be reporting on your organization's accomplishments all the time, you need to know the difference between a true accomplishment (in the donor's eye) and what is merely an activity. Consider this statement:

> Began the new "Youth in Transition" program with a five-year grant from the U.S. Health and Human Services agency to establish a residential treatment program to help homeless teenagers and young adults.

The preceding is not yet an accomplishment. As far as a donor is concerned, it is merely an activity you're engaged in, since the description does not reveal what the program hopes to accomplish or why it matters. Three additional words, "model" and "become self-sufficient," make all the difference:

> Began the new "Youth in Transition" program with a five-year grant from the U.S. Health and Human Services agency to establish a model residential treatment program to help homeless teenagers and young adults become self-sufficient.

Now the donor sees where you're going with this: The program will serve as a model for others to learn from (wonderful), and it will transform homeless youth into self-supporting members of society (hooray).

SEVEN COMMON FLAWS THAT UNDERMINE DONOR NEWSLETTERS: A CHECKLIST

"Almost every donor newsletter I see suffers from at least one of the following flaws," I reported in my first book, *Raising More Money with Newsletters than You Ever Thought Possible.*[5] "You would be shocked by how many newsletters suffer from all seven."

Don't be discouraged, though. You can easily remedy these flaws without earning a degree in journalism.

Flaw #1: Doesn't Deliver News that Donors Care About

Here's the deal: When you call it a *news* letter, you're making a promise to your readers that you'll bring them news that speaks to their special interests. A *donor* newsletter, therefore, should include accomplishments and the rest, as noted earlier. If you're new to donor newsletters, here's an easy-to-follow "editorial prescription": Devote roughly a quarter of your space to accomplishments, a quarter to need, a quarter to recognition, and leave the rest for vision and efficiency.

- **Your current newsletter suffers from flaw #1 if:** You slather your front page with a "from the desk of . . ." column, written by your executive director or board chair. Ninety-nine times out of 100 (oh, yes, we've seen that many and more; they're epidemic), "from the desk of" columns do not focus on core donor interests. Your front page is for your most important news. It's not the place to set up a rocking chair for a good-old-fashioned cracker-barrel chat.

Flaw #2: Doesn't Put the Donor Center Stage

Many nonprofit newsletters unwittingly hog the credit just by the way they tell their stories. "We did this," they report. "We did that," they say. "We're changing the world for the better."

But where's the donor? Off to the side, a bystander with cash. "Thank you very much for that," the newsletter adds. "Now we can get back to our important work."

Donors want to feel they've made a difference. Give them the credit as well as your thanks. In a donor-centered newsletter, the donor is unquestionably the hero. The donor is essential. "See how your gifts are changing the world." The donor-centric way of looking at things is this: "With you, we can do wonders. But without you, we're sunk."

- **Check whether your current newsletter suffers from flaw #2:** Examine your front-page headlines, lead paragraphs, and captions. Do donors get enthusiastic credit for making your accomplishments possible? If not, your newsletter probably isn't donor-centric.

Flaw #3: Isn't Very Friendly

Get out the latest issue of your newsletter. Take a red pen in hand. Circle every instance of the word "you": *you'd, you'll, your, you're, yours, yourself, you've.*

Now, are there red circles everywhere? In the headlines, captions, the first sentence of articles, your bullet lists? If yes, you've passed the all-important "you" test mentioned in Chapter 13. If red circles are few and far between (less than six per page, say), you've failed.

A good donor newsletter is friendly, even intimate, in tone. Frequent use of the word "you" closes the distance between you and the reader. This is especially important at institutions that hate the very idea of using the word "you" in their newsletter. Aloof, distant, cold, haughty, stuffed shirt, wind-baggy, and fearful of a conversational tone: None will win the hearts of donors.

- **Your current newsletter suffers from flaw #3 if:** You have few red circles.

Flaw #4: Skimps on Emotional Triggers

There's certainly no reason to skimp. Professor W. Gerrod Parrott (you met him in Chapter 9) counted up 135 possible emotions your newsletter might seize on as way to incite a gift. On your next visit to the tattoo parlor, have this inked on your wrist: Charity starts when you move a heart. In a profitable donor newsletter, tugging heartstrings is a round-the-clock obligation.

- **Your current newsletter suffers from flaw #4 if:** No anger, fear, hope, salvation, exclusivity, greed, guilt, or other gift-inciting emotional triggers appear in your newsletter headlines.

Flaw #5: Doesn't Tell Stories

Reread Chapter 15 on storytelling.

Organizations put far too much faith in statistical evidence to make their case. Statistics *are* important. But they're slow. People jump on your bandwagon far faster when the message comes in story form. Most articles on the front page of the *Wall Street Journal* begin with an anecdote, for good reason. You can understand anything instantly, without translation—a new trend, a new science, a new political puzzle—when it's reduced to one or two people in a situation.

- **Your current newsletter suffers from flaw #5 if:** Headlines celebrate big numbers. Real-life example: "Unrestricted grants reach $5.7 million in 20th year." To insiders that meant something. To outsiders it read like an algebra problem. Stick to telling stories.

Flaw #6: Expects People to Read in Depth

Sorry. Most of your audience won't give your newsletter careful attention. They'll glance at a few headlines, photos, and captions (any stuff that's bolder, briefer, and quicker), then get on with their lives. If you bury important information in long articles, most people will miss it.

- **Your current newsletter suffers from flaw #6 if:** It has short headlines, long articles.

Flaw #7: Doesn't Have Real Headlines

We've saved the worst for last. If you could fix only one flaw in your donor newsletter, this would be the one to fix. Why? Because it's a safe bet that most people (editors assume 80 percent a least) read only the headline and maybe a nibble of the first sentence in your article. To have any hope of getting a message across, you will strong headlines.

- **Your current newsletter suffers from flaw #7 if:** You ask someone to read a headline and tell you what the story's about . . . and they guess wrong.

THE FLAW YOU FIX FIRST: HEADLINES

The list that follows aren't really headlines, although they all pretended to be in one donor newsletter or another:

- Adoption Works!
- An Inclusive Approach to Excellence
- Strategic Plan on the Move
- Strong Men for Strong Families
- The Value of Volunteering
- From the Development Department
- We'd Love to Say Thank You!

What disqualifies them from being headlines?

In journalism, headlines have a job. They exist as an essential reader convenience. The headline sums up the story so the reader can quickly and confidently decide whether to stay or go. Counterintuitive as it might seem, headlines exist so you *don't* have to read the story. And putting "any old words" into large type at the top of an article will not automatically create a headline for you, not by a long shot.

Pay attention to your own reading behavior the next time you open a newspaper. You scan the headlines. Some stories interest you. Some don't.

As you sort through the headlines, you're making instant decisions about how you'll spend your "discretionary attention span." Will you dig deeper into the story? Or do you already know enough? Headlines make those instant decisions possible. By giving you the gist at a glance, they have done their job and done you a service.

"A good headline," writes Dr. Mario R. Garcia, a world-famous designer of major newspapers and their online reincarnations, "[has] enticing words, good action verbs, the best possible summary of what the content is about, and, if possible, a surprise or 'hook' that pulls us in."[6] In his book, *Heads You Win: An Easy Guide to Better Headline and Caption Writing*, veteran journalist Paul LaRocque concludes, "Good headlines do two things: They capture reader interest. They capture the essence of the story."[7]

A good headline explains the point of the story. A bad headline leaves lots of obvious questions unanswered. Consider the headline "Adoption Works!" For whom? For the child? For the parents? What does "works" mean? Why does it matter to the donor? You can *assume* some of the answers to these questions, but you don't *know* the answers. That's when you rewrite.

HIGH-VOLTAGE HEADLINE VERBS

Newspaper editors have a saying: "The verb in the headline *is* the story." The difference between professionally selected verbs and the verbs favored in nonprofit newsletters is striking.

The following verbs ran in front-page headlines over articles in the *Wall Street Journal*:

mauled, devour, looms, spark, threaten, embrace, sputters, sowing, surge, reject, retools, blames, clash

Compare them to the verbs found in typical nonprofit front-page headlines:

establishes, listed, use, reach, plan, unifies, build, sets, visits, shares, administer, awards, help, benefits

Wall Street Journal headline verbs describe physical action (devour, embrace). They suggest conflict (mauled, reject, blames) and tension (looms, threaten). They're easy to imagine because they are sensory: You can hear them (clash, sputters), you can see them (surge, spark).

The nonprofit headline verbs are safe, serene, and cerebral, guaranteed not to raise a single hair on the back of anyone's neck. Nonprofessionals sometimes assume blandness is desirable, as an option to the manufactured sense of alarm that characterizes nightly television news. The thinking: "Why would we want to upset our donors? The world's already stressful enough."

That assumption is dead wrong. Psychology killed it. Our minds pay special attention to differences in our environment. They are designed to do so. When the mind encounters things it knows all too well, it tends to ignore them. So playing it safe in your newsletter—no edges, no excitement, no surprises, everything predictable and drained of shock value—is actually the fastest way to train readers to ignore you.

How to Find the Story Behind the Headline

A good headline explains the story's gist. But what, exactly, *is* your story's gist? What point does the story make? How do you find the best angle for your target audience, which is donors?

Let's walk through the process together. Let's take a story idea and develop it for a donor newsletter.

Pretend for the moment that you're a domestic violence agency. Your next donor newsletter comes out in September. And you have what you think is the perfect front-page story: October Is Domestic Violence Prevention Month. Okay, write that down: *October Is Domestic Violence Prevention Month.* Now write down this question: *So what?*

That's how you develop a raw idea into a publishable story: You ask yourself blunt questions like "So what?" and "Why would a donor care?"

"Well," you answer yourself with chipper enthusiasm (see how much fun this is?), "in October we're hoping to go into sixth-grade classes and hold domestic violence workshops."

But your tough-editor side isn't buying it. "Look, workshops are fine. But donors don't care about what we *do*. They care about what we *accomplish*. We have to tell them why these workshops matter." Seeing that this is a bit deflating, your tough-editor side relents just a bit. "I'll admit, though, you've hooked me with the sixth-grade thing. You're saying that kids that young need domestic violence classes? I'm surprised."

Your enthusiasm roars back. "These programs work! When those sixth-graders grow up and get adult partners, they'll be far less likely to abuse their mates if they've had this training. That's what studies found. But you have to reach kids before puberty, or it's no good."

Suddenly, your tough-editor side grins. "Right! Now you're talking results. Exactly what the donor wants to hear." But there's a frown attached, too. "Where do I, the donor, come in? How can I be the hero?"

"That one's easy. It's a new program. We don't have it in the budget. The schools sure can't afford it, though they'd love to have us come in and do it. The donors are our only hope. We can't do it without them." Bingo!

Now you've uncovered a story angle that promises results and involves the donor. And see how far you've come from your original story idea. *Finally* you're ready to write the headline. "Did I hear you correctly? You're saying I should write the headline before I write the story itself?" Absolutely. And it might read something like this (the four elements labeled with bracketed numbers together comprise the headline unit):

OCTOBER IS DOMESTIC VIOLENCE PREVENTION MONTH (1)

Is It Possible to Stop Domestic Violence Before It Starts? Yes, Studies Show...If You Can Get Inside Pre-Pubescent Heads (2)

Proven "Early Intervention" Program for Sixth-Graders Ready to Go in Our Schools...If You'll Help With The Cost. (3)

With your help, we can all celebrate Domestic Violence Prevention Month the best way possible: by halting violence before it begins. (4) [article continues...][8]

A few observations about this example:

- Four elements work together as a unit to deliver a complete message.
  1. The top element is called, in the newspaper business, a "kicker" or "eyebrow." It sets the broad context: "October Is Domestic Violence Prevention Month."
  2. The biggest type ("Is it possible . . .") is the actual headline.
  3. The next biggest type ("Proven 'early intervention' program . . .") is called a "deck" in the newspaper business. The average person calls a deck a "subhead." But in publishing, "subheads" actually refer to those small, boldface phrases that break an article into smaller chunks.
  4. The lead sentence of the article ("With your help . . ."). The lead is often the *only* sentence of an article that gets read, so it is uniquely important.
- In newspapers and magazines, feature articles almost always run with both a headline and a deck. Both elements contribute something essential: facts, or point of view. The headline sums up the story, the deck offers commentary. Or vice versa. Many donor newsletters seem unaware that decks exist, a serious shortcoming.

Together, the headline and deck number 38 words. In a great newspaper like the *Wall Street Journal*, a headline-deck combination that long wouldn't earn a second glance. Headlines in most donor newsletters, though, are very tight-lipped. They restrict their heads to a handful of words ("Adoption Works!"). Understand: Very few stories will compress to just a few words (okay: "*Titanic Sinks*"). Use as many words as you need to get your point across. Dr. Barbara Ellis, author of *The Copy-Editing and Headline Handbook*, has this advice: "write a short sentence summing up the story and then delete the extra words."[9]

ELECTRONS OR PAPER? HIGH-PERFORMANCE E-MAILED NEWSLETTERS

It's the most common question now asked in my donor newsletter workshops: "Should I switch from printed newsletters to some kind of e-news?"

It's not that simple. E-news and paper newsletters are not either/or equivalents. Kris Hermanns, director of development at the National Center for Lesbian Rights (NCLR), offers this easy test: "Ask yourself. Are you raising money with your newsletter now? If not, don't expect to do better with an e-newsletter." Ted Hart, founder and president of the ePhilanthropy Foundation, points out:

> Use of the Internet as a stand-alone solution is not effective. Although some have predicted that ePhilanthropy will replace many traditional approaches to

soliciting support, this will not be the case. Just as television failed to kill radio, yet changed it significantly, so, too, will the Internet change traditional forms of fundraising, not by eliminating them but by changing their utility and increasing their effectiveness.[10]

He advises nonprofit organizations to see things like Web sites and e-mail "as a set of relationship-building tools first and fundraising tools second."

What's the potential if you do take this view? Hart points to the case of KVIE public television in California. "KVIE launched a weekly Viewer's Club [e-mailed newsletter] in 2001." The e-news was personalized around the viewer's specific program interests, alerting the viewer to upcoming shows. "Just two years into a comprehensive effort to improve online relationship building, KVIE has seen its online membership grow by 68 percent and has turned just $2,000 in online gifts in 2001 into nearly $200,000 in 2003."

Kris Hermanns oversees a rapidly expanding online giving program, begun in 2001. In 2006, NCLR expected to raise more than 10 percent of its $3.1 million budget online, a huge leap over the year previous. NCLR pursues landmark court cases that advance civil and human rights for the lesbian, gay, bisexual, and transgender (LGBT) community. Early victories included custody battles where lesbian moms were denied rights to their children.

E-newsletters play a part, but only a part, in the NCLR donor cultivation program. NCLR has a twice-a-year paper newsletter for bigger articles, "of real substance." Inside is a reply envelope for gifts. The NCLR e-newsletter goes out every other month. It includes three items, each about 100 words long. Each links back to the Web site. "NCLR is news-driven," says Kris. "And the Web site is all about content." Each e-news item leads to a host of documentation, such as complaints to court motions and briefs, rulings; news articles about ongoing cases; and a library of "how-to" materials, such as how to create safe schools, seek asylum, or write anti–hate crime legislation.

"The problem with some e-newsletters," Kris says, "is you get too many, and the content doesn't seem all that relevant." NCLR works to stay relevant. When people sign up for the NCLR e-newsletter, they fill out a "subscriber profile" that notes, among other things, what they do—or do not—wish to receive, and where they live. NCLR segments its e-news list geographically, so when there's an event nearby, or an action alert that matters to just one part of the country, those subscribers get a special bulletin.

To wring any great, *immediate* financial advantage from e-newsletters requires good data management. It is expensive to manage data at this level. "NCLR has two people who do nothing but think about how to slice and dice the data," Kris notes. "You have to be data-driven, to personalize, segment, and target."

There are two major payoffs. One, you can mine your data for new asking opportunities. Two, you can easily use your data to build relationships that are much stronger, by making personal thank-yous—the typical missing ingredient in most giving programs—routine and systematic.

Each month, NCLR's system spits out a report of every new gift above $5,000, so the executive director can call that person with thanks. Any gift above $500 gets a personal note card or a phone call. And that's just for starters.

NCLR knows what events someone's attended, what and whether they've given, who solicited them. And all this data, combed for insights, yields hundreds of thousands more dollars in support annually, through specially tailored custom appeals. Their planned "30 by 30" campaign, for instance, will spot donors who are close to $30,000 in lifetime giving, so they can be asked to bump up to that goal. Reaching $30,000 apiece aptly celebrates NCLR's thirtieth anniversary of fighting long and hard for fair and just treatment in America's courts, made possible by such steadfast donors.

When consultant Patricia Kern was vice president of marketing and development at the Boys & Girls Clubs of Greater Kansas City, her e-newsletter went out monthly to more than 1,000 e-mail addresses. "We used it to highlight three programs or activities each month. The December e-newsletter was an annual recap and a very soft ask." The important observation she makes: "All of our conventional fundraising (letters of appeal, grant applications, events) went up every year we were consistently doing the e-newsletter. It was free. It worked. And more money was raised. A good combo."

The monthly schedule said "Look. We're busy. We're organized." It reminded people of the clubs' existence. It fed twigs of information to its target audiences, keeping a warm little fire of recognition and appreciation burning. It built trust. When a hard ask came, like an event invitation or a grant application, prospects and donor had a stronger, clearer, positive image in their minds.

Just don't expect to reach everybody you'd like to with e-newsletters alone. "Keep in mind that not all donors are electronic savvy," Kern says.

Keep in mind, too, that readership of e-newsletters is quite low.

The vast majority of people will not open any particular issue. Even when you do a wonderful job, results are modest.

The Rhode Island Foundation probably does a better e-newsletter than most. The foundation's secrets: Stick to one topic per issue; keep that single article concise (a couple of brief paragraphs); and use the e-newsletter as a welcome mat that links people to the website. Don't overlook, too, that the foundation gives away more than $20 million a year in grants; many readers are well motivated to see what's inside. Yet only around 35 percent of recipients open the foundation's e-newsletter.

Consultant Rick Schwartz, who helped develop that particular e-newsletter, believes brevity is the key to higher-than-dismal opening rates. It doesn't take long to train people to ignore you, either. "If they know it's a monster," he predicts, "they won't open it."

YOUR E-NEWSLETTER'S SUBJECT LINE MAKES ALL THE DIFFERENCE

Schwartz also pointed out that one early change dramatically boosted opening rates. At first, the foundation sent out its e-newsletter under a bare-bones title. The "subject" line of the e-mailed newsletter told the number of the issue and that's all. When the foundation expanded the subject heading to include a tiny teaser headline, as well, opening rates jumped immediately.

The most important message in your e-newsletter is the message in your subject box. That message acts as both your "masthead" (the name of your e-newsletter) and your irresistible come-on. In direct mail, the "job" of the envelope is to get opened; protecting the enclosures is secondary. Similarly, in an e-newsletter, the job of the subject line is to get opened, to persuade the largest percentage of your target audience to spend a bit of their discretionary attention span on seeing what you have to say. If you can get someone to play with your e-newsletter a few seconds more, you'll leave a stronger impression.

Take some comfort. Even if people *don't* open your e-mailed newsletter, your organization can derive some benefit.

After all, before recipients can delete the latest issue, they *will* have to glance at the e-mail address and read your organization's name and almost certainly read your subject line, as well. It's only a moment. But still. They're reminded you exist. They remember that your mission and organization can from time to time be interesting or even amazing. And from time to time, if you properly ask, and it's convenient for the donor and volunteer, each of those microscopic fleeting impressions might contribute to the decision that you are worthy of support.

And while we're on the subject: Reminding people you exist once a year, with a solicitation letter say, means in most minds you really *don't* exist.

To produce good to great results in fund development, organizations need a communications plan that puts them in frequent touch with prospects and donors. Six times a year, by various means, is probably a minimum. And four of these communications are probably just making contact; they are not hard solicitations.[11] An e-mailed newsletter can help you flesh out a communications plan, with minimum commitment of time and cost.

EXHIBIT 19.1	**MONTHLY E-NEWS FROM THE WOMEN'S FUND OF RHODE ISLAND**

As a social justice organization, the Women's Fund works to build a sense of community. In January 2007 the fund launched a monthly e-news program. The monthly e-news augments the Women's Fund's printed quarterly "newsyletter," sent by postal mail.

The e-news includes engagement activities, not just information sharing. The Women's Fund also encourages viral marketing by asking recipients to forward the e-news to those who might be interested.

The fund's e-news:

- Highlights results produced by the work of the Women's Fund
- Invites the reader to attend activities
- Shares donor testimonials
- Shares social justice quotations
- Recommends books and promotes women's rights book clubs
- Invites subscribers to recommend, among other things, books as well as speakers for future events
- Asks subscribers to take action, which might include telephone and letter-writing campaigns
- Asks subscribers to answer fact-finding questions
- Asks subscribers for their opinions

See Exhibit 19.1 for a list of ways the Women's Fund of Rhode Island uses its e-newsletter.

ELECTRONS *AND* PAPER: OTHER ADVANTAGES OF E-NEWSLETTERS

Even if you claim only a modest donor base and minimal data management, adding an e-newsletter to your donor and prospect communications schedule has advantages. For instance:

- **Easily increases the number of donor contacts in your annual schedule.** E-newsletters help you stay in frequent touch with your donors without the expense of postage and printing. An every-other-month e-news adds six contacts to your annual donor communications schedule. Heed, though, Kris Hermanns' words: "Relevance makes the difference. Sending something of little interest, simply to stay on schedule, will quickly demote your e-news to delete-on-sight status. You stay in frequent touch so you can nurture a sense of accomplishment, ownership, and pride in your donors. Once people begin actively avoiding your communications, you're going in reverse."

- **Fastest format for emergency appeals.** E-newsletters give you a way to make emergency appeals NOW! while your issue is red hot. Have crisis, write e-mail, send e-mail: Within an hour, you can hustle a call to action into your supporters' hands. (And urgency is a great emotional trigger. Urgency is a direct-to-the-brain stimulant that, by itself, increases giving.)

- **Brief enough for a busy world. Perfect for the writing-challenged.**
E-newsletters can be extraordinarily brief. Translation: less writing for you. In fact, they probably *should* be brief. It's part of online culture. If you still think the term "sound bite" is pejorative, you're two decades out of date. Reading habits have changed. Expectations, too. With the Internet, the sound bite entered a Golden Age. For their e-news editions, major newspapers shrink every story to one headline and a teaser, with a clickable link to the Web site where the full story waits. A typical example from the *New York Times* e-news:

At Churches Nationwide, Good Words for Evolution

Ministers at hundreds of churches preached that the opposition many Christians say exists between science and faith is false.

- **Entice people to your Web site.** E-newsletters invite people to visit your Website, for information or to make gifts. You may have hidden extraordinary riches there: archives, news clippings, directories, tips, how-tos, guides, studies, photos, maps . . . the possibilities seem endless. The Rhode Island Foundation's e-newsletter, for instance, regularly reminds subscribers of three popular databases: for the nonprofit market, there's a list of other grantmakers; for the donor market, there's a directory of state nonprofits; for parents and their college-bound offspring, there's a directory of the foundation's numerous scholarship funds.

Tip: You will never exhaust the public's interest in real-life stories of people you've helped, thanks to donor support. Include these on your site and promote them in your e-news.

Also: You will be surprised by how much interest people will show in your finances, if you post them on your Web site. Encourage people to take a peek in your e-news. Inviting them into your books radiates openness, honesty, transparency, authenticity.

Finally: Your Web site is the first place people (including reporters, lawyers and financial advisors, donors of all sizes, and volunteers) go to get information on you. The more you satisfy their curiosity, the quicker you will form a strong bond. On your Web site, include past issues of your newsletters, annual reports, mission, vision, history, staff bios, contact information . . . anything that will help people get comfortable with you or get in touch. Remind your e-news subscribers in every issue: "Want to know more about us? Want to get in touch with the right person? Visit our

Web site . . . ." Think of your e-newsletter and your Web site as a tightly knit, codependent team.

A 2006 study by Donordigital (San Francisco) and Target Analysis Group (Cambridge, MA) found that "online giving mainly serves as a source for acquiring news donors." Furthermore, and perhaps a bit of a surprise, "Donors who give online are generally spread out evenly across all age groups." But online is not where they continue to give, once the relationship has begun.

According to the 2006 report, "The longer a direct mail donor has been giving to an organization, the less likely they are to start giving online. Direct mail donors do not renew online, and lapsed direct mail donors do not reactivate online." The opposite doesn't hold true for online donors. Instead, significant numbers tend to migrate to direct mail as they continue to support the nonprofit. For online donors acquired in 2005, a median 46% gave by mail in 2006. While only 2% of mail-acquired donors in 2005 gave online the following year.[12]

- **Speak and show.** You can now bring e-newsletters to life, with embedded audio and video. These need not be large files, incidentally: Advanced technology can compress files so small that they'll download painlessly even through slow connections. Imagine: Your subscribers can actually hear a child say thanks or a soldier in Africa deliver a "you are there" firsthand account of a conflict or an artist invite them to a show. The impact can be stunning. Donor click-through rates for special appeals introduced in this fashion have been tantalizingly above average.

E-Newsletters Must Be Opt-in (A Good Idea for Everything, Really)

The Internet is about choice: "I choose to search for this. I choose to click on this. I choose to read your e-mailed newsletter."

Or I choose not to.

Ethical (i.e., smart) e-news subscriber programs are always "opt-in" programs. In other words, donors say yes or no to their subscription. That's half the secret to success. To avoid irritating donors and prospects, e-news subscriptions must also be supremely easy to drop. Include some version of the following statement in every issue of your e-news:

> You have subscribed to this e-newsletter. If you wish to unsubscribe, simply reply by e-mail and say "unsubscribe" in the subject line.

Research indicates that asking donors and others on your mailing list whether they wish to receive any, some, or all of your communications materials can actually *increase* giving. People appreciate being asked their preferences, particularly now that information glut in everyone's complaint.

An opt-in e-news subscriber program also weeds out the disinterested, yielding a more realistic, better-qualified database of the predisposed. There might be minor public relations value to placing a few, carefully selected individuals (such as reporters or politicians) on your e-news subscriber list without first asking if they wish to be there or not. But with donors, this is a clear line in the sand: If they do not actively say yes to an e-news subscription, they should not be on your subscriber list.

FAST, EASY, STILL ON PAPER: THE "NEWSYLETTER"

There is a cheap, fast, easier-to-do alternative to the newsletter that can be quite effective in keeping donors well informed about your accomplishments.

Simone calls it a "newsyletter." She invented it for clients who don't have much in the way of staff and resources. Anyone can do a newsyletter today. It's not designed. It's not corseted by columns and departments. It has no photos. It's a small production instead of a big production. It's just a quick letter from you to a friend. (See Appendices 19B and C for two newsyletters published by the Women's Fund of Rhode Island.)

You write your newsyletter in a conversational voice. One page, two pages, four pages, whatever it takes. And it's *all* news. There's no ask. (Feel free to enclose a gift envelope, however.) It could be a letter that begins something like this . . .

> Dear Jane,
>
> What do you know. . . .
>
> A letter where I'm NOT asking you for money.
>
> Today, I am just writing to report. I wanted you to know how we used your generous gift, to make progress on a problem we know you care about: our state's sick environment.
>
> That environment can be healed, we promised—with your help. And the healing has begun—thanks to you and other donors who took on this mission.
>
> Here's what we've accomplished in your name since I last wrote you . . . .

The newsyletter doesn't have to report only *new* news, either. The writer can also revisit triumphs previously mentioned in a regular newsletter or appeal. Those triumphs form the backbone of your organization's story. They *should* be mentioned more than once.

How often should you mail your newsletter to donors?

As often as possible if it's good, the Merkle | Domain executive said. Six times a year isn't an uncommon schedule.

But it's actually a question you might want to ask your donors.

"Commitment is...built through the *exercise of choice*," Adrian Sargeant and Elaine Jay assert in their 2004 book, *Building Donor Loyalty*. "Donors who are afforded the opportunity to choose the frequency and the content of the communications they receive from a nonprofit develop more commitment than those who are not offered such choices."

They cite the enviable example of Botton Village in the United Kingdom where every fundraising measure (response rates, lifetime value, donor loyalty) is significantly above the norm. "This record has been achieved because, in offering donors choices, Botton Village has moved away from 'intrusion' in fundraising activity to 'invitation.'"

Botton Village invites new donors to choose between two delivery schedules for newsletters, either four times a year or "just once a year, at Christmas." The same choices are offered in every subsequent communication "so that donors can change their minds at any point in the relationship."[13]

SIMPLICITY ITSELF: A PROVEN FORMULA FOR A DONOR NEWSLETTER

At a fund development conference a few years back, an executive from what is now Merkle | Domain shared the formula they'd perfected for profitable donor newsletters. Before you go off reinventing the wheel, realize that, using this formula, some Merkle | Domain clients now make more money via their donor newsletters than via their appeal letters.

The formula:

- 11 × 17 format, folding to four 8½ × 11 pages, sometimes with an extra sheet slipped in if you need more room.
- Two-color printing or full-color both work.
- Not on glossy paper.
- Not a self-mailer (self-mailers appear to have "low perceived value").
- Mail in a #10 envelope with some variation of this teaser copy: "Your newsletter enclosed."

- Send exclusively to current donors.

- Include a reply envelope and reply device.

- Mail as often as possible.

- Focus on "accomplishment reporting"; offer proof of effectiveness by telling the stories of those you've helped.

In Conclusion

You can do more with the 35 words of a good headline-and-deck combination than you can with a 500-word article.

Donors need to be inspired, moved, and informed—AQAP, as quickly as possible. Almost no one reads the articles: Donors don't have the time, and nonprofits don't write all that entertainingly. Explosions of interest or enthusiasm begin when some headline lights a fuse. Focus your attention there.

▓ ENDNOTES

1. Done wrong, which seems to be the case 99 times out of 100, it's a punishing waste of everyone's time and money. But there is no substitute.
2. Jeff Brooks, "Loyalty-Building Newsletters: Four Principles for Making Your Newsletter a Powerful Fundraising Tool," online: www.merkledomain.com Merkle | Domain Group, 2005.
3. Penelope Burk, *Donor-Centered Fundraising* (Chicago: Burk & Associates, 2003), p. 87.
4. Jeff Brooks, Loyalty-Building Newsletters, an "orange paper" online: www. merkle-doman.com Merkle|Domain, p. 3–4.
5. Tom Ahern, *The Mercifully Brief Real-World Guide to Raising More Money with Newsletters than You Ever Thought Possible* (Medfield, MA: Emerson & Church, 2005), p. 15.
6. Dr. Mario R. Garcia, *Redesigning Print for the Web* (Indianapolis: Hayden Books, 1997), p. 117.
7. Paul LaRocque, *Heads You Win: An Easy Guide to Better Headline and Caption Writing* (Oak Park, IL: Marion Street Press, 2003), p. 10.
8. The article could make an offer, for instance: inviting donors to join the kids in the classroom for the program (assuming you can get permission for such a visit). Another relationship-building opportunity: Ask the teacher and kids to send the donors thank-you notes once the program is given.
9. Dr. Barbara Ellis, *The Copy-Editing and Headline Handbook* (New York: Perseus Publishing, 2001), p. 14.
10. Ted Hart, James M. Greenfield, and Michael Johnston, *Nonprofit Internet Strategies* (Hoboken, NJ: John Wiley & Sons, 2005), pp. 7, 9, 91.
11. Consider offering donors the choice of how often they wish to hear from you. In tests, giving them that choice has improved overall giving.
12. Reported in *Mal Warwick's Newsletter* (March 2007): 1–2.
13. Sargeant and Jay, *Building Donor Loyalty.*

Boys & Girls Club of Pawtucket Newsletter

Boys & Girls Club of Pawtucket **News**

Winter 2005

One Moeller Place, Pawtucket, RI 02860 • 401-722-8840 • www.bgcpawt.org

NOW is best time to give. Why? Your gift automatically **DOUBLES!**

Three new "challenge" grants could spur Club's 2005 fiscal comeback

- Within reach (with your help): $210,000 in cash for Pawtucket kids
- Philanthropic alum and his novelist wife put $50,000 on the line; their personal biggest
- Club's board president and Citizens Bank add to challenge

DONORS, START YOUR CHECKBOOKS... and DOUBLE your giving instantly. NEW challenge grants:

- **Anthony Ruddy and Lisa Baumgarten (husband and wife, both Club alums, in his case from Pawtucket; she's a best-selling novelist under the pen name Lisa Gardner):**
  $50,000 CHALLENGE

- **Pawtucket Club board president Philip A. Ayoub:**
  $30,000 CHALLENGE

- **Citizens Bank, led by President and CEO (and Pawtucket Club alum) Joseph J. MarcAurele:**
  $25,000 CHALLENGE

Are YOU ready to meet the challenge for Pawtucket's boys and girls? Call Nisia Hanson at 722-8840.

Club alums have pledged $105,000 in 2005 if other donors can be found to make matching gifts. The total take (challenge and full match) amounts to $210,000. At stake: the future of the Pawtucket Club.

Increasing the level of community support has become a top priority at the Boys & Girls Club of Pawtucket. After the schools, the Club is Pawtucket's busiest child development agency, with 3,050 children and teens now enrolled in programs.

But it has struggled to find enough funding to keep pace with surging growth and a red-hot demand for services.

The three challenge grants hope to spur current donors to increase their giving, by offering people who care about the mission of the Club a chance to double the impact of their gifts.

Job #1: replacing bygone funding

Most of the private philanthropy the Pawtucket Club could count on 20 and 30 years ago has disappeared along with the city's manufacturing base.

The competition for grant funding in Rhode Island has intensified as well. The number of IRS-registered charities here now exceeds 5,000, more than double what it was in 1990.

With all these mouths to feed, traditional sources of support like the United Way, which pools charitable gifts collected from workplaces throughout the state, have found less and less every year to give the Pawtucket Club. (Though 2005 will see a temporary reversal of fortune. The United Way has awarded the Club two separate 21-month grants, recognizing the unusual effectiveness of our afterschool and preschool programs.)

It's left to each community to support vital social services. Developing a broader base of individual and business support from the community it serves has become essential for the Boys & Girls Club's financial health.

Finding $1,000 per child per year

Every child costs the Club more than $1,000 annually. The Club provides a safe and supervised place after school; year-round

...CHALLENGE continues on back

2 • Boys & Girls Club of Pawtucket News • Winter 2005 • www.bgcpawt.org • 401-722-8840

Number of single-parent households soars in Pawtucket; many are poor

Pawtucket's percentage leap is biggest by far among Rhode Island's cities

- The new reality: majority of Club members live with single moms, often in low-wage jobs
- Child poverty linked to variety of risks including teen pregnancy and adult joblessness

Why kids need the help they get at the Boys & Girls Club, now more than ever . . .

1996
26% of Pawtucket's kids live in SINGLE-PARENT households

Now
42% of Pawtucket's kids live in SINGLE-PARENT households

The percentage of single-parent households grew faster in Pawtucket than in any other Rhode Island city, reports the 2004 Rhode Island Kids Count Factbook. Rhode Island Kids Count is the state's leading researcher of child development issues.

From 1996 to 2004, the number of single-parent households in Pawtucket jumped from 26% to 42%, a steep 62% increase. Second-place Woonsocket's total grew just 48% in the same period.

At least 65% of the Club's members, we estimate, now live in single-parent households, most often led by a mom.

As a group, single moms have the lowest median income in Rhode Island, $17,252 a year (the single dad median is $29,776; the married couple with kids median is $63,706).

Studies show that children from poor, single-parent households face numerous disadvantages.

They are at higher risk for health and behavioral problems. They experience difficulty more often in school, are more often teen parents, earn less as adults, and are more often unemployed as adults.

Grants received since last we spoke...

- **Alperin/Hirsch Family Foundation**...$500...for general programming
- **Billy Andrade-Brad Faxon Charities for Children**...$9,625...for food for teens and transportation to and from the Elson Branch for after-school programs *(Thanks to Board Member, Paul Keating!)*
- **Boys & Girls Club of America**...$2,000...for a photography program, IMAGE MAKERS

- **Bristol County Savings Charitable Foundation**... $10,000...for teen homework, food and career planning *(Thanks to Board Member, Mike Tamburro!)*
- **Carter Family Charitable Trust**...$5,000...for All Children's Theatre collaboration
- **June Rockwell Levy Foundation** ...$7,500... for arts for all ages
- **MacAdams Charitable Foundation**...$250... for general programming
- **Ocean State Charities**...$3,000...for teen arts program
- **RBC Dain Rauscher**...$2,000...for arts
- **Stop & Shop, Cottage Street, Pawtucket** ...$3,611...for general programming *(Thanks to the employees there!)*
- **United Way of Rhode Island**...$180,000 over 21 months...for after-school programs
- **United Way of Rhode Island**...$20,000 over 21 months...for the Growing and Learning Center: The Creative Curriculum

Thank you!

Pawtucket Club member Alvin Andrade

Photo by John C. Meyers

www.bgcpawt.org • 401-722-8840 • Boys & Girls Club of Pawtucket News • Winter 2005 • 3

Trustee Representative Peter F. Kilmartin presents a House of Representatives Legislative Grant for $10,000 to Jim Hoyt, Club CEO. The grant helps pay for sports, fitness and recreation activities in the Club's after-school programs. Looking on, a brass relief of Club benefactor Robert Moeller.

New board members named

Newly elected to the board:

- William A. Cateli, Jr., state aid and finance specialist, Rhode Island Office of Municipal Affairs
- Augusto "Cookie" Rojas, Jr., assistant vice president and community development officer, Pawtucket Credit Union (and Club alum)
- Kathleen S. Sullivan, community relations, Collette Vacations

Inducted as 2005 trustees:

- Richard J. Blockson, general manager of The Times
- J. Jeffrey Calista, owner and president of LJC Sales, Inc., Pawtucket
- Robert Lee Williams, family service coordinator, Pawtucket Housing Authority (and Club alum)

53 East Avenue closes

Opened in 1902, building became too costly to maintain and update; teen programs shift to other facilities

Electric lights were still novel enough to make the news.

There was an "anti-cigarette league" because a "great many of the boys are addicted to it." The heated "natatorium" (swimming pool) was a wonder, holding 70,000 gallons of water "so clear…that a 10-cent piece laying on the bottom is magnified to the size of a half-dollar." And Col. Lyman B. Goff, the Pawtucket Boys' Club founder and principal philanthropist, handed over 400 shares of Pennsylvania Railway stock to start an endowment.

When the original Pawtucket Boys' Club opened its doors in 1902, Col. Goff's dream building was state of the art.

But 103 years later, antiquated systems, safety concerns, strict new fire codes, and rehabilitations estimated to exceed $500,000 doomed the building to mothballs. The recommendation to close the Club's oldest facility was approved in December by the board of directors.

Closing the building won't change programming, however. Programs for the 600 teens who used 53 East Avenue have already moved either to the Club's Arts Center a few doors away or to the Elson Branch on School Street.

A club for "unhappy boys"

"The club is designed for unhappy boys," speaker Thomas Chew said at its dedication, as the *Pawtucket Times* reported in July 1902. Boys Clubs were a relatively new phenomenon, meant for the cities, "designed to fight the street for the possession of the boy, that it might save him from vice, from crime and prison," said Chew.

Unhappy boys were those "who have little or no chance to see and hear the best things. The drunkard's child; the fatherless or motherless boy; the dull boy; the poor boy; the shiftless, the lazy, the cigarette fiend…the bad boy. Here they will all find a welcome."

Mr. Chew compared bad boys to that other "delicate piece of mechanism," a watch.

"If I were to put a sign on this building, so that every passer-by could tell what was being done within, it would be this: 'Boys Cleaned, Regulated and Repaired.'"

In 1923, boys line up at 53 East Avenue, the Club's original building.

4 • Boys & Girls Club of Pawtucket News • Winter 2005 • www.bgcpawt.org • 401-722-8840

Challenge Grants...continues

athletics; tutoring (Pawtucket's high school graduation rate is 67%, second lowest in Rhode Island); career counseling for teens; an intensely popular arts program; even hot meals.

Membership costs the child just $30. Yet some Pawtucket families have trouble affording even that modest amount. Nearly half of Pawtucket's children live in single-parent households. Almost a quarter of the city's kids live in poverty (versus 7% statewide).

"Who you calling a baby?"

New Baby Boom hits Pawtucket Club -- only this time it's 6 to 8 year olds

- Youngest member group grows 209% in just one year
- "The younger you get them, the better," comments Jim Hoyt, Pawtucket Club CEO

It's raining kids in Pawtucket.

And they're really young.

In 2003, the Boys & Girls Club of Pawtucket welcomed 179 members ages 6 to 8.

In 2004, that number jumped 209%, as 554 members ages 6 to 8 participated in Club activities.

This bulge heralds more growth for the Club. It also puts additional pressure on facilities already stretched to accommodate the migration from the Teen Center.

The Boys & Girls Club of Pawtucket
One Moeller Place, Pawtucket, RI 02860
phone 401-722-8840
www.bgcpawt.org

New Hampshire couple invests in Pawtucket kids' potential

"Why my wife and I chose to make our largest charitable contribution ever, to the Boys & Girls Club of Pawtucket."

- Bottom line, says Pawtucket Club alum, since the community reaps the benefits, "it is up to us to pay for the services that the Club provides."

Anthony Ruddy spoke at our annual meeting on November 24 about why he and his wife, Lisa Baumgarten, residents of New Hampshire, pledged their largest-ever charitable gift to a Boys & Girls Club in Pawtucket.

"I grew up here in Pawtucket. I'm a second generation alumnus of the Boys & Girls Club. Both my mother and father were involved with the Club as children. And my father was not only a member, but worked five days a week at the East Avenue Branch through the 1940s and 50s.

"My sister and I became members of the Boys & Girls Club at the Elson Branch and joined the swim team with Jim Hoyt as coach and aquatics director. Over the years Jim has been coach, mentor, and friend.

"As business people, my wife and I look at philanthropy as investments. We look at organization and leadership. The Boys & Girls Club of Pawtucket excels in both of those areas.

"Although the Club is a non-profit entity, it must run as a business. But unlike a regular business, it offers a service - at a loss. You heard Phil [Ayoub] and Jim [Hoyt] say that it costs $1,000 per child, yet the Club charges $30 per child. That may seem like a strange business model, but make note...the children are not the customers of the Club - it is us, the community. We reap the benefits of the services the Club provides...by helping our children in need excel to their greatest potential, to secure their future. The Club does this with after-school programs, sports activities, tutoring, mentoring, and preparing our teenagers for college. The Club gives children a place to go, in a society where many children come home to an empty house during the day.

"The Club has met the challenges of a changing community, by changing with it. But the financial needs of the Club are greater than ever. As the community, it is up to us to pay for the services that the Club provides."

Example 1: Women's Fund of Rhode Island Newsyletter

Characteristics of a newsyletter:

- Alternative to a traditional newsletter
- Donor/volunteer update
- Printed on letterhead and personalized to each individual
- In order to be more personal, includes salutation only, no address
- Outside envelope includes statement "Your personal update"

Dear _____:

Welcome to fall. I hope this new season finds you all in good health.

As I write this update to you, my thoughts keep focusing on the 2004 election.

Please encourage your friends, neighbors, colleagues, and strangers to vote. Perhaps you do vote and always have. But ask around. I've been talking about voting since the spring—and continue to encounter women and men of all ages who do not vote. And these are people of diverse race/ethnicity, education, and socioeconomics.

The United States has one of the worst voting records of any nation in the world.

Sure, I hear all about disgust with politics and apathy. But let's never forget what happened in November 1917. Women did not have the vote at that point. They'd been fighting for the vote for decades. The opposition was vicious.

The story was retold vividly when HBO premiered its film *Iron Jawed Angels*. I'd like to share it with you.

> The women were innocent and defenseless. And by the end of the night, they were barely alive. Forty prison guards wielding clubs and with their warden's

EXAMPLE I   347

blessing went on a rampage against the 33 women wrongly convicted of "obstructing sidewalk traffic . . ."

Affidavits describe the guards grabbing, dragging, beating, choking, slamming, pinching, twisting and kicking the women . . . When one of the leaders, Alice Paul, embarked on a hunger strike, they tied her to a chair, forced a tube down her throat, and poured liquid into her until she vomited.

Thus unfolded the "Night of Terror" on November 15, 1917, when the warden at the Occoquan Workhouse in Virginia ordered his guards to teach a lesson to the suffragists imprisoned there because they dared to picket Woodrow Wilson's White House for the right to vote. [Source unknown]

The horrors of that night were leaked to the press, changing minds. Finally, women won the right to vote.

Can you imagine what Alice Paul and her 32 colleagues would think of the millions of women who were registered to vote but did not vote in 2000? Think of the people of color who continue to suffer intimidation at the polls? Can you imagine what they must think of the white people who don't at least try to vote?

Of course voting is part of the business of the Women's Fund. The Women's Fund champions fairness, impartiality, opportunity, shared power and responsibility in all spheres of personal and community life—including economic, cultural, educational, social, and political.

All I can say is please vote. And encourage others to do so. And remind people of the past and current battles to secure equitable rights for all.

So what's happening at the Women's Fund these days?

We're in the final stages of planning **our annual celebration gathering**. As I told you in my June update, our guest speaker is Marcia Ann Gillespie, a frequent speaker about the national and international women's movements. Advance registration (with payment) is required. This is a sell-out event so make your purchases early!

In August, the Women's Fund **decided its third round of grants**. We awarded $82,100 to 7 organizations. Four of the grants made are to continue projects that we had previously funded. The Women's Fund also gave its first grant to a program for girls. Please see the enclosed description of our 2004 grants.

Thank you for your own interest in the Women's Fund. If you have questions or comments, please feel free to contact me personally via telephone to 397-2534 or via email at spjoyaux@aol.com. I'll see you at the voting booth!

Regards,

Simone P. Joyaux, ACFRE, Founder and Chair

Women's Fund of Rhode Island

Example 2: Women's Fund of Rhode Island Newsyletter

Dear ____ :

I'm sorry it's taken me so long to send you an update from your Women's Fund. This has been a particularly busy time—the transition into an independent organization.

But before I tell you what's been happening...

Mark your calendars now for our 4th annual Fall Celebration: Thursday, November 17, 5:30—9 p.m. at the Crowne Plaza. Laura Flanders, journalist and author, is our keynote speaker.

You will receive your invitation soon. And if you want a reserved table for 10, contact Marcia Coné-Tighe, Executive Director, immediately! Tables are already selling. Marcia has an order form that she can e-mail to you.

So what has happened at the Women's Fund since last I wrote you?

We've spent an enormous amount of time on the required activities for independence.

- The Women's Fund was certified as a nonprofit Rhode Island corporation on March 2. We received our IRS 501c3 letter of determination in June.

- Marcia Coné-Tighe is the first fulltime Executive Director of the Women's Fund. The Board is thrilled.

- We relocated our office. Come and visit us at One Union Station! We are located on the first floor, in The Rhode Island Foundation building. Special thanks to The Rhode Island Foundation for making this new space possible.

And you can imagine all the other transition work we've been doing! Obtaining insurance and setting up our own financial bookkeeping system. Establishing

EXAMPLE 2   349

personnel policies and opening bank accounts. Setting up our own database and moving the website. Lots of work!

Please bookmark the Women's Fund website in your computer.www.wfri.org. We have lots of plans to improve the website. That will take time—but do visit us periodically to see the progress.

Even during this transition period, we continued our work to help level the playing field:

We regularly host *Conversations With the Women's Fund*. One Conversation focused on Rhode Island's 2005 legislative proposals that affected women and girls. Another Conversation focused on women's political participation. If you want to receive invitations to these Conversations, please provide your e-mail address to Marcia at mctighe@wfri.org.

Please congratulate our new grantees. The Women's Fund awarded its grants early this month. Take a look at the enclosed descriptions.

We introduced our new *Marking Milestones Program*. This program lets you mark an important milestone in your own life and the lives of your friends and colleagues. You can recognize a bar or bat mitzvah, a marriage or birthday, a special favor or any other occasion. Contact Marcia to obtain these special invitations.

We continue to raise money. Your gifts are critical, now more than ever. The Women's Fund raises money to support its core activities like grantmaking, Conversations and other special initiatives to help level the playing field for women and girls.

We also continue to raise money to build our endowment. The endowment is close to $3 million now, held at The Rhode Island Foundation. The endowment makes sure that there are funds in perpetuity to address the unique needs of women and girls.

The Women's Fund received its first bequests a few months ago. How exciting! One family and one individual made bequests in their wills, directed to the Women's Fund.

The founding vision of the Women's Fund was to create an independent nonprofit social justice organization that would help level the playing field for women and girls. Now, with your support, we will build this organization.

There is much work to do. Regularly, someone contacts the Women's Fund with a new idea for us to take on. Individuals and organizations ask us to join coalitions, launch new initiatives, and convene others to talk about issues.

All of us at the Women's Fund are excited by these ideas. But our resources are limited. Only one staff person and a great group of volunteers. A budget of less than $300,000.

Please know that your Women's Fund is doing all that we can. We plan carefully each year. We consider all the suggestions. We manage our resources carefully and do all that is possible.

Your support—as a volunteer and donor of money—is critical. Only with your continued support can the Women's Fund maintain its current level of activity. And with your increased support, the Women's Fund can do more.

I'll end, again, with a quote: *Hope is a state of mind, not of the world. Hope, in this deep and powerful sense, is not the same as joy that things are going well, or willingness to invest in enterprises that are obviously heading for success, but rather an ability to work for something because it is good.* —Vaclav Havel

Thank you. If you have questions or comments, please feel free to contact either Marcia or me.

Regards,

Simone P. Joyaux, ACFRE, Founder and Chair

Women's Fund of Rhode Island

CHAPTER 20

The Web Site Home Page

CLICK. SEARCH. DO. READ? NOT SO MUCH

DEAR READER Online philanthropy is a huge, evolving topic for your consideration. This chapter touches just on a Web site's home page. For a thorough overview of philanthropy over the Internet and the latest developments, visit www.ephilanthropy.org.
Tom

WHY WEB SITES ARE COMPLETELY DIFFERENT

Web sites are fundamentally different from other kinds of communications.

With direct mail or other forms of advertising, for instance, you *go* to your target audience, bearing a message.

With Web sites, however, your target audience *comes* to you. The visitor is motivated to make contact for a personal reason:

- **To find something I want.** *For instance:* the season's schedule (theater, dance, music); a class in photography (education); financial aid (education); a grant (foundation); a list of indigenous birds (nature society); free health care (clinic); heart-healthy tips (hospital); a list of homeless shelters (human service); directions to your location, contact information, hours of operation, job openings (anyone).

- **To do something now.** *For instance:* make a gift from a donor-advised fund (community foundation); purchase a ticket for a performance (theater, dance, music); enroll in a class (education); make a donation to disaster relief (aid agency); order a professional book (association); request materials be sent, sign up for a mailing list (anyone).

- **To research something I'm curious about.** *For instance:* how to build a butterfly garden (nature society); how various types of birth control work (family planning); what a candidate's position is on a certain issue (political);

what are the warning signs of Alzheimer's (association); to check out your history, board, staff, newsletters, financials (anyone).[1]

Very few Web site visitors wander in by accident. Most are there to accomplish something. And they will judge you by one thing: How easy and fast was it to do what I wanted to do? Good customer service means everything on a Web site: How well did you anticipate and deal with a visitor's questions, confusions, expectations, desires, and demands? Good customer service helps build a positive brand. Bad customer service helps build a negative brand.

Meet Ginger. Ginger has come to your site, looking for something, and she has easily accomplished her goal. She's impressed and grateful. Your organization rises in Ginger's opinion. She is likely to speak kindly of you in conversation if the relevant topic should arise ("Hey, Ginger, do you know where I can find . . . ?"). And Ginger is likely to return to your site.

Now meet Fred. Fred has come to your site, looking for something. But he has failed to accomplish easily what he set out to do. Fred leaves frustrated, disappointed, and unimpressed. Your organization, in his uncensored private view, is stupid and worthless. If someone brings you up in conversation, he'll be sure to mention his bad experience. He is unlikely to return. Game over for Fred.

Is Your Home Page Ready for Newcomers?

Web-usability guru Steve Krug advises: "As quickly and clearly as possible, the home page needs to answer the four questions I have in my head when I enter a new site for the first time." They are:

- **What is this?** What's the site about? And who *are* you people anyway? What's my bottom-line impression? Is this for me?

- **What do you *have* here?** What's listed in the navigation? What are all these items begging for my attention? Are they interesting? Where's the stuff I came looking for?

- **What can I *do* here?** Where's *me* and *my* task? (That's if you've come to *do* something. If you've landed here for no particular reason, the thought becomes): What's intriguingly click-worthy?

- **Why should I be here—and not somewhere else?** What makes you folks unique, compelling, surprising, entertaining, and different than your competitors?[2]

The home page is *so* many things: your virtual reception desk *slash* welcome committee *slash* directory of departments *slash* public spokesperson *slash* helpful tour guide *slash* sales associate *slash* wise counselor.

The critical decisions by the first-time visitor (whether to spend time, dig deeper, or turn right around and leave) all happen on the home page. Getting your inside pages right is child's play compared to making the home page wonderful for your various target audiences.

Relative to fund development, those target audiences include, at a minimum:

- Individual donor prospects who are investigating your worthiness

- Individual donors coming to do something (make a gift) or check on something (your accomplishments)

- Lawyers, bankers, financial advisors, and others who are counseling a client who is considering a planned gift to you

- Foundations and other grantmakers doing a background check

- Reporters (because they might tell your story to their audiences; at a minimum, a reporter expects to find financial information such as your 990 or annual report, staff lists, press releases, and an obvious media contact)

GETTING OFF ON THE RIGHT FOOT: THE IMPORTANCE OF A TAGLINE

Meet Philanthropy Customer X, a prospective donor. It's X's first visit to your site, driven there by a friend, an ad, a referral by a financial advisor, something in the news (disaster relief, for instance), word of mouth, or maybe a Google search.

There's little you can safely assume about this first-time visitor.

The person's demographics—income, age, education, race, gender—are still a mystery. Maybe you can jump to a likely conclusion or two.

If you're a liberal charity, Philanthropy Customer X probably holds similar views. (You'll never raise money from the other side, certainly.) If you're a faith-based charity, you might assume Philanthropy Customer X is of the same faith—but not necessarily, if your mission is a relief charity. Effective relief agencies attract an ecumenical mix of donors. There are plenty of atheists giving to Christian and Muslim relief work.

So, what might this total stranger—Philanthropy Customer X—want to know . . . and find . . . and do?

For starters, X wants to know who you are.

For that you need more than a name. You need a tagline.

Here is Steve Krug's well-informed opinion (with italic emphases added):

> One of the most valuable bits of real estate is the space *right next* to the Site ID [i.e., the logo]. When we see a phrase that's *visually connected* to the ID, we know it's meant to be a tagline, and we read it as a description of the whole site.[3]

His definition: "A tagline is a pithy phrase that characterizes the whole enterprise, summing up what it is and what makes it great."

Great tagline: "A mind is a terrible thing to waste." Introduced by the United Negro College Fund in 1972, it is still powerful today.

Also nice: "Changing lives, changing minds." Used by the Greater Hartford Association for Retarded Citizens. This tagline also comes in an extended version: "Changing the lives of those who have mental retardation, and the minds of those who don't."

Not as clear, though, is the tagline used by the New York Community Trust. It reads: "Building an endowment"—endowment? That's something a college has, right?—"for the City"—what is an endowment for a city?—". . . and making it easy"—nothing wrong with easy, I guess—"for New Yorkers to be philan-thropists"—okay, I'm not getting a real good mental picture here. What exactly is a philanthropist? Is that supposed to be me?—"today and tomorrow." And that means?

Pithy? Squishy maybe. Those 19 words raise a bunch of questions. The trust knows exactly what it means. But will the visitor guess right? Steve Krug again: "When you're involved in building a site, it's so obvious to you what you're offering and why it's insanely great that it's hard to remember that it's not obvious to everybody."[4]

Take precautions. Test your tagline on a few people who are completely unaware of what your organization does. Don't be shocked if unlikely misin-terpretations emerge.

Test more than your tagline, too. Ask people who are unfamiliar with your organization to view your home page. See if they instantly, and without prompting, understand your mission and what you seek to accomplish.

You're not indulging idle curiosity. You're proofing your home page against failure. Krug warns:

> The one thing you can't afford to lose in the shuffle—and the thing that most often gets lost—is **conveying the big picture**. Whenever someone hands me a home page design to look at, there's one thing I can almost always count on: They haven't made [the big picture] clear enough.[5]

What Must Be on the Home Page, Krug Says

Steve Krug says a good home page will include:

- Your name and tagline
- Navigation to the features of the site[6]
- A search function

- Teases ("Like the cover of a magazine, the home page needs to entice me with hints of the 'good stuff' inside," Krug says)
- Timely content ("signs of life," Krug calls them)
- Offers (such as events, campaigns, news, booklets, other publications)
- Shortcuts to the most frequently requested things on the site

Those are the tangibles. The home page must also measure up to these expectations, according to Krug:

- Show me what I'm looking for.
- ...and what I'm not looking for. Expose me to some of the wonderful things the site has to offer even if I'm not looking for them.
- Show me where to start.
- Establish credibility and trust. Hint: If your organization was awarded "the Nobel Peace Prize" or was "founded 1916" (a testament to your enduring relevance), display that fact right under your logo.

In Conclusion

Think of your Web site as a 24-hour information booth and ticket window, offering donors and prospects a convenient, intriguing selection of ways to participate in your mission and vision.

And don't wait, either. We don't have a firm date on when Web sites became mandatory in any serious communications effort, but it was years ago.

ENDNOTES

1. Research among journalists around 2004 discovered that almost 100 percent of the time they visited an organization's Web site first, before phoning, to read old press releases, review newsletters, and check on personnel, the board, and financials. And that was in 2004.
2. Steve Krug, *Don't Make Me Think: A Common Sense Approach to Web Usability* (Indianapolis: New Riders, 2000), p. 101. Steve Krug has been called a "web-usability guru" so often it might as well be his middle name. He has consulted with AOL and Apple on their wonderfully easy-to-navigate Web sites. His book has sold more than 100,000 copies, a notable best seller in the field of design. The title refers to his First Law: Make everything obvious to everyone. The ideal web visit involves zero confusion and none of the consequent frustration.
3. Ibid., p. 103.
4. Ibid., p. 102
5. Ibid., p. 100
6. Navigation comes in several flavors. There is *persistent* navigation, which includes major items such as tabs that appear on every page. There is *utility* navigation, which includes minor but useful conventions such as "About Us" and "Contact." And there is *local* navigation, which applies to just a special page or section.

Tips for Writing

THINK FIRST. WRITE LATER

Writing is easy. All you do is stare at a blank sheet of paper until drops of blood form on your forehead.

—ATTRIBUTED TO GENE FOWLER, JOURNALIST
AND SCREENWRITER

Writing . . . is but a different name for conversation.

—LAURENCE STERNE, THE LIFE AND OPINIONS
OF TRISTRAM SHANDY, GENTLEMAN

DEAR READER The biggest barrier to good writing is murky thinking. If you don't know what your message is before you begin to write, you won't write well. It's simply not possible. Probably a third of my "writing" time is spent staring into thin air or doodling, trying to get my thoughts organized and clarified. I write myself little questions like "Why would a donor care about any of this?"
Tom

INTRODUCTION

Most nonprofits don't have the budget to hire professional writers for every communications task. Fundraisers, executive directors, board members, and other volunteers often end up writing materials meant to inform or persuade donors and prospects. These tips will help even occasional writers get good results.

YOUR FIFTH-GRADE TEACHER WAS RIGHT: OUTLINE

Gene Fowler described the feeling perfectly. And little has changed, from an anxiety standpoint, since his days bleeding over a mechanical typewriter. The difference now: A blinking cursor on a blank computer document is the invitation to despair.

But, frankly, the torment associated with writing is exaggerated. After all, hundreds of thousands of professional writers sit down daily and work at their craft without hesitation. They know how to start. They know where they're going. They meet their deadlines. They get the job done in a reasonable amount of time.

Anyone can share their confidence. Writing effective, readable nonfiction is easy enough. You learned the basic trick as a child in school: Outline your topic before you begin writing. The good habit of making an outline first can save you hours of grief, confusion, and false starts. Much of the anguish associated with writing disappears when you have an outline. "There's no such thing as writer's block," writing coach David Fryxell chides. "There are only disorganized writers—writers who don't know where their next sentence is going."[1]

"Writing is thinking on paper," William Zinsser famously said; he authored the best-seller, *On Writing Well*.[2] And so it goes: If your thoughts are tied up in knots, you won't—can't—write clearly, simply, or briefly, all of which are hallmarks of good nonfiction. And until you can *tell* it (your message, your story, your case), you can't *sell* it.

If, instead, your donor newsletters, e-news alerts, editorials, annual reports, funding appeals, press releases, grant applications, and/or Web sites are (say) vague, awkward, and miles too long, then your target audience will not respond at full strength. Remember: We're not trying to get people to read for the sake of reading. We're trying to get them to read enough to act, sooner or later, on what we have to say.

An outline undoes the knots in your thinking and straightens out the string. With an outline, you'll see at a glance: *This comes first, this comes second, this comes third* as you write your article, tell your story, argue your point, announce your event, make your ask, and so on.

AN EASY WAY TO OUTLINE: ASK YOURSELF QUESTIONS FIRST

It's quick and easy to create an outline. It might take only 10 or 15 minutes if you ask yourself a series of questions like these:

- What is my topic?

- Who is my target reader? (If it's a donor, now would be a good time to review Chapter 13, the section titled "How to Interest Donors and Prospects: The Big Four"; and Chapter 19, the section titled "What Do Donors Want from Your Newsletter?.")

- Why would the target reader be interested in this particular topic? (You might find yourself searching for a new topic once you've wrestled with this question.)

- What kind of questions will the target reader have?

- What's the most *important* thing I can tell the reader about this topic? (Has there been a change for the better or the worse, for instance? Why does it matter that the target reader know about this change?)

- What's the most *surprising* thing I can tell the target reader about this topic? (Having news value guarantees heightened interest.)

- Can I show instead of tell? (Let's hope so. Show is much faster than tell, when you're trying to bring a reader up to speed. Can you, for instance, start your letter or article with an anecdote that shows a person struggling with the very problem that your agency solves? And there are many kinds of "show": The right photo is indeed worth a thousand words.)

- Do I have any offer I can make that relates to this topic? (Offers cause responses. Responses help you track whether anyone's paying attention to what you say.)

- Does the topic lead naturally to some call to action? (News about a challenge grant would lead naturally, for instance, to an urgent gift request.)

- Which of our themes does this topic illustrate? (Every topic should illustrate *some* key theme. See Chapter 13 for a quick review of themes.)

Using these questions as the skeleton, let's flesh out a hypothetical outline, in this case for a symphony that plans to announce an endowment campaign.

What Is My Topic?   We desperately need an endowment for our symphony. We have a structural deficit we can't erase through ticket sales. We need income from an endowment to bridge the gap, if we want to keep our standards high.

Who Are My Target Readers?   Our current donors. Plus anyone who loves live classical music.

Why Would This Particular Topic Interest Them?   The symphony's future depends on this. Without it, we really can't survive. If donors and music lovers want high-quality live performance close at hand, the proposed endowment is the only guarantee.

What Kind of Questions Will They Have?   They'll for sure wonder whether we're bad at managing money. We have to explain the structural deficit in such a way that it makes sense. For one thing, we have to show them that it's perfectly normal in the symphony business.

What's the Most Important Thing to Tell Them about This Topic?   It's actually two things, the two things we said before: The symphony has no future without an endowment, and a structural deficit is normal.

What's the Most *Surprising* Thing?   Every time you perform, you lose money.

Can I Show as Well as Tell?   We have gorgeous photos of performances. Which gives us a great place to stick a caption where we can repeat the theme, maybe something like "Big, beautiful music costs money. Ticket sales now pay for just 60 percent of the symphony's bills. The newly launched endowment campaigns can make up the difference, though—forever."

Do I Have an Offer?   We've been talking about doing preconcert informational events. Maybe this would be a good time to announce these events where people could come in early, mingle and snack, in exchange for a five-minute chat about the endowment. We also need to make sure people who are interested can get their hands on our case statement. It will be available both in a printed version and online, in a downloadable format. Oh, and we should have a special season's subscription that includes a built-in donation to the endowment campaign: We can promote that, too.

Can I Do a Call to Action?   A few, actually. We want people to give to the endowment campaign, of course. But maybe there could be different kinds of gifts. Maybe they could endow their favorite instruments. Or maybe they could endow scholarship chairs in the audience so that music-loving youngsters from low-income families can attend performances. What about a call to action for volunteers? Maybe there are music lovers out there who would volunteer to host a donor cultivation get-together in their home. We'd handle the logistics, if they'd be willing to invite a dozen or so friends in for an hour of hors d'oeuvres and a quick briefing on the endowment. And don't forget to promote a visit to the Web site. They'll be delighted! We've got some live performance video there and a wonderful musical campaign thermometer that shows how well the campaign is going.

Which Themes Does This Topic Illustrate?   Our major theme: Donors make it all possible. With donor participation, the symphony's future is guaranteed. But if donors don't build an endowment, it's only a matter of time before the symphony goes out of business.

Now we have an outline that can easily blossom into many intriguing things: a case statement, a bunch of newsletter articles and items, a press release, a web page or two, a letter to the editor, or several appeal letters. Now that our thoughts on this topic are in good working order, *now* we're ready to write.

And so we begin, with one easily absorbed, conversational sentence that frames the discussion. Followed by another simple statement that reveals the problem: the surprising truth about ticket sales versus costs. Followed by enough proof to answer the prospect's predictable doubts about the symphony's financial management. Followed by the solution:

> A symphony is a tough business.
>
> Every time you perform, you lose money... If you depend on ticket sales alone.
>
> Consider the National Symphony Orchestra, resident at the Kennedy Center in Washington, DC. The National Symphony earns just 60% of its income from ticket sales.
>
> And that's pretty typical. Here we do a bit better. Here, subscriptions and single-ticket sales earn back 65% of our cost.
>
> Still, it's clearly not enough.
>
> We have what's called a "structural deficit." In the symphony business, we can never earn enough to pay our bills. Costs rise much faster than ticket prices can. And that's the problem. But there is a solution. It's called a permanent endowment... [etc.]

Writing nonfiction is not about choosing words. It is about presenting your thoughts clearly, briefly, and simply to a target audience. Outlining helps you develop and organize your thoughts about any topic into a coherent whole. The more detailed you make your outline, the less you have to write, too. Writing without an outline is self-inflicted torture. Write with an outline, and you'll never have a moment's doubt about what to say next.

KNOW THE POINT OF YOUR STORY AND START THERE

Let's reduce outlining to its most essential question: *What's the point of your story?* Why are you bothering to tell your readers about this event, person, result, anecdote?

"I want volunteers to know how important they are." Or: "I want them to know how much good even a small gift does."

Start your story by coming right to the point:

> You wouldn't think $39.50 could change a life. But in the case of Maria, $39.50 donated to the XYZ shelter meant she could afford a good, secondhand suit.

That suit built her confidence. Her newfound confidence helped her land the job that lifted her out of poverty and into a career as a real estate broker. Not bad for $39.50.

There are primary messages; and then there are secondary, supporting, or less consequential messages. Until people understand the primary message, the secondary messages are meaningless. Until you've mastered writing, do not violate the first principle of hierarchy: Start with the most important stuff, and get to the less important stuff later.

WRITE ABOUT BENEFITS, NOT FEATURES

"The first step in writing copy that sells," says marketing consultant Robert W. Bly, "is to write about *benefits* and not about features."[3]

For fundraisers, that translates to: "The first step in writing or speaking persuasively to prospects and donors about your programs, services, activities, mission, and vision, is to talk or write about *benefits* and not about features."

"A feature is a descriptive fact," Bly explains. "A benefit is what the user. . . gains as a result of the feature." A *feature* is what you do. A *benefit* reveals why it matters. Keep in mind that while insiders (staff and board) care a lot about "what you do," donors and prospects care mostly about "why it matters."

Translating features into benefits couldn't be easier. Use this simple formula to reveal to yourself the benefit lurking within: "Why do we have [fill in the feature]? Because [fill in the benefit]." For example, "Why do we have a 24-hour hotline? Because crises don't just happen 9 to 5."

What you do: "We offer 24-hour crisis intervention, information and referrals."

Why it matters: "So a woman in trouble will never hear 'Sorry, we're closed.'"

What you do: "This manual provides a list of over 200 useful and sustainable landscape plants that may be found in local garden centers and nurseries."

Why it matters: "Consult this guide when your planning your next plantings. You'll end up with far better looking gardens and landscaping, for far less work and water. Plus you'll eliminate the need for potentially harmful pesticides in the bargain. Help the environment while you help yourself. And enjoy your garden more while you labor less."

What you do: "The Museum depends on the efforts of over 200 volunteers to conduct tours, assist in the library, museum collections, the Museum Shop, and with many special programs throughout the year."

Why it matters: "The Museum needs you. We're holding your place." You might be wondering, what's the benefit here? It's an emotional one: People want to feel needed.

What you do: "Your membership entitles you to unlimited free admission to all Museum-sponsored events for a full year."

Why it matters: "Stop by whenever you're in the neighborhood. Relax in front of your favorite painting. Take a closer, unhurried look at that new exhibit (one of 20 each year). Shut out the world and turn up your imagination full volume."

WRITE LESS

Advertising sage Bruce Bendinger says a lot of problems with writing start early.[4] "In school, most of your writing assignments have been exercises in grammar, vocabulary and reading comprehension, done for the approval of a teacher. In most cases, you were required to fill a certain number of pages, so brevity was penalized. As a result, you've been taught to over-write."

But that's not all you've learned that's bad for readers, says Bendinger.

> In school, long words are preferred to short ones. Complex concepts win out over simple statements. And the lecturing language of education is preferred to the conversation of everyday life. This tendency toward verbal inflation has been encouraged by bureaucrats, lawyers, politicians and the academic community.

He goes on to say that the real world won't stand for it. Your audience has its choice of thousands of other messages each day. And it prefers things fast, vivid, and easy to understand.

Keep this note-to-self prominently displayed next to your keyboard:

> Use fewer words.[5]

It's the reader-friendly thing to do. Your writing is probably not all *that* interesting (no offense, but let's be honest). Your target audience is pressed for time. And you're a supplicant: You're coming to them, asking for something. The audience owes you nothing, least of all its attention span.

On Web sites, the situation is even more dire. Visitors come for a reason: They come to find something out, or they come to accomplish something. Useless words only get in the way. Web-usability guru Steve Krug offers this as his "Third Law": "Get rid of half the words on each page, then get rid of half of what's left." He's not kidding. "I find I have no trouble getting rid of half the words on most Web pages without losing anything of value. [While] the idea of removing half of what's left is just my way of trying to encourage people to be ruthless about it."[6]

Krug is a particularly fierce foe of "happy talk." Do you have a welcome on your home page? That's usually a prime example of happy talk. Introductions to sections are usually happy talk. Still not sure what qualifies as happy talk? Says Krug, "There's one sure-fire test: If you listen very closely while you're reading it, you can actually hear a tiny voice in the back of your head saying, 'Blah blah blah blah blah. . . .'"[7] Words on Web sites are strictly functional: They tell you things you *need* to know. Happy talk is any writing you can remove, and no one will notice it's gone.

WRITE FOR SPEEDY READING

People don't have any great desire to *read* your stuff. What they really want to do is *process* your stuff AQAP—*as quickly as possible*. To squeeze from your donor newsletters, annual reports, appeals, and other communications a few drops of interesting information or good feeling, then continue on with their fast-lane lives, now reassured (if they're donors) that their gift is doing good work, glad that they've helped, and slightly better informed.

AQAP is not optional, by the way. The faster you make the reading experience, the more readers you will have. It's that simple. And like Death Valley on a hot day, it's that unforgiving.

Grade level governs reading speed. The two things are directly linked. The *higher* the grade level of your prose, the *slower* it will read. The *lower* the grade level, the *quicker* it will read. Newspapers aim for the eighth-grade level. Direct mail aims for the sixth-grade level. Popular novels can score at the fourth-grade level; that's why they're "page-turners," and you fly right through them.

Don't be surprised if your own writing tests near or at the twelfth-grade level. It's common. But it's far too high for fund development materials.

People can *understand* material written at elevated grade levels; that's not the problem. The real problem is the ponderous nature of the reading experience. Prose at the twelfth-grade level tends toward convoluted sentences; big, dull words; jargon (an insiders-only language); and fuzzy thinking. Altogether, a bore and a chore. Until you can write about your ideas and programs at the eighth-grade level, you're not ready to talk to donors and prospects.

At this point, you might be wondering: "But if I lower my grade level, don't I risk talking down to my readers?"

Relax: Grade level has nothing to do with your topic. the *Wall Street Journal* writes about the world's most complex subjects, yet rarely writes above the tenth-grade level and often nearer the eighth-grade level.

The standard Flesch-Kincaid scoring system uses averages to gauge the grade level of a piece of prose: average characters per word, average words per sentence, average sentences per paragraph.[8] The lower your averages, the lower your grade level, and the faster your writing reads. A piece of writing with, on average, three sentences per paragraph, 13 words per sentence, and five characters per word, for instance, scores at the sixth-grade level—no matter what the writing's about.

You *can* use big words and long sentences. But keep them to a minimum. And be especially suspicious of two words: "and" and "including."

The conjunction "and" often joins two perfectly clear, brief sentences into one long, not-so-clear, dangling sentence.

"Including" (also "includes") is often prelude to a long train of items separated by commas or semicolons that would be better displayed as a bullet list. A bullet list is intrinsically a much quicker reading experience than a long, congested paragraph that uses exactly the same words. Encountering a bullet list, the eye can skip briskly from item to item and never get lost, as it often does in a dense paragraph.

BULLET YOUR LISTS AND READING SPEEDS UP

Keep an eye out for "bullet lists in disguise." These are chains of items separated by commas or semicolons. These chains are mischievous, because they slow the reader down. Often words like "includes" or "including" introduce them. But not always. In the following real-life example, the words "you can" kicked off the parade.

Bullet lists are intrinsically faster to read than dense paragraphs. Bullet lists help lower your Flesch-Kincaid grade levels and improve your Flesch reading ease. Here's proof.

Both versions of the example text are the same. We haven't changed a word. We've simply added a colon and recast most of the second sentence as a list.

We work in partnership with your coalition, school, faith organization, board of health, or health and human services provider group to develop plans to improve the health of your community. Using the latest prevention research, data, curricula, and tools, you can establish health priorities, design new initiatives, form working partnerships, and evaluate the success of your efforts.

(scores at the twelfth-grade level, with a miserable reading ease of 29)

We work in partnership with your coalition, school, faith organization, board of health, or health and human services provider group to develop plans to improve the health of your community. Using the latest prevention research, data, curricula, and tools, you can:

- Establish health priorities
- Design new initiatives
- Form working partnerships
- Evaluate the success of your efforts

(scores at the tenth-grade level, with an acceptable reading ease of 52)

BEGINNING WITH A HISTORY LESSON, AND OTHER COMMON FLAWS

Here's how the lead article in a nonprofit newsletter begins:

> The lack of housing affordability impacts a broad swath of society, from the very poor striving to get ahead to middle class families battling long commutes and a desire to live near where they work to seniors struggling to survive on a fixed income while their property values increase in a rapidly expanding market. Many years ago, our city aggressively pursued the creation of low-income housing. In recent years, our city has demonstrated a strong desire to maintain and encourage affordability; with funding and subsidies, we have promoted diversity of income in very tangible ways. It is useful to step back and examine what areas we can improve and to review alternative approaches to some of our challenges. Below, I will outline some key areas for consideration as our city and the region continue to grapple with the many challenges of affordability.

If you define "ineffective" writing as writing that will fail to attract and hold readers, then this article is doomed to be ineffective. It assumes readers are scholars and will patiently endure a tedious lecture for the sake of knowledge.

Writing like this is incredibly common, almost a default, in the nonprofit publications we see.[9] Yet most of these publications are *not* meant for a scholarly audience. Instead, they hope to influence nonspecialist, nonacademic target audiences such as donors, prospects, members, the media, politicians, parents, past patients and their families, alumni, and so on.

Let's remember: None of these target audiences is obliged to read your stuff. Everyone has busy lives and crowded minds. Here are several reasons why this kind of writing won't work for them:

- **How we write and how we prefer to read are two different things.** Consider the example just shown. It starts with both a history and an economics lesson. No surprise, really. This is how we're all taught to write, from the time we wrote our earliest grade-school essay: Start at the beginning, move logically toward the end.

  But that approach does not mirror how we actually like to read. When we read, we prefer to start in the middle of the action. We want to get right to the point, the good stuff, the controversy, the conflict.

  Your job as a writer, as far as the reader is concerned, is to entertain. *Not* to educate. If you successfully hook the reader, yes, the reader might indulge, maybe even enjoy, being educated. But not until the hook is set.

  One last point about the difference between writing and reading: They go at different speeds.

  While we *write* at a snail's pace, with each word sometimes painfully extracted, we *read* at light speed. Furthermore, as readers, we're not really dealing with words, we're dealing with *thoughts*, at the ideal pace of one thought per sentence.

You might find that the act of writing moves along more briskly if you stop worrying about word choices and instead focus on forging clear, brief, and simple thoughts. A paragraph is not a heap of words. It is a sequence of linked thoughts that together make one point.

- **Tedium is always a bad idea.** Reading is already a form of labor—mental labor. Don't make it harder. Readers want to speed through everyday prose. In reading, speed and grade level are directly, though inversely, related, as we noted. For speedy reading, a single-digit grade level is required. Our sample on affordable housing scores at the twelfth-grade level, as slow as it goes.

  The first sentence in the housing article is 55 words long. The typical first sentence of a professionally written direct mail letter is about 8 words long. Short sentences produce quick reading. Long sentences produce slow reading. Don't start with long sentences.

- **You have three seconds to make me care.** Communications is a brutal world, where few things merit more than a glance. Direct mail professionals assume, for instance, that an appeal receives no more than four seconds of attention. Start counting. . .

One Mississippi.
Two Mississippi.
Three Mississippi.
Four Mississippi.

Have you hooked my interest? If not, I don't open the envelope. And your appeal sinks into oblivion, ignored forever.

It's really no different for any piece of writing: a newsletter, an e-mail, an annual report, a Web site. Inexperienced writers at nonprofits sometimes assume that a *responsible* reader, someone who really *cares* about the cause, *should* take time with every word and endure until a point gets made.

That is absolutely, positively, dangerously wrong. A trained professional writer, however, assumes that if she can't intrigue you in the first dozen words, she has failed to do her job.

WHERE YOUR ORGANIZATION'S HISTORY *SHOULD* GO. . . .

Your organization's history has an important role.

Your history speaks volumes to the skeptical mind about your organization's staying power, evolution, responsiveness, and continued relevance. But since donors are interested primarily in your current accomplishments, it's "what did you do for the world *lately*?" that matters more.

Accomplishments belong in the driver's seat, while history rides in the trunk. Unless the details of your organization's founding are fairly amazing—"Extraterrestials from the Planet Quahzmos actually put up most of the cash for our first soup kitchen"—put the history at the end, not the beginning.

Old news is intrinsically more boring than *real news*. Don't let history get in the way of your readers' enjoyment. History buffs are *not* the bulk of your audience. Time-pressed people are. They want you to get to the point.

In Conclusion

Readers are a pretty intolerant bunch. These days, you have just a few seconds to hook their fleeting attention. Think longer before you write, and you'll write better. Write less, and you'll write better . . . from the reader's point of view.

ENDNOTES

1. David Fryxell, *How to Write Fast (While Writing Well)* (Cincinnati: Writer's Digest Books, 1992), p. 93.
2. William K. Zinsser authored the million-copy-seller, *On Writing Well* 30th anniversary edition; New York: Harper Collins, 2006). Many consider this the best book ever published on how to write nonfiction. Simplicity is Zinsser's watchword. His practical suggestions include reading your writing aloud to help you develop a conversational style.
3. Robert W. Bly, *The Copywriter's Handbook* (New York: Henry Holt, 1990), p. 57.
4. Bruce Bendinger, *The Copy Workshop Workbook* (Chicago: The Copy Workshop, 1988), p. 149.
5. And if you're engaged in a conversation, write this on your hand: "Listen more."
6. Steve Krug, *Don't Make Me Think* (Indianapolis: New Riders, 2000), p. 45.
7. Ibid., p. 46.
8. Built into Microsoft Word. Look for "Readability Statistics."
9. This opinion is backed by uncommonly wide experience. In our work we review publications from hundreds of nonprofits of all shapes and sizes.

Readability

VISUAL ASPECTS OF GOOD COMMUNICATIONS

DEAR READER   If nonprofits paid serious attention to readability in their donor materials, the sector as a whole would raise more money. It's that simple. I've reviewed thousands of printed pieces and Web sites intended for donors and prospects. My sworn testimony to you: Fundraising materials that are a chore to read are depressingly common. And costly design is no cure; expensive graphic designers continue to be among the worst offenders against fast, easy reading. There's a price to pay when you make things hard to read: fewer gifts.
Tom

WELCOME, BROWSERS!

Doug Dolan of Viva Dolan, an award-winning communications firm with an international client base and a specialty in gorgeous high-end catalogs, once remarked, "Our theory is that people . . . fall into three groups: flippers, skimmers and readers."[1]

Pretty much in that order, too. People habitually browse before they begin to read. They're looking for things that interest them. Observe your own behavior next time you pick up a strange magazine.

Thanks to this "browse first, read later (maybe)" habit, a lot rides on how compelling or intriguing your publication's so-called browser level is. The browser level is where any desire to read in depth starts.

And, truth be told, it's where most reading starts *and* ends. The vast majority of your time-pressed target audience will give your materials little more than a quick once-over. You have one shot to squirt something into their impatient brains as they fly through your pages. For the vast majority, that flight will last no more than a minute.

Understandably, then, a strong browser level—one that is articulate; beguiling; inspirational; shocking; enjoyable; surprising; entertaining; informative; and, *particularly*, one that contains benefits for the target audience—is indispensable.

What *is* the browser level? All the stuff that's bigger, bolder, briefer. Anything that's *easy* to absorb on a quick fly-by. The wandering eye jumps to those bigger, bolder, briefer elements first, motion studies tell us.

The browser level of a newsletter includes:

- The teasing little inside-this-issue list on the front cover
- Headline-and-deck combinations (see Chapter 19 for an explanation)
- Overline (also called a kicker or an eyebrow; a brief statement above the headline, e.g., *Breaking News*, that categorizes the story)
- Lead sentences (visually, because white space precedes it, the easiest line to read in the article)
- Subheads inserted into the body of the text (these help two ways: to break up the text's mass, and to guide the reader step by step through the major ideas in the article)
- Pull quotes (also known as breakouts; they're sentences or passages excerpted from the body copy and set in large type)
- Captions
- Bullet lists
- Photos, maps, graphs, illustrations, and other art

The browser level of an appeal letter includes:

- The address on the envelope (if you've misspelled the recipient's name, your appeal is immediately trashed)
- The return address on the envelope
- The envelope teaser, if any
- The letter's salutation ("Dear . . .")
- The Johnson box, if you have one (named for its purported originator, the Johnson box is a paragraph, sometimes boxed or in bigger type, that appears above the salutation)
- The opening paragraph (keep it brief; somewhere between 5 to 10 words is not uncommon in a professionally written letter)
- Underlined and boldfaced words (use sparingly; if you emphasize too often, emphases loses their impact)
- Bullet lists (faster to skim than dense paragraphs)
- Subheads

- The closing
- The signature
- The P.S.

This fact can't be overemphasized: People will skim before they read. If you don't hook the person somehow during that quick skim, your game could well be over before it even begins.

HOW WE LOOK

In the 1980s Siegfried Vögele[2] published his pioneering eye-motion research—and shed new light on one of the great mysteries in communications: how we browse. This professor at the Direct Mail Institute in Munich, Germany, rigged cameras to record how the eye acted in the first few seconds of confronting an unfamiliar page of graphics and print.

The eye follows a typical downward arc. The glance starts at the upper right-hand corner of the page and zips instantly (and involuntarily) to the largest graphic on the page. The eye then concludes its reconnaissance by exiting at the lower right-hand corner.

Dr. Vögele also found that eyes go to:

- Photographs or drawings first, before they go to text
- Close-ups first, before they go to photos showing the entire person (eyes go to eyes)
- Children first, before they go to adults
- Big text (i.e., headlines) first, before they go to small text
- Short words, short lines, and short paragraphs first (i.e., headlines, captions, pull quotes)

The implications? Well, for one thing, you have far more control over what the viewer looks at than you might have realized. You can drag the reader's eye (and mind and heart) around on a leash, if you know what you're doing.

FROM GUTENBERG TO WHEILDON

Real knowledge about readability is quite recent.

Johann Gutenberg introduced movable type in the 1440s, paving the way for a massive publishing industry, widespread literacy, and modern information-based economies.

Yet, from then until almost now, any discussion of readability lacked one thing: valid, scientific data. In a debate between designers promoting opposing design solutions, for instance, no one could authoritatively answer a basic question, Which of these two design solutions is easier to read? Opinion thrived, of course, as it always does in a vacuum. But no one knew for sure.

Colin Wheildon set out to remedy that lamentable lack. Maybe he'd heard one too many baseless arguments down at some Sydney watering hole where newspaper types hung out. The estimable Mr. Wheildon was the precociously young editor of a major Australian daily, then a television news editor, then managing editor of Australia's most popular magazine.

Beginning in 1982 and continuing for nine years, he researched readability issues using rigorous scientific methods. This one-of-a-kind research, conducted Down Under, was unknown by the rest of the world. Then Harvey McKinnon, a Canadian fundraising consultant visiting Australia, stumbled on a copy of the study. He passed it along to U.S. direct mail fundraiser Mal Warwick, who realized the data was indispensable. In 1995 he published it as a book called *Type & Layout: How Typography and Design Can Get Your Message Across—or Get in the Way*, with a foreword by advertising legend (and readability advocate) David Ogilvy. The same book under a slightly different title reappeared in a 2005 second edition.[3]

The table that follows summarizes a selection of some of his key findings. What seem like innocuous aesthetic possibilities ("Maybe we should have colored headlines in our donor newsletter to make it more visually exciting.") can seriously degrade ease of reading.

Design Choice	"How Easy is the Text to Read?"		
Article in black ink on white paper	Good: 70%	Fair: 19%	Poor: 11%
Article in white on black (i.e., reverse type)	Good: 0%	Fair: 12%	Poor: 88%
Article in serif type	Good: 67%	Fair: 19%	Poor: 14%
Article in sans serif type	Good: 12%	Fair: 23%	Poor: 65%
Article in black ink on white paper	Good: 70%	Fair: 19%	Poor: 11%
Article in black ink on pale blue paper	Good: 38%	Fair: 19%	Poor: 43%
Article in black ink on white paper	Good: 70%	Fair: 19%	Poor: 11%
Article in purple ink on white paper	Good: 51%	Fair: 13%	Poor: 36%
Headlines in black	Good: 67%	Fair: 19%	Poor: 14%
Headlines in bright colors	Good: 17%	Fair: 18%	Poor: 65%
Headlines in dark colors	Good: 52%	Fair: 28%	Poor: 20%

(reprinted with permission from Colin Wheildon)

Reading is already a form of mental labor. When you make it yet more laborious through reader-unfriendly typographic choices, people will find other ways to spend their precious time. They are all volunteers, with dictatorial control of their attention spans. And they are under no obligation to struggle with your stuff.

The goal of competent typographic design is always the same: to inject a clear message into the reader's head as fast as possible. Making comprehension easy and swift in your publications and on your Web site is one sure way your organization can deliver good customer service. That has advantages: Being the bearer of good customer service builds a positive brand. First impressions do count. Will that first impression be painless or frustrating? Your typography often decides.

With regard to typography, graphic designers are not always your friends. Few know Colin Wheildon's research. Many (particularly suspect are designers without any rigorous background creating books, magazines, or newspapers) treat language almost disdainfully, as an unwelcome intrusion into what otherwise would be a garden of purely visual delights. Poor typography will cost you money, though, because it spoils your efforts to convey a message quickly and clearly.

"Typography exists to honor content," says Robert Bringhurst, an acclaimed book designer and type historian. "In a world rife with unsolicited messages, typography must often draw attention to itself before it will be read. Yet in order to be read, it must relinquish the attention it has drawn. Typography with anything to say therefore aspires to a kind of statuesque transparency. Its other traditional goal is durability: not immunity to change, but a clear superiority to fashion."[4]

ANATOMY OF A FAILED ANNUAL REPORT

Reader-unfriendly print materials are surprisingly common in the nonprofit world.[5]

It's not for lack of cash. Well-heeled nonprofits, able to afford luscious printing and dearly expensive graphic designers, still manage to turn out readability disasters almost by default.

Sadly, these printed pieces are often *unsuspected* disasters. They look good at first glance. They boast enviable production values. Staff and board are thrilled that their organization's publications "look so professional." But are these publications easily read and understood? And are they getting your message across? Often no and no.

Annual reports and case statements are among the worst offenders. A butcher's bill of flaws detected during a readability audit of a fairly typical high-priced annual report published by a community foundation in the United States follows.[6] This expensive report, mailed to tens of thousands of well-targeted individuals, never had a chance. It was dead on arrival, thanks to its dogged reader-unfriendliness, both visually and verbally.

Visually, the flaws included:

- Using a sans serif typeface for the body copy (we read a serif face such as Times New Roman four times faster than a sans serif face like Arial or Helvetica, according to Wheildon's research[7]).

- Setting the articles in a point size that looked small (an irritant for older eyes).

- Line measures that extended up to 90 characters in width (versus an ideal in the 40- to 60-character range[8]).

- Double spacing between lines of type, destroying the visual unity of the paragraph.

- Omitting indents (which are a reader convenience; speedy reading depends heavily on pattern recognition, and indents are part of the pattern).

- Generous helpings of reverse type. Reverse type slashes good comprehension from 70 percent (for black type on white) to 0 percent (for white type on a dark background), Wheildon found. Which pretty much doomed the messages from both the chair and the president, both set in reverse. Customarily, of course, these sorts of messages are bland, predictable, and hence skipped. So a bad typographic treatment might be forgiven. But that wasn't the case here. Here, the chair's message set up the theme for the book: the involvement of this foundation in environmental issues. That key theme deserved prominence, not a burial.

On the writing side, the flaws included:

- The captions weren't captions at all, but labels. Real captions tell stories.[9] And they're hugely important, because they're one of the few items of text that almost everyone reads, Dr. Vögele discovered.

- The shortest opening paragraph in the annual report was more than 40 words long. The sight of a first paragraph the size of a bus looks exhausting. Direct mail copywriters learn to begin letters with a one-sentence paragraph of 10 words or less. They want to make sure the reader's first little mental commitment is effortless. If a piece of writing looks like work, most people simply won't read it.

- An absence of any headlines or decks. Instead, the annual report merely ran headings to mark major divisions: "welcome," "message from the president," "giving," "selected grants," and so on; basically, a series of tabs like you'd see on file folders. They didn't tell any story, a big missed opportunity. Headline-and-deck combos are the best (only) way to reach a large number of readers. Without headlines, the annual report was effectively mute. It said nothing.

The final tally: nine major crimes against easy reading. Is this uncommonly bad? Not at all. Work equally flawed is probably more the rule than the exception in nonprofit communications.

THE INDENT: REPORTS OF ITS DEATH ARE GREATLY EXAGGERATED

The advent of desktop publishing in the 1980s permitted huge steps forward for nonprofits in the cost and convenience of printed materials by opening up two tight and expensive trades, graphic design and layout, to anyone with a computer and a copy of Microsoft Word.

But desktop publishing was also one undoubted step backward for readability.

The poor indent began to die, partly (modish designers share the blame) at the hands of those with the tools to publish but not the training to realize how important this reader convention truly is.

Indents are not optional, at least not in the North American market (the only one we know well), where readers, their minds hurrying to chew through the daily verbiage, have learned to depend on such things to ease the labor.

The reading brain is a creature of habit. It relies on conventions it's come to recognize over the years. One of those conventions—prevailing in virtually all professionally produced books, newspapers, and magazines—is the indent.

Think of the indent as a rung on a ladder. The indent helps the eye climb through the text, by breaking up the solid, rectangular mass of the paragraphs. Professional typographers sometimes refer to the indent as the visual equivalent of a building's front door. It clearly signals to the wandering eye: *This is where you enter.*

Indents are never optional, if you wish to be rigidly reader-friendly. But missing indents sometimes bring no particular penalty. On Web sites, for instance, indents aren't conventional. Viewers have adjusted.

Appeal letters, however, make a bad mistake when they delete indents. Without indents, your heartwarming letter looks at a glance just like standard business correspondence, where the convention of unindented paragraphs now holds sway.

A business letter is the *last* thing you want to resemble. What could be more *un*heartwarming?

A letter asking for money is *personal* correspondence. From some *me* to some *you*, just the two of us having a chat. That's the idea. It's intimate. Unindented paragraphs break the mood.

There's another reason for using indents in fundraising letters, Mal Warwick says. "The eye needs rest," he notes in his Cardinal Rule #6 (Format Your Letter for Easy Reading), "so be conscious of the white space you're leaving around your copy."

First on his list of things that add white space: "Indent every paragraph."

Mal Warwick, *How to Write Successful Fundraising Letters*, (San Francisco: Jossey-Bass, 2001), p. 110

In Conclusion

In self-defense, read Colin Wheildon's research. Learn to spot the ways that second-rate (if superficially pretty) design choices sabotage easy reading.

Keep in mind: If you don't have a strong browser level, you don't have a prayer of communicating well.

⬛ ENDNOTES

1. "The Road Less Traveled," *issue* 8, No. 2 (Fall 2002): 12.
2. What happens during the crucial first moments when your appeal letter arrives at its destination? Dr. Siegfried Vögele studied that encounter and found it consisted of three swift appraisals: examining and opening the envelope (eight seconds on average), unfolding the letter (four seconds), browsing the letter at a glance (another eight seconds). His findings are well summarized in Mal Warwick's book, *How to Write Successful Fundraising Letters,* rev. and updated (San Francisco: Jossey-Bass, 2001).
3. Mal Warwick, *Type & Layout: Are You Communicating or Just Making Pretty Shapes.* (Corporate Design Foundation, Boston.)
4. Robert Bringhurst, *The Elements of Typographic Style* (Vancouver, BC: Hartley & Marks, 2005), p. 17
5. How common? A review of printed materials from hundreds of nonprofits found that about one in 20 was producing work that would consistently pass a readability audit.
6. The "butcher's bill" is the count of dead and wounded at battle's end.
7. Why? We have a theory. Serif type isn't intrinsically "better" than sans serif type. It's just far more common. In the United States and in Australia, where Wheildon did his research, serif type is the choice for most newspapers, books, and magazine articles. Our brains have become highly efficient at rapidly deciphering serif type.
8. James Felici, *The Complete Manual of Typography* (Berkeley, CA: Adobe Press, 2003), p. 120.
9. The Associated Press standard photo caption uses two sentences. The first sentence describes what the photo shows, in the present tense, and states where and when the photo was made. The second sentence gives background on the news event or describes why the photo is significant. *The Associated Press Stylebook and Libel Manual* (Reading, MA: Perseus Books, 1998), p. 307.

Monitoring Progress And
Measuring Results

HOW EFFECTIVE ARE *YOUR* COMMUNICATIONS

When it is obvious that the goals cannot be reached, don't adjust the goals, adjust the action steps.

—CONFUCIUS

DEAR READER   Measurement is not about getting it perfect. It's about getting it "righter." On my best day I expect to get no more than 70 percent of the things right in my communications. (And I'm probably guessing high, to keep my ego intact.) Still, that's all I need to do: 70 percent right will work fine.

Maybe there are 20 things I need to take into account. If I get 70 percent (14) of them right—and they are the most important things to get right, like emotional triggers—then I'm grazing in sweet clover. The communications will work.

What you don't want to do is get just 30 percent of your donor and prospect communications right. Then your income will suffer. This chapter covers the two ways to rapidly improve your communications: Prepare well and measure your results.

Tom ■

"IS IT WORKING?" HOW TO MEASURE YOUR RESULTS

Are you getting the results you need from your newsletter, your advertising, your direct mail, your public relations, your Web site, your chats with prospects? Are the critical indicators pointing up or down? As for the bigger picture: What are the strengths and weaknesses of your communications plan?

To answer these questions, you need proper measures. A communications program without proper measurement is like a car without wheels: It gets you nowhere.

And definitely beware people complimenting you on the *look* of your publications. Not because it's flattery; we're all entitled to flattery. But because a compliment about the attractiveness of your Web site, newsletter, case statement, or annual report might not mean what you hope it means. To paraphrase someone: You can't eat compliments. Unless they turn into action, they're beside the point.

Style—but without substance that is donor-relevant—is a common flaw in fund development materials, especially when budgets are big enough to afford professional graphic design. Viewers (we hesitate to call them readers) will react, "Wow! That's gorgeous!" But is that all you get? A striking first impression without any subsequent gift?

Often, yes. Steve Herlich, as vice president of development at Southwest Mental Health Center in San Antonio, noticed the phenomenon with his splashy donor newsletter. "I get a lot of positive feedback about how nice-looking it is," he said. "Almost no donations as a result, though."

In a nutshell: Pretty printed materials by themselves do not produce results. Don't be fooled by flash; it's not enough. First make your communications donor-centric. *Then* make them look good.

Which brings us full circle, back to the first thing this chapter talked about, which is *action*. Fund development communications, oral and written, are ultimately about action; if not now, then sometime. You want people to do things, to act on your behalf, to become your investors: donors and volunteers, people who give you their "time, treasure, or talent," the trinity of philanthropy.

Measuring results is relatively straightforward. (At the rudimentary level; at the upper levels it can become as mathematical as physics, and there are books on the right techniques for measuring and improving results.[1]). There are two essentials.

1. You need to quantify (count or measure in some way) the actions that resulted from your communication attempt.

2. Then you need to interpret your quantification correctly, by having handy a benchmark against which to compare your results. That way you'll know if you're running above or below reasonable expectations.

Let's say yours is a local charity, and your goal is to acquire new donors. After all, it's a basic obligation in any fund development program. "At every organization, some level of donor attrition is inevitable," says Stephen Hitchcock, a longtime senior executive at Mal Warwick Associates. "In any given year, at least 10 percent and more likely 20 percent of your donor base will fade away." If you neglect acquisition, you seal your organization's charitable fate. "If you stop acquiring donors now, in as few as five years you could end up with next to none. Therefore any organization desiring a long-term future must invest in some level of acquisition."[2]

So you take the conventional route: You do a mailing. You send out a direct mail solicitation to households in your area not already on your list. Not just any households, of course, but households you feel might be predisposed to your cause for some reason. If you're trying to acquire new donors for a family planning clinic, for instance, you might target women.

You mail your solicitation. Within 12 to 14 days, you have most of your return. Over the next six months, a couple more responses will wander in; but pretty much all your response will be in your hands within two weeks. How exciting . . . and fast.

Let's assume the solicitation was good enough to achieve a routine response. In 2007, in the United States, experts say an okay (not flaming great, not miserable) response to an acquisition mailing is one half of 1 percent (0.5 percent). Thus, if you mailed 20,000 pieces, your response yields for your organization 100 new donors. Is that enough?

That depends on your goal. What are you measuring?

If you're measuring immediate cash income, you might conclude that the effort wasn't worth the trouble and cost. If, for instance, the average gift from these 100 new donors was $25, you've just brought in $2,500. Which might not even cover the cost of printing and postage.

By another standard, though, you've done fine.

Wasn't the real purpose of the mailing to plug a hole? You set out to replace your annual 10 to 20 percent donor attrition. If you have 500 donors in your current base, and you lose the full 20 percent (i.e., 100 donors depart), then your acquisition mailing has at least broken even, which is the goal. Those 100 new donors replace your loss.

But a no-growth goal doesn't get you far. You probably want to do more with your acquisition mailing than simply make up a loss; you want to *expand* your base.

Now you have to recalculate. You work out the problem on a scrap of paper. You currently have those 500 donors in your base. *(You write down the number 500.)* You're going to lose 20 percent of them, worst case. *(You multiply 500 by 20 percent, which equals 100.)* So you need 100 new donors to make up that difference. *Plus* you want to grow your base by 10 percent, which translates into 50 new donors. *(You add your replacement goal of 100 to your growth goal of 50.)* Your *total* goal has become: 150 new donors acquired.

Mailing to 20,000 households, you won't make your goal. If you mail to 30,000 households instead, you will, since one-half of 1 percent multiplied by 30,000 equals 150.

To measure how effective any kind of communication has been, you have to know first what constitutes success *for you*. For the fundraiser who sends out the acquisition mailing just described, immediate monetary success is beyond reach. But a different kind of success beckons: dealing with the problem of attrition. Furthermore, fund development veterans like Stephen Hitchcock know that acquiring a new donor is worth any price because the proper measure of a donor's worth is lifetime value, not first gift. Before you can measure properly, you need to decide what really matters.

Avoid false, pointless, and unrealistic goals. To be useful, goals must be (1) measurable; (2) achievable with the resources you have at your disposal; and (3) worth doing.

Pursuits such as "raising awareness in the community of who we are" are favorites of untrained would-be marketers. But goals like these are not very useful. For one thing, to track the "raising," you'd need to survey the community before and after your communications efforts, to measure things like "prompted" and "unprompted" awareness. That level of sophistication requires professional researchers. Costly, and to what end? Unless you can tie "increased awareness" to some specific fund development objective, it's information not worth knowing.

At the beginning, stick to numerical goals for your communications. State them as "wants" or "needs." Such as:

- **Monetary goals.** These measure *how much*. "We want to increase the average gift to our spring appeal from $25 to $30." Or: "We need our fundraising income to match inflation of 4 percent. To account for that, this year's minimum (level-funded) goal will be 4 percent higher than last year's." Or: "We want to increase the average-dollar-per-newsletter-subscriber from $5 to $6."[3]

- **Participation goals.** These measure *how many*. "Every time 20 people attend one of our cultivation gatherings, we get at least one new donor who's pretty serious. We want to persuade six people to host those gatherings this year."[4] Or: "For every 100 people who visit our Web site, 10 click through to the giving page, and 2 make gifts. We want to attract 1,000 people a month to our Web site."

Many goals are attained by a mix of written and oral communications methods: event invitations, acquisition mailings, informational meetings, newsletters, letters to the editors, emails, grant applications, and so on. A goal that states "We need to increase giving to our agency by 10 percent this year" won't be met by just one means.

Have precise goals. Measure whatever you can. And *don't* be seduced by the idea that "building your image" produces hard fund-development results.

Image-building promotions simply cannot do the job of raising money because they do not require a response. Building your image is *not* a call to action.

A surprising number of nonprofits find the wherewithal to buy advertising in the newspaper and then waste the money completely by running image-building ads that include no ask, no response mechanism of any kind, and make no offer. Unless you have fortunes to spend (on the scale of, say, oil producers), image advertising of this sort does you no measurable good in fund development.

MEASURING THE UNMEASURABLE

There are things you cannot easily measure.

Take donor newsletters. What's measurable about them?

Well, you can measure response to *specific* items in the newsletter. If an issue advertises an offer for, say, a bequest booklet, you can count how many people respond. Offers are always measurable. (Word to the wise: In focus groups, disgusted donors occasionally refer to this booklet as the "death brochure." Make yours ungloomy.)

Or you can measure income directly generated by your newsletter. When you include a reply envelope in your newsletter, you can measure the number and size of the gifts you get back. (Note: If you use the same gift envelope for more than one solicitation, make sure you somehow specially mark the one slipped into the newsletter. That way you'll be able to distinguish newsletter gift envelopes when they return.)

So those are two measures of a newsletter's mettle. But *neither* tells you *anything* about the one thing that really matters to the health and cost effectiveness of your fund development program: Is your newsletter effectively building donor loyalty? Was your annual report effective? Did the Web site do its bit?

You'll know . . . eventually.

But in the near term, all you can do is produce good, strong communications work and hope for the best.

Bottom line, only one numerical measure matters. And everything contributes to it—every oral and written communication in your fund development effort, every interaction your organization has with donors.

That royal measure is retention.

If five years from now, you've retained 40 percent of the donors you acquire this year, well, that is better than if you've kept just 30 percent of the donors. And you'll have brought in far more money. Acquiring donors is expensive. Retaining donors is relatively cheap. To pay back the original cost of acquiring them, you need to retain your donors as long as possible, all the way to a bequest or other planned gift, if you can. Some good communications and honest attention do the trick.

What's the real benchmark for retention?

Actual results vary, of course. The biggest hemorrhage typically happens after the first gift, on your second attempt to get a gift. That's when bonds are loosest and newly acquired donors flee you in the largest numbers. With second and subsequent gifts, donors tend to stabilize and linger a bit.

So, let's pretend you've acquired 100 new donors. If you lose them at the reasonably common attrition rate of 50 percent every year, by the fifth year *just three* of the original 100 donors will still be giving to you.[5]

Get Your Thoughts in Order *Before* You Begin to Write: A Checklist

Your best defense against poor results is to mount a good offense: Communicate well, in ways that have a high likelihood of piercing the inertia, indifference, and clutter standing between you and your target audience.

There are two big, basic challenges in fund development: (1) acquiring new donors, and (2) keeping those donors interested and active as long as possible. Much of your success depends on your communications, oral and written. They are how you bring in new people and sustain a healthy relationship with them.

The following checklist summarizes advice from previous chapters. Use it to help you get your thoughts in good working order before you begin to write.

1. **Write a creative brief.** See Chapter 13 for a review of this all-important first step. Here's the formula:

    This [insert item name; say, article in your donor newsletter] **will convince** [insert specific target audience; say, those with 45 and older, who should have wills] **that** [insert action you want reader to take; say, request your informative brochure about bequests] **will result in** [insert any benefit that the reader might value; say, guaranteeing that your mission has an enduring future by strengthening your endowment].

2. **Decide which emotional triggers to include.** *Fear* and *anger* are favorites. So are *hope* and *salvation*. Any form of membership (in, say, a planned giving society) puts *exclusivity* to work. There are 135 emotional states to choose from. See Chapter 9.

3. **Be clear about the problem your organization is solving.** Emotional triggers work in pairs. There's a negative emotion: That's the problem. Countered by a positive emotion: That's the solution. Your mission, your cause, your accomplishments are the *solution* to some *problem*. What is that problem(s)?

4. **Figure out the "reading order" for your piece.** Most people will look at your materials in a certain sequence. And on first encounter they'll be

skimming quickly. Give serious thought to what your target audience will see first, second, last. Make sure you're starting from strength: What's your hook in the first thing they encounter? Does it start with a bang? What happens if readers start from the back instead of the front? Is there a strong message at both ends?

5. **Think through your response mechanisms.** You want your readers to *do* something, right? You've got to help them. How will they do it? How will they complete the action that you'd like them to take? If, for instance, you're asking people to go online to give, is your Web site ready to receive these visitors? Is everything perfectly obvious on the receiving end? Use willing friends to road test all your response mechanisms, to see what unsuspected impediments and confusions they encounter.

6. **Translate features into benefits.** There's an old saying in commercial copywriting: "Features tell. Benefits sell." Features are the things you do. Benefits are why any of it matters. Feature: "We have a 24-hour hot line." Benefit: "Because crises do not happen on a 9-to-5 basis." Benefits often speak to a reader's self-interest: "What's in it for me?" For instance: "We now offer you a monthly giving option so you'll never have to write a check again. You can now support your favorite cause every month automatically, no muss or fuss. Make a powerful difference—at your convenience." Before you write or talk about anything, ask yourself: *Why will the reader care?*

7. **Write your browser level before you write your body copy.** Write the bigger, bolder, briefer stuff first: headlines, decks, captions, offers, calls to action, and so on. Much of the time, your browser level is all that people will read. If people need to read your articles to understand your message, you *will* fail to connect.

8. **Don't forget to promote your themes.** For example, are you anxious to remind readers that charity plays an important role in your mission? Include that message in your browser level.

9. **Don't forget to highlight your offers.** An offer is anything a reader can get by responding. Offers include discounts (e.g., three tickets for the price of two); premiums (e.g., a T-shirt for a $100 gift); information (e.g., a brochure); new ways of giving (e.g., online); chances to multiply a donor's impact (e.g., challenge campaigns); tours; and so on. Your only limit is your imagination.

10. **Don't forget to use testimonials.** Testimonials prove how well you do your work, in a fast, credible way. Testimonials also easily switch off the skeptical in your reader.

EVALUATING YOUR DONOR NEWSLETTER: EIGHT TESTS

There are four general criteria for evaluating donor newsletters:

1. **Is the newsletter reader-friendly?** Is it easy to skim? Is the language accessible, written for speed? Did the design choices enhance readability? Is its "personality" warm and inviting?

2. **Is the newsletter clear about the benefits of supporting your mission?** Does it answer the most basic question: What's in it for me? if I give.

3. **Is the newsletter "donor-centric"?** Does it recognize and celebrate donors in a way that would be emotionally satisfying? Does it answer key questions that donors typically have regarding your business efficiency, your accomplishments, and your vision?

4. **Is the newsletter action-oriented?** Does the reader know what to do next? Are there offers to respond to? Is the contact information obvious?

Then there are eight specific tests you can apply to make sure your donor newsletter goes out the door as effective as can be:

1. **The "emotional trigger" test.** Profitable donor newsletters work because the reader's skimming eye trips across lots of emotional triggers, particularly in the "browser level." For example, this trigger-laden headline/deck combination that appeared in the newsletter of the Drug Policy Alliance: "Senior Republican Wants to Draft You in the War on Drugs. Outrageous New Bill Makes Americans Choose Between Spying on Their Neighbors and Jail Time." Or something fear-resonant like "The 10 Warning Signs of Childhood Depression."

2. **The "news hook" test.** A newsletter (or any other publication that promises news) needs to shout its NEWS! loud and clear. The human brain craves the new: *Tell me something I don't know. Make my life more interesting for a few moments.* Neuroscience says the human mind will respond involuntarily even to the mere mention of the word *new.*

   A few practical words of advice, then.

   You cannot overuse the word *new,* for one. Sprinkle the word everywhere, with special attention to the browser level.

   Use other words and phrases that carry the same electric charge: words like *secret, hidden, hints, tips, update, private, confidential, mystery, discover, unveil, expose, reveal, divulge*; phrases like "Did you know?" "Myths and Facts," "Frequently Asked Questions," "Heard on the Blog."

Don't shout NO NEWS! by running the same old things over and over, like a recurring "Letter from the Executive Director" column parked ostentatiously on the front page of every issue.

3. **The "you" test.** UK fundraising superstar George Smith notes, "All fundraising copy should sound like someone talking."[6] This applies to donor newsletters, too, because they are fundraising copy, of a special kind.

   Donor newsletters are a hybrid form of news publication. They are not "pure" news vehicles, tell it like is whatever "it" happens to be. Nor are they simple chronicles of agency activities (i.e., "In March we did this. In April we did that. In May we did these other things.").

   Donor newsletters are actually a form of direct mail appeal. Though an appeal as soft as silk: The "asks" are secondary to the news. And utterly respectful of the donor's valuable time: Each issue conveys all the right information as quickly as it can.

   As with all direct mail appeals, frequent use of the word *you* (in any form) is mandatory. *You* is glue. *You* keeps people reading. *You* personalizes the newsletter in a way no other word can. *You* makes the newsletter sound like George Smith's required conversational voice. (In contrast: A pure news publication, to bring us back to the earlier point, consciously maintains a neutral distance.)

   Circle each instance of the word *you* in red. Red makes them easy to spot. You should have red circles all over the place. Dozens of circles per page is a worthy goal. Red circles should be especially common in the browser level. Try hard to write at least two-thirds of your headlines so they include the word *you*.

4. **The "obvious offers" test.** Offers must be obvious ("obvious" meaning displayed inside boxes or with big type) to draw a good response. Offers that are buried in text are dead on arrival, because only a small percentage of recipients read any particular article.

   Common newsletter offers include invitations to give online, to write a bequest, to sign up for an e-alert, to request an informative brochure, to join a special society, to renew membership, to register for an event, to switch to monthly giving, to volunteer, and so on. When you make an offer, celebrate it. Shy, retiring offers don't get asked to dance.

5. **The "accomplishments" test.** Donors have one overwhelming interest regarding the charities they support: What did you do with my money? Did I make the world a better place by giving you a gift?

   The best sort of accomplishment reporting is both obvious (in the headlines) and directly linked to the donor (as in "With your help, we can do all these wonderful things. And without your help, we can't.")

It's important that you learn to distinguish between "accomplishments" and "activities." Donors don't care that much about your activities. Donors really care about results. For instance, purchasing equipment because you've received a grant is merely an activity; donors will be mildly interested at best. Activities only become true accomplishments when your stories talk about why the activity *matters*. For example, "With this new equipment, purchased thanks to the generosity of donors like you, people who are now in pain 24 hours a day will finally find some blessed relief." Similarly, announcing that you've created a committee or a task force or a plan or a club, these are all just activities and pretty ho-hum by donor standards. They become accomplishments only when the reader understands why the committee or task force or plan or club was urgently needed to help change the world, fix a problem, right a wrong.

Testimonials, by the way, are a form of accomplishment reporting. Positive testimonials, in fact, are one of the best forms of accomplishment reporting. They're usually short, so they're fast. And they are by nature usually somewhat anecdotal. It's real person telling a story. Witness this statement written in a waiting room book by a patient at a Planned Parenthood clinic: "My experience here was difficult. However, the staff was supportive, knowledgeable and nonjudgmental. Thank you!" Exactly the results that donors hope to buy with their gifts.

6. **The visual test.** This test evaluates how fast someone can absorb the key messages in an issue of the newsletter, thanks to two things: (1) exploitation of the browser level; and (2) design issues that aid or defeat easy reading. This test guarantees your newsletter is visually reader-friendly. Reading is labor; when it's *hard* labor, people find other things to do with their discretionary attention span.

The browser level includes all the bigger, bolder, briefer things. Eye motion studies demonstrated that people quickly scan a publication before they start reading.[7] And their eyes (this is the important part) go immediately to graphically prominent information, either verbal (e.g., headlines) or visual (e.g., photographs).

Have Colin Wheildon's book, *Type & Layout*,[8] handy when you conduct this test. If your newsletter is set, for instance, in a sans serif typeface, you will learn from Mr. Wheildon's readability research that a sans serif typeface like Arial is five times harder to comprehend than a serif typeface like Times New Roman. And you will learn a host of other important findings about colored type, colored backgrounds, reverse type, and the habits of the eye.

A couple of other things to check on:

The ideal line measure (the number of characters and spaces in a single line of type) is somewhere in the 40- to 60-character range. Newsletter columns of 85 characters are far too wide.

Generally speaking, all photos should run with adjacent captions. Dr. Vögele proved that eyes flit first to dominant graphic elements, with photos leading the list. Photos are "eyeball traps." When—as it predictably will—the eye zips right to a photo, have a message waiting to pounce in the caption.

One last thing: Headlines should look like headlines. In newspapers it is common to find headlines set in a type size two or three times bigger than the type size of the articles. If the articles are set in 12-point type, for example, then the headlines introducing them are 24 to 36 points in size. Headlines have to be powerful and dramatic looking to be taken seriously (or even noticed, for that matter). Headlines that are just a few points larger than the article do not command attention.

7. **The "donor-centric" test.** This test evaluates your newsletter's donor-appreciation factor. And it's simple: Just count the times you've been donor-centric when you talk about your mission, vision, accomplishments, and needs.

    Truth is, most newsletters are donor-*optional* rather than donor-*centered*.

    A typical nonprofit newsletter talks something like this: "We did this. We did that. We were amazing. Oh, by the way, thanks, if you've given."

    A "donor-centric" newsletter, however, takes pains to put the donor center stage. Donor-centric newsletters go beyond just sharing the credit: they make the donor the hero of the story.

    Donor-centric newsletters repeat two messages constantly, both overtly and between the lines: "With your help, all these amazing things happened (or will happen). And without your help, they won't."

    The first message focuses on mission and vision, accomplishments and needs. The second message shifts the burden for all that onto the donors' shoulders. When donors believe they are responsible for your success, giving starts to bloom. Then it's just a matter of providing the donors with many opportunities to participate, along with frequent feedings of appreciation and (of course) reporting on accomplishments. Fund development is never easy. But it becomes much "less hard" when all your communications are donor-centered.

8. **The "headlines" test.** Headlines are the most important element of any news publication. When the headlines are good, the newsletter works. Or vice versa.

    What makes a good headline?

- **Good headlines are efficient.** They are a key reader convenience. They give time-pressed people the gist of the story in just a few seconds. I traverse four daily newspapers without strain and with total confidence for one reason: their very excellent headlines.
- **Good headlines are as long as they need to be to convey the whole story.** A typical *Wall Street Journal* headline/deck combination clocks in at 20 to 35 words. The *whole* story, by the way, is not simply what happened, but also why it *matters* to the reader. There's always an angle. And the target audience determines what the angle is.

    The paramount flaw in nonprofit newsletters is bad headlines: headlines that tell half a story, a vague story, or no story at all.

    For example: A headline such as "Judge Samuel Alito Confirmed to the U.S. Supreme Court" is half a story. What's missing is *why* his appointment matters to your particular donors. It is never safe to assume "well, everyone knows why *that* matters." A good headline sums up the entire story. It leaves nothing unsaid. It doesn't rely on the article to fill in important blanks.

    Furthermore, in a donor newsletter, headlines take a position. When an organization promoting, say, reproductive rights reports on an event like Judge Alito's confirmation, the donor newsletter isn't neutral. It advocates a certain position. Supporters of advocacy groups *want* you to express an opinion. Through their donations, they *pay* you to express an opinion. For a reproductive rights audience, a suitable rewrite then might be: "'Worst-case' Supreme Court Appointment Confirmed: Alito's In. What's Next? New Conservation Majority Has Abortion Rights in Its Sights. Threat to Roe v. Wade Highest in 30 Years."

MEASURING THE EFFECTIVENESS OF PUBLIC RELATIONS

The old unit for measuring success in the PR trade was column inches, since news articles were considered "free advertising." It made a certain sense to measure the space occupied by an article and equate that to an ad size. It allowed PR folks to attach a plausible monetary value to the coverage they managed to obtain. For instance, a news article that ran for 10 column inches would equal, in square inches, a two-column ad that was 5 inches deep. And an ad that size in a newspaper or magazine had a price tag. This led to statements like "That front-page article about your organization was worth $6,000 in advertising."

Yes and no. Yes, an equivalent ad might *cost* that much. But if it appeared just once, as news articles will, that ad would be *worth* almost nothing, since most advertising requires repetition to work at all well. In truth, the full value of articles lauding your organization can only be realized through repetition: by photocopying those articles (thus extending their lifespan) and distributing them in abundance to prospects and donors.

A more sophisticated measure of public relations is what might be called "message penetration." Which is to say: How often do your key messages appear in the media? Have your key messages penetrated so deeply and widely that they've become part of the story?

For Roger Williams Park Zoo (Providence, RI), message penetration became effective when newspaper and magazine articles about the zoo began to routinely repeat phrases like "New England's best zoo" and "one of the top ten zoos in the country," messages that the zoo had pushed long and hard.

For HousingWorks RI, an advocacy group working to change attitudes and increase public support for affordable housing, message penetration became effective when every news article and political speech mentioned the group's basic theme, that affordable housing was an economic development issue. Previously, the issue of affordable housing had been linked most prominently to homelessness or treated as a social justice issue. When the issue was linked instead to economic development, it became possible to seek a $50 million bond for construction, which ultimately voters approved.

For the Audubon Society of Rhode Island, which is trying to increase charitable contributions, message penetration will be effective, and giving will rise, when donors begin routinely echoing the theme "Achieving the Audubon Society's mission depends on donor support: 75 percent of the Society's income is from charitable gifts." Right now that critical fact is a best-kept secret. Donors don't yet realize how much they mean to the organization. When they *do* realize how much they're needed, they will respond.

STANDARDS FOR E-MAIL SOLICITATIONS

Madeline Stanionis is the voice of experience where e-mail solicitations are concerned. "If you want your email to generate 10 donations," she writes in *Raising Thousands (if Not Tens of Thousands) of Dollars with Email*, at least 1,000 people need to receive your message, 250 people need to open your message, and 50 people need to click on the link to your donation page.[9]

That equals a 1-percent response from your e-mail list, a 4-percent response from the people who then open your e-mail, and a 20-percent response from the fraction who make it all the way through to your donation page.

"It's a numbers game, of course, just like other direct marketing media," Stanionis explains. And no one guarantees that your numbers will do as well as her example. Your particular results rely on just one thing: the quality of your e-mail list. "Who they are, how they got there, what they want, and how deeply they're connected to your cause," as she says. If you add lots of e-mail addresses to your list without knowing or verifying that these people have an interest in your cause, your income from e-mail solicitations will likely be disappointing.

IN CONCLUSION

Good professional communications are built backward: from (1) the target audience and (2) what you want that audience to do. In pursuit of success, you consider a few dozen things, from emotional triggers to convenience.

But it is not a piece of machinery you're building as you work to improve your communications. What you are trying to build really are stronger, more determined relationships with your donors and volunteers. You desperately want those generous people to understand, at a heart level, that your mission *needs* them to succeed and can't live without them.

That's foremost. But you're building something else, too, *also* vitally important. You're building inside your organization, at the very same time, a so-called culture of philanthropy: a mature awareness and appreciation that your organization's supporters, your donors and volunteers, like investors in a company, make the mission and vision possible, at least in part and sometimes in whole.

With that awareness and appreciation, and those strong relationships, unimaginably wonderful results will irresistibly bloom.

ENDNOTES

1. For help evaluating direct mail, see Mal Warwick's *Testing, Testing, 1, 2, 3* (San Francisco: Jossey-Bass, 2003). For help evaluating fund development programs with many different components, see James M. Greenfield's *Fund-Raising Cost Effectiveness: A Self-Assessment Workbook* (New York: John Wiley & Sons, 1996).
2. Stephen Hitchcock, *Open Immediately! Straight Talk on Direct Mail Fundraising* (Medfield, MA: Emerson & Church, 2004), p. 87.
3. Say you have 400 people on your donor newsletter's mailing list, and when you mail an issue, $2,000 in gifts come back in the return envelopes you've enclosed. That gives you "an average-dollar-per-subscriber" of $5 (2,000 divided by 400). If the next issue to the same 400 brings in $2,400, your average-per-subscriber rises to $6.
4. These meetings are described in detail in Chapter 7. No solicitation occurs. In fact, people are told to leave their checkbooks home. They are asked to simply come and listen to a brief presentation in a relaxed setting.
5. Best Friends, an animal welfare group, in 2006 published on its Web site the results of a survey regarding donor retention. A "nationally recognized fund raising consultant" had advised that the "typical" donor retention rate was around 10 percent. That seemed ominously low, with huge financial implications, "since it is clearly much more expensive

to acquire a new donor than it is to renew a past supporter." So Best Friends "took a rather unscientific sampling, looking at data sets from 20 organizations to see what kind of retention rates were typical in this group. These organizations vary in annual dollars raised from a few hundred thousand to over ten million. The number of donors ranges from several hundred to several thousand. The group includes just about every type of nonprofit, from art museums and environmental groups to human service providers and religious organizations. We looked only at cash received, including gifts, membership dues and pledge payments, but ignoring pledges. The average year-to-year retention rate across the organizations over the years from 1999 to 2004 was just over 50%. The lowest average for a single organization was around 25% and the highest over 67%."

6. George Smith, *Tiny Essentials of Writing for Fundraising* (Kermarquer, France: White Lion Press), 2003.
7. Conducted by Siegfried Vögele, at the Direct Mail Institute in Munich, Germany.
8. Colin Wheildon, *Type and Layout*, 2nd edition (Mentone, Australia: The Worsley Press) 2005
9. Madeline Stanionis, *Raising Thousands (if Not Tens of Thousands) of Dollars with Email* (Medfield, MA: Emerson & Church) 2006, p. 15.

Monitoring Progress and Measuring Results

HOW GOOD IS YOUR RELATIONSHIP-BUILDING PROGRAM?

Da an ce da kare tuwo ya yi yawa a gidan biki, y ace "Ma gani a kas!" (When the dog was told that there was food for everyone at the wedding feast, he replied, "We'll check that out at the ground level!")

—PROVERB FROM NIGER

Data itself is nothing unless one uses it as a resource from which to draw conclusions.
—BRIAN HERBERT AND KEVIN J. ANDERSON, *DUNE: THE MACHINE CRUSADE*

DEAR READER   This chapter is not a comprehensive exposé of evaluation. I'm just providing some ideas for you to explore. Send me your comments and examples. Together we could develop this further. *Simone*

Everyone knows it's important to monitor progress and measure results.

Interestingly, however, the actual process isn't all that successful in many organizations. Staff complains about the lack of time. Board members focus on their own opinions rather than objective, verifiable assessment. Some organizations do not have the capacity or the capability to design and execute evaluation.

Others recognize the complexity and focus on quantitative evaluation only, the easier stuff. These organizations avoid the difficulties of qualitative evaluation, like donor emotions and donor satisfaction.

The bottom line, though: Organizations must improve their evaluation processes. Zero evaluation is not an option.

Doing just a bit is better than doing none. Your organization decides what it can handle. Don't take on too much but do something. Not just because your funders demand it, but because you know evaluation can make your organization stronger.

Read through the suggestions in this chapter—and in Chapter 23 on evaluating your communications. Identify what your organization evaluates now and decide what improvements you can make.

Find out what your colleagues assess. Ask them for sample tools. Collect samples from the Internet and in publications (see Exhibit 24.1).

Evaluate. And then evaluate more when you are able.

> *In a metric-minded organization, it's very tempting to focus on things that are easy to measure instead of those things that are important to measure.*
>
> —GROUP OF 33, *THE BIG MOO*

Colleague Tina Palmer, CFRE, suggested that employment retention is an important performance measure. I agree! Here's what Tina shared with me as she reviewed this chapter:

> I've seen so many organizations run through multiple development officers. If donors meet with multiple gift officers because of staff turnover, do these donors lose faith in the organization's abilities? This could affect donor retention and size of gifts.
>
> Also, what does this kind of change say about the professionals leading development efforts? Should organizations look carefully at leaders who have high employee turnover within their departments? Is the leader causing the turnover and why?

EXHIBIT 24.1   WHAT DOES YOUR ORGANIZATION EVALUATE?

The most effective organizations regularly evaluate these sorts of things:

- Organization relevancy and mission
- Alignment of programs and services with mission
- Quality of programs and services
- Board and individual board member performance
- Performance of each staff person, of teams, and of operations in general
- Financial performance
- Communications and marketing
- Fund development performance, including relationship building

What would you add to this list?

I suspect that some development leaders are not organizational development specialists, described in Chapter 3. These professionals look to financial results only and seek employees who produce money.

Tina asks another important question: "Why does our profession consistently lose development officers within the initial two to three years?"

I think it's because many entry-level professionals are stranded with the kind of leaders that Tina describes in her first comment. Too much fundraising focuses on financial strategies and tactics rather than the organizational development perspective. With those limits, people often cannot perform effectively, don't experience success, and leave the profession. This book hopes to fight Tina's critique and advance the profession.

WHY EVALUATION MATTERS

Evaluation tests the quality of your decision-making and the competency of your execution. Evaluation of past performance allows you to forecast future results. The most effective evaluation raises meaningful questions, generates critical conversation, and produces organizational learning and change. See the useful definitions in Exhibit 24.2.

Certain evaluation results can provide vital information to your various stakeholders. This transparency—as well as the results themselves—serves as a relationship-building strategy. The information shows your stakeholders the value of your services, the difference their participation makes, and the reliability of your performance.

EXHIBIT 24.2 USEFUL DEFINITIONS

Accountability: Responsible for something. Synonyms include responsibility, liability, and answerability.

Evaluation: Examining something to judge its value, quality, importance, and effect. Synonyms include appraisal, assessment, and measurement.

Competence or competency: The ability to do something well or to meet a particular standard. Synonyms include capability and proficiency.

Measure: A way of evaluating something. Synonyms include assess, evaluate, and appraise.

Performance: How something or someone functions or operates or behaves. The effectiveness of how a job is done. Synonyms include achievement and action.

Result(s): To produce a particular outcome. The desired outcome from an action. Synonyms include outcome and consequence.

Standard(s): Level of quality or excellence that is accepted as a norm. Synonyms include principles and values.

> *Meeting and exceeding performance standards adds confidence to the performance measurement process and reinforces the decisions made by board, management, and staff. Reliable expectations also permit the uninterrupted deliver of program and services.*
>
> —JAMES M. GREENFIELD, *FUND-RAISING COST EFFECTIVENESS*

In his workbook, Greenfield outlines a useful evaluation scenario comprised of five key elements.[1] These elements can apply to diverse evaluation processes, from charitable gifts to relationship building to client services.

1. **Effectiveness.** The degree to which your effort produces your desired result(s)

2. **Efficiency.** The quality of your execution, for example, how well you carried out the effective strategies

3. **Productivity.** The effort required (output) to achieve your desired results, also called outcomes

4. **Profitability.** The level of use, benefit, or advantage produced, not exclusively financial return

5. **Predictability.** The reliability to predict future results

> *In ba k'ira, me ya ci gawai? (If nothing has been forged, then what happened to the charcoal?)*
>
> —PROVERB FROM THE HAUSA, WEST AFRICA

DECIDING WHAT TO MEASURE

What will you measure? How will you even decide what to measure?

Let's start with *how* you decide what to measure. First, you pose strategic questions. At the same time, you decide who is necessary to help answer the questions. Fund development staff leads these conversations. The CEO participates in some manner at some level. The board endorses the proposed performance results for the institution.

Start with this question: What does your organization want to achieve? Then move on to these six questions.

1. What will you measure? Why does each measure you've chosen matter?

2. What are the most important measures? Why?

3. How do these measures relate to your organization's values, mission, vision, and strategic plan? Why is this important?

4. How will you use the information to take future action?

5. How will the information help you improve your strategies and tactics?

6. How will the information help your board and staff understand what is most important?

The easiest performance measures to define are the quantitative ones. You know: how many, what percent, the number of, and so forth. Measuring the qualitative is always harder. For example: satisfaction, closeness, interest, and so forth.

Of course, you can draw conclusions about the qualitative measures from the quantitative results. But often that's limiting. Some of your performance measures will be "soft" rather than hard data. For example, you want to know how donor values align with your organization's values. You'll evaluate the degree of intimacy between the donor and your organization, in order to decide if it's time to solicit.

> *Numbers-based innovations are easy to sell ... but numbers-based innovations are rarely home runs. They rarely cause people to look back in awe at the amazing thing they've done. It's the emotional stuff—the stuff that some smart people don't think will work—that you need to be part of.*
>
> —GROUP OF 33, *THE BIG MOO*

Effective evaluation typically includes multiple measures. A single measure produces a limited perspective. For example, evaluating total money raised is not sufficient to determine if an organization's fund development program is effective. You would expect to look at other measures such as retention.

MEASURING PERFORMANCE AND EVALUATING RESULTS

Performance measures may remain unchanged for years. Think about all the traditional measures fundraisers use to evaluate these results. For example:

- Donor attrition, acquisition, retention rates
- Retention trends after first gift
- Average gift size, percent of donors who increase their gifts, frequency of donor upgrades

- Number of donors, and number of donors who give multiple gifts per year
- Return on investment and cost effectiveness
- Participation rates of board members and other volunteers in fund development activities
- Application of well-established research and practice in fund development and fundraising communications; consistent use of the body of knowledge

Now think about these additional performance measures:

- Staff and board member behaviors that demonstrate a culture of philanthropy
- Diversity of prospects and donors reflective of a diverse community
- Donor-centered fund development program
- Satisfaction trends of fundraising volunteers, donors, event participants, and so on
- Customer satisfaction with the organization as a whole, a critical under-girding for acquiring and retaining any donor
- Donor loyalty trends (active loyalty versus passive loyalty/easy givers)

Results, however, change regularly. Once you've defined what you're trying to achieve and what measures would best evaluate performance, you forecast results. Often organizations do this annually. You forecast results based on results achieved previously plus reasonable ambitions. (Some organizations use the term "results"; others use the term "outcomes." Still other organizations may use the term "benchmarks.")

A Practical Example

The best organizations commit to quality customer service. In the nonprofit/ NGO sector, customers include lots of different stakeholders: for example, donors, volunteers, and clients. Each expects quality customer service. Your organization understands that stakeholder perception of customer service depends upon all the interactions with various people and departments. Exhibit 24.3 shows some of your performance measures and the results you've set as benchmarks for quality customer service this year.

You've outlined five strategies and tactics to promote and evaluate the status of your customer service:

1. Conduct annual customer service training for all staff once per year.
2. Collect examples of good and bad customer service from throughout the organization. Analyze what happened and outline how to capitalize on success and improve weakness.

EXHIBIT 24.3   AN EXAMPLE OF PERFORMANCE MEASURES AND PERFORMANCE RESULTS

Performance Measures for Customer Service in Fund Development	Performance Results Targeted for the Fiscal Year
Donor satisfaction with communications from the organization	Donors rate the organization a 4–5 (on a scale of 1–5 with 5 being high)
Compliments received from donors	A minimum of 25 compliments received from donors about customer service
Complaints received from donors	No donor complaints received
Donor retention, upgrade, and longevity rates in giving	25% increase in each area

3. Ensure that all program participants complete a customer service/program satisfaction survey after every program.

4. Conduct an annual telephone survey with randomly selected donors to evaluate their experience with the organization.

5. Include customer service questions in the annual donor survey.

See Appendix 10B "Member Survey of Audubon Society of Rhode Island" for examples of questions for donors and volunteers. Look at all the research reports throughout the sector and use some of their questions.

A Suggestion for Measuring Some of Your Qualitative Results

You might use ratings of 1 to 5 or 1 to 10 with the higher number indicating better performance. For example: "How satisfied are you with our donor recognition program? Please circle your level of satisfaction on the scale of 1–5, with 5 being high."

You can also use Likert scales, a type of survey question where respondents rate the extent to which they agree or disagree with a given statement. The Likert method of measuring attitudes is the most widely used scale in survey research.[2]

This scaling method is called "bipolar." It measures either a positive or negative response to a question by offering exhaustive and mutually exclusive response categories. The response includes two positives and two negatives. Sometimes the response includes a neutral or "no opinion" choice. Likert scales can also force respondents to choose by eliminating the neutral or "no opinion" from the scale, for example, "neither agree nor disagree." See examples of commonly used Likert scale responses in Exhibit 24.4.

EXHIBIT 24.4   **EXAMPLES OF COMMONLY USED LIKERT SCALE RESPONSE OPTIONS**

Very good / Adequate / Inadequate / Very inadequate
Very good / Good / No opinion / Poor / Very poor
Strongly agree / Agree / Undecided / Disagree / Strongly disagree
Very good quality / Good quality / Uncertain / Poor quality / Very poor quality
Strongly encourage / Encourage / No opinion / Discourage / Strongly discourage
Definitely yes / Probably yes / Uncertain / Probably no / Definitely no

Courtesy of our market research guru Bob Harris, Harris Marketing

ANALYZING AND INTERPRETING EVALUATION RESULTS

Of course, performance measures and results are just data unless you analyze and interpret the information. What matters most are the trends and their implications.

When I analyze information, I think about these things:

- Analyzing multiyear trends within your organization.

- Analyzing comparisons against, for example, standards in the fundraising profession and comparable organizations. Remember, standards may differ based on the size of your organization or your particular cause. And standards across the profession don't remain static over the years. Read sector publications to find the most current standards.

- Comparing results against your goals in order to determine—for example—if you set goals appropriately and have the capacity and capability to do the work.

When identifying the implications, consider these eight questions:

1. What will be the consequences if we continue on this path?

2. Why do we achieve some results and not others?

3. What are the consequences of these trends and implications?

4. What kind of changes must we make to improve our results?

5. What resources and competencies will these changes require?

6. What are the barriers to making changes?

7. How will we mobilize the resources and competencies we have on hand, and acquire and/or outsource the additional necessary resources and competencies?

8. What are our next steps and how will we monitor the progress and results from our next steps?

To close the loop, always ask why. Consider question #6, for example. Once you've identified the barriers to making change, you need to understand why these barriers exist and how you can eliminate them).

> *Fund development is not about money only. Include performance measures and proposed results that reflect the humanity of philanthropy.*

COMMUNICATING EVALUATION RESULTS

Once you've completed your analysis and interpretation, communicate the information to those who participate in strategic dialogue and decision making. Provide for them an in-depth narrative that accompanies the quantitative and qualitative data.

As I always say, organizational effectiveness depends on quality information transformed into knowledge and learning. The development staff helps others transform information into knowledge and learning. That's function #6 in my enabling functions, "helping board and staff to take meaningful action on behalf of your organization." See Appendix A, "Enabling Functions." For further details on enabling, in *Strategic Fund Development: Building Profitable Relationships That Last.*

Competent professionals make the time to do this important work. And the best professionals know full well that the measures and results go far beyond money. These professionals—those organizational development specialists referred to in Chapter 4—know that the entire system affects fundraising performance.

POSSIBLE PERFORMANCE MEASURES FOR RELATIONSHIP BUILDING

Now let's narrow the focus to nurturing relationships and look at that from various angles:

- How the prospect or donor responds and feels
- What you do to nurture relationships
- Charitable giving measures that reveal donor loyalty

Combine the results from these three areas of measurement, and you should know whether your organization is sufficiently donor-centric.

> *Your purpose is to understand donor and volunteer expectations, and then measure their experiences with your organization. You want to know how your performance compares to their expectations.*

When you review the data produced by your measures, analyze. Keep probing. Keep asking "why," which can take you to an expanded level of analysis and thinking. For example: "Why did we achieve our desired 25 compliments for customer service? What did we do differently and why do we think that made a difference?"

From the Prospect/Donor Perspective

"What do they really think of us?" These measures depend on the donor's perception of his or her experience with your organization. As previously noted, you decide when and how to evaluate, using the measures you've selected.

Try these measures with your donors of both time and money. And remember, you're asking them "What do you think of us?"

Here are six satisfaction measures.

1. Satisfaction with your organization's execution of its mission and the progress made on your mission

2. Satisfaction with your organization's customer service (and not just from the development office)

3. Satisfaction with your thank-you process and your recognition program

4. Satisfaction with and participation in your organization's activities (e.g., attendance at programs, fundraising events, cultivation gatherings, synergy of giving and volunteering, etc.)

5. Satisfaction with the quality of conversations they have with you

6. Satisfaction with your organization's communications

Here are 10 performance measures for your relationship-building program:

1. Different ways the individual participates in your organization (e.g., volunteering and giving money, attending events, etc.)

2. The degree to which the donor feels connected to the ultimate beneficiaries and the results produced by your organization

3. The degree to which donors' personal values align with your organization's values

4. Donor-initiated contact with your organization (e.g., stopping by to say hello, calling you with questions and ideas, etc.)

5. Donor response to your contacts (e.g., returning bounce-back cards, completing surveys, responding to your invitations even if they do not actually participate, etc.)

6. How often the donor refers others to your organization

7. How often the donor compliments or complains about your organization
8. Donor's level of confidence in your organization
9. Donor's perception of your organization's trustworthiness
10. Position of your organization/cause within the donor's priorities

What You Do to Nurture Relationships

"What are we doing to improve the relationship?" These measures focus on what your organization does to nurture relationships. You're measuring how effective and efficient your strategies are. You can apply these to both donors and volunteers, too. Thirteen measures include:

1. Breadth and depth of information in your files, with an emphasis on interests and disinterests, motivations and aspirations
2. Diversity, regularity, and frequency of organization contacts with prospects, and, most especially, with donors
3. Level of personalization in communications and cultivation
   a. "Dear Jane," not "Dear Friend." And "Dear Simone," not "Dear Ms. Joyaux" if I've been giving for years
   b. You know Tom and I dislike special events, so what kind of personalized cultivation are you doing, based on our interests, if you want to retain that bequest?
4. Effectiveness of cultivation at fundraising events (e.g., gathering more information about prospects and donors, good conversations, candid questions, etc.)
5. Board and staff value the relationship-building program and behave accordingly
   a. Board and staff demonstrate understanding of relationship building
   b. Board member and staff participation in nurturing relationships
6. Effectiveness of communications strategies and content (see Tom's measures in Chapter 23)
7. Frequency and regularity of cultivation activities, attendance and quality of conversation, number of attendees who joined the mailing list or followed up with a gift
8. Frequency of your contact with prospects and donors without asking for a gift
9. Effective identification of the predisposed (e.g., number regularly identified)
10. Percent of the predisposed qualified as prospects
11. Percent of prospects transitioned into donors

12. Diversity of donors reflective of your organization's cultural competency

13. Quality of conversations you have with prospects and donors (remember, conversation means lots of listening from you. Do they ask lots of questions? Do they respond in detail when you ask them questions? Does the conversation seem to flow naturally? How candid and honest was the conversation?)

Charitable Giving Measures that Reflect Donor Loyalty

Here are 10 measures that reflect donor loyalty:

1. Donor retention rate

2. Rate of transition from first-time donor to regular donor

3. Percent of donors who increase their gift size and/or number of gifts per year

4. Size of gift from the donor's perspective

5. Size of gift compared to donor's giving elsewhere

6. Size of gift compared to donor's estimated capacity

7. Size of gift compared to your estimation of donor's level of interest and commitment

8. Frequency of giving per 12-month period

9. Loyalty (e.g., number of years giving, percent who make a bequest or some other form of legacy gift)

10. Consistency in giving (e.g., frequency and size)

In addition to considering these measures, take a look at the measures in Jim Greenfield's book. Jim has lots of great ideas about what to measure and how to measure. Many of his examples can be modified for your relationship-building program.

Monitoring Progress

This is your job. Yes, it takes time. But how else will you make quality decisions and forecast realistic results? Without ongoing evaluation, how will you understand your return on investment and justify your costs? Without measuring what is important, how will you enable others to understand and commit to change? And the bottom line: Without evaluation, how will others hold you accountable and how will you demonstrate your accountability?

Professional fundraisers design and manage this evaluation process. You ensure that your staff colleagues and the board understand the value and participate in the process. You ensure understanding and ownership for the evaluation process by explaining the why and the how-to.

You facilitate conversation with key internal constituencies in order to develop the performance measures. You outline the process, including a calendar for regular reporting and strategic dialogue.

You design formats for communicating the data and analyses. You review this with key constituencies to ensure their understanding and support for this important communication.

Also, you facilitate the process to forecast performance results. Typically this is done annually, based on the previous year's results.

In Conclusion

It seems fitting to end this chapter by returning to the value of relationships.

In his book on multicultural marketing and communications, Clotaire Rapaille talks about the best relationships.[3] I've paraphrased his words and applied them to philanthropy:

> In the best philanthropic relationships, your prospects and donors know that you care more about them than their money. And you actually do! You understand their interests and priorities. And these prospects and donors know you'll be there when their interests and priorities match what your organization has to offer.

ENDNOTES

1. James M. Greenfield, *Fund-Raising Cost Effectiveness: A Self-Assessment Workbook* (New York: John Wiley & Sons, 1996).
2. The scales are named after Rensis Likert (1903–1981), an American educator and organizational psychologist best known for his research on management styles. A founder of the University of Michigan's Institute for Social Research, Likert served as the institute's director from its founding in 1946 until his retirement in 1970. His 1960s and 1970s books on management theory were very popular in Japan and still affect modern Japanese organizations.
3. G. Clotaire Rapaille, *The 7 Secrets of Marketing in a Multi-Cultural World* (Provo, Utah: Executive Excellence Publishing, 2001), pp. 42–43.

You and Your Organization:
Sprinting into the Future

Put on your red pants.

Embrace the *folie du pourquoi.*

Learn and change. And help others to do the same.

Aficionados of learning organization theory talk as much about *un*learning as learning. The *un*learning is often hardest. Maybe even impossible.

After all, one's experiences create a mind-set, the frames through which we interpret and live our lives. At best, we *un*learn by parking assumptions and ideas in a separate place. They're no longer relevant and we work hard to ignore them.

The challenge is to think and behave differently. More than tweaks here and there. More like *metanoia*, a Greek word meaning a fundamental transformation.

For change to happen, the cost of *not* changing has to be higher than the cost of changing. Take a look at this change management theory, shared with me by Peter Duschinsky, U.K. change management consultant.

"Giving people an exciting vision of the future is okay but not sufficient to achieve change. Why not? Because the excitement soon evaporates as people get back to the day-to-day demands of their jobs.

"So something more is needed. Perhaps a clear structure for how to get there? An outline of next steps help, but doesn't seem to generate the necessary energy for change.

"After all, change is not just financially costly—it is also costly in personal terms. New and different ways of doing things scare people. Much easier to stay in one's comfort zone.

"So what will generate that energy? Only a recognition that things can't stay as they are. And that recognition has to come from the people involved, not from an external consultant or manager."[1]

This can be expressed in shorthand, as an equation:

$$\text{Vision} \times \text{Next steps} \times \text{Dissatisfaction} > \text{Cost of change}$$

Post this nifty equation on your bulletin board as you work through your own change and help your organization change. Imagine using the change equation as a rallying cry to help your organization move into the future confidently.

What's the key in this equation? Dissatisfaction. For example: Dissatisfaction with your donor retention rates or with your communications. Dissatisfaction with how little you know about your donors' interests or how well you nurture the relationship.

Capitalize on the dissatisfaction. Without it, inertia always wins. It's just easier not to change.

Most people use the word "change." But let's up the ante to "transformation." What does transformation look like? Instead of renovating a few rooms of the house, the owners tear down walls, relocate the kitchen, and raise the roof. Or maybe, the owners build a new house. Transformation is about reconceptualizing. Transformation is all encompassing and system wide.

It's what colleague Jon Duschinsky was talking about with me one day. He asked if we have a responsibility to scare charities and those who work in them. I took the "we" to mean "we fundraisers, we leaders in philanthropy." And my answer is yes. The sector is making progress, but more is necessary. As Jon noted, enormous cultural and structural changes are still required. I'd say that's transformation.

Throughout this book, Tom and I have talked about questions, the fundamental value of "why." We began by saying that a question-driven fund development program lodged inside a questioning organization will *always* outperform and certainly outlast a complacent program inside a complacent organization.

This book is about moving into the future. It's about asking meaningful questions to stimulate deep conversation. Asking the cage-rattling questions. Using conversation to produce learning. Stimulating innovation to create transformation.

For me, great fundraisers are catalysts and change agents. Great fundraisers are more radical than conventional. Armed with their red pants and the *folie du pourquoi,* they rebel against norms. Using judicious subversive activities, these fundraisers start a revolution whenever necessary. They do this for themselves and for their organizations, for the profession, the sector, and the world.

■ ENDNOTE

1. Adapted by Peter Duschinsky from Gleicher, referenced by Beckhard and Harris (1987). For those of you who know French fundraiser Jon Duschinsky, Peter is Jon's father.

Coda

PHILANTHROPY'S MORAL DILEMMA

Justice comes before charity.

—POPE JOHN XXIII

Giving isn't a posture reserved for the rich or the powerful. It is the responsibility and privilege of every man, woman, and child to participate in the task of building more just and humane societies.

—ALFRE WOODARD, *ROBIN HOOD WAS RIGHT*

Small acts of resistance to authority, if persisted in, may lead to large social movements . . . ordinary people are capable of extraordinary acts of courage . . . those in power who confidently say "never" to the possibility of change may live to be embarrassed by those words . . . the world of social struggle is full of surprises, as the common moral sense of people germinates invisibly, bubbles up, and at certain points in history brings about victories that may be small, but carry large promise.

—HOWARD ZINN, *YOU CAN'T BE NEUTRAL ON A MOVING TRAIN*

DEAR READER   This chapter is like the bonus cut on a CD. You might not like it or listen to it. Or maybe you will.

Colleagues in the U.K. and Canada might call this chapter a "rant." It certainly expresses my concern about the overall state of philanthropy.

Others might call this chapter a political position. But I'm talking about everyday politics, the politics of you and me and our relationships. These relationships inevitably involve power, authority, and influence.

I'm talking about the politics of philanthropy—and what I believe is the resulting moral dilemma. This chapter closes the circle of this book. *Simone*

POLITICS OF POWER IN PHILANTHROPY

As in any human endeavor, politics are alive and well in philanthropy. NGOs seek power, just like everyone else. Witness these actions by nonprofit/NGOs. They:

- Recruit people of influence for the board to help get big gifts and special favors.

- Retain board members who do nothing but give big gifts, despite this violation of good governance principles.

- Depend on executive committees without considering the negative power dynamics, and effect on other board members.

- Admit unqualified kids from socially powerful families to elite schools because social capital is so important.

- Recognize donors by gift amount, with no discussion about any possible negative impact.

- Treat big donors and their major gifts differently than other donors.

- Use terms like "major gifts" and "major gifts officer" with donors, with little thought about the messages communicated.

Each of these actions reflects some form of privilege, defined as an advantage or benefit not available to everyone. When (rarely) confronted about these (often) unquestioned acts, organizations may respond: We need money because we do good. Politics makes the world go round so we act accordingly. It's a typical example of the end-justifying-the-means thinking.

Nonprofits accept these politics as the status quo, the way of doing business. Organizations often reinforce this approach, either intentionally or unconsciously. Or because the sector doesn't talk much about the issue, let alone alternatives.

Perhaps politics aren't hidden in philanthropy, merely masked with a hint of entitlement and self-righteousness. Power, authority, and influence *do* offer advantages, but not without one big consequence, what I call the moral dilemma and crisis of philanthropy.

MORAL DILEMMA FACING PHILANTHROPY

Despite efforts to the contrary, the United Nations Declaration of Human Rights often seems as far away as it must have in 1948 when adopted. Even as philanthropy flourishes, the "inherent dignity and the equal and inalienable rights of all" founder.

Which is both ironic and linked. Linked because so many nonprofits and NGOs see philanthropy as the "pathway through global political, social, and economic barriers to make change."[1] But ironic because philanthropy is part of the status quo that erects those very barriers.

For me, this is the moral dilemma: In general, philanthropy and fund development reinforce the status quo. The haves remain haves. The have-nots remain have-nots. By depending on power, both philanthropy and fund development honor privilege, which destroys the likelihood of a level playing field. And finally, philanthropy's transformational capacity too rarely touches equity and social justice.

Don't get me wrong. There is so much to admire and value in philanthropy. But I'm increasingly concerned about privilege and power, the fashion of the world. Philanthropy uses both to move its mission forward. As it does so, philanthropy embroils itself in a moral dilemma, an actual crisis in my opinion.

POWER, THE SILENT HAUNTING

None of this is a secret. It's just not mentioned much. And discussed even less, except in special circumstances.

What exactly does "power" mean? Easily stated: a controlling influence, the ability to influence others. Look up "power" at www.visualthesaurus.com. Click on the diagram and watch the various synonyms reconfigure. Words like: baron, big businessman, king, magnate, mogul, tycoon. What's not to like? Or how about "so powerful that you can influence events around the world?" Personally, I want that one.

Then click on the little dotted line that leads to "powerlessness." There you'll see "impotence," "lack of strength," and "weak and feeble."

The most common origin of power is based on privilege. For example, the privilege of being equipped with money, being male, being born to the majority race, and being able-bodied, just to name a few.

The use of this traditional privilege and power reinforces the status quo, devaluing those with less (or different) privilege and power. Traditional privilege excludes other community voices, reducing the possibility of change. All this conflicts with the broader purpose of philanthropy: building community—and that pesky UN Declaration of inherent and inalienable rights for all.

Privilege, the Driving Nature of Power

It's privilege that people don't want to talk about, because privilege is personal. But keep in mind: Some of your privilege and mine comes at the expense of others.

Without a fundamental awareness of privilege, it's almost impossible to understand the politics of human relationships. It's hard to ask the tough questions about power, and then change if you want to.

So let's start at the beginning: Each person experiences life differently. Often a person's experience produces some disadvantage: for example, ethnicity, gender, socioeconomics, religion, and so forth.

But there's something perhaps more important than disadvantage: its opposite, advantage. Advantage is rarely mentioned, let alone closely examined.

Advantage—unearned, unrecognized, invisible—captured the attention of author and consultant Peggy McIntosh.[2] She challenges us to "unpack the invisible knapsack of personal privilege." She dares us to acknowledge that privilege is not a result of something a person has done. On the contrary, privilege is the result of "invisible systems conferring dominance on a particular group."

> *You know what's really compelling about these unearned and invisible privileges? All should be the norm in a just society.*

Then all these unearned privileges become the norm. A culture's socialization about norms produces hierarchies and power dynamics that are often unquestioned and accepted as reality. The norms of our respective cultures advantage some and disadvantage others.[3]

Racism, for example, causes a disadvantage for people of color in the United States. At the same time, racism provides unearned and generally invisible advantages to white people, illustrated in Exhibit 25.1. Of course, the same holds true for other differences, illustrated in Exhibit 25.2.

Here's my recommendation: Take a private moment to identify your own privilege. Write down your unearned advantages. This helps increase personal awareness, a critical first step. Then do the same thing with a friend. Sharing and talking about privilege increases sensitivity.

Now comes the harder step: expanding the conversation and awareness. Discuss privilege in the development office. Discuss privilege with the development committee and even your board. (Yes, I've had the privilege discussion with a board.)

Here's the hardest step: Talk about the implications of privilege, for board members and donors, for staff and clients. Explore ideas about what you might do to minimize the negative affects of privilege. Then make those changes.

UNDERSTANDING THE TWO TYPES OF PHILANTHROPY

There are two kinds of philanthropy: traditional philanthropy and social change (also called progressive) philanthropy.

EXHIBIT 25.1   **UNEARNED PRIVILEGES OF A WHITE WOMAN**

One day in the late 1980s, Peggy McIntosh began writing down all her unearned privileges as a white woman in the United States. Here are just a few of the more than 50 she identified. Twenty years later, these still hold true.

1. If I should need to move, I can be pretty sure of renting or purchasing housing in an area which I can afford and in which I would want to live.
2. I can be pretty sure of having my voice heard in a group in which I am the only member of my race.
3. I do not have to educate my children to be aware of systemic racism for their own daily physical protection.
4. I can do well in a challenging situation without being called a credit to my race.
5. I can remain oblivious of the language and customs of persons of color who constitute the world's majority without feeling in my culture any penalty for such oblivion.
6. If I declare there is a racial issue at hand, or there isn't a racial issue at hand, my race will lend me more credibility for either position than a person of color will have.
7. I can choose blemish cover or bandages in 'flesh' color and have them more or less match my skin.

Source: Peggy McIntosh, Unpacking the Invisible Knapsack.

EXHIBIT 25.2   **A FEW OTHER EXAMPLES OF PRIVILEGE**

- Watch Tony Kushner's *Angels in America*, either on stage or on DVD. Roy Cohn, once one of the most powerful men in the United States, says he doesn't have AIDS because homosexuals have AIDS and homosexuals have no power—and he, Roy Cohn, has power. (Cohn died of AIDS in 1986.)
- Even young boys know it's better not to be a girl. In the 1990s, the Michigan Board of Education published findings from a statewide survey of boys and girls, asking them what it means to be male or female. Nearly 50 percent of the girls noted the advantages of being a boy. Only 7 percent of the boys saw any advantages to being a girl. Most disturbing, a significant number of boys said they would commit suicide if they woke up as a girl.[*] This is a frightening indictment of being female in the United States.
- The privilege of money (and its likely unearned privileges) can give special power. The donor may appear worthier than those who need help. Soon donors and professional experts decide how to use money for the disadvantaged. Often those deemed "disadvantaged" are not at the table or even in the room making decisions about their futures. This is a travesty of privilege, power, authority, and influence. An un-level playing field if ever there was one.

[*]Statistics from Marie C. Wilson, *Closing the Leadership Gap: Why Women Can and Must Help Run the World*, (New York: Viking/Penguin, 2004), p. 103.

I'm using the term "traditional" in the sense that this philanthropy is the most prevalent, most common. Operating in the mainstream, it uses no adjective. This is simply philanthropy, including the full gamut of endeavors: for example, healthcare, education, arts, environment, human service, and so forth. This is voluntary action for the common good, to address community needs and improve the quality of life.

Then there's social change/progressive philanthropy, requiring an adjective to distinguish its focus and approach. This kind of philanthropy focuses on root causes and supports systemic change.

An often-told story illustrates the difference between the two types of philanthropy.

Imagine that you're walking along a riverbank. Suddenly you notice babies floating down the river, drowning. You wade into the river and rescue them. But there are still more, so many. Soon you see another person walking along the riverbank. You call out to her, "Come and help me save the babies who are drowning in the river." But she hurries on, saying "I'm going to the head of the river to figure out who is throwing them in and stop them."

"Rescuing the babies" is the traditional and dominant approach in philanthropy. Going to the head of the river to fix the root cause is less common and often controversial.

Of course, the choice is not either/or. Every society needs both. And some organizations do both. Equally important, everyone chooses his or her own interests and causes, as it should be.

My complaint, however, is that social change philanthropy is not well enough known in the sector. Nor is there enough of it to fulfill part of philanthropy's purpose, building community in terms of that UN Declaration of "inherent and inalienable rights for all." Moreover, philanthropy itself succumbs to the politics of power and privilege.

But more on all this in subsequent sections of this chapter. For the moment, back to clarifying the distinction between what I'm calling traditional mainstream philanthropy and social change/progressive philanthropy. Exhibit 25.3 illustrates the two philanthropic approaches. And so does this citation, one of my favorites:

> Traditional philanthropy is based on responding to, treating and managing the consequences of life in a society with a capital-based economy. Progressive philanthropy, on the other hand, analyzes and responds more to cause then effect. Progressive philanthropy supports . . . social change . . . actions that seek to right the imbalances of an unjust society or unequal distribution of resources . . . often making people, institutions, and government uncomfortable. Progressive philanthropy strives to fund work that is proactive rather than reactive. Progressive philanthropy . . . challenges the assumptions that economic and social inequities are somehow unavoidable as the price of progress or prosperity.[4]

EXHIBIT 25.3 **COMPARISON OF TRADITIONAL AND SOCIAL CHANGE PHILANTHROPY**

Traditional Philanthropy	Social Change/Progressive Philanthropy
Give money to feed the hungry	Give money to lobby for public policy that ensures a living wage and affordable housing, thereby making sure that people can pay for food, shelter, and clothing
Give money to clean up the rivers	Give money to educate voters about the need for environmental protection
Give money for education scholarships	Give money develop a funding model that ensures education for all

TRADITION DOMINATES

More than 100 books fill the walls of my office. Countless articles fill my files. Great books and great articles. Some of the best in the field.

But most don't mention anything but mainstream philanthropy. Same experience with all my continuing education over 30+ years. There's limited exposure to social justice or social change/progressive philanthropy, except in specialized publications or at special conferences.

This isn't my experience alone. Most fundraisers I encounter aren't familiar with the concepts of social change philanthropy or social justice, the purpose of this other philanthropy. Most fundraisers that I know talk about mainstream traditional philanthropy, not the full spectrum of philanthropy, which includes social change.

That's my concern: the lack of familiarity with social change philanthropy. We're missing part of history, an essential component of our practice, a critical element of building community.

The dominant culture, the voice of the "majority," wins. The status quo reinvents the status quo. I think that's a shame. I expect a fairer approach from philanthropy and fund development and the nonprofit/NGO sector. I hope the globalization of fund development will introduce new experiences that can fight these dominant voices.

> *Research in the United States shows that more than 90 percent of philanthropic gifts go to what may be called traditional philanthropy. I'll bet that's the case in most places around the world.*

HAVE YOU NOTICED: THE LESS SOCIAL JUSTICE WE HAVE, THE MORE PHILANTHROPY WE NEED?

Ironic, isn't it? We need more philanthropy because we refuse to deal with social injustice.

Martin Luther King Jr., said it well, "Philanthropy is commendable, but it must not cause the philanthropist to overlook the circumstances of economic injustice that make philanthropy necessary."[5]

Social injustice. What does that actually mean? Unfairness. Inequity. Privilege and advantages available to some but not all.

Perhaps the best way to describe *in*justice is describing what the opposite, social justice, looks like. John Rawls, one of the twentieth century's most important political philosophers, proposed two key principles in his theory of justice: (1) the right of each person to have as much liberty as possible without compromising the liberty of others; and (2) social and economic positions should advantage everyone and be available to all.

At the Women's Fund of Rhode Island, we describe social justice as equity: fairness, impartiality, opportunity, shared power and responsibility in all spheres of personal and community life. And all spheres include economic, cultural, educational, social, political, safety, and everything else.

The thing is, *in*justice is contagious. To quote King again, "Injustice anywhere is a threat to justice everywhere. We are caught in an inescapable network of mutuality, tied in a single garment of destiny. Whatever affects one directly, affects all indirectly."[6]

If we gave more money to stop injustice, then we would have less injustice and less need to compensate for injustice through traditional mainstream philanthropy. Surely that's what Martin Luther King Jr. meant when he said philanthropy was commendable, but . . .

And if the nonprofit/NGO sector spoke out more and more loudly, then justice could prevail more often (see Exhibit 25.4).

Social change means community empowerment, redistribution of resources, and transformation of social and institutional systems that perpetuate all forms of inequity.

—FRANK J. OMOWALE SATTERWHITE, PH.D., PRESIDENT AND CHIEF EXECUTIVE OFFICER, NATIONAL COMMUNITY DEVELOPMENT INSTITUTE

EXHIBIT 25.4   **NONPROFITS AND ACTIVISM**

Some sector literature decries the loss of nonprofit activism and speaking out. I suspect there are three reasons for this decreasing attention to activism:

- Many nonprofits allocate their resources to direct service—whether protecting the environment, caring for the poor, or any other worthy cause. The focus on rescue, coupled with limited resources, stops these NGOs from working on systems change.
- Many nonprofits partner with government for service delivery. Government, more conservative by nature, may inhibit or prohibit work on systems change.
- In the panic for more money, many organizations avoid remarks or actions that may cause controversy.

We Are Complicit

Candidly, I think much of the sector is complicit in social injustice. That's part of the sector's moral dilemma (see Exhibit 25.5).

Complicit because we don't acknowledge the harm of privilege and power and figure out how to discuss these issues. Complicit because we're comfortable with the status quo and have figured out how to use politics. Complicit because it's easier and less risky to be conventional than it is to question.

Injustice demands social change, a leveling of the playing field. But this is hard to do.

Why? Because social change is about my personal privilege and yours. Because it's about the personal privilege of our donors and our friends and neighbors and families. Because change could hurt those of us who are privileged.

This is risky business, discussing privilege and power. So I'll start.

I'm a white, heterosexual, well-educated, affluent woman. White, heterosexual, well educated, affluent: all privileges that offer me rights and benefits in the United States, Canada, and most everywhere in the world. Unearned advantages provided to me through birth, via my parents. Sure, I've worked hard. But I had a head start, a really big one.

I do have one glaring disadvantage: I'm a woman. It's a disadvantage in every country of the world to be a woman—yes, even in the United States of America, that bastion of democracy and freedom. But at least I'm white, heterosexual, well-educated, and affluent, compensating somewhat for the gender disadvantage.

I can get married and I can buy a nice house. I can get lots of different jobs—although I won't get paid as much as a man for doing the same thing. Also, I've hit the age when age is a problem again, too old. But I'm still enormously privileged.

Yet everyday I think about Pamela and Clare and Peg and Brian and Ron who cannot get married except in parts of Canada or in Massachusetts (U.S.), and for

---

EXHIBIT 25.5   **SIX ELEMENTS OF PHILANTHROPY'S MORAL DILEMMA**

1. In general, we focus on privilege in philanthropy, fund development, and governance. Privilege is mostly unearned. And privilege is most often found at the intersection of socioeconomics, gender, ethnicity/race, and sexual orientation.

2. Many fund development strategies and tactics reinforce privilege. What impact does this have on constituents, the organization, a philanthropic culture, the sector, the profession, and the world?

3. Most gifts are given to traditional philanthropy to fund things like the arts and education, healthcare, the environment, and helping those in need. This is wonderful, but it needn't be so dominant, obscuring the full range of philanthropy.

4. The gifts given to help those in need often ignore systemic change. Giving is a rescue operation rather than a problem solver. It's time to revitalize the activist nature of nonprofits. We need systemic change to build strong communities.

5. Mainstream traditional philanthropy dominates the history and practice of the nonprofit/NGO sector, leaving many sector professionals and organizations ill informed. Learning about social change/progressive philanthropy typically requires reading specialized publications and attending conferences.

6. Philanthropy has not done enough to transform injustice. The mainstream traditional focus inhibits sufficient investment in social change.

---

how long there, I wonder. I think about Miriam, Sharon, Ingrid, and Cynthia who are Latina and Black and always have to be aware and wary.

PHILANTHROPY AS A DEMOCRATIZING ACT

My view is that philanthropy is *not* particularly democratic. I believe that usually we accept (and design) philanthropy as an act of traditional power and privilege.

Instead, I think philanthropy can, should, and must amplify all voices, especially those that are traditionally ignored. I expect philanthropy to behave as an empowerment tool. I want philanthropy to be a strategy to democratize our communities and our organizations. A strategy to fight the haves/have nots model of society. A strategy to democratize our communities and organizations.

> *Philanthropy means shared power, not the power of privilege.*

ATTACKING THE MORAL DILEMMA

Rest assured, I'm not naive. Fundraisers *will* focus more on the donors who are most loyal and who give more money. Nonprofits *will* recruit board members with connections. And on and on and on.

But we can certainly better manage power and privilege in our organizations, and in our society. That's my challenge and my battle cry directed to myself and to you. Directed to all nonprofits/NGOs and people working with them. That's my challenge and battle cry to donors of time and money. Certainly we can better manage power and privilege!

I think philanthropy could better stimulate the evolution of society. Maintain traditional mainstream philanthropy in its full panoply. But also embrace progressive philanthropy that fights for social change.

I think the nonprofit/NGO sector must examine itself and how organizations and professionals are complicit in privilege and power. Let's use the philanthropic process—including fund development—to question privilege and power in the doing of this work.

Leaders can raise these issues at every opportunity. In organizations where we work and give money and time. Within our professional associations and in writings and presenting.

It's amazing what can happen when you raise issues like these. Concerns from others come into the open. Uncomfortable dynamics change. New ideas surface.

We can demand recognition for both types of philanthropy. We can incorporate both types of philanthropy, mingled together, not as separate specialty topics.

> *Charity is good, but supporting and creating social change are about power. Power can infuse lives with purpose and dignity. That opens up the possibility of joy. The life of the giver, as well as that of the receiver, is transformed. . . . No matter who we are, no matter how much money we have, whatever our color, gender, age, religion, or language, we can bring change to the world around us. We can open our minds, roll up our sleeves, and reach out our hands.*
>
> —ALFRE WOODARD, *ROBIN HOOD WAS RIGHT*

Philanthropy has enormous power for good—as long as donors, volunteers, professionals, and organizations don't get confused about the distinction between social change philanthropy and traditional mainstream philanthropy.

Yes, it's up to the donor and volunteer and organization which philanthropy to engage in. But I think it's up to all of us in the sector to demand broad recognition of both kinds of philanthropy.

For me, this is an obligation. A bit like the obligation of the cured, explained by a Harlem doctor.[7] It's about choosing to speak out, to tell one's story for the benefit of others. It's a moral obligation to confront "what we know" and "what we do."

Morality falls between the knowing and the doing. So the moral failure is when we don't *do* what we *know.* I'd add to this, that's the moment when we must stand up and speak out. Petition and demonstrate. Volunteer time and send money. Is this not the obligation of the privileged and the obligation of philanthropy?

> *I'm more and more convinced that one of the obligations and glories of philanthropy is questioning privilege and its resulting power. I'm convinced that philanthropy can and should be—more often—a subversive act.*

In Conclusion

Chapter 1 is called "Beginning at the Beginning." Beginning with building communities.

This chapter is the other bookend. Returning to building community by conquering the moral dilemma. Ending at a new beginning.

Here is one of my favorite stories. Apply this to the moral dilemma of philanthropy.

> Imagine that it's 24 hours before you were born. A genie appears and says: "You get to set the rules of the society into which you will be born. You can set the economic rules and the social rules and all the other rules. The rules you set will apply during your lifetime and for the lifetime of your children and even grandchildren."
>
> Just imagine how thrilled you are with this offer! But you're smart. You ask, "What's the catch?"
>
> And the genie says: "You don't know if you're going to be born poor or rich, White or of color, infirm or able bodied, homosexual or heterosexual, or female or male."
>
> So what rules do you want?[8]

I know what rules I want: equity and social justice for all.

I know that to create this world requires social change/progressive philanthropy, not only traditional mainstream philanthropy.

And I know that this means transformation, more probably revolution. I think it's time for more subversive acts like asking cage-rattling questions. Confronting complicity and challenging privilege and power. Exploring morality and speaking out. Increasing philanthropy for social change.

Revolution is hard.

But I have hope.

"La esperanza muere última." Hope dies last.[9]

■ ENDNOTES

1. Leland R. Kaiser, Ph.D., is founder and president of Kaiser Consulting, a healthcare consulting firm located in Brighton, Colorado. Writer, lecturer, health policy analyst, and futurist, Dr. Kaiser sparks the imagination of audiences worldwide to change obsolete mind-sets. He made this statement at the April 2007 Kaiser Institute in Ponte Vedra, Florida.

2. Peggy McIntosh is the associate director of the Wellesley Centers for Women, Wellesley College, Massachusetts. She consults widely in the United States and throughout the world with college school and faculty to create more gender-fair and multicultural curricula. In 1988 she published a groundbreaking article on white and male privilege. The original article and its shorter version, "White Privilege: Unpacking the Invisible Knapsack," have helped put privilege into discussions about gender, race, and sexuality. Available at http://seamonkey.ed.asu.edu/~mcisaac/emc598ge/unpacking.html#power.

3. Explained by Capek and Mead, *Effective Philanthropy: Organizational Success through Deep Diversity and Gender Equality.* (Cambridge: MIT Press, 2006).

4. Tracy Gary and Melissa Kohner, *Inspired Philanthropy: Creating A Giving Plan* (Berkeley, CA: Chardon Press, 1998), p. 2.

5. Martin Luther King, Jr., quoted in Alfre Woodard, *Robin Hood Was Right* (New York: W. W. Norton, 2000), p. 31.

6. Ibid., p. 15.

7. Lance Armstrong described the obligation of the cured in his keynote address at the 2007 AFP Conference in Dallas, Texas.

8. Modified by Joyaux from a news clipping of a Warren Buffett. This story illustrates John Rawls' Theory of Justice. *A Theory of Justice* (first published in 1971.)

9. Jessie de la Cruz, retired farm worker, recounting the days before César Chavez and the founding of the United Farm Workers. Quoted by Studs Terkel, *Hope Dies Last: Keeping Faith in Difficult Times* (New York: The New Press, 2003).

Questions About Privilege And Power

Do these questions have meaning for you personally or professionally? How might you use them?

1. How do the politics of philanthropy affect professionals? How do the politics of power affect careers and a sense of vocation in this work?

2. What is power? Why does it matter?

3. How does power affect organizations, communications, and relationships?

4. How are privilege, power, and politics linked among themselves? How are they linked to philanthropy, fund development, and governance? How do privilege and power affect organizational dynamics, fund development, and governance?

5. How do privilege and power affect civil society and civic capacity?

6. What is the nature of power when we discuss diversity and inclusion?

7. How is power important or not?

8. What are the implications of not having power?

9. How do power/power dynamics affect others? How does power affect process and conversation and decision making?

10. Why do people want power?

11. What are the different kinds of privilege and power?

12. What is the language of power, and how does language include or exclude people?

13. What is the "currency" of power, for example, money and what else? How is power measured?

Developed over the years while teaching and presenting. With particular thanks to Cohort 15, Saint Mary's University Master's Program in Philanthropy and Development.

14. What is the relationship between power and control, and between power, authority, and accountability?

15. What is the nature of responsibility from those holding power to those without power?

16. What is the responsibility of the individual or group to take power/become empowered?

17. How is power acquired? How do we create power? How do we share power? How do we give away power?

18. How could/should philanthropy serve as an empowering tool?

19. To what extent do professionals have an obligation to ask these questions and encourage this kind of conversation? Why and why not?

20. What is the connection between power and the impact an organization has in its community?

21. What is the nature of your own personal privilege and advantage? How does this affect your life experience and the way you interact with others?

22. How have you been taught and socialized to remain oblivious or aware of your privilege?

23. How can each of us better perceive/acknowledge our own privilege? How can we use this awareness?

24. How do you hold yourself accountable to manage your privilege and avoid disempowering others? How do you lessen the affect of your own privilege on others?

25. How do life experiences factor into the need to achieve or repel power?

26. How does the social/cultural context empower or disempower people?

27. Why do people seek control? What is their motivation?

28. How do leaders create safety so a group can honestly discuss privilege and power?

29. What does your organization mean by "diversity"? How will diversity affect your organization?

30. What is the relationship between leadership and power?

31. How familiar are you with traditional philanthropy and social change/progressive philanthropy? Is traditional philanthropy enough to create a civil society and civic capacity?

32. How does the history of philanthropy and the body of knowledge reflect traditional philanthropy and exclude social change/progressive philanthropy? Why is social change/progressive philanthropy the poor and often forgotten stepchild in our communities and in our nations?

33. How do professional associations reinforce the status quo or facilitate dialogue about social change? Why does this matter or not?

34. What level of risk are you able to take when it comes to asking any cage-rattling questions, especially questions about privilege and power? (And remember, ability to take risk often depends on a person's privilege.)

35. How might your organization "live its life differently" if it happened "in public"? For example, if the media examined your fund development and governance procedures; if donors of varying amounts examined your relationship building, etc.?

Joyaux's Concept of Enabling Functions, Skills, and Attitudes

Staff enable volunteers. Volunteers should expect this of staff. Also, good leaders enable their staff in the same way.

Enabling Functions

1. Transmit the organization's values.

2. Engage volunteers in the meaning of your organization.

3. Respect and use the skills, expertise, experience and insights of volunteers.

4. Provide direction and resources, remove barriers and help develop skills.

5. Articulate expectations and clarify roles and relationships.

6. Communicate (which includes helping people transform information into knowledge and learning).

7. Encourage people to question organizational assumptions and ask strategic questions.

8. Ensure quality decision making.

9. Anticipate conflicts and facilitate resolution.

10. Engage volunteers in process as well as tasks.

11. Encourage volunteers to use their power, practice their authority, and accept their responsibility.

12. Model behavior.

Originally developed by Simone Joyaux, "Voluntary Association and Volunteer Leadership," *Nonprofit Organizational Culture: What Fundraisers Need to Know,* no. 5 (Fall 1994). Further developed and expanded in Simone Joyaux, *Strategic Fund Development: Building Profitable Relationships That Last* (Sudbury, MA: Jones & Bartlett 2001).

13. Coach people to succeed.

14. Manage.

15. Enhance attrition.

16. Monitor, evaluate, and enhance enabling.

17. Create opportunities/strategies to buy more time to think things through. (Proposed by members of Cohort 14 of the Master's in Philanthropy and Development Program, Saint Mary's University)

Enablers Have the Right Attitude

Enablers:

1. Respect and trust others.

2. Are trustworthy themselves.

3. Are comfortable with diversity and complexity.

4. Welcome divergent opinions.

5. Are flexible and comfortable with change.

6. Commit to process as well as outcome.

7. Appreciate conversation and disagreement.

8. Share responsibility for success.

9. Acknowledge responsibility for failure.

10. Balance personal ego with egos of others.

11. Persevere.

12. Are patient.

Enablers Possess Essential Skills

Enablers are:

1. Organizational development specialists.

2. Proficient teachers and learners.

3. Effective communicators (listening, informing and helping to transform information into knowledge).

4. Critical thinkers (anticipating problems, identifying solutions, and redirecting volunteer energies).

5. Strategists (analyzing situations, identifying barriers and opportunities, capitalizing on strengths, and ensuring action and results).

6. Comfortable with conflict and resolve conflict through shared power with as many individuals as possible.

7. Effective motivators and can focus and manage people well.

Basic Principles of Fund Development

1. Why do most people give? Because they are asked. It's that simple. But only ask those who are interested.

2. Each year, individuals give the largest portion of philanthropic gifts in North America.

3. Focus on the donor or prospective donor. "It's not what your organization is selling, it's what I'm buying that counts. I'm interested in my interests, my motivations and my aspirations. Match those and then I'll give to you."

    Don't universalize your own passion. Not everyone is interested in your particular cause, no matter how convincing you are. And please do not try to convince them! That's offensive. Find those who share your passion.

4. Don't trespass on personal and professional relationships. Use your connections to identify those who are predisposed and build relationships between the cause and those who are predisposed. And if your connections are not interested, leave them alone. (See #3.)

5. What is fund development? Asking the right prospect for the right amount at the right time for the right project in the right way with the right solicitor.

6. Giving is an emotional act, not a financial transaction. Your organization is the means by which donors live out their own interests and aspirations.

    a. Psychological research and neuroscience say that all human decisions are triggered by emotions. "Emotion is multidimensional: It focuses on a person's core goals, directs attention and interest, arouses the body for action, and integrates social group and cultural factors. It is thus a central component of meaning making." —Carol Saunders, PhD, Brookfield Zoo

b. Research from the direct mail industry says that people give in response to one or more of seven emotions: greed, guilt, anger, fear, flattery, exclusivity, and salvation.

7. Remember: People move from one emotion—for example, anger—to hope, by using your agency as the means to make change. Tom Ahern calls that process emotional twinsets. Your agency is the means by which donors express their own interests and live out their own aspirations. Direct mail expert Mal Warwick talks about five emotions: hope, faith, love, duty, and compassion.

8. More visibility does not produce more contributions. People (and businesses, etc.) focus on what interests them. Your agency can be more and more visible—but if I'm not interested, I'm not paying attention. And I sure won't send money.

   a. It's okay if someone doesn't know who your agency is or what it does. Tell them, if they're interested! You are trying to identify the predisposed.

   b. Do *not* solicit someone unless you are assured that the person knows about your agency.

   c. Where do you need to be visible? Within your current donors, because you want to build their loyalty. Absence does *not* make the heart grow fonder—instead, it's out of sight and out of mind! Your agency must nurture relationships with current donors.

9. *You* have to give first. (*You* means each board member, the CEO and development officers, and fundraising volunteers.) Why? Because you cannot represent an agency or cause without demonstrating your own commitment—and you show that commitment by giving money, not just time.

10. Most fund development problems are actually *not* fund development problems. Most problems relate to other areas of operation Fix the real problem. (See monograph on Joyaux Web site:www.simonejoyaux.com Click on Resources, Free Library, Fund development, *Choosing your road.*)

11. The mission of fund development is to secure donors, not donations. It's about loyalty and commitment.

12. Fund development is a process and a profession. The profession is founded on ethical principles and standards, based on a body of knowledge and best practice, and protects the public through voluntary certification of professionals.

13. Philanthropy is defined as voluntary action for the common good—and hence volunteers are critical to the process. Volunteers help cultivate

relationships and solicit gifts. Professional staff enable volunteers to identify, cultivate and solicit.

14. A balanced funding mix of solicitation strategies and donor sources ensures stability and credibility. Whenever possible, the best way to solicit a gift is through face-to-face solicitation.

Resources

We strongly recommend the following books and articles because we've found them unusually helpful in our work. Some are recent, some are classics. All are worth reading (even ours, we shamelessly assert). This resource list includes some of our personal favorites; it is not meant to be comprehensive.

ON COMMUNICATIONS

Books

Tom Ahern, *How to Write Fundraising Materials That Raise More Money* (Medfield, MA: Emerson & Church, 2007)

Tom Ahern, *The Mercifully Brief Real World Guide to Raising More Money Through Newsletters Than You Ever Thought Possible* (Medfield, MA: Emerson & Church, 2005)

Robert W. Bly, *The Copywriter's Handbook* (New York: Owl Books, 2006)

John Caples, *Tested Advertising Methods* (Englewood Cliffs, NJ: Prentice Hall, 1974)

Barbara G. Ellis, *The Copy Editing and Headline Handbook* (New York: Basic Books, 2001)

Rudolf Flesch, *The Art of Readable Writing* (New York: Harper & Row, 1949)

Malcolm Gladwell, *Blink: The Power of Thinking Without Thinking* (New York: Back Bay Books, 2007)

Malcolm Gladwell, *The Tipping Point* (New York: Back Bay Books, 2002)

Ted Hart, James Greenfield, and Michael Johnston, *Nonprofit Internet Strategies: Best Practices for Marketing, Communications, and Fundraising Success* (Hoboken, NJ: Wiley, 2005)

Stephen Hitchcock, *Open Immediately! Straight Talk on Direct Mail Fundraising* (Medfield, MA: Emerson & Church, 2004)

Steve Krug, *Don't Make Me Think: A Common Sense Approach to Web Usability* (Berkeley, CA: New Riders Press, 2005)

Roland Kuniholm, *The Complete Book of Model Fund-Raising Letters* (Englewood Cliffs, NJ: Prentice Hall, 1995)

George Lakoff, *Don't Think of an Elephant: Know Your Values and Frame the Debate* (White River Junction, VT: Chelsea Green, 2004)

Harvey McKinnon, *Hidden Gold: How Monthly Giving Will Build Donor Loyalty, Boost Your Organization's Income, and Increase Financial Stability* (Chicago: Bonus Books, 1999)

Marty Neumeier, *The Brand Gap* (Berkeley, CA: New Riders Press, 2006)

David Ogilvy, *Confessions of an Advertising Man* (New York: Atheneum, 1988)

Jerold Panas, *Making the Case: The No-Nonsense Guide to Writing the Perfect Case Statement* (Chicago: Institutions Press, 2003)

George Smith, *Tiny Essentials of Writing for Fundraising* (Kermarquer, France: The White Lion Press, 2003)

Madeline Stanionis, *Raising Thousands (if Not Tens of Thousands) of Dollars with Email* (Medfield, MA: Emerson & Church, 2006)

Joseph Sugarman, *Advertising Secrets of the Written Word* (Las Vegas: DelStar Books, 1998)

Mal Warwick, *How to Write Successful Fundraising Letters* (San Francisco: Jossey-Bass, 2001)

Mal Warwick, *Testing, Testing, 1, 2, 3: Raise More Money with Direct Mail Tests* (San Francisco: Jossey-Bass, 2003)

Colin Wheildon, *Type & Layout: Are You Communicating or Just Making Pretty Shapes* (Mentone, Australia: The Worsley Press, 2005)

Articles

Susan Nall Bales, "Wanted: Master Storytellers," *Nonprofit Quarterly* (Fall 2005). www.nonprofitquarterly.org.

Stephen Denning, "Telling Tales," *Harvard Business Review* (May 2004). www.hbr.org.

Chip Heath, "Loud and Clear: Crafting Messages That Stick," *Standard Social Innovation Review* (Winter 2003). www.ssireview.com.

Nonprofit Quarterly (Fall 2005). Theme of the issue is "Amplifying Democracy: Nonprofits and Communications."

ON RELATIONSHIPS AND A BIT MORE

Books

Penelope Burk, *Donor-Centered Fundraising* (Chicago: Burk & Associates, 2003)

Ken Burnett, *Relationship Fundraising* (San Francisco: Jossey-Bass, 2002)

Mary Ellen S. Capek and Molly Mead, *Effective Philanthropy: Organizational Success through Deep Diversity and Gender Equality* (Cambridge, MA: The MIT Press, 2006)

Chuck Collins, Pam Rogers with Joan P. Garner, *Robin Hood Was Right: A Guide to Giving Your Money for Social Change* (New York: W. W. Norton, 2000)

Jim Collins, *Good to Great: Why Some Companies Make the Leap. . .and Others Don't* (New York: HarperCollins, 2001)

Jim Collins, with Jerry I. Porras, *Built to Last: Successful Habits of Visionary Companies* (New York: HarperBusiness, 1994)

USA Giving Foundation, *Giving USA 2007: The Annual Report on Philanthropy for the Year 2006* (Glenview, IL: Giving USA Foundation, 2007)

Daniel Goleman, *Emotional Intelligence: Why It Can Matter More Than IQ* (New York: Bantam, 2006)

Daniel Goleman, *Social Intelligence: The New Science of Human Relationships* (New York: Bantam, 2006)

Kay Sprinkel Grace, *The Ultimate Board Member's Book: A 1-Hour Guide to Understanding and Fulfilling Your Role and Responsibilities* (Medfield, MA: Emerson & Church, 2005)

Group of 33, *The Big Moo: Stop Trying to Be Perfect and Start Being Remarkable*, edited by Seth Godin, (New York: Portfolio, 2005)

Simone P. Joyaux, *Strategic Fund Development: Building Profitable Relationships That Last* (Sudbury, MA: Jones and Bartlett, 2001)

Lynne C. Lancaster and David Stillman, *When Generations Collide: Who They Are. Why They Clash. How to Solve the Generational Puzzle at Work* (New York: HarperCollins, 2005)

Paul Light, *The Four Pillars of High Performance: How Robust Organizations Achieve Extraordinary Results* (New York: McGraw-Hill, 2005)

Jerold Panas, *Asking: A 59-Minute Guide to Everything Board Members, Volunteers, and Staff Must Know to Secure the Gift* (Medfield, MA: Emerson & Church, 2004)

David Pottruck and Terry Pearce, *Clicks and Mortar: Passion-Driven Growth in an Internet Driven World* (San Francisco: Jossey-Bass, 2000)

Robert D. Putnam, *Bowling Alone: The Collapse and Revival of American Community* (New York: Simon & Schuster, 2000)

G. Clotaire Rapaille, *7 Secrets of Marketing in a Multi-Cultural World* (Provo, UT: Executive Excellence Publishing, 2001)

Ellis M. M. Robinson, *The Nonprofit Membership Toolkit* (San Francisco: Jossey-Bass, 2003)

Adrian Sargeant and Elaine Jay, *Building Donor Loyalty* (San Francisco: Jossey-Bass, 2004)

Dick Whitney and Melissa Giovagnoli, *75 Cage-Rattling questions to Change the Way You Work* (New York: McGraw-Hill, 1997)

Karla A. Williams, *Donor Focused Annual Giving Strategies* (Sudbury, MA: Jones and Bartlett, 2003)

Wilson Learning Library, *The Social Styles Handbook* (Herentals, Belgium: Nova Vista Publishing, 2004)

Howard Zinn, *You Can't Be Neutral on a Moving Train: A Personal History of Our Times* (Boston: Beacon Press, 2002)

Articles

P. Christopher Earley and Elaine Mosakowski, "Cultural Intelligence," *Harvard Business Review* (October 2004). www.hbr.org.

John W. Gardner, "Building Community," *Independent Sector* (September 1991). www.independentsector.

Carl Sussman, "Making Change: How to Build Adaptive Capacity," *Nonprofit Quarterly* (Winter 2003)

Nonprofit Quarterly (Fall 2001). The entire issue focuses on building strategic relationships, including an article by Daniel Yankelovich, "The Magic of Dialogue."

Nonprofit Quarterly (Summer 2003). Articles on the role of the nonprofit sector in a democracy and the advocacy/lobbying relationship. Roger Lohmann, "The Commons: Our Mission If We Choose to Accept It"; Scott Harshbarger, "The Greatest Leadership Challenge: Renewing our Belief in Democracy and Political Advocacy"; and Jeff Madrick, "Who's Promoting the General Welfare?"

ON THE WEB

Donor Bill of Rights, available at www.simonejoyaux.com

International Statement of Ethical Principles, available at www.afpnet.org

Standards of Ethical Conduct and Professional Practice, available at www.afpnet.org

Index

Lightning Source UK Ltd.
Milton Keynes UK
UKOW02n2338200514

232002UK00001B/13/P